Sacred Sonics

**Natural, Geometric Tuning Systems
and Simplified Theory**
for
**Performers, Composers, and Sonic
Therapy Professionals**

Proposing A Practical, Theoretical Basis for a Return
to Ancient Traditions of Sound and Frequency

Dr. Kenneth O. Holliday

Available Light Press • Ancient Traditions to Harmonize Our Future

Sacred Sonics:
Natural, Geometric Tuning Systems and Simplified Theory for Performers, Composers, and Sonic Therapy Professionals

And

Proposing A Practical, Theoretical Basis for a Return
to Ancient Traditions of Sound and Frequency

by Dr. Kenneth O. Holliday

Published by Available Light Press

Available Light (Intl.)

https://www.sacredsonics.com
https://www.availablelight.jp

Cover Design by Rob Williams
Layout Design and Internal Illustration by Dr. Kenneth O. Holliday
Cover Photography by Makiko Nagamine (STUDIO WEST, Okinawa)
Technical Consultant, Dr. Ceabert J. Griffith

ISBN: 979-8-9853437-0-0 (paperback)

Printed in United States of America

First Edition (2021)

Tyler Riese, whose focus and persistence inspired a father
to do better... to *be* better.

Erika Tiffany, who reminded me to do what you love,
and love what you do. No matter what.
So much like your father; it's frightening.

Mitsuki Lee, who showed me that life *can still* be fun,
and an adventure worth having.

Thank you all for your Love.

and...

To every mother who has ever recognized
and nurtured a child's potential,
decades before that child realizes it for themselves.

Thank you for never losing faith.

And finally, to Dad; Guess what? I finally 'get' it.

This page is intentionally blank

Forward

For over a decade, your writer has been plagued by a notion. At times, it has led to extreme distraction. At others, it has been merely a persistently gnawing sensation in the back of my mind. It has been at most times, in thought and action, a constant, disquieting presence for much of my life, more so over this past decade.

The issue itself can be summarized in the proverbial nutshell by voicing the question: How is it possible to possess such a deep desire to create music yet, lack any ability to fully appreciate the music itself?

Creation is satisfying to the extreme. And, I deeply enjoy playing certain music. However, there is something deeply unsettling about modern music's tonal structure that renders the listening experience *less than* uplifting and at times, irritating — even stressful.

I have found myself constantly migrating from one instrument to another, never truly mastering any. Yet, the same limitations always surface, once again triggering yet-another move to a new instrument… always searching for my place — my sound in the world of music.

On one particular day, some ten years ago, while listening to a sitar being played live, I experienced resonances and fundamental pitches for which I had no prior frame of reference, having been steeped in the traditional 'western' musical traditions. The sitar was magical, exotic, and (in this case and particular performer) masterfully played. The tones and harmonics produced by the instrument were simply hypnotic…mesmerizing… expansive… and meditative.

The experience triggered a series of thought processes, dreams, and outright meditative revelations that have led (more like; pushed and prodded) this writer inexorably to the point of questioning everything that he was ever taught about music, how it should be constructed, and how it should sound. Research ensued, and continues to this very moment.

The frustrating, decades-long process of questioning everything has taken me around the world of sound and frequency, and back again. The intended destination was *personal* truth and deeper understanding. What was eventually discovered is that such a journey is a lifetime in the doing, and never embarked upon simply for one's self. It is the underlying search for the honest-truth that is fraught with such paradigm-shifting experiences and the questioning of the very foundations of how most people 'think' about modern music.

The text you hold in your hands is the result of but one of several side-trips taken in the journey. A voyage that continues to breathe new life into a deep love of music. It somewhat quiets the mind to finally realize concepts that have now taken solid form – to be put on the page and conveyed to others who may use it, improve it, and perfect it — to be utilized in the wider world, and in each individual practitioner's relaxation and wellness practice.

It seems that attempting to create (re-discover) a way of formulating tone and structure based upon the principles of nature's math, is not by any means, an original quest. The same path has been trodden many times before, and by far more exceptional philosophers than the one putting these words down. However, in this particular journey, the reader will find that we deviate significantly from the paths blazed by those previous, intrepid seekers.

Despite those who have embarked upon a similar journey, there remains a lot that musicians and artists seem to repeatedly forget. Therefore, an additional objective of this work is to serve as a friendly reminder that there is (so much) more to music and the world than that which you have been taught in a standardized education process.

By re-examining the relationship of our human experience to nature, energy, tone and frequency, we regain the ability as well as the tools with which to redefine our musical experience with the universe and possibly our civilization. So, instead of merely recounting the quest for a better holistic tonal system, the writer invites you, kind reader, to come with - along the musical path seldom taken.

Each page of this text will act as a sort of guide along the harmonic path; a quest that is not intended for the entrenched mindset, nor for the feint of heart. It is a path all-to frequently abandoned by those who attempt the journey. That there are other footprints on the lower trail is not in dispute. However, the unique destinations we seek are seldom found, much less, thoroughly excavated.

What we will find is a wealth of possibilities that possess real potential to forever change the world of therapeutic music as well as sound and frequency healing — for the betterment of all humankind.

This text is geared towards the practitioners of sound and frequency healing, as that is the world the writer has chosen. However, most of the concepts, theories, and systemic constructs contained herein, are eminently and equally applicable to general music and composition.

The curious reader, the sound and frequency practitioner, as well as the budding composer are all invited to come along, on this journey into alternate tonality and natural frequency. The work contained herein is intended for everyone to use, refine, customize, and enjoy...

For the betterment and enjoyment of human-kind.

Dr. Ken Holliday

"Ac yno yn y nyffryn tawl mi glywaf gân yn swn yr awel"
-<u>Ysbryd y Nos</u> by Edward H. Dafis

"And there, in a quiet valley, I hear a
song in the sound of the breeze."
(Translated from the original Welsh)

This page is intentionally blank

Introduction

In recent years, significant attention has been directed toward the holistic arts and our treasured, indigenous healing traditions. Much of this refocused attention has been beneficial to the advancement of holistic technique and practice. Some of it, quite frankly, stretches the limits of imagination - inviting more profound, focused investigation. Both are steps in the right direction, in this writer's opinion.

Among the holistic areas of particular interest, one may specifically recognize a certain level of renewed scientific rigor as well as much-needed validation of many of the more 'fringe' practices. Of the more promising of these fields is that of electromagnetic energy, frequency, and sound – as *healing modalities*.

This renewed vigor is primarily due to science painting itself into a logical corner while simultaneously, creating more sensitive instruments with which to measure the world around us... as well as to shed light upon false assumptions and errant conclusions. What I am pointing to here, is the proverbial stacks of scientific assumptions, which due to technological advances in measurement and observation, have been revisited and turned completely inside-out. Yet, the new discoveries have never been corrected in the mainstream scientific narrative nor, edited in the textbooks from which new generations are being taught.

One example of this is found in the conclusions of the Michaelson & Morley experiments conducted in the 1890s. These experiments were designed to prove, once and for all that the concept of the universal Aether (The medium by which everything is surrounded and by which All is connected) was patently false. These two very respected scientists designed an experiment with late 19th century technology that *failed to detect* any expected effects that could be attributed to the Universal Aether. From that point forward, any mention of the Aether, by any scientist has been tantamount to career suicide.

This is how ridiculously pedantic modern science has become.

Thus, science painted itself into that corner. And, when significantly more advanced and sensitive instrumentation, in the 20th century, discovered the required evidence, and confirmed the existence of the universal aether medium... crickets! And, *still* few want to discuss it, even though the expected effects of the Aether have been confirmed. The discovery of the Universal Aether, now called the 'Quantum Vacuum Effect', posits a vastly superior explanation for common phenomena than the currently accepted mainstream explanations. Yet physicists are still petrified of even speaking of the implications of the discovery of this unifying 'Field' of energy. The overriding attitude is; "Shut up and calculate."

Yes! New discoveries, due to improved observation techniques have emerged. Discoveries that allow us deeper understanding of these energies and their affects. Some of the more exciting developments have been observed in methods that can be utilized in applications ranging from pure relaxation to focused healing.

The observed results of these studies are real. And, we only need to embrace the lost, forgotten, falsely-debunked, and as-yet unproven theories in order to usher the human race into a new age of science that accepts and confirms the existence of that which has been ignored due to its inconvenient status as one of many, 'forbidden topics.'

To many, it will come as no surprise that the ancient cultures, which both precede and inform our modern cultures, made meaningful, effective use of sound and frequency, among other mysterious energies. That these energies were not merely used as entertainment per se but, as a formal wellness practice is established through their own words. The healing aspects of sound and frequency are to be found elucidated in several examples such as the healing and teaching centers founded by honored masters such as Plato and Pythagoras.

On the darker side, however, there are also emerging sonic technologies developed for depleting purposes as well as outright demolition (à la the walls of Jericho). This is not to mention several distasteful military applications explicitly designed to 'do harm', such as the SASER program at CalTech, announced in 2009 - and just as quickly removed from their public-facing research website.

SASER is an acronym for "Sound Amplification by Stimulated Emission of Radiation." And, much like its cousin, the laser, a SASER device, tightly focuses *sonic* radiation in a 'beam' that could just as easily be utilized as a constructive, holistic tool as it is a destructive weapon. Upon which of these applications do you suppose our greatest scientific minds will focus their energies?

Sound is already… readily accepted as a massively-destructive force, but not even seriously viewed as a positive, constructive, and healing tool. This, despite the extant examples found within ultrasonography, which is almost exclusively relegated to a mere diagnostic tool. (Why?) This mentality is typical of the modern western worldview - struggling to comprehend the universe through reductionist logic and, seemingly, hopelessly and completely mired within the attitudes of the Kali Yuga cycle of civilization.

On the lighter side of the topic, much evidence has been amassed on the wellness front, that demonstrates a clear correlation between specific sonic methods and some pretty remarkable results. However, as we repeatedly observe, expensive research is challenging to accomplish, especially when there is nothing to be patented for profit.

Additionally, any valid findings that corporations deem objectionable or threatening to the prevalent narrative, or their precious revenue stream(s), are routinely relegated, without due-process, to the realm of 'anecdotal' results or outright 'pseudo-science.'

Therefore, despite increasingly numerous historical accounts and modern reports of positive results indicating significant progress in the field of sound and frequency therapy, there seems to be not one shred of deep-pocket interest in performing high-profile, well funded, well designed research into the wellness applications of sound and frequency.

The apparent exception to this rule is the research specifically designed to denigrate and discredit various holistic practices and practitioners who are on the front lines researching these phenomena — on our own.

This irritating habit of discrediting anything that is not accepted doctrine is precisely what the entrenched corporate academics are doing. Millions of dollars are spent to debunk and vilify dietary supplements, holistic practice, and spiritual concepts when just a little honest research into the topics would benefit humanity far more - and likely cost society far less in the currency of pain and suffering. Profit is the only motivation that seems to operate in the modern corporate mindset. The wellbeing of humanity is not their problem unless they can find a way to make it more profitable than pharmacology.

Fortunately, our abundant universe doesn't really work this way. Truth always finds a way to be heard and vindicated. In this work, we will strive to bring forth a very simple truth and, demonstrate how to begin applying it in your musical life as well as sound and frequency healing work.

In the field of sound and frequency healing, we already understand that specific healing frequencies promote and support positive responses within the human body and society. We also know that there are techniques that work well for some individuals but, curiously, not for others.

The reasons for this phenomenon are not entirely clear (and truly warrant serious study.) Still, these effects are likely, deeply rooted in our energetic individuality. What we do see is that there is no known, perfect tone, no ideal amplitude, and no magic frequency that will enable every body to respond in the same way every time. Just as in pharmaceutical medicine, there is no magic pill or elixir that promises perfect results to every patient.

Our ancient past is replete with pioneering masters of science, mathematics, mysticism, and healing who have charted a path through the burning briar patch of civilization's various incarnations of orthodoxy and faux-legitimacy. I propose that we only need to retrace the steps of these heroic masters to understand more deeply their thought processes and therefore, the relevance of their lives' work. Only then may we hope to mirror their significant successes.

In recent years, we have clearly seen a trend in which the monolithic academic power-and-control mechanisms, used for centuries as a bludgeon against any non-canonical theories, have begun to break down significantly. The result has been that independent researchers in every field, from anthropology to zoology, have taken the lead in critically re-evaluating the official narratives regarding the history of the human race, our origins, technology, *and* our healing traditions.

This renewed interest in 'forgotten' texts, disregarded evidence, and 'out-of-place' artifacts, has led to a virtual groundswell of new, logical, and innovative theoretical constructs in academic fields tangentially related to ancient healing methods and their theory. One of my personal favorites involves recent theories, which propose that the Osirium in Abydos, Egypt, as well as Hatshepsut's mortuary temple' annex in Deir El Bahri, were not 'temples' per se - but centers of healing, spiritual wellness, and initiation. Centers of healing, whose techniques revolved around sound and frequency!

The mentioned theory suggests that, what we call the Osirion and Hatshepsut's mortuary temple 'annex' were actually sonically tuned structures built for the purpose of initiations and healing. This sonic-tuning theory also extends to the Great Pyramid on the Giza plateau albeit for different purposes.

I anxiously await further confirmation before jumping on that particular bandwagon. But, I have hope that this will prove to be as valid a hypothesis as that tiresome habit of naming everything that remains standing, in Egypt, a 'tomb' or 'temple.' Unfortunately, the Egyptian office of Antiquities has blocked much of the more esoteric research in Egypt. Additionally, ongoing hostilities in parts of the middle east have resulted in a complete stoppage of excavations and analyses in the nations of the region once known as Mesopotamia.

Although the 'academic' establishment has fought a pitched battle to preserve their precious historical narratives (along with their individual tenures), truth is slowly winning the day. Previously 'settled' science is now decidedly 'unsettled' as ample new evidence, much of it once hidden away in dark rooms under the world's museums and private collections, has been placed under increasing scrutiny by extremely vocal, independent researchers.

Fortunately, we currently live in a time where literally, any researcher can, at the press of a key publish their analyses to be seen and critiqued by a far wider audience than has ever been possible. In fact, that is exactly what has been done with this text.

This wider, open-source level of scrutiny is crucial to advancing our understanding of history, precisely because much of this once-hidden and still-unacknowledged evidence directly contradicts established, and often facetious, established narratives. Much of this contradictory evidence is now finally, slowly, and inexorably being allowed to tell its version of the human story. That story, very likely contradicts what you have learned from current, mainstream sources and, may not at all, be what you expect.

One of the great masters of history, Aesculapius, was a student of Hippocrates and a legendary healer in his own time. Aesculapius was responsible for establishing several 'hospitals' (with schools) throughout the ancient Mediterranean world. After his death, Aesculapius was 'deified' by the people for his work. He is remembered as the rightful Greek 'god' of medicine. Yet, it is Hippocrates who is most commonly associated with healing medicine today. The student apparently surpassed the teacher by a wide margin.

Some historical accounts suggest that the Greek god of medicine, Aesculapius, was a renamed Egyptian god by the name of Imhotep. However, there are several accounts of a 'living' Aesculapius as a student of Hippocrates. I speculate that Aesculapius was human, precisely as described above and that his legendary status as a healer associated him with the Egyptian healer/god Imhotep. This phenomenon is actually a common occurrence throughout ancient history.

We can see several, revered gods and demi-gods who assume different names in other cultures, i.e., Enki --> Osirus --> Quetzalcoatl or, Innana --> Ishtar --> Aphrodite.

Among the healing tools traditionally utilized by Aesculapian physicians were herbals, specific 'movement,' 'solar' treatment, and sacred sound. Yet, in our typical human hubris, such holistic techniques are considered outmoded, superstitious, fringe, or are summarily dismissed as ineffectual, without even a hint of due process. How is it that something so wildly effective as to provoke people to venerate a practitioner as a god of healing, becomes so easily relegated to the realm of superstitious hyperbole?

So-called 'modern' medicine, currently boasts the most horrifically abhorrent failure rates and unacceptable iatrogenic death rates in human history. It produces not one pharmaceutical that actually *cures* anything. Yet, somehow our modern pharmacological medicine is considered the 'gold standard' of healthcare and modern philosophy. I ask the reader; Which of these systems is truly the outmoded, superstitious, and ineffective practice?

When we consider the landmark works of the Ancient masters such as Pythagoras, Aesculapius, Archimedes, Thoth, Hermes Trismegistus, Plato, et al.; We are often confronted with the words 'myth', 'allegory,' and 'metaphor.' These utterances are dog-whistles that expose the cognitive dissonance that abounds in the modern, reductionist mindset, and by direct extension in our corporate academia. These ancient heroes are the same legendary masters who gave us philosophy, Euclidean geometry, advanced 3D geometry, architecture, cosmology, and even rudimentary physics. Masters from the middle east, Africa, Macedonia, Greece, as well as the Indus and Asiatic cultures, have created (or preserved) a body of wisdom and knowledge that we again, are only now beginning to look upon seriously - much less comprehend.

The point is; These masters were *far* from 'mythical,' farther still from being intellectually lazy. They were far too prolific to be mere pulp-fiction publishers. However, organized academia wastefully relegates much of their historical, spiritual, and essay works to metaphorical lessons or worse, outright allegorical fiction.

We are repeatedly told that most of their (non-mathematical) work is not 'meant to be taken literally.' To that, I can say no more or less, than any among us. Therefore, I merely shake my head at the willful ignorance stubbornly displayed by so many who have firmly shuttered their minds against even the most minor considerations of historical fact.

These same great masters we have named, are those who received and passed down knowledge from their ancestors; the Mesopotamian, Indus, Egyptian, and the great Western and Central African civilizations, who built astonishing structures, and we are just now rediscovering that they were not nearly as primitive as we have been led to believe. The civilizations of northwest Africa alone, would require a lifetime of study to fully understand the grand majesty of their world.

Subsequently, one of the many, common themes in ancient civilizations that I regularly bump into, is this concept of sound and frequency healing. A growing body of evidence suggests that (among other 'advanced' technologies) sound and electro-magnetic frequency were in widespread use in these civilizations as therapeutic modalities! Indeed, the Greeks continued these more ancient traditions for centuries. However, a significant portion of the more profound and detailed knowledge was forever lost to the sands of time and conflict.

Piece by piece, we attempt to salvage or re-invent what we can of this knowledge; much of it hidden away in museum basements or left unexcavated out of academic malfeasance. We use what little we have learned, and attempt to rebuild upon the foundations laid millennia ago by the great, enlightened masters of the Golden and Silver Ages of civilization. It is some small part of that lofty and ultimately unattainable purpose that this book is intended to serve.

The work that you now hold is not intended to serve as a textbook instructing how to perform sound and frequency healing. Far better practitioners than I have already laid that solid foundation and made it pretty firm and level. Although the structure of my work may seem to reflect such a purpose.

It is instead, intended to be part of a mildly-entertaining, engaging, informative, thought-provoking, and ever-evolving discussion of the knowledge regarding sound and frequency healing concepts retrieved from history as well as developed (perhaps rediscovered) in the author's research and work.

The experienced practitioner can undoubtedly draw upon this data to enhance their practice and skills. The novice can absolutely supplement their development by learning from it. The curious will likely find interest and value in the information. But, this text will not teach you how to apply sound healing techniques. Such skills as is proper, must be learned from an experienced practitioner.

Instead, we seek to tap into those deep, mysterious connections between ancient knowledge; primarily Pythagorean and Euclidean mathematics, Platonic theory, various indigenous traditions, music, mathematics, geometry, and their current applications in actual practice.

We will overlay this 'harder' knowledge with some few esoteric understandings to peer deeper into the implications. It is up to the reader to determine if and how the information might be applicable in any musical composition or wellness practice.

A definitive evaluation of all tonal systems and their correlations to ancient mathematical structures would require an in-depth analysis of every construct; ultimately, an unfeasible task. Instead, we are looking for reasonable, mathematical correlations and general themes that correspond to ancient, holistic principles. I do not wish to (nor will I) debate from generalities to conclusions for each specific instance. Instead of pointless, rhetorical posturing, it is my hope that these data, assorted generalities, and the resulting theories may suggest some coherent pattern or firm basis, from which we may become at least mindful in further considering the ideas proposed herein.

The writer shall present the thesis for the reader to judge independently.

From the few examples we examine herein, the following recurring themes exist:

- Correlations existing between ancient mathematics and musical constructs and how we may apply them to achieve superior tonality.
- Mathematical symbolisms and their significance present in 'geometric' sound frequencies.
- Tonal systems, standards, and their bases - as well as some historical variations.
- Incompatibility (at the emotional and physiological level) of modern tonal standards with human wellness and healing.
- Establishing a structure and rationale for a tonal standard to be used in contemporary sonic therapy and healing practice.
- Applications of modern technologies in the delivery of healing, therapeutic sound.

As we do exist in a modern, technological age, we will certainly delve into the practical aspects of some of the associated sound reproduction and recording technology. We will explore how we may appropriate, and incorporate both, electronic and acoustic instruments to serve a higher, if supplemental, purpose in human wellness.

This, above all, is the passion that drives this work.

This page is intentionally blank

Contents

Contents (cont.)

Appendices:

This page is intentionally blank

1

A Very Brief History

...of Sound and Frequency Healing

Much like their Mesopotamian predecessors, the Egyptian, Indus, African, and later, Greek civilizations understood that sound, especially certain vowel sounds produced by the human voice and through breath, were deeply powerful tools for human well-being. Therefore, one could reasonably conclude that sound, music, and chanting held a deep significance for them. This fact is especially obvious of the Indus and Egyptian cultures and, by association, Mesopotamian, Semitic, Aegean healers, and priests.

To further underscore the importance of sound in lifestyle, wellness, and healing; In a letter of rebuttal (to an unknown slight) from the legendary healer cum deity, Aesculapius, to King Amman, it was written, "...as for us, we do not use simple words but sounds *[that are]* filled with power." (Brackets for clarity)

That the ancients understood and utilized the power of both, instrumental and vocalized sound is therefore, established fact and not mere supposition.

We will discuss human-produced sound more completely in our *'Chapter 34 - Vocalization, Chanting and Humming'* later in this text.

In more recent times, an audio researcher by the name of John Stuart Reid, also of significant *cymatics* reputation, detailed his work, performing acoustic testing in the Giza pyramids.

The details of Reid's interesting work are currently outlined at: *www.cymascope.com/cyma_research/egyptology.html.*

Among several enlightening findings, Reid's research strongly suggests actual *intent* in the acoustic design of these ancient structures, such that they are highly resonant, and very likely, architecturally-optimized to enhance certain acoustic properties. This suggestion has been echoed by several researchers engaged in related study.

The author recalls that; Reid, at one point reported that he had experienced a personal, significant healing during acoustic experiments performed in the King's Chamber of the Great Giza Pyramid.

He hypothesized that this personal experience may be a direct result of the resonant properties of the so-called sarcophagus, which he apparently entered during some of his resonance experiments.

Nowadays, even if you could obtain permission to enter the Great Pyramid, it is forbidden to bodily, enter into the 'sarcophagus.' The relevant authorities generally have it roped off like some fragile artifact - to enforce this curious prohibition.

That the sarcophagus itself, being made of a single block of red granite, is unlikely to be harmed in any way by human contact is a fact ignored by the rule-makers at the Office of Egyptian Antiquities, who also stubbornly cling to the facetious narrative that the pyramids were originally constructed as tombs and, that there is nothing under the Sphinx. (Hidden knowledge preserves the prevalent narrative.)

However, we do know from Reid's observation(s) that the sarcophagus within the King's chamber, in the presence of specific primary or resonant frequencies, indeed "rings like a bell — albeit at low frequency." Furthermore, certain tones projected within and along the ascending passageway cause the sarcophagus and surrounding chamber to create documented, amazing resonances, which additionally possess extremely long, natural decay rates.

This ringing of the structure, and resonance of the environs, occurs despite significant damage from the destructive negligence of unknown, early explorers.

However, Reid reports that specific, temporary 'patches' were applied to the damaged sarcophagus to complete the acoustic studies.

Figure 1.1 - The sarcophagus in the 'restored' King's Chamber of the Great Pyramid on the Giza Plateau.
(Photograph by Jon Bodsworth, distributed under a CC-BY 2.0 license)

As if there were not already enough un-citable information regarding work within the Great Pyramid, there have also been multiple reports contemporary to the nineteenth and twentieth centuries, of nine discorporeal manifestations in the King's Chamber when certain tones were made to resonate within the structure. The figures are said to have emerged on all sides from 'beyond' the walls of the King's Chamber. They were also reported to have remained present until the resonance tones were dissipated. These reports are fascinating if true. But, we are unlikely to be allowed to try it ourselves.

Further resonance research within the Giza pyramid complex has been banned by the Egyptian antiquities officials. To date, there have been no satisfactory rationale for this decision, released to the various researchers nor, to the general public. It's almost as if there is something that certain individuals wish to remain hidden.

Reid hypothesized that the pyramid builders deliberately and specifically engineered the existing, acoustic resonance. The implication is that they were well aware of sound's power and healing properties, long before the Greeks came to learn these 'mysteries' from what remained of the declining priestly hierarchy and civilization of Egypt.

The writer agrees wholeheartedly with this hypothesis and hopes that research will soon emerge to definitively validate the thesis. The writer would add that; the Egyptians (at least those of the dynastic era) were not the originators of this technology but, inherited the knowledge from the earlier, more advanced pre-dynastic, Mesopotamian and early Semitic culture(s).

Pythagoras c. 500BC (The same genius who gave us the Pythagorean Theorem, $\alpha2 = \beta2 + \gamma2$) is considered the 'Father of Sonic Healing.' After fleeing Samos due to a standing conflict with the tyrant Polycrates, Pythagoras lived in self-imposed exile in (the now Italian) district of Croton.

There he established the Pythagorean Mystery School, where among other esoteric practices, the use of musical instruments as tools of healing was commonly taught and practiced. The instruments in common use during this period, were mainly the flute and the lyre, along with some type of tuned percussion.

The hero of our story, Pythagoras, believed that, adherence to the three 'Golden Verses' required 'Preparation, Purification and, Perfection.' Pythagorean aesthetic discipline also taught that the proper kind of music contributed significantly to human wellness, if used in a specific and prescribed manner. His technique of sonic healing was dubbed 'musical medicine.'

It is imagined that; As Pythagoras, or his advanced students, played various instruments, they would lead attendees in performing meditations and chanting exercises intended to balance or heal. At other times, these 'followers' employed specially-structured music as a medicine for *passions* such as anger, aggression, and anxiety.

Unfortunately, all the writer can do is imagine the process — as none of Pythagoras' written methods or instructions have survived.

Despite the tragic fact that none of Pythagoras' direct writings on the subject have survived into modern times. We do learn something of his life and work in Croton, as well as his teachings and techniques, thanks to the work of contemporary authors such as Philolaus and, from the writings of some few of his 'disciples.' This quilting together of historical information is, admittedly, an inexact process.

Directly related to our purpose in this text; With the device dubbed 'the monochord,' a single-stringed musical instrument, Pythagoras was able to deduce the theory of musical intervals still in use today. That this was a rediscovery of more ancient knowledge, there is little reasonable doubt.

Figure 1.2 - Modern reconstruction of Pythagoras' monochord instrument. Photo courtesy of the *Whipple Museum of the History of Science, at Cambridge University.*

Pythagoras reportedly first observed the formation of musical intervals with his monochord instrument - that halving a string's length would produce a tone an octave higher than the original tone. Using this methodology, he was able to systematize the common musical intervals, such as the 3rd, 5th, octave, etc., which allowed for the creation of complete tetra-chords on multi-stringed instruments.

If only we were privy to the exact root tone used on the original monochord instrument, this text might be very short, indeed.

It seems logical that, before this rediscovery of musical intervals by Pythagoras, that stringed instruments were 'free-tuned' depending on the situation. If accompanying a flute or other fixed-tuning instrument, the stringed instrumentalist would likely adjust the tone of their primary string relative to the specific flute (or other fixed-tuning instruments) in use before tuning the instrument's secondary strings in a manner that was again, relative to the tone of the first string. Before the rediscovery of musical intervals however, it is a mystery how harmonic music could have existed at all.

One theory is that Pythagoras of Samos rediscovered this information as part of his research, which was likely based upon previous records and writings in early-Greek as well as other contemporary languages. Unfortunately, this is also information that cannot be directly confirmed because, the great majority of pre-Magna Grecia period writings have suffered the same fate as those of Pythagoras himself.

We do know that Pythagoras founded his mystery school in Croton, Italy where the curriculum included the concept of his 'musica universalis.' *Musica Universalis* teaches that the planets move according to mathematical rules and therefore are said to resonate, inaudibly, in a kind of 'cosmic' symphony.

This Pythagorean concept of Musica Universalis, is reminiscent of the mechanism by which we receive the so-called 'Cosmic Octave', developed by Hans Cousto. We will discuss and examine the 'Cosmic Octave' later, in Chapter Thirty-Five of this text.

While it is debated whether it was Pythagoras directly, or his talented student, Philolaus, who was responsible for much of the musical theory and techniques developed in Croton's mystery school, the role of the Croton school and its focus on therapeutic, esoteric musical systems is undeniable.

Again, we are left to pick at the bones of innumerable historical fragments, to construct theories, and endlessly-conjecture as to the state of sound and frequency healing arts in the Macedonian and Greek periods as well as all periods prior.

The one thing that we do know for sure is that the practice definitely existed, and that it was an honored practice worthy of a somewhat elevated status for many of its practitioners. If only the Greek masters had followed the example of Sumerian cultures — enshrining critical teachings upon baked tablets or stone rather than mere papyrus.

Multi-stringed instruments of the Greek and later periods *must* have required some standard method of 'relative' tuning — in which one master string sets the reference pitch for an entire ensemble. This practice is still in use today for solo performance and practice on stringed instruments when no *absolute* tuning reference is available.

A systematic tuning reference, such as that developed by Pythagoras, would have been extremely helpful in the process of tuning instruments for group performance. A standard reference pitch for all instruments was made much more accessible by his work. Due to Pythagoras' body of work in this discipline, his student, musician-philosopher, Philolaus is known to have subsequently, designed a system in which Pythagorean tetra-chords were 'merged' in a kind of proto-scale system. His work was the origin of the twelve-tone scale that remains the standard octave division to this day.

Unfortunately, the mathematical units (such as 'Hz' or 'cycles per second' in common use today) used to describe these ancient reference pitches are lost to history. Therefore, the *precise* tone frequencies are also subject to the same constructed theories and endless conjecture – giving rise to no lack of animated debate.

While it seems unlikely that the modern second (as a unit of time equal to one-sixtieth of a minute) has changed since the Mesopotamian civilizations standardized metrics of the passage of time, it is equally improbable that a method of actually measuring wavelength versus time existed in the era of ancient Egyptians, or to the later Hellenistic civilizations.

However, there have been professional reconstructions of the monochord, also called the sonometer. These historical reconstructions allow us to produce the intervals of Pythagorean tuning with little difficulty. It is significantly more challenging to determine the specific frequencies *actually* used by Pythagoras, to derive the intervals because such determination is dependent upon the string's length and diameter, not to mention the actual material from which it was made.

You see, we would need a standard reference tone and a method to reliably determine the actual tones yielded by the early masters. Otherwise, we are just making educated (and some uneducated) guesses as to what exact tones were used in ancient healing music. It is those 'educated' guesses upon which this text concentrates.

We have precious few indications of the actual methods that Pythagoras, Plato, and several others, used to establish standard units of measure for the root tones. And, those that survive, are from third-party sources. This is where we have come. Therefore, *this* is where we ultimately stand, despite no shortage of conjecture and theorizing from the so-called 'experts.'

Indeed, judging from the wide variety of standards common throughout the period, root standardization *may* have been attempted by some means common to all practitioners. Whether this is the actual case or not has not been factually determined.

The several Greek musical scale structures were based upon intervals. The intervals themselves were apparently, derived from this unknown reference tone. However, it seems reasonable to assume, given Pythagoras' et al., mathematical skills, that they established (or inherited from earlier cultures) some standard method derived from some other famous passion. Perhaps... Geometry. (Thus, the entire premise for this text.)

During the Greco-Roman period, healing centers were often used for periods of 'incubation.' Incubation was a practice in which participants were treated to some method or methods that created a state of 'dream sleep.' It has been suggested that hypnotic or even psychedelic substances were utilized to induce the preferred state.

However, it is noted that other therapeutic modalities, as well as spiritual initiations, were also performed in these 'sanitoria' utilizing the same or similar methods.

Based on the layout and evident structure of known sanitoria, it is readily apparent that they were designed with acoustic properties. This writer suspects that sonic-frequency and other, similar modalities were utilized therapeutically, within their walls.

These acoustically-resonant spaces, intentionally integrated into the architecture of these sanitoria, could serve to significantly enhance the effectiveness (and the propagation) of therapeutic, or other sound, throughout the entire structure.

Figure 1.3 - Temple of Hathor Complex with healing sanatorium (Roman Era) located at Dendera, and adjacent to the Mortuary Temple Complex of Hatshepsut. Inset indicates cellular structure of the complex.
(Image: Wikipedia Commons, distributed under a CC-BY 2.0 license)

The hypothesized resonances would have primarily been a function of the parallel stone walls, the 'cellular' arrangement of the rooms, and the overall length versus (estimated) height of the building itself. Even having a conversation in one of these rooms without being overheard in several others would seem unlikely.

To gain a deeper understanding of the tones that may have been utilized in these sonitoria, we would need to know the exact dimensions of the structure. To date, I have not located any such specific, detailed information regarding sanitoria, Hathor's temple' at Dendera, or the Osirium in Abydos. In fact, there is such disinterest in this structure that public images are surprisingly uncommon.

We clearly see just such a 'cellular' architecture reflected in the Byzantine Era's architecture and, even later in the medieval Christian monastic structures, where the properties of sound were also well-understood and extensively utilized. The sonorous, echoing performances of 'Gregorian' chants are a perfect example of how the 'spiritual' healing power of sound continued to be understood and practiced well into and beyond the Middle Ages.

Although brief, even this short tour of sound healing history is mildly intriguing. We can now understand that the historical and cultural precedent for using sound as 'medicine' for body, emotion, and spirit is well and firmly established in our cultural heritage.

So, what happened? How did the human species forget it's traditional, intimate, historical, and treasured connection to sound and frequency? The full answer to that question is as long as it is complicated and convoluted.

So, just this once, I will attempt to keep it brief.

The brief version:

Empire, war, banning of reading, banning the teaching of reading, prohibitions on the education of the 'unclean' masses, monolithic religious authority, destruction of the Alexandria Library, marginalization of the sacred feminine, and the resultant apathy of entire desperate, fearful peoples have certainly been the short list of causes for this current 'cultural amnesia' and the subsequent loss of any significant, historical context for the basis of sonic medicine.

To continue with the longer version:

In so many ways, we no longer remember who we are as a species. Therefore, we have forgotten from whence we came. All of the knowledge, history, and spirituality of our distant cultural past has been burned, pillaged, edited, redacted, or simply hidden from inquiring minds in vast, hidden archives. Seems absurd, doesn't it?

These rightful legacies have been pillaged from the consciousness of humankind and supplanted by impotent cultural and religious narratives promoted by the 'winners' over the ensuing millennia. Invariably, these controlling narratives promote increasing levels of ignorance by fomenting division and separateness among the good People of this world. It is the author's considered opinion regarding society's existing narratives that; nothing could be farther from the truth of the matter. The success of one, is the success of all. Therefore, it is cooperation and sharing, rather than competition and conflict which serve humanity's highest aspirations.

And, nothing places us farther from the purest-possible 'light' than some false belief that we are anything but deeply connected to each other, and the entirety of the harmonious universe.

To be sure, there were wars and corruption in our ancient past. Yet, it was the rise of some curious obsession for domination and control of others - as well as the ultimate fall of secondary empire that truly put the final nails in human history's coffin.

'Secondary empire' is a term the writer uses to describe so-called empires that arose from the disintegration of previous civilizations. A few examples are the Akkadian, Babylonian, Dynastic Egypt, Macedonian, Byzantine, Ottoman, and Holy Roman empires. All were mere shadows of their predecessor-cultures.

For whatever reason, these secondary empires were, undoubtedly, even less tolerant than their predecessors, and most notably disinterested in promoting the more esoteric humanistic practices. Any practice, which empowers the individual, necessarily serves to weaken the iron grip of the elite class upon those very peoples. Thus we see that the ruling classes certainly had sufficient motivation to suppress any traditional, esoteric practices that conveyed power and higher consciousness to the people whom they wished to continue dominating into perpetuity.

There are other reasons and rationale for humanity's decline, to be sure. The point is that when struggles and wars for power and control over territory, trade routes, racial identity, and tax revenue turn to the focused destruction and obfuscation of knowledge, the only likely outcome, is the intentional suppression of individual empowerment, for the ultimate purpose of appropriating that power for the controlling class.

We have seen this cycle play out through our various historical events, such as the unnecessary, twice destruction of Solomon's Temple in Jerusalem, the senseless, intentional burning of the Library of Alexandria, the mass extermination (suppression) of the Knights Templar, and the destruction of critical ancient structures in Palmyra as recently as 2011; Just to name a few.

The suppression and eventual vilification, of ancient, esoteric knowledge, are common features of both the Arian and Piscean ages

(approximately 2500BCE until Present.)

It is no wonder, then, that the history of the last five millennia of human history has been little more than the continuous story of war, oppression, and control of others. The concept and practice of centralized authority has become the very hallmark, rather than the exception, in human culture – much more so, since the time of the Universal Church's (aka: Roman Catholic Church) rise to power.

Let's hope that a more ecumenical Aquarian age dawns very soon.

Going forward, we will be examining the natural, mathematical, and technological bases of tone. We will explore the theoretical relationships between geometry, sacred geometry, and sound.

If we manage to keep an eye on the proverbial ball, the end result *should* be a better understanding of a mathematically (geometrically) 'perfect' basis for healing sound, as well as essential, playable musical tuning systems.

We may never be able to verify the actual, precise tones created and utilized by the ancient masters. But, we can certainly do better at *trying* to recreate them than our civilization and its feckless, monolithic musical associations, have thus far managed.

2D Geometry of Sound

Tonal Resonances of Polygonal Geometry

Euclid, a student of Plato, was born circa 325 BCE. This would have been approximately 275 years before Julius Caesar 'accidentally on purpose' burned the main library in Alexandria circa 48 BCE. A common belief is that Euclid was initially a student in Plato's school in Athens, and, later taught mathematics in this same library on the shores of Alexandria, Egypt.

Euclid has long been credited with developing the class of mathematics related to simple shapes in two dimensions. His name is generally associated with the branch of two-dimensional geometry known as 'Euclidean Geometry.' At the foundation of this work are the so-called 'regular' geometric shapes. An example of a regular polygon is simply a shape where every side meets with two other vertices without any of the line segments intersecting except at the endpoints. In our examples we refer to polygons where each side is equal in length to all others. The most basic example of such a regular polygon is the equilateral triangle.

When we look closely at the characteristics of these regular polygons, we encounter an interesting correlation between the sum of the internal angles and the number nine. The resulting, associated resonances and harmonics, derived from the math, naturally display the same characteristic affinity for the number nine - considering that they are geometric numbers themselves. This general observation is an interesting correlation and, it is exactly that correlation, which is especially relevant to the work about which this text is written.

Specifically: When we add the individual digits found in the sums of the angles and associated resonance tones, the resulting numerical reduction is always nine. Additionally, the sum itself, is associated with a specific tone value expressed in Hertz, which the polygon depicts graphically.

For example; The dodecagon relates to a resonance of 1800Hz. This resonance is assigned because 1800° is the sum of the dodecagon's internal angles. Additionally, the second harmonic of 1800Hz is 3600Hz, which is a harmonic value that describes the octave tone above 1800Hz. The sum of the digits' 3+6+0+0' still gives us '9.' And, as we will later see, all of the resonance frequencies derived from more peripheral extra-geometric analysis, generally display the same characteristic of direct reduction to the number nine — despite their having no direct geometric correlation.

Some few remaining acceptable frequencies derived in this work however, may instead reduce directly '3' or '6.' These values are still considered part of the family, as they are direct divisors of nine and *360*. The 260 value is the geometric expression of the full radian system that governs the measurement of degrees in any geometric object and, is discussed in some depth in the next chapter.

However, some regular polygons with a significantly large number of sides do not reduce directly to nine. Some reduce to eighteen, while others reduce to twenty-seven. The more astute observers among us will surmise my next observation; Continuing the reduction of digits reveals that the sum of digits in the numbers '18' and '27' does reduce to... You got it! Nine. Therefore, the reduction to nine is a consistent and predictable feature of geometrically-derived resonances.

All regular Euclidean polygons have a value of the sums of their angles that *always* reduces numerically to the number nine. How does that work?

This 'universal' divisibility by nine (as well as three and six,) is built in to the formula for calculating the sum of angles. This effect was explained by someone significantly more versed in the mathematics than this writer, as seen in the following quote:

"Any number multiplied by 180 would 'inherit' this divisibility property because 180 is itself, divisible by 3, 6, and 9. Additionally, the same numbers are divisible by 2, 4, and 5 but not 7 or 8, for the same reason."

Notwithstanding this perfectly logical explanation, it certainly doesn't diminish any sense of wonder derived from such a perfectly ordered geometric system - based upon a system that was originally designed at least six millenia in the past! (Probably further) Imagine if your geometry teacher had pointed out this little tidbit to you. Would it have made geometry any more interesting? In this writer's opinion, the answer would be a resounding "Yes!"

Additionally, because the geometry of the five, three-dimensional Platonic solids (discussed later) is based upon objects constructed from these same regular polygons, we will see this relationship with the numbers three, six, and nine continue in *'Chapter 4 - 3D Geometry of Sound.'*

The fact that each nominal resonance frequency, derived from the sum of internal angles, reduces to the number nine is essential once we begin constructing a theoretical 'Geometric Tuning Grid' later in our exploration. We will also repeatedly, observe this strong relationship with 3, 6, 9, as well as 12, and 72 when we start playing around with the math.

While correlation does not necessarily equate to causation, we will see several more of these little mathematical coincidences accumulate as we continue our exploration of geometry, frequency, and tone.

For now, let us consider the first eleven regular polygons to see just how they start to fit into our system.

For clarity, the writer will point out that; any variation of a specific regular polygon, such as those below, will demonstrate the same sum of internal angles. We will keep the analysis uncluttered by evaluating the *equilateral* versions of each shape. One could construct a 'regular' *pentagon* with any number of assorted internal vertice angles. However, the total value of those angles would always calculate to 540°, as the total *sum of internal angles*.

The following figures demonstrate the theoretical correlation between polygonal geometry, the internal angles, and resulting theoretical resonances.

Examining The First Eleven Regular Polygons

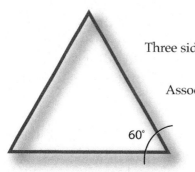

<u>Triangle</u>

Three sides intersecting at 60° each

Sum of internal angles 3 x 60° = 180°

Associated Tones: 180Hz & 360Hz (octave)

60°

The most basic of the regular polygons with the least number of sides possible

Fig 2.1

<u>Circle</u>

Encompasses one complete arc of 360°

Sum of internal angles = 360°

Associated Tones: 360Hz & 720Hz (octave)

The foundational shape of two dimensional geometry, possessessing no sides and no vertices

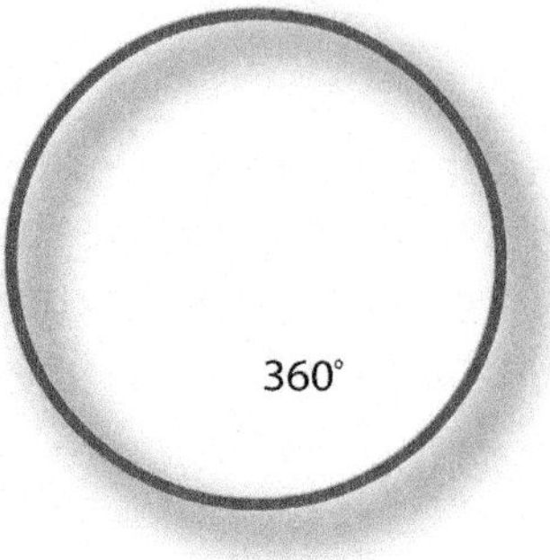

Fig 2.2

360°

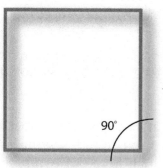

<u>Square</u>

Four sides intersecting at 90° each

Sum of internal angles 4 x 90° = 360°

Associated Tones: 360Hz & 720Hz (octave)

90°

The seeming antithesis to the circle yet encompassing an identical resonance

Fig 2.3

Pentagon

Five sides intersecting at 108° each

Sum of internal angles 5 x 108° = 540°

Associated Tones: 540Hz & 1080Hz (octave)

The pentagon, a traditional symbol of power,
encompasses the points of the pentacle, a very
ancient symbol of protection

Fig 2.4

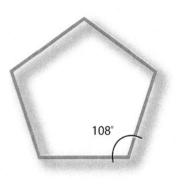

108°

Hexagon

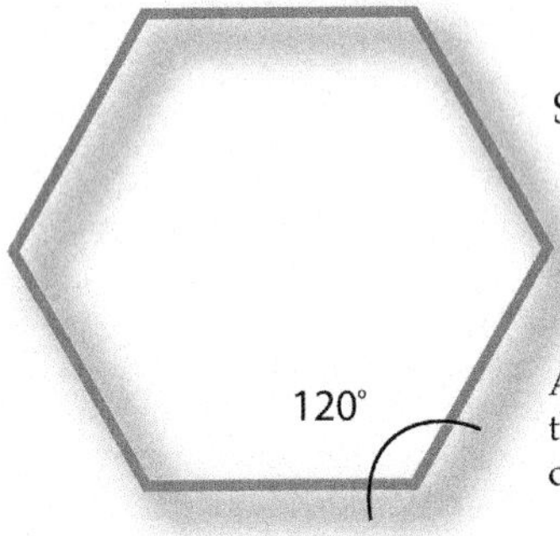

Six vertices intersecting at 120° each

Sum of internal angles 6 x 120° = 720°

Associated Tones: 720Hz & 1440Hz (octave)

120°

Arguably the most prolific polygon in nature composing
the structures of snowflakes, organic molecules, quartz
crystals, natural basalts, and the structure of bee-hives

Fig 2.5

Heptagon

Seven vertices with internal angles of 128.57° each

Sum of internal angles 7 x 128.57° = 900°

Associated Tones: 900Hz & 1800Hz (octave)

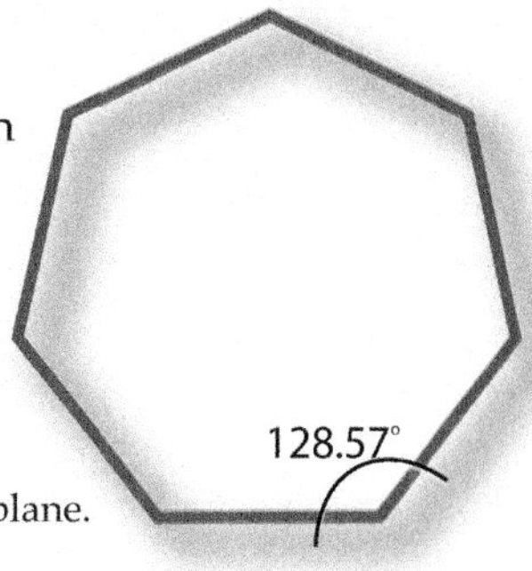

The regular heptagram, sixth in the heirarchy of regular
polygons, also encloses the shape of the seven-point star,
commonly symbolic of protective forces within the material plane.

Fig 2.6

128.57°

Octagon

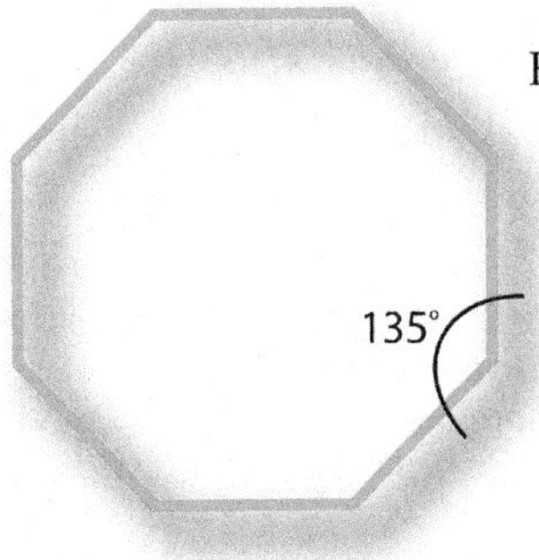

Eight vertices of 135° each

Sum of internal angles 8 x 135° = 1080°

Associated Tones: 1080Hz & 2160Hz (octave)

135°

This eight-sided polygon is easily recognizable as
symbolizing shielding or stopping things. It is the
shape adopted by many nations' stop signs as well
as the common shape of a standard umbrella

Fig 2.7

Nonagon

Nine sides intersecting at vertices of 140° each

Sum of internal angles 9 x 140° = 1260°

Associated Tones: 1260Hz & 630Hz (lower octave)

The regular nonagon, associated with the number nine,
is numerically, the end of a series or a cycle of completion as
the number cycle is seen to begin with one and end with nine.

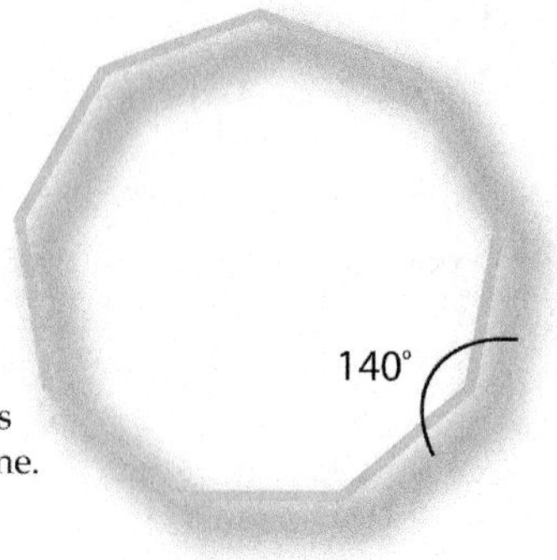

140°

Fig 2.8

Decagon

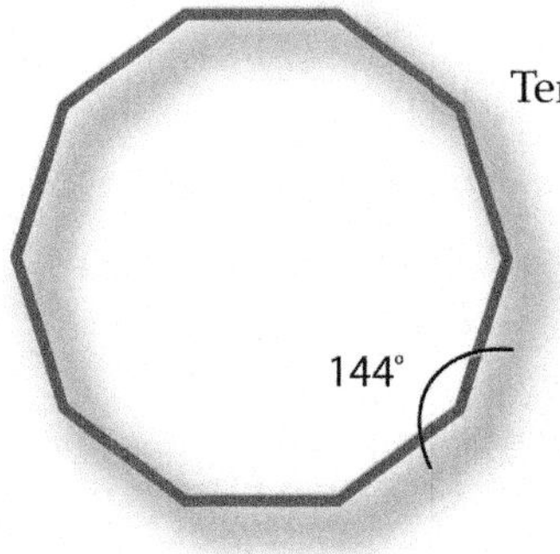

Ten segments with matching vertices of 144° each

Sum of internal angles 10 x 144° = 1440°

Associated Tones: 1440Hz & 2880Hz (octave)

144°

The decagon represents the start of a new cycle of
higher frequency potential than the previous cycle
ending with the nonagon. Symbology includes new
beginnings,progress, and initiation to new concepts
and energies.

Fig 2.9

Hendecagon

Eleven sides intersecting at vertices of 147.27° each

Sum of internal angles 11 x 147.27° = 1620°

Associated Tones: 1620Hz & 3240Hz (octave)

Our tenth polygon is more important than it may seem.
However, the resonance of 1620Hz will be giving us a nice
challenge later in our work.

147.27°

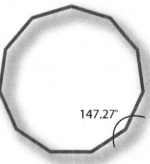

Fig 2.10

Dodecagon

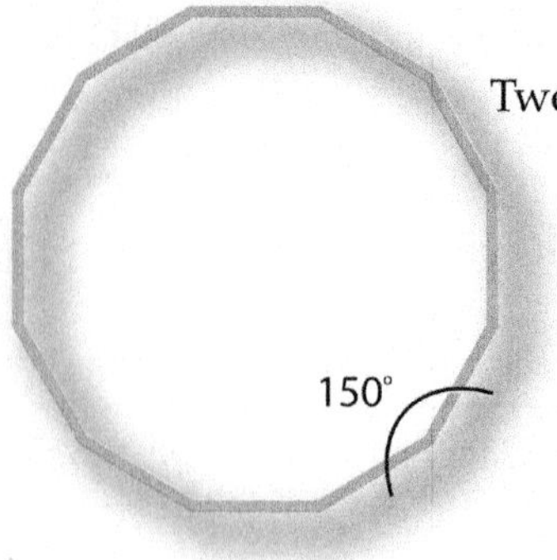

Twelve segments with vertices of 150° each

Sum of internal angles 12 x 150° = 1800°

Associated Tones: 1800Hz & 3600Hz (octave)

150°

The dodecagon was considered by ancient cultures to
be such a sacred shape that it is rumored that Plato
advocated capitol punishment for any student found to
reveal its secrets or even draw the shape.

Fig 2.11

There exists a theoretically, infinite array of regular polygons. What we have detailed above are just the first eleven.

Based on this analysis, we now have several candidate resonance frequencies derived from simple geometry, which we will later link to actual musical tones — even full scales and working chords, for use in sound and frequency applications, intended for relaxation, wellness, and healing.

Again, you will notice that each frequency reduces to the number nine, as do the indicated associated tones.

Let's test the limits of this so-called relationship to the number nine. But, this time, let's throw the three and the six in the mix as well. Allow me to explain...

We've already seen that the internal sum of angles of the triangle (3 sides), hexagon (6 sides), and nonagon (9 sides) are all perfectly divisible by 9. So, it comes as no surprise to learn that they are also divisible by 3 and 6. We will always assume that our polygons have no intersecting line segments (i.e., that they are 'regular' polygons). If, then, we search the theoretically infinite polygons, what interesting surprises lie in wait?

Let's see what happens when we evaluate some regular polygons to put this rule to the test. We will evaluate each sum of angles for divisibility by 3, 6, and 9. The results are displayed in the right-hand columns in *Table 2.12*, below.

Table 2.12 lists the vertex angles, the sum of the internal angles, and the results of a simple division by each of our key geometric divisors. This exercise illustrates the desired level of natural, geometric 'purity' of the numeric sequence(s) and therefore, each of the subsequent associated tones revealed by basic geometric fundamentals.

Although the author has confirmed the consistent results by performing these calculations for every polygon up to 5000 sides, the following, demonstrates the first twenty-eight regular polygons, as examples of the 3, 6, 9 reduction phenomenon:

Table of The First Twenty-Eight Regular Polygons

Sides	Single Vertex Angle	Sum of Internal Angles	3	6	9
3	60°	180°	Y	Y	Y
4	90°	360°	Y	Y	Y
5	108°	540°	Y	Y	Y
6	120°	720°	Y	Y	Y
7	128.5714286°	900°	Y	Y	Y
8	135°	1080°	Y	Y	Y
9	140°	1260°	Y	Y	Y
10	144°	1440°	Y	Y	Y
11	147.2727273°	1620°	Y	Y	Y
12	150°	1800°	Y	Y	Y
13	152.3076923°	1980°	Y	Y	Y
14	154.2857143°	2160°	Y	Y	Y
15	156°	2340°	Y	Y	Y
16	157.5°	2520°	Y	Y	Y
17	158.8235294°	2700°	Y	Y	Y
18	160°	2880°	Y	Y	Y
19	161.0526316°	3060°	Y	Y	Y
20	162°	3240°	Y	Y	Y
21	162.8571429°	3420°	Y	Y	Y
22	163.6363636°	3600°	Y	Y	Y
23	164.3478261°	3780°	Y	Y	Y
24	165°	3960°	Y	Y	Y
25	165.6°	4140°	Y	Y	Y
26	166.1538462°	4320°	Y	Y	Y
27	166.6666667°	4500°	Y	Y	Y
28	167.1428571°	4680°	Y	Y	Y
29	167.5862069°	4860°	Y	Y	Y
30	168°	5040°	Y	Y	Y

Table 2.12 - Table of the first twenty-eight regular polygons demonstrating the universality of the 3, 6, 9 divisibility phenomenon.

We could go on ad-infinitum with this little exercise. But I am sure you kind readers get the point. And, incredible as it may seem at first, we learn that *every* regular polygon imaginable has several common characteristics that my math teachers never pointed out:

- No matter how many sides (odd or even), All regular polygons have a sum of internal angles that numerically reduces to the number '9.' This reduction is performed by adding the individual digits together. (i.e., 360° reduces as 3+6+0=9)

- No matter how many decimal places are used to express the individual internal (vertex) angles, the sum of the interior angles is always a whole number. (This is logical but bears highlighting.)

- None of the resulting frequency equivalents exist in the modern, even-tempered western musical scales based on A^4-440Hz.
  (See: *Appendix II - Piano Key Tones Using 'Equal-Tempered' Methodology*)

- The only useful frequency equivalents that exist in the calculations of *any* twelve-tone equal-tempered (12TET) system, is within the equal-tempered tones based upon the vaunted A^4-432Hz. Of course, These are the 'A' tones.
  (See: *Chapter 6 - The 432Hz Question*) You need so much more than just a new reference tone.

- In a regular polygon, the resulting sum of angles is always fully divisible by 3, 6, *and* 9. No exceptions. Again, this is a logical consequence of the math.
  (See: *Appendix VII - Table of Polygonal Frequency Data.*)

To further expand our understanding of the significance of the divisibility effect, it is essential to recognize that our use of a radial standard of 360° in a full circle is most certainly due to the simple fact that the original system is derived from $Base_{60}$ (sexagesimal) and closely associated with $Base_{12}$ (duodecimal) mathematics.

$Base_{60}$ (and its little sibling $Base_{12}$) is incredibly useful because, the 'basis' number, '60' possesses more divisors than any smaller positive integer. The complete list of the divisors of '60' is:

1, 2, 3, 4, 5, 6, 9, 10, 12, 15, 20, 30, 60

Thus, a 360° (**3** x 120° = 360°, **6** x 60° = 360° or even **9** x 40° = 360°) radius standard remains the rock-solid foundation of an eloquently designed geometry. The previous reference to the divisors '5' and '10', offer a 'hook' into the prevalent Base$_{10}$ geometry with which most of us are more familiar.

Alternative geometric standards based on other base-system numbers are theoretically possible. But they are demonstrably cumbersome, and would require a complete revision of literally everything pertaining to higher mathematics.

Another wonderful side-benefit of Base$_{60}$ math is that it significantly reduces the mathematical dependence upon remainders i.e., fractions. Yes. There are significantly less fractions to deal with in Base$_{60}$ math. Third graders rejoice!

These facts definitely make it less cumbersome to work with the math. But, we are, nevertheless saddled with Base$_{10}$ mathematics for whatever historical and cultural reasons. But, what a benefit it is to have our geometry so firmly rooted in the Base$_{60}$ and Base$_{12}$ systems.

A perfect radius of 360° reduces to our 3, 6, and 9 target divisors. Additionally, the number is also perfectly divisible by '12' (i.e., 360 ÷ 12 = 30) as well as by '72.' The significance of the latter number (72) is a bit more esoteric and ancient but, is again rooted in Base$_{12}$ math where **72 ÷ 12 = 6.** That result of six bringing us right back to our Base$_{60}$ correlates. I will leave most of the esoteric discussion for others more versed in that topic.

The 360° standard has been with humankind since the earliest *known* civilizations. Yet, to the casual mathematician, this standard seems somehow arbitrary, considering that we generally use Base$_{10}$ mathematics for nearly everything (with the exception of computer science where binary (Base$_{2}$), octal (Base$_{8}$), and Hexadecimal (Base$_{16}$) are the prevalent maths.

So why not use ten or even 1,000 as the basis for our radian system? Would that not be a more efficient approach considering our Base$_{10}$ mathematical leanings?

The quick and easy answer would be: "No!"

Such ill-advised approach, would be a complete disaster.

There is simply no other radial standard that provides the elegance, precision, and simplicity of 360° based geometry while simultaneously remaining compatible with Base$_{10}$ math and its modern derivatives.

Additionally, the many correlations to other extant disciplines and practices would not be possible using any other standard as they all assume the same 360° system. We would essentially need an overhaul of our civilization's mathematical foundations. And, why would we do something like that?

Further, while '60' has twelve perfect divisors, the number '10' has only four (1, 2, 5, and 10.) This fact alone would significantly limit the usefulness of a strictly Base$_{10}$ radial geometry.

Our most ancient ancestors knew what they were doing. And, they chose well.

A Complete '360'

A Series of Numerical Coincidences or Just Darn Good Math?

We now know that the same ancestors who gave us the 360° radial system, routinely applied the $Base_{60}$ (and $Base_{12}$) mathematical systems to much more than just counting days and measuring circles. A majority of the critical numbers they seemed to use often (and 'often' cannot be overstated in this case) were the numbers '72', and its divisors, especially the number '12.'

To be clear, the writer seeks to discuss and analyze the implications of these number values without assigning any mystical import to them. The frequent application of these values in ancient times is merely the result of their pervasively efficient $Base_{60}$ and subordinate $Base_{12}$ mathematical systems upon which these ancient civilizations based everything they did. And, while it is immensely interesting to consider the deeper implications vis-a-vis esoteric spirituality, that is not why this text has been written.

Assigning a mystical meaning to a number such as '12' or '72' in this case would be counter-productive and, would be analogous to some later civilization enshrining our own $Base_{10}$ system numbers '5' and '10' as holy relics. While the writer does possess a significant esoteric bent, in this particular case, we must dispassionately regard them as just standard numbers in a mathematical context.

Notwithstanding the preceding disclaimer, understanding the importance of key values is pertinent to the work presented here if only to comprehend the deep significance placed in them by earlier cultures… and ours.

Therefore, we will indulge briefly in an abridged discussion of certain key number values and their pervasive application as well as the apparent cultural fixation upon them, throughout the preceding millennia.

———————

The number '72' is extensively referenced in practically every esoteric, spiritual tradition on the planet. Mesopotamian religion(s), Confucianism, Judaism, Taoism, Islam, Buddhism, Christianity, Egyptian mysticism, Qabbalah, and many (if not all) others.

The number also appears often, in historical folklore. In his book detailing Chinese folklore of the Hui Muslims in China, one B. Riftin* refers to 72 halls in an underwater palace, 72 merits of a hero, and 72 specific stars in the night sky.

*B. Riftin, '_Review: Mythology and Folklore of the Hui_: A Muslim Chinese People (L. Shujiang and K. Luckert),' Asian Folklore Studies 57. 2, 1998, p.371.

And, let's not forget the '72' virgins that await all martyrs of Allah in modern Islam.

The Mayan 'long count' calendar consists of 1,872,000 days. When divided by '72,' we get precisely 26,000, a nicely-round number, which (in years) was the Mayan calculation indicating one full precessional cycle of the Earth's polar axis. This metric is astonishingly accurate to within some few years in each of the 2000-year zodiacal cycles depending upon which source you read.

This 26,000-year number represents thirteen smaller cycles of 2000 years each, which all totaled, equals a Mayan 'Great Year.' The '72' in this case, represents the number of years required for the Earth's axis to shift 1° in its precessional cycle, and is amazingly accurate especially when one considers the assumed, primitive nature of the society as professed within mainstream archeology.

Interestingly, the thirteen smaller, 2600 year divisions of the precessional cycle allow each 'Great Year' to begin in a different Zodiacal age.

Whereas the last Great Year began in the Age of Pisces, the following will be (or already has been, depending upon the source) initiated in the Age of Aquarius. Also of note is the fact that we recently concluded a Great Year cycle in 2012 and, are, according to the Mayan calendar, now entering the Age of Aquarius at the beginning of a new 'Great Year' cycle.

Architectural symbolism involving the number '72' is also typical. For example, the Temple of the Holy Grail had '72' chapels, and the royal reception hall of Persepolis had '72' pillars...

The number '72' is deeply enshrined in our 360° geometrical foundations. Note that 360° divided by 72 gives us 5. And, when divided by 12 gives us 30... Again, always a whole number. This fact is not surprising at all once you analyze the underlying math. However, as musicians, we must give pause at the utter symmetry of the system. It is, on its own, already a harmonic structure if not yet fully formed music. When we then take a more in-depth look at the resulting sums of our internal polygonal angles, a clear pattern emerges, which must be further explored.

We could go on with hundreds of examples of the number '72.' But I promise not to. However, it is imperative that the reader understand the importance of all the significant numbers pulled from ancient customs and mathematics. Their cultural and esoteric significance however, is to be viewed as secondary to their actual usefulness.

Not to be outdone by any means, the number '12' is repeatedly expressed in cultural and historical references such as the number of months in a year, zodiacal divisions, average hours of daylight, and darkness in a single day. Twelve is also the number of the Tribes of Israel, enshrined in the twelve days of Christmas, and reflected in the number of apostles who are said to have followed The Christ.

There are many more relevant, cultural, and spiritual references from which to illustrate the deep significance of the number twelve in our many cultural systems. But, there is one specifically that applies to our work here. And, it refers directly to musical structure.

Thus, the reader will also note that the traditional musical octave is predominantly seen as being divided into twelve 'notes' or tones, plus one; just like the Great Zodical Year. This particular work will continue with this twelve-tone tradition as it is both systematically relevant and incredibly convenient for the modern musician.

Just for kicks, we will demonstrate yet another interesting quirk of the 360° system that we will now demonstrate.

Pick a polygon. Any of them will do. I'll wait...

Case 1: Regard your chosen polygon. If the number of sides is an even number, divide the sum of internal angles by 72.

For example, a decagon has ten sides. Since '10' is an even number, we will divide the sum of the internal angles by '72' like so:

$$1440° \div 72 = 20.00$$

Then, divide the same number by '12':

$$1440° \div 12 = 120.00$$

With even-numbered polygons, there is *never* a remainder when dividing by 12 or 72.

Case 2: If the number of sides is odd, divide the sum of angles by 12.

For example, a nonagon has nine sides. Because '9' is an odd number, we will divide the sum of the internal angles by '12' like so:

$$1260° \div 12 = 105.00$$

Then, divide the same number by '72':

$$1260° \div 72 = 17.5!$$

Dividing by '72', leaves a remainder of 0.5 when the polygon has an odd number of sides. And, that remainder is always 0.5.

So, with odd-numbered polygons, there is never a remainder when dividing by 12. But there is *always* a remainder of 0.5 when dividing by 72.

To Explain, Perchance to Clarify:

In Case 1: (even-sided polygons), dividing by 72 leaves no remainder.

In Case 2: (odd-sided polygons), dividing by 72 always leaves a remainder. And, that remainder is always 0.5.

In either case, division by '12' results in a whole number result. This occurs because 360° is divisible by '12' (and '72' for that matter.) However, in the case of odd-sided polygons, dividing by '72' leaves a remainder. Initially, this apparent, outlying case was a bit of a disappointment to this author. It seemed to indicate some preference for even-sided polygons. In the end, however, this was not the case. It is just another interesting artifact of the math. Or so it now seems.

The fact that only the even-numbered polygons are divisible by '72' threatened to throw a wrench in the early, working theories regarding the vaunted, ancient, and sacrosanct nature of the number seventy-two. So, a re-evaluation of the basic premise was in order.

Then, I realized something worth noting. When division by '72' leaves a remainder, the remainder is always 0.5... Wait for it! ... If you do the work by long-division, the actual, whole-number remainder value is always '36!' I have found no exceptions to this within the first one-thousand polygons.

First, '36' is divisible by 12. So, that part of the phenomenon is a now-resolved mystery. However, '36' is obviously not divisible by '72.' But, '72' is divisible by '36.' This demonstrates an apparent and deeply cyclical nature, built in to these systems that we can certainly exploit for our current project.

So, the 0.5 remainder is always '36' when rendered by long division. This fact hangs out like a sore thumb and, the effect occurs with the odd-sided polygons.

It also indicates that any purely-geometric resonance frequencies with decimal remainders should also reduce numerically (to nine) just as well as those with no remainder at all.

Those constructs that reveal The thirty-six (or 0.5) remainder represent the odd side - the unpaired, 'extra' side of our regular polygon. Perhaps, this is in some way symbolizing the imperfection seeking resolution within the whole. I will stop philosophizing there and allow the subsequent work to speak for itself on this matter.

So, while the writer may not be able to fully explain why the remainder is always '36', it is a convenient outcome because, thirty-six is a number we can work with as it reduces to nine and is a perfect divisor of '72' and '360.' We've come full-circle back to that semi-magical reduction to the number '9.'

"If you only knew the magnificence of the 3, 6, 9, then you would have the key to the universe." - Nikola Tesla

In summary

360 is a base$_{60}$ multiple passed down to (or rediscovered by) our ancestors over 6000 years ago by their Mesopotamian progenitors.

It has the undeniable benefit of working well in Base$_{10}$ math (because **360 ÷ 10 = 36**), which is probably why most people never consider the standard's origins in Base$_{60}$. Dating from our deepest antiquity, it has been applied to far more than simple geometry. The consequences of the 360°, Base$_{60}$ foundation, and the 3, 6, 9, 12, and 72 connections have profound implications in math, physics, architecture, rocket science, spirituality, music, and metaphysics. The main implication is that; Base$_{60}$ and the 360° radial math, renders all of these disciplines easier to understand and to manage while serving to interconnect them and make them completely cohesive.

Based on all of this, I am prone to believe that there is more than just a passing significance in these many numerical relationships. Nikola Tesla thought so too. But I wish to see more validation.

For whatever reason, our ancestors made the very wise decision to use Base$_{60}$ as the foundation of their math. And a 360° radial standard for the circle is the resulting system that works most elegantly and efficiently - even when using derivative Base$_{10}$ math.

This writer is convinced that these facts are not just a set of convenient coincidences. Our ancestors possessed significantly more profound knowledge than we have been led to believe. Their deep understanding of math, physics, music, and cosmology potentially dwarfs our own 'modern' understanding of these subjects. It behooves us to listen and 'hear' what these facts are saying to us.

One more salient point about the phenomena thus-far explored: The Mesopotamian origin of our geometrical system is undeniable. And the Sumerian originators had a very predictable habit of connecting everything back to this single mathematical system. A few examples would be:

- The number of major divisions in a day. For example; the total hours in a day: (72 ÷ 3 = 24) as well as the *twelve* average hours of daylight and, *twelve* average hours of darkness.

- The number of minutes in a day: (24hr x 60minutes = 1,440 minutes in a day (1,440 ÷ 72 = 20.00 which is a whole number divisor of '360'.) Also, 1,440Hz is one of the central frequencies in the tuning systems, resulting from our work here.

- The number of seconds in a day (1,440 minutes x 60 seconds per minute = 864,000 seconds (43,200 in the day and 43,200 in the night) Curiously, 43,200 ÷ 10 = 432. This example points us toward a significant, foundational number that we will encounter a bit later; 432.

Mathematical 'coincidences' continue to accumulate. It is not possible, at this point, to see how all of this dovetails into a complete and cohesive tonal system. Yet, we are setting the foundation for some fascinating correlations, which will allow us to construct just such a system.

All of these associations and others, still in common-use today, have their origins with our Mesopotamian ancestors.

The number of months and days in a year is an extended example of their strict adherence to this numerical system. They used a 360-day calendar (with an extra 'leap' month added every few years to reset for the seasons.) We can keep the examples flowing by pointing out that the Earth's geographic coordinate system is still based on the ancient Sumerians' planetary grid system. Yes! They knew that the Earth is a sphere. And, they were clearly aware of the remaining planets of the solar system — even those that were not 'discovered' until much later in our current civilization cycle.

The repeated illustrations of the $Base_{60}$ and $Base_{12}$ mathematical prowess of the ancients are seemingly endless, with applications in agriculture, animal husbandry, accounting, architecture, personnel ranking systems, etc.

Literally, everything of cultural significance was connected back to their $Base_{60}$ (and its subset of $Base_{12}$) math.

And, yes! It makes perfect sense that the science of music, tone, and frequency would also be rooted in the same $Base_{60}$ geometry. That is to say; Why wouldn't it follow the pattern of every other significant cultural construct of the eras in question? How could one consider that this single discipline escaped notice and, somehow developed completely independent from the cultural standards applied to every other discipline?

I would argue that this deep connectivity extends directly to the *twelve* notes of the musical octave, which is but one of the significant reasons why the twelve-tone system is where we will concentrate our subsequent efforts.

What's next?

In a later section, *Chapter 6 - The 432Hz Question*, we will discuss an 'adjusted' musical tuning grid system based upon this work. At that point, it will not be necessary to remember all of the minutiae suggested in the math and its origins.

The constructed systems outlined in this text, will be, essentially self-managing in this regard.

The purpose of the preceding and somewhat ponderous demonstration, is merely to provide some small portion of a 'proof of concept' demonstrating the beautiful, harmonious connection between disciplines such as geometry, music, and extended cultural norms - as well as specific relationships to nature and therefore the very foundations of society.

At this time, however, it is time for us to consider some of the 3D geometry and resonances related to our nascent thesis.

3D Geometry of Sound

The Platonic Solids

As the name 'Platonic Solids' implies, the Greek philosopher, mathematician, and all-around uber-genius of his time, Plato, became obsessed with determining what three-dimensional polyhedrons might be considered the perfect geometric solids.

His work produced five perfectly symmetrical 3D shapes, each of which are formed by identical polygons, making up each face of the individual constructs. A curious property of these Platonic solids (Sometimes referred to as 'sacred' solids,) is that when properly aligned and to proper scale, the shapes 'nest' inside one other, forming a single amazingly-complex structure. This construct is roughly analogous to a three-dimensional version of a *more* complicated construct known in sacred geometry, as 'Metatron's Cube.'

Plato discovered these three-dimensional shapes in his work. I suppose the coincidence was simply too much for him to bear. The belief that his five perfect solids somehow correlated with the five 'humors' (or elements) of Earth, Air, Fire, Water, and Aether was just too tempting. He, therefore, assigned each of the Platonic solids as representative of one of these elements. His rationale for assigning each of these 'humours' is unknown. However, these primal elements are seen, indicated in each of the Platonic solids' details in the charts below.

Some modern thinkers seem to take great satisfaction in calling out Plato for claiming that he could illustrate the structure and harmony of the entire universe by this assembly of five solids.

It must make armchair physicists feel superior to one of the ancient world's greatest minds by belatedly poking holes in his more esoteric theories, utilizing modern, reductionist logic, and basing their argument on the visible universe's Newtonian paradigm.

Well, as it turns out, the field of quantum mechanics has a few things to say about this topic. Perhaps these great modern thinkers should pick up a text, or read recent papers regarding advances in quantum mechanics and modern cosmology; of which study strongly indicates that the underlying, energetic *substructure* of the universe, the radiating energies, and the molecular structures arising from them, are indeed based upon just such geometries.

"Philosophy is written in this grand book, the universe, which stands continually open to our gaze. But the book cannot be understood unless one first learns to comprehend the language and read the letters in which it is composed. It is written in the language of mathematics, and its characters are triangles, circles and other geometric figures without which it is humanly impossible to understand a single word of it; without these, one wanders about in a dark labyrinth." — Galileo Galilei

In any case, we will predicate our examination of 3D geometry on these Platonic Solids. Our brief analysis of each shape will be based on the sum of the internal angles and the number of polygons required to construct it. The product of which will reveal the particular structure's resonance frequency.

Each of the Platonic Solids will yield three significant pieces of frequency data. The first is the 'Associated Primary Resonance,' which is numerically identical to the sum of all internal angles, and is expressed in Hertz (Hz).

The second and third data pieces are some of the octavated frequencies, determined to correspond to the associated frequency; one octave up and one octave down. These values are also expressed in Hertz (Hz).

This subsequent analysis of 'octavation' or 'octavization' is based upon Pythagoras' detailed observations of octaves and intervals using his 'monochord' instrument. As a result of simple math, octaves are easily calculated respectively, as twice the base frequency $(2 \times f_1)$ and one-half the base frequency $(f_1 \div 2)$.

We cannot yet determine other harmonic intervals, such as the scalar thirds or fifths, because we do not yet know what the proper mathematical frequency intervals may be. But not to worry. The kind reader will see that the data, surprisingly and simply, falls into place.

We will also attempt to identify any obvious or apparent correlations between the geometry and which of the infinite regular polygons might share resonant frequencies based on our root frequency calculations. This data is displayed as 'Associated Polygons.'

So. With all this in mind, let's take a closer look at the details of these Platonic solids.

The Platonic or Sacred Solids

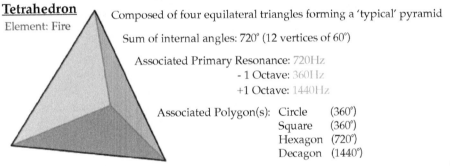

Tetrahedron
Element: Fire

Composed of four equilateral triangles forming a 'typical' pyramid

Sum of internal angles: 720° (12 vertices of 60°)

Associated Primary Resonance: 720Hz
    - 1 Octave: 360Hz
    +1 Octave: 1440Hz

Associated Polygon(s): Circle   (360°)
                      Square   (360°)
                      Hexagon (720°)
                      Decagon (1440°)

Fig 4.1

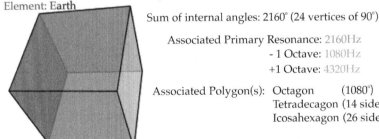

Hexahedron
Element: Earth

Composed of six squares forming a typical cube shape

Sum of internal angles: 2160° (24 vertices of 90°)

Associated Primary Resonance: 2160Hz
    - 1 Octave: 1080Hz
    +1 Octave: 4320Hz

Associated Polygon(s): Octagon   (1080°)
                      Tetradecagon (14 sides - 2160°)
                      Icosahexagon (26 sides - 4320°)

Fig 4.2

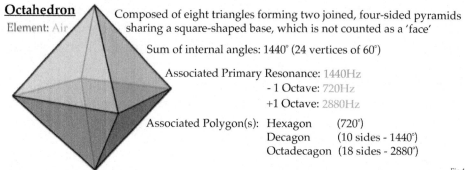

Octahedron
Element: Air

Composed of eight triangles forming two joined, four-sided pyramids sharing a square-shaped base, which is not counted as a 'face'

Sum of internal angles: 1440° (24 vertices of 60°)

Associated Primary Resonance: 1440Hz
- 1 Octave: 720Hz
+1 Octave: 2880Hz

Associated Polygon(s): Hexagon   (720°)
Decagon   (10 sides - 1440°)
Octadecagon (18 sides - 2880°)

Fig 4.3

Icosahedron
Element: Water

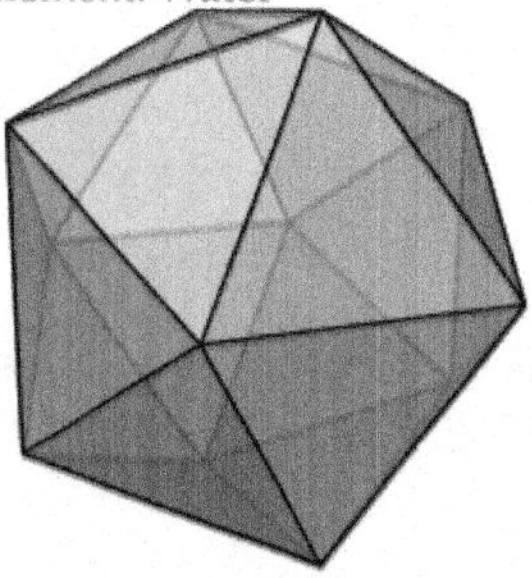

Composed of twenty triangles joined at each side

Sum of internal angles: 3600° (60 vertices of 60°)

Associated Primary Resonance: 3600Hz
- 1 Octave: 1800Hz
+1 Octave: 7200Hz

Associated Polygon(s): Dodecagon   (12 sides - 1800°)
Icosidigon   (22 sides - 3600°)
Tetracontagon (40 sides - 7200°)

Fig 4.4

Dodecahedron
Element: Aether

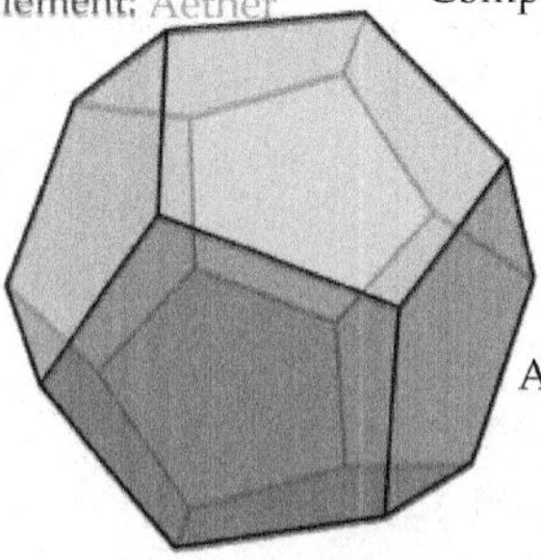

Composed of twelve pentagons joined at each side

Sum of internal angles: 6480° (60 vertices of 108°)

Associated Primary Resonance: 6480Hz
- 1 Octave: 3240Hz
+1 Octave: 12960Hz

Associated Polygon(s): Icosagon   (20 sides - 3240°)
Triacontaoctagon   (38 sides - 6480°)
Heptacontatetragon (74 sides - 12960°)

Fig 4.5

Platonic Solid Imagery, courtesy of Wikipedia Commons in original article located at: https://en.wikipedia.org/wiki/Platonic_solid

Regarding Other 3D Solids

There exist other sets of three-dimensional constructs, that bear some mention in our current analysis. Among these are the thirteen Archimedean solids, various sacred geometries, folding geometries, Fibonacci spirals, and vortex geometries... among others.

Some may cry, "foul!" as the writer chooses to *not* delve into any deeper study of the myriad, complex, 3D geometric solids. "Why not?"; If for no other reason than to bolster the developing thesis.

First and foremost; far better mathematicians have already blazed that particular trail. The interested seeker will find hundreds of extant volumes detailing the wonders of nature and geometry — both symmetrical and asymmetrical.

And, while we *will* touch upon some analysis and speculation on specific sacred geometries, symbology, harmonic series, and even touch ever-so lightly, upon toroidal energy fields in this text, most of the more-complicated, three-dimensional constructs are simply harmonics of the more basic two-dimensional geometry.

Therefore, any deeper consideration of these constructs would contribute nothing of significance to the thesis except, perhaps, a data set of potentially confusing cross-correlations. All significant resonances and harmonics are contained and reflected in the foundational, Euclidean and Platonic geometries.

Our work here centers on the simplicity and elegance of basic geometry and its proposed relationship to tone and frequency. In actuality, we are exploring geometry's universal connection to almost everything, just as Galileo suggested.

Therefore, the answer to the question is simple: The additional, complex geometries arise from Euclidean and Pythagorean geometry. Even Plato's sacred solids could be considered derivative because, all of the foundational maths are Euclidean in origin.

As such, these more intricate constructs are simply extensions of the primary geometry. Thus, it seems pointless to 'muddy the waters' by delving too deeply into what are ultimately, peripheral topics that after some cursory analysis, reveal no additional, compelling data to support or contradict this text's thesis. (*No disrespect to Archimedes.*)

Notwithstanding the above, some interesting correlative tidbits are to be found in a set of geometric constructs called Sacred Geometry.

Sacred Geometry and Sound

Deep Esoteric Connections

Our analysis of Sacred Geometry is no more complicated than the previous mathematical dissections - performed on the Euclidean and Platonic constructs. The 'sacred' constructs are primarily collections of complex, two-dimensional polygons that convey a specific, traditional, cultural, or esoteric message. Their study rests as much in the pervue of symbology as geometry.

However, the writer has selected a few of these particular geometric constructs for study, primarily because of their historical, symbolic, and cultural significance; both in ancient tradition and modern esoteric studies. Let's examine what these forms have to say to us regarding our journey into frequency and sound.

"Geometry, which before the origin of things, was co-eternal with the divine mind and, is God himself... and supplied God with the patterns for the creation of the world..."

— Johannes Kepler, The Harmony of the World, 1619

The Seed of Life

We will begin our discussion of the sacred geometric patterns with the *Seed of Life* construct. The Seed of Life pattern consists of seven circles, each of identical radius. One circle forms the central core of the construct. Six are arranged in an overlapping, equi-radial manner to create a central, flower-like pattern, consequently forming six 'petal' shapes radiating from the origin. The Seed of Life does not generally, have an enclosing circle. However, some sources erroneously construct it with an enclosing eighth circle. This enclosing circle represents *restriction* and *limitation*. The symbology inherent in enclosing the Seed of Life in a circle, is not at all what we are working towards here.

Therefore, we omit that particular, restricted version even though it is often seen in an enclosed form.

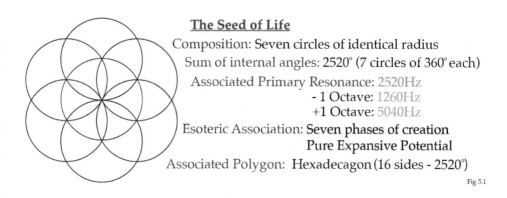

The Seed of Life
Composition: **Seven circles of identical radius**
Sum of internal angles: 2520° (7 circles of 360° each)
Associated Primary Resonance: 2520Hz
            - 1 Octave: 1260Hz
            +1 Octave: 5040Hz
Esoteric Association: **Seven phases of creation**
            Pure Expansive Potential
Associated Polygon: Hexadecagon (16 sides - 2520°)

Fig 5.1

Given the historically-stated implications of the symbol, it is no mystery that the Seed of Life is present, in some form, within many esoteric traditions. It is seen carved into ancient walls and pillars and, it is additionally recreated in some of the stained-glass and stonework of Templar, Gothic, and Byzantine era churches. Some examples of its *symbolic* significance are:

- Seven phases (days) of creation
- Seven human chakra
- Seven colors of the rainbow
- Seven ancient musical scales
- The seed of Creation in which the template of the holographic universe is based

The Egg of Life

Similar to the Seed of Life, the *Egg of Life* is the name commonly given to what is the second iteration of transition toward the Flower of Life construct. Those who enjoy meditatively recreating these symbols, may recognize that the Egg of Life is one step removed from the Seed. As the seed begins its expansion process, it swells with potential before springing forth as new life. Thus, the altered intersections representing the expansive energy of the construct.

In another perspective, the Egg of Life symbolizes the creative power(s) of the sacred feminine, while the Seed of Life embodies the potentiality of the sacred masculine. Such opinions seem to vary within and among various, esoteric belief systems.

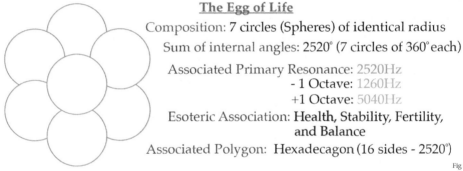

The Egg of Life
Composition: 7 circles (Spheres) of identical radius

Sum of internal angles: 2520° (7 circles of 360° each)

Associated Primary Resonance: 2520Hz
- 1 Octave: 1260Hz
+1 Octave: 5040Hz

Esoteric Association: **Health, Stability, Fertility, and Balance**

Associated Polygon: Hexadecagon (16 sides - 2520°)

Fig 5.2

The Egg of Life is represented initially, as seven circles that are in the beginning stages of expressing this creation potential.

Some practitioners are fond of expanding the image of the Egg of Life to a 3D image of a cluster of spheres. This is a decidedly more accurate, modern, yet non-traditional way of viewing the Egg of Life construction. The writer makes no judgment as to whether this is good, bad, right, or wrong. However, as it is a non-traditional representation of the symbol, which reveals little additional information, we will adhere to the more traditional representation.

To those who would protest such a dismissal, consider the following: Due to the fact that the three-dimensional image would contain either ten or twelve spheres, depending upon how it is rendered, the inherent resonances are already accounted for and included in our original geometric analysis.

This is because, 3600Hz and its lower octave of 1800Hz, for the former construct, as well as 4320Hz with its lower octave of 1080Hz, for the latter version, are all harmonic constructs for which resonances are already accounted for in the simpler constructs previously outlined.

Therefore, in regards to all recognized forms of the Egg of Life, we are in very good standing regardless of which position one may feel is technically correct.

The Fruit of Life

Despite all of the wonderful imagery and associations, the Fruit of Life represents the only resonant frequency (from sacred geometry) that does not appear naturally in the various tuning systems created in this text. This makes the Fruit of Life a bit of a mystery as the other sacred geometries are well-represented in the systems we will soon be creating. The resonance tone of the Fruit of Life consistently hovers between a 'D' and a 'D#.' Yet, in no instance do we see it actually resolve into a specific, usable tone in our twelve-tone systems.

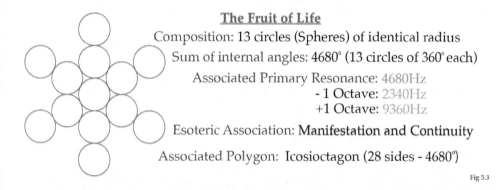

The Fruit of Life
Composition: 13 circles (Spheres) of identical radius
Sum of internal angles: 4680° (13 circles of 360° each)
Associated Primary Resonance: 4680Hz
- 1 Octave: 2340Hz
+1 Octave: 9360Hz
Esoteric Association: **Manifestation and Continuity**
Associated Polygon: Icosioctagon (28 sides - 4680°)

Fig 5.3

Additionally, any attempt to force its resonance of 4680Hz, into any of the created tuning systems results in some violation of the 'rules' of the game (which we will soon enumerate) as well as significant dissonance and harmonic failure. The primary and secondary tones of the Fruit of Life do however, occasionally pop up among the harmonics of herein-constructed systems. (i.e., 13th harmonic of 180Hz and, 26th harmonic of 720Hz) And, are thus implicitly, if peripherally included in the harmonic systems we will soon be building.

A quick check reveals that the primary resonance of the Fruit of Life, 4680Hz, turns out to be the 13th harmonic of 180Hz. This is why it appears in the harmonics, which we will be explaining in *Chapter 21 - Harmonics and Overtones.*

So, apparently, there is 'nothing to see here.' Therefore, we simply move on! The Fruit of Life resonance will be well-represented in the system(s) we are building in this work albeit in a largely harmonic capacity, and uncoupled from what would be its primary, fourth octave frequency of 585Hz, which again places it in-between a D and D# in our developing system.

This stubborn lack of cooperation, makes the Fruit of Life an even stranger work of sacred geometry. And honestly, this writer has become fascinated by the resonance values being strictly harmonic in nature. While checking for an interval that would allow the fourth-octave 585Hz to become a player in our system, the writer found that a perfect fit *could* be achieved using a 13:8 interval ratio, which would give us a workable interval width of 840.528ᶜ. Coincidentally, that interval is *designated* as an 'Overtone 6th - 13th Harmonic.' Knowing that we are getting well ahead of ourselves with that explanation, let's just say that the math indicates that no matter what, the Fruit of Life's resonance is destined to be a harmonic tone, nothing more.

However, as the Flower of Life construct inherently incorporates both the Seed of Life and the Fruit of Life geometries, the Fruit of Life's harmonic resonances, popping up (as it were) in the harmonics, does not come as a complete surprise. In fact, it is a kind of back-handed vindication to the developing thesis. However, the Fruit of Life construct is definitely unique; especially in these regards.

The Fruit of Life is full of rich, protective, and nurturing symbolism. Thirteen, a number that has received a lot of undeserved, bad press, carries an ancient association with over-watching, protective forces, natural cycles, and just overall, good fortune. Fitting, it seems.

Additionally, the Fruit of Life is metaphorically significant as the natural result of a fertile 'Seed' and it's cyclical journey to manifesting 'Fruit' and, from which you come full circle back to the seed… "As above, so below" — The end is merely the beginning of a new cycle.

The Flower of Life

This ancient construct is a veritable masterpiece of geometric symbolism that consists of nineteen evenly spaced and intertwined circles constrained within a single enclosing circle making for a total of twenty.

The inclusion of an enclosing circle is a bit of a surprise considering its previously noted implications regarding the Seed of Life. Yet, that is how the base image is generally and traditionally represented. The nineteen circles forming the main image, are arranged in the same repeating, flower-like arrangement and identical proportions as the Seed of Life pattern, which forms the core of the image. This somewhat fractal/holographic construction makes perfect sense as; in nature, the flower always contains the perfected seed of the next generation and, remains an ideal reflection of its source.

The Flower of Life

Composition: 19 circles of identical radius & one enclosing circle to complete

Sum of internal angles: 7200° (20 circles of 360° each)

Associated Primary Resonance: 7200Hz
- 1 Octave: 3600Hz
+1 Octave: 14400Hz

Esoteric Association: Underlying structure and order of life and universe, Connection with All

Associated Polygon: Tetracontadigon (42 sides - 7200°)

Fig 5.5

Each circle of the Flower of Life has its central axis on equidistant points of the perimeter of the six circles surrounding it, all possessing identical diameters. Connecting these points reveals the underlying pentagonal feature, indicating the sacred feminine basis of the Flower's design. Essentially, the 'Flower of Life' is multiple 'Seed of Life' images interlocked and overlapping to form an expanded geometry. No amount of analysis can diminish the mesmerizing effect of the overall construct.

The Flower of Life is a powerfully symbolic construct noted to be inscribed upon the stonework of many ancient structures, including the Osirion at Abydos, the gates of the Forbidden City in China, and many ancient, sacred structures of nearly every major spiritual tradition.

The 'Flower' represents the most notable and easily-recognized construct within the group of sacred geometric 'Unity' symbols.

In the archaeological context, it is seemingly impossible to explore an ancient spiritual structure without running across some representation of the Flower of Life — as the image has been found in multiple excavations, on every continent. Of significant note, is the fact that it is consistently found in the form that includes the enclosing circle. Therefore, this is the generally accepted form of the construct. Thus, we have used the enclosed version in this analysis.

Figure 5.4 - The Flower of Life etched into the granite of the Osirion in Abydos, Egypt
The Osirion at Abydos, Egypt boasts some of the earliest known examples of the Flower of Life. The engravings inscribed into red granite, one of the hardest stones in the world, are in excess of 6,000 years old and, may date back as far as 10,500 B.C.

The Merkabah

Next, we will consider the sacred geometry construct known as the Merkabah (məː ˈkaːbə) or Merkavah. This intricate design, also known as the star tetrahedron or, in its more familiar, two-dimensional representation, the Star of David. The three-dimensional geometry is basically constructed with one tetrahedron inverted *through* another.

Therefore, the internal angles of **2 x 1200° = 2400°,** would yield a resonance of 2400Hz, which is already included in our analysis as the octavated value for the single tetrahedron resonance, which is of course, 1200Hz.

The merkabah construct possesses extremely deep, esoteric symbolism and additionally, represents our first, and somewhat obvious encounter with a toroidal energy field.

These two nested tetrahedrons are not considered as one static image. Instead, they represent counter-rotational energy fields. One tetrahedron 'rotates' within its energy vortex while the other counter-rotates within its own field. The superimposed energies symbolized in the image, theoretically create a dual toroidal energy field — literally, one toroidal vortex, intersecting with another. In some meditational practices, this is a visualization tool to imagine the interplay of the cerebral energy vortex and the heart energy vortex.

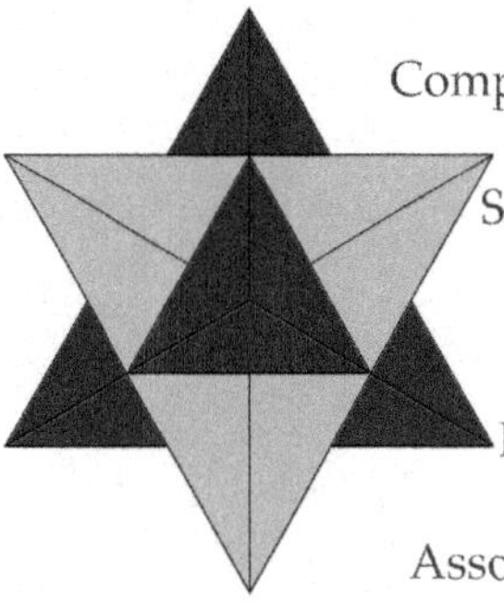

The Merkabah (aka Star Tetrahedron)
Composition: Two tetrahedrons inverted within each other, forming a 3D star with eight tetrahedral points

Sum of internal angles: 1440° (2 tetrahedrons of 720°)

Associated Primary Resonance: 1440Hz (Octahedron)
- 1 Octave: 720Hz
+1 Octave: 2880Hz

Esoteric Association: **Represents the light-spirit body and the Merkabah Light Throne/chariot**

Associated Polygon: Decagon (10 sides - 1440°)

Fig 5.6

This is all very fascinating to consider, since this construct has been around for an exceedingly long time. How did ancient people know about these two energy vortices and their intimate relationship?

In its two-dimensional form, the Merkabah construct is represented by the upright triangle of the sacred masculine (Mace or Sword) and the inverted triangle of the sacred feminine (Vessel or Chalice).

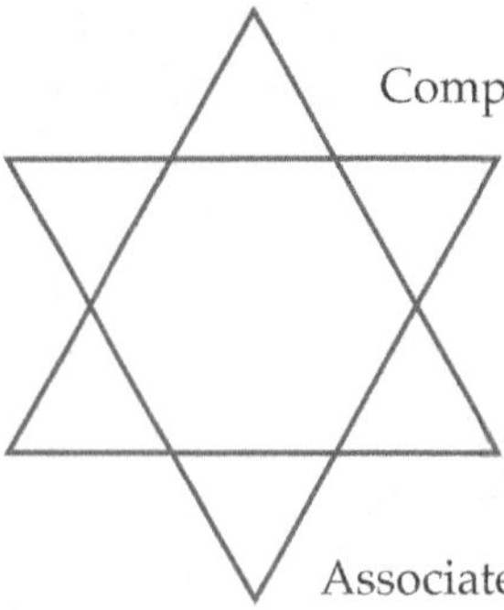

The Star of David
Composition: Two triangles inverted within each other, forming a 2D star with six triangular points

Sum of internal angles: 360° (2 triangles of 180° each)

Associated Primary Resonance: 360Hz
- 1 Octave: 180Hz
+1 Octave: 720Hz

Esoteric Association: **Union of sacred aspects of sacred feminine and sacred masculine**

Associated Polygons: Circle & Square (both 360°)

Fig 5.7

In this form, the resonance is simply calculated as two regular triangles of 180° each — resulting in a familiar 360° resonance that we will continue to see quite often.

Alternately, one may feel that the central hexagon, outlined by and, formed from the intersections of both triangles, requires special treatment. In such case, the resonance would be calculated as six triangles and one hexagon;

$$(6 \times 180°) + 720° = 1800° \text{ or } 1800\text{Hz} \ldots$$

This analysis reveals a value that is merely a higher octave manifestation of the dodecagon's base resonance and, as such, is already included in the basic analysis used to derive tonal frequencies for the system that we are here to explore.

Interestingly, not only is 1800Hz a primary resonance value of the dodecagon, it just so happens to be the fifth harmonic of the original 360Hz, circle resonance and, is thus well represented in the basic geometry.

We will be discussing harmonics and their vital importance to tonal systems in *Chapter 21 - Harmonics and Overtones.*

Vesica Piscis

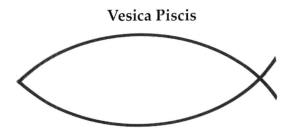

The Vesica Piscis (lit: bladder+fish) is a deceptively simple construct formed from two circles of identical radius, which intersect at each other's radial origin (center-point). The resulting figure has been adapted to many different disciplines and esoteric schools of thought. The figure displayed above, is one form of the (truncated) vesica piscis, which many will recognize as the symbol for the early Christian movement, the 'icthyus.' Because the icthyus is not strictly-speaking a regular polygonal construct, it is presented here as one example of the many versions of the vesica piscis construct.

In other esoteric belief, the vesica piscis symbolizes a portal through which the manifestation of the merged energies of sacred masculine (the first circle) and the sacred feminine (the second circle) are brought into physical being. Basically, conception. The vesica piscis construct has also been described as another illustration of a type of vortex-energy portal.

This is conceptually similar to a black hole/white hole combination where 'information' is transported through a energetic singularity and consolidated in the quantum 'Field.' Subsequently, the renewed, manifested, and enhanced data re-emerges into the physical universe from the other (white hole) aperture. We should always keep in mind that sacred geometries are largely two-dimensional representations of multi-dimensional concepts and phenomena.

Consequently, there are several 'interpretations' of meaning for the basic vesica piscis symbol. And, there are just as many ways of representing the symbol itself. However, every explanation of its meaning seems to revolve around the union of masculine (god) and feminine (goddess or Sophia) for the purpose of creative co-manifestation.

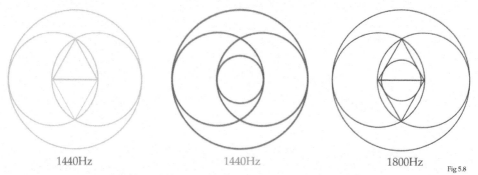

1440Hz   1440Hz   1800Hz   Fig 5.8

Fig. 5.8 - A few of the variations of the vesica piscis one might encounter

The basic version of the vesica piscis, Being formed from two circles, the math would be easily expressed as:

$$2 \times 360° = 720°$$

Of course, this results in a resonance value of 720Hz. But, like so many things in life; ultimately, it doesn't appear to be quite so simple.

The reason for this is that the various methods of illustrating the vesica piscis throw some additional geometry into the mix. *Figure 5.8*, illustrates just a few of the examples of extended geometry within the extant versions of the vesica piscis construct.

The vesica piscis construct is commonly found in nature, although generally 'hidden' *within* nature itself. Cut an apple or a pear in half vertically. The core of a 'natural' apple or pear contains a vesica piscis geometry, the center contains the seeds of new creation.

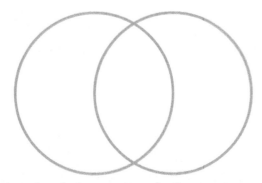

Fig. 5.9 - Basic vesica piscis geometry reflecting a resonance of 720Hz, which just happens to be the 2nd Harmonic of 360Hz.

This example is pretty much the epitome of the symbol's basic meaning. Also, if one were to cut the fruit in half horizontally, it would reveal the pentagon and the pentacle star geometries, prominently displayed. It is also relevant to point out that genetically modified fruits do not always properly display these internal geometries. Therefore and theoretically, such genetically-modified fruit may not share the proper, healthy resonance with nature.

Examples of the vesica piscis symbol in nature and architecture abound. All you have to do is start looking around. Just about any Gothic or neoclassical portal for windows or passageways, incorporates at least, the upper half of the central symbol. And, it seems that; once you take notice of one example, the symbol of the vesica piscis is suddenly everywhere — inherent in nature and much of human-manifested structure. The one notable exception being modern architecture, which has largely forsworn the use of graceful arcs, arches, and portal stylizations in the tradition of the vesica piscis within common, architectural geometry.

When one considers the wide variation in the presentation of the vesica piscis geometry, the underlying fact remains that the most basic form of the symbol, two circles intersecting at each of their radial origins as shown in *Figure 5.9*, is the most readily recognized variation of the vesica piscis.

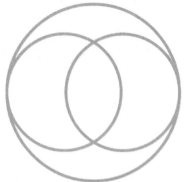

Fig. 5.10 - Vesica piscis geometry reflecting a resonance of 1080Hz
(3rd Harmonic of 360Hz and the 2nd Harmonic of 540Hz)

The resulting resonance again, is 720Hz. At times, the figure includes an enclosing circle as shown in *Figure 5.10*. This merely adds another harmonic layer, which again, has previously been encountered and is already incorporated into our basic resonance data. The resonance inherent in this enclosed version calculates to 1080Hz.

The unenclosed version's resonance of 720Hz, presents as the 2nd harmonic (one octave higher) of 360Hz, which is a very important tone in our tonal series, reflecting the resonance of the basic circle.

Additionally, 1080Hz is the 3rd harmonic of 360Hz while also being the 2nd harmonic of 540Hz, yet another critical tone in the work we are doing here, which reflects the resonance of the pentagon.

The purpose for pointing to this fact at this early stage, is merely to illustrate the graceful, cyclical nature of these tonal relationships and the natural harmonic balance that is revealed when working with geometric resonances in this way.

Considering the various resonances and harmonics outlined above, the math resulting in a resonance of 720Hz and consisting of harmonic ties to 360Hz, 540Hz, and 1080Hz, will be our reference for this particular sacred geometry construct.

This primary resonance value has, again, already been encountered as the inherent resonance of the tetrahedron as well as the hexagon in Euclidean geometry. This fact was previously explored in our analysis of the basic two-dimensional geometry, first examined in the second chapter of this text.

In Conclusion

From this brief analysis of the sacred geometry constructs above, one could be forgiven for making the observation that; as fascinating as the analysis of sacred geometries may be, each construct (or symbolic glyph) reveals little in the way of unique geometric resonance data and therefore, usable geometric resonance frequencies. To be quite clear, we've already 'been there and done that.'

Each of the constructs, being derived from the existing, foundational geometries, reveal intrinsic, resonant octaves and harmonics of the same Euclidean and Platonic origins that we have previously examined.

That each of the specific resonances is significant to the broader interpretation of each symbol's inherent, esoteric meaning is a given.

However, while their esoteric impressions and interpretations may be culturally-fascinating and significant; individually, these ancient symbols contribute little that is unique in the way of novel resonance frequencies to the purpose of this text.

What these constructs *do* provide, is an entire catalog of correlating harmonic data that will prove instrumental in validating the work we will soon be doing. That work is; the construction of unique geometric-based tuning systems for the purpose of relaxation, healing, and wellness applications.

That the sacred geometry frequencies are culturally significant, spiritually indispensable, and mentally compelling, the author concurs. However, if we arrive at a resonance frequency of 360Hz for a circle, the octave tones and harmonics resulting from, for instance, two, sixteen or any number of circles, is implied in the initial work by way of octavation, math, and naturally-occurring harmonics.

It therefore follows that; we should *expect* to see those frequencies either in the main tuning systems or at minimum, in the harmonics, preferably both.

The described scenario of harmonics, resulting from primary resonance values, is precisely what we have observed during this brief analysis of sacred geometries.

We will soon bear witness to solid verification that the vast majority of these frequencies naturally appear in certain geometric tonal systems — once the basic geometric resonances and tone correlations are ironed out. This leads us directly into systems of tuning instruments such that they can exist and play naturally within a geometric tuning paradigm.

That many of the exposed resonances appear in the geometric tuning grids created later in this work, is a matter of math and logic — not magic. The mathematical effects themselves are exclusively due to an incredibly well-designed system of geometry originating in deepest antiquity.

For those interested in further exploring sacred geometries and their resonances, here is a brief listing of other notable, complex sacred geometries:

- Triquetrium (Variation of the Vesica Pisces construct)
- Germ of Life (Closely related to the Seed of Life)
- Metatron's Cube (A fusion of Platonic solids)
- Pentacle (Five pointed star of protection/warding)
- Grid of Life (Multiple Flower of Life patterns interwoven into an expanded, multi-verse pattern)
- Vector Equilibrium (Two interesting fusions of 3D geometries)
- Tree of Life (From the Qaballic Studies)
- Sacred Feminine - Essentially an inverted triangle or pyramid
- Sacred Masculine - Essentially an upright triangle or pyramid
- Pillar of Power (Closely related to the Tree of Life construct)

Caution: Sacred geometry is a rabbit hole of great depth. But, well worth the effort.

The 432Hz Question

A Problem Compounded by Standardization and Even Temperament

There has been significant debate, talk, speculation, and no shortage of authoritative works proposing the utilization of an alternate tuning standard based on an A^4 fixed at 432Hz; meaning that the 'A' above middle 'C' on the standard keyboard, commonly referred to as the 'fourth-octave-A' or 'A^4', should be *re*-standardized to 432Hz. Most of the information is interesting, some of it compelling, but not all of it entirely factual.

It should be noted that the 432Hz issue is altogether separate from the 'equal temperament' discussion. However, they are necessarily discussed together because, the adoption of the concert tuning standard and the standardization of the equal temperament tuning system seem to have occurred somewhat concurrently on the historical timeline.

The Concert Tuning Standard and 432Hz

The concert tuning standard was fixed at 440Hz (for A^4) circa 1936 in the Americas and other countries. The standard was eventually adopted and instituted as the international concert pitch standard in 1955. However, many European and American orchestras were already using this standard (although certainly not universally) since the late 1890s.

Prior to that time, tuning fundamentals from as low as 430Hz to as high as 452Hz were in scattered use worldwide.

The range of demands precipitated by these random tuning standards had continued to be a significant source of difficulties among composers, conductors, and performers as well as instrument designers. The situation was particularly hard-felt among operatic singers who were often expected to sing in much higher and brighter registers that consequently harmed their voices and tragically threatened to shorten their careers. For some perspective, think for a moment about Mozart's aria titled '*Queen of the Night*' from **_The Magic Flute_**. Now, imagine if it were performed in a tuning that was even higher than the commonly-heard standard A^4-440Hz tuning. One word immediately comes to mind; Brutal!

Owners of stringed instruments were also constantly frustrated by breaking strings and instrument damage caused by the more stressful tunings at the higher end of the standardization range.

To further complicate the situation; Pianos, when included in a production, force all performers to play to whatever tuning standard the piano is using. Because the piano is a fixed-tuning instrument, its presence *dictates* the tuning for every other instrument on-stage. The tuned keyboard became much the tyrant of the orchestral world.

As if the situation could not get any worse, we learn that it certainly did. Tuning difficulties were further exacerbated by the unfortunate reality that pianos do not utilize a single string to create their tones. Yes, you read that correctly. A layman's image of the piano's function is one felted hammer striking one string yielding one tone. However, this is not actually the case.

Most concert pianos, whatever the stated tuning standard, utilize either two or three strings for each note or piano key. Generally, the arrangement would be three strings for the treble tones and two strings for the lower registers. While multiple strings make for a fuller tone, rendering the somewhat 'choral' tonal texture of the piano, there is absolutely no way to keep multiple strings tuned to the same pitch for any period of time. Most professional piano tuners don't even try. Instead, they generally tune same-key strings to within a certain 'tolerance' that is considered the acceptable standard. This wiggle-room can be as much as a 7$^¢$ difference. So, there's that little complication with creating pure tone within modern standards.

To *ridiculously* complicate matters, piano tunings prior to the late nineteenth or early twentieth centuries were not yet standardized in any meaningful way. The tuning *and* temperament of that piano tuning, rested mainly with those professional masters who maintained the piano's tuning in any particular venue. Some master piano tuners used 'Mean Tone' variants while others used their own interpretations of 'equal temperament' with a twist... sometimes, including their personally-preferred fundamental tone. To say all of this caused confusion and frustration might be considered a bit of an understatement. Fortunately, most composer's scores included specific tuning instructions for the performance of their music, which of course didn't add to the confusion at all.

Standardization was an apparent necessity. However, the choice of the 440Hz concert tuning pitch may not have been the ideal or even the logical solution. One gets the feeling that 440Hz standardization may have been an uneasy compromise between argumentative voices rather than any logically considered solution to the problem.

The popular 'alternate' of 432Hz tuning standard has gained a lot of positive attention in recent years. Much of it is, in this writer's opinion, well-deserved. And, we will therefore, lay out a logical case for adopting a 432Hz tuning standard in this very chapter.

Music performed in equal-temperament tuning with the 432Hz, alternative tuning standard takes on a different, more subjectively pleasing texture when compared to the same music played in the international 440Hz concert tuning standard. To the writer, it just sounds more colorful and calming. Your mileage may vary. But, there is much more to the story.

While its superior tonal quality is an entirely subjective assessment, it is one that has been reluctantly echoed by some professional musicians in the meditative and sound healing arena, such as Mr. Steven Halpern. At the time of this writing, Halpern is a forty-six-year veteran of meditative and relaxation music production. His catalog boasts over thirty unique productions spanning those decades.

In recent years, Mr. Halpern has produced several masterful and very popular meditation and relaxation compilations, some of which have been 'down-tuned' to the 432Hz even-tempered tuning.

In an interview that appeared on the network streaming service, *Gaia.com*, an initially skeptical Halpern while not expressly stating a preference, did confess that 432Hz had a certain appeal to him.

Having listened to both the 440Hz and 432Hz versions of Mr. Halpern's works, this writer concurs with his expressed opinion vis-a-vis the 432Hz standard, if not the methodology used for digitally down-tuning 440Hz standard productions.

Concurrently, when considering the 'controversy' over 440Hz vs. 432Hz tunings, one must understand that the international 440Hz concert tuning standard is just as arbitrary as any other choice while having the distinction of being just as complicated and, factually, possessing little or no scientific basis.

So, if it were merely a matter of making a logical choice, how did western music manage to get it so horribly, completely wrong?

In contrast to the 440Hz tuning standard's lack of basis, logic, and reason, a 432Hz standard does have a rational basis. That basis is contained within some of the math we have already seen and more of which we will soon examine. And it is that very subject that we are here to address.

Mathematics (specifically; geometry) was considered the foundation of everything in the Golden Age of the ancient world. Music was by no means an exception. It would make no logical sense to posit that music was somehow exempt from this pan-cultural norm — given the fact that *so much* of what the ancient cultures built and historically recorded for posterity was always and in some way, based upon their fundamental understanding of these same mathematical principles.

In *Chapter 9 - 'The Case for 432Hz'*, we will attempt to further bolster the claims regarding the 432Hz standard with a more in-depth analysis of tuning standards.

Adding to the issues and debate surrounding concert tuning standards, another main challenge with tuning systems is the concept of 'temperament' specifically, 'even temperament' as used in modern music.

However, the overriding consideration for any tuning system is that of the 'fundamental' tone upon which the tuning system is based; as this is the foundation upon which all subsequent harmonies are constructed. The word *temperament* can be viewed as the underlying mathematics that determine the intervals between successive tones in relation to the fundamental tone.

These separate-but-critical considerations are the primary reasons why it is oftentimes difficult to discuss temperament without the subject of tuning standards being automatically included in the conversation.

Equal (or even) temperament is a progressive, tonal construct where each successive tone in a scale is mathematically, 'evenly spaced' by a fixed mathematical constant. By carefully varying frequency over an acoustic interval, we construct a tuning standard that meets the necessary criteria. In 'even temperament,' the tonal difference (that we hear) from C^4 to $C^{\#4}$ is mathematically equal to the tonal contrast of every other semitone throughout the entire audible range - regardless of the nominal differences in Frequency expressed in Hertz.

In the modern standard of equal temperament, the intervals are forced to be exactly 1/12th of the octave. That is to say that each semitone carries a mathematically equivalent interval value to every other semitone interval in the system.

This, however, is not how nature seems to operate. If it did, the nautilus shell would probably look much different and likely be far less interesting.

The math of even-tempered scales is accomplished by some reasonably complicated ratios which involve square roots used to calculate the relationships between tones. As a young musician, I never really understood any of it. I just played by the stated rules. Eventually, I grew tired of the constant dissonance of the standardized, pre-packaged tones, and moved on to other pursuits.

At any rate; to make such a system universal, there must be a consensus among performers as to the frequency of the fundamental tone. In the case of our standardized, modern music, the *root* or fundamental frequency is primarily understood to be 440Hz for the A above middle C (aka A⁴).

Applying the subsequent even-tempered math, yields frequencies of unnatural, cumbersome frequency values and reveals some unfortunate compromises made to wedge the proper number of intervals into the octave. Nature was never intended to be confined to a one-size-fits-all methodology. And, in this writer's opinion, it hasn't really turned out well for those who have tried.

In modern tuning, this gerrymandering of frequency to achieve the illusion of 'even-temperedness' is required regardless of the root frequency chosen, and is decidedly lacking in elegant qualities. Therefore, simply changing the tuning standard from 440Hz to say... a 432Hz value yields no improvement whatsoever, since the same shoehorn... Rather; the same *math,* is used to create any tuning system based on the equal temperament standard.

For most musicians, equal temperament is what we have to work with. And, honestly, it works *reasonably* well for commercial music. But, when considering meditative, relaxation, or healing sound and holistic objectives, the equal tempered tonal structure is wholly inadequate, as it provides no physiologically-relevant resonances with which to work. That is, unless you happen to be using the 432Hz-based even-tempered system, in which case, every 'A' tone is useful. *(See: Appendix IV for a comprehensive listing of the actual tones used in both 440Hz, 12TET and 432Hz, 12TET systems.)*

To further validate this claim, one learns of a standing controversy in music theory. There has been some significant professional angst over, for example, a 'missing' tone that resides 'somewhere' between G♯ and A in the 12-TET system. Additionally, there are most-certainly other imperfect intervals created by the current system, that are also a bone of contention for many.

Some musicians go so far as to designate this missing note as G♯A♭ to indicate that G♯ is not enharmonic with and, therefore not the same tone as A♭ (which it certainly is not.) As for the other imperfect intervals, the tone frequency difference for a perfect 5ᵗʰ should, in one theory, be 702ᶜ. In actual, 12-TET practice, this modern standardization forces this interval to 700ᶜ.

It is a commonly repeated trope that the average ear cannot hear differences less than 5¢. (Sometimes this is said to be 6¢ or even 7¢ depending on who is doing the talking.) However, other critical intervals, such as the Major 6th, in the twelve-tone, even temperament (12-TET) system are as much as 15¢ off according to more harmonically balanced systems. Now, that is a noticeable difference.

A cent (¢) is a specific metric used for such tonal intervals. In even-tempered scales, there are exactly 100¢ between each semitone. Consequently, there being twelve intervals within an octave, we arrive at a perfect 1200¢ for a complete octave. Unfortunately, there is no direct way to convert a frequency to cents or vice-versa - as cents are a measure of the 'distance' between two frequencies and not a metric that is specific to the frequencies themselves.

Again, detractors of pure-tone and micro-tonal tuning systems will again, hawk the old narrative that most cannot hear a difference in tone where the interval is 'less than a nickle' (5¢) in any case. Who comes up with these ridiculous tropes anyway? In this writer's opinion, this is a baseless and completely nonsensical argument against using the purest and most natural tones reasonably attainable.

The ear may not be able discern the difference but, nature and your brain certainly can sense the difference, and they *do* differentiate between even closely adjacent tones.

The equal-tempered system in general usage is, in-part achieved by incidentally compromising an entire 'tonal structure' somewhere between 'G' and 'A,' as well as the purity of many essential harmonic intervals. The interval calculations - being shoehorned (as it were) into the modern approach, is the final straw as far as this writer is concerned, driving home the point that the current standard is decidedly imperfect. And many musicians know this as fact.

So… Why don't we 'regular' folks know about any of this?

Well, most people simply do not (or cannot) notice the off tones and imperfect intervals; because our incredibly-adaptive ears and brains have the unique ability to fill in the blanks for us — albeit with significant effort. Our sensory systems and their associated neurology, often make necessary corrections without our awareness.

Ironically, the people who are considered the 'best' at hearing modern pitches as-played, are said to have 'perfect pitch.' Nothing could be farther from reality, in this writer's opinion. They may have 'perfect pitch' relative to the 440Hz, equal-temperament standard. But, since we have shown that 12-TET is decidedly imperfect, these people are simply trained to hone in to these *im*perfect pitches.

Of significant note is the above-referenced phenomenon of the nervous system's automatic compensations for sounds that are heard. This phenomenon may also go a long way to explain why instruments that sound wonderful to one person are 'chalkboard-fingernails' to others. For this writer, the latter would definitely apply to the 440Hz, 12-TET tuned piano. That instrument and your mild-mannered author have never gotten along.

One could theorize we could suppose, that the compensatory effect is somewhat different for everyone, which is why we must be especially mindful when attempting to create a one-size-fits-all system for sound and frequency work. This compensatory effect itself, is solidly within the realm of neuroscience. Thus, the writer will leave this theory in their capable hands to further explore.

Those who possess so-called perfect pitch, relative to 440Hz, 12-TET, are entrenched in an illusion created by a deeply flawed system.

In the case of modern, equal-temperament, ignorance may seem to be bliss. However, Galileo had a lot to say about such an imperfect system of tones. His position is made clear in the following quote:

To paraphrase the words of Galileo: Tones that are played together, but do not *naturally* and *perfectly* harmonize, maintain the ear (and the associated neurological, auditory pathways) in a state of constant physical and neurological compensation. In his words, "perpetual torment" in other words, a constant irritation.

From a relaxation and sound healing perspective, this is completely unacceptable. If the clients' ears cannot relax, then the client's mind and body cannot rest.

"Agreeable consonances are pairs of tones which strike the ear with a certain regularity; this regularity consists in the fact that the pulses delivered by the two tones, in the same interval of time, shall be commensurate in number, so as not to keep the eardrum in perpetual torment, bending in two different directions in order to yield to the ever discordant impulses." - Galileo Galilee

Under such conditions, the client will never fully benefit from any of the intended relaxation and healing effects. We must use better, more natural harmonies.

Additionally, Galileo asserts that the "two tones..." must be "commensurate in number..." In order to prevent this "perpetual torment" of the ear and the neurological processes that allow us to 'hear' sound. Commensurate means: "corresponding in size or degree; [to exist] in proper proportion." *(Brackets mine)*

So what can we take away from Galileo's sage advice?

The phrase 'commensurate in number', strongly implies a proportional yet natural mathematical correlation between these tones. Therefore, such a proportional relationship strongly implies a *natural* mathematical and (dare I say?) *geometric* relationship.

We must now seize upon these words, and their interpretation, to assert that there must be a consistent, commensurate, geometric proportion in successive tones, in any scale intended to trigger a positive physiological response as well as to promote relaxation and, therefore, healing. Furthermore, this text proposes that such proportion is to be *commonly* found in nature and the related math.

The writer proposes just such a basis, which is to be achieved via universal geometry.

The current equal-tempered tonal system is, decidedly insufficient to promote the necessary, desired response at the neurological level. And, the commonly used tone values are not, in any way, naturally 'commensurate.' i.e., 'proportional' to any natural, neurological, or physiological process. In the prevalent, modern tuning standard, complex math using irrational numbers is employed to calculate the individual tones that make up these even-tempered tuning systems.

The resulting wave-form values are wildly fragmented with decimal remainders that often extend to six or even eight digits.

You can easily demonstrate the harmonic discord spoken of by Galileo simply by playing two random notes on the piano and then selecting two more - repeat as desired or necessary. Whenever you strike two notes that do not share 'consonance,' (i.e., harmonize) the ears and brain react unpleasantly. We say that the notes sound 'out of tune', when in fact, they may be in tune for that particular system but, are simply not harmonically compatible. This is what we find in 440Hz, 12-TET systems. The notes are technically in-tune for that system. But, they are not quite what one could call perfectly harmonic.

If you focus on the disharmony in the played notes, you may be able to 'feel' how hard your senses are working behind the scenes to resolve the dissonance — to make it work. The human brain is hard-wired to attempt to resolve dissonance into a consonant signal.

But it requires a lot of neurological horsepower to accomplish this task. And, it's not always possible. The theory then is that; repeated exposure to the same *micro*dissonances such as those prevalent in the 440Hz, 12-TET system, forces a more permanent neurological compensation (i.e., Desensitization) to occur.

At this point, some of you kind readers may be starting to understand the writer's deeper point regarding consonance and the prevalent standards.

Such compensatory mechanisms are how we have become accustomed over a lifetime, to modern music's inherent dissonances. And, to commercial music, it is an arguably irrelevant discussion. Yet, when one considers the potential healing aspects of sound and frequency, the usual musical tuning methods are wholly insufficient and, the writer will argue, wildly inappropriate for the task.

The modern even-tempered tuning system, based upon 440Hz, was not the common standard until the early twentieth century. Most contemporary musicians are utterly unaware that any alternative exists due to the singular academic focus on the modern 440Hz, 12-TET system.

Why was this obviously-flawed system ever adopted? We will likely never find a clear answer to that question. However, it is apparent that we are supposed to accept the 'fact' that these tones are the only possibilities for making music. Otherwise, why aren't other tuning options routinely taught in music schools? The 440Hz, 12-TET system is almost exclusively presented in the vast majority of music schools. Oh, certain teachers may briefly expose students to the fact that other systems 'once existed.' But, that is usually where it ends.

Now, you know better. We are not limited to just the eighty-eight notes of the modern piano for creating musical tone. There exists a quite literally unlimited, abundant supply of consonant tones for us to explore and, with which to compose our life's masterpiece.

I say that we go find them and, use them.

Ignorance and Fear are the parents of twin evils; Limitation and Self-Doubt.
-Author

7

Equal Temperament

Systematically Destroying Harmony for Over a Century

Equal or 'even' temperament is familiar to everyone, to at least some extent because, it is actually the system in which virtually all modern music is composed. The system itself, standardized in North America circa 1930, is one in which the octave is strictly divided into twelve equal tones of 100$^{\rm c}$ each. The cent ($^{\rm c}$) is a seemingly arbitrary unit that applies to the 'distance' between frequencies. A full octave is comprised of 1200$^{\rm c}$ and, in equal-temperament, each semitone is determined to be separated by *precisely* 100$^{\rm c}$ without compromise or regard to the inconvenient realities of nature.

The implementation of the twelve-tone equal temperament (12-TET) standard, also referred to interchangeably as 'even-temperament' within this work, addressed a few serious problems regarding the standardization of instrumental design, orchestral performance, and composition but consequently created many other problems with the actual music.

Conscientious performers and composers throughout the latter half of the 19$^{\rm th}$ century and up to the present time, have been engaged in debates over temperament and tonal harmony issues arising from 12-TET tuning from the moment the system was introduced.

Because the current standard, 12-TET system is now the sole system taught in most musical schools, any other tuning systems have all but disappeared as historical footnotes. As previously stated, most modern musicians are completely unaware that other tuning systems exist, much less possess the knowledge and tools with which to design and implement custom tuning artistically. In this writer's opinion, contemporary music is stagnating - our musicians having been thoroughly indoctrinated into the cult of 440Hz, 12-TET with few legitimate methods by which to individualize their expression through their music.

Modern (popular) music often appears dry and monotonous because almost every piece of music is now written by rote-formulas using the same old, limited 88-piano-key tonal structure, which is now being generated for the musician by high-tech computing devices called 'beat boxes' or 'Digital Audio Workstations.'

So-called 'artists' with very little knowledge of music, can now use computerized 'loops' and 'beats' derived from prepackaged 'instrument packs.' Their only limitation is the significant financial outlay required to purchase the latest and greatest equipment and software add-ons. The tracks most often resulting from such a system reflect the minimal skill required to create them and, more often than not, demonstrate a general absence of imagination as well as a significant lack of comprehension of the entire concept of tonal variation and musical phrasing. In comparison, the writer is reminded of small children playing with their little, colorful music toys.

To be fair, when 'real' musicians choose to work with these modern systems, you get far better results. But, this writer observes that; real musicians generally prefer real instruments (as well as preferring to perform with other real musicians) to create their music, with heart-and-hand.

However, when talented musicians adopt modern technology in their workflow, the results *can* be magnificent. After all, an instrument is only as good as those who choose to master it. Therefore, any instrument is eminently useful for making artistic compositions. The point here is that the prevalent, chronically-assistive technologies can make otherwise talented artists complacent and outright lazy.

Obviously, the results are less than stellar when the technology is in charge of the creative flow, rather than the musician artistically bending the technology to their unique vision.

Whatever the case may be, there are only so many ways to combine eighty-eight piano keys. As an unintended consequence, 12-TET has destroyed harmony, limited creativity, and has incarcerated a great many, otherwise talented musicians in a tarnished, technological, 12-TET cage.

The most well-trained and educated musicians are often too rigidly technical (and technological) in their approach to sound. Personally, this writer is drawn to artists who paint with unique, random brushes, strongly preferring raw creativity over listening to a music stream and being unable to discern the difference between one track and the next.

The modern 12-TET standard has only been *the* standard for about a hundred years. We have an entire cultural legacy, a vast library of music composed in the hundreds of years prior that no one living has ever heard as the composers intended. There is one exception to this rule that I find fascinating. And, that is the wealth of compositions exclusively for the bowed string instrument ensemble. These instruments in the absence of a restricting piano accompaniment, are capable of producing the far wider and significantly more harmonic performance that the composer originally intended.

This is true for bowed instruments specifically because, non-fretted string instruments have the ability to produce the actually-intended note rather than the compromised tone offered by 12-TET. Sometimes it will be a D$^\sharp$ and sometimes it will be a E$\flat$. Those who are fortunate enough to have learned music on a violin, viola, cello, or even a fretless classical guitar, already understand what is being discussed here. And, many of you may also be nodding your heads in agreement with the basic arguments of the thesis, if not the specifics.

In this writer's opinion, the reality of 'lost tone' is the actual tragedy resulting from these myriad compromises thrust upon music by international musical associations in the name of 'standardization.'

Yet, there *is* an uncompromising solution to the compromise of standardization. And, that is one of the main things we intend to explore in this work.

The consequences of 12-TET standardized tuning have not been all negative, however. Since the spread of these tuning standards in the late 19th and early 20th centuries, manufacturers of musical instruments have achieved explosive innovation on the hardware side of music. Keyboards, which had been mainstays in upper-class homes since the late 1600s, were suddenly, within reach of more middle-class households; primarily because manufacturers had a somewhat-formalized format with which to standardize and subsequently mass-produce their instruments at lower costs.

The upright piano was suddenly more practical and relevant to the middle class. All of this served to bring prices down from 'unattainable' to most households, to become seen as just a 'major purchase.' This fact alone allowed the significant development of varied musical styles in the Americas, Britain (especially) and in other hotbeds of musical innovation around the world. I would go so far as to hypothesize that the Blues and Ragtime's evolution into Jazz, Rockabilly, and ultimately Rock 'n Roll would not have been possible without the widespread, inherent imperfections of the early implementation of equal-temperament tuning. Every cloud does seem to have a silver lining.

For hundreds of years prior to the standardization of 12-TET, we see an arguably minimal variation in the instruments and musical styles available. In just the past one hundred years or so, the proliferation of and accessibility to musical instruments (of all types) has served to allow just about anyone the opportunity to experience group and individual musical performance at earlier ages than ever in history. This was once a privilege reserved for the somewhat wealthier population. This writer also doubts that this universalization of music would have been possible without the widespread standardization such as seen within the gilded cage of equal-temperament.

These observations are presented for background and context. We are not trying to reinvent the wheel here. We are trying to make a brand new kind of wheel altogether.

What we are here to accomplish is the discovery of a more human-friendly tonal system; one that is to be adopted if we expect to make 'music' that truly enhances human health and wellbeing.

Back to the issues with equal-tempered systems

In equal temperament, all intervals are made up of semitone units. Each semitone is set precisely at 1/12th of an octave, which is 100¢ in the technical language. A 12-TET fifth is built upon seven semitones, therefore, it is measured at 700¢ exactly. And, relative to a pure, perfect fifth, it is always 2¢ flat. An even-tempered, major third is built upon four semitones and is therefore, 400¢ wide. However, compared to a pure major third, it is a whopping 14¢ sharp. The major sixth is constructed upon nine semitones (900¢) and turns out to be 16¢ sharp. We could continue with the examples. But, the kind reader certainly gets the point.

The common assertion that the human ear is unable to discern differences between tones separated by less than a 'nickel' (aka 5¢), is a poor excuse and, seems like nothing more than a rationalization for the inherent imperfections in the 12-TET system.

However, as was previously stated and, is just as likely to be noted many more times, the modern equal-tempered tuning system works well for commercial music and entertainment. However, whatever system we end up with during this exploration will generally consist of what this writer, and the research consider to be 'pure' tones and intervals. These will be derived from the mathematics of geometry and nature. How's that for a systematic basis?

Because in equal temperament, the intervals are identical in all parts of the chromatic scale - despite the natural harmonics, many may feel that the system is not only one most familiar to musicians but, the only system that can navigate modern music's expanded harmonies. Melodically, it achieves the ideal situation of being standardized while having somewhat perceptually equal steps for every semitone.

But the price for these significant advantages, is the absence of more perfectly tuned intervals, with the obvious exception of the octave.

Therefore, the complete absence of pure harmony in many intervals in the 12-TET standard, is a compensatory artifact from ruthlessly calculating an objectively 'equal-tempered' tuning system. It's all in the math used to calculate them, and it is all a compromise.

Merely inserting the 'missing' tone(s) or correcting the mis-tuned intervals in an ad-hoc manner, would likely cause the whole house of cards to come crashing down. The math just doesn't work that way. We need better math... And, therefore, better resulting tones.

Perhaps this inherent lack of harmonic richness is why ancient musicians used an uneven temperament in their compositions and scales. However, given an infinite selection of tone frequencies, it is a daunting task to ascertain what calculations each ancient culture may have utilized. Therefore, we can only imagine how such music may have sounded in reality. Additionally, this writer challenges the absurd assertion that *complex harmonies* can be achieved with no system other than 12-TET.

Fortunately, much of the historical interval data has survived through history. The Pythagorean and some of the Platonic theories have survived, due to the extensive writings of other authors contemporary to the common period(s). While we will endeavor to honor these contributions and attempt to use this information (in spirit at least), it is not possible to recreate the exact tones used by Plato, for example. This writer is privy to no sources that can verify any formula or procedure for replicating the actual, authentic tones used in antiquity. So, we only have our modern vocabulary and ancient geometry to guide us.

In other words, we must make educated estimations. Yet, other aspects of the work will remain decidedly familiar as we do not seek to raze theory to its foundations — merely to renovate the main structure a bit.

To such end, throughout the work contained herein, the reader will notice a distinct bias towards a twelve-tone system. And, there are several reasons why the writer believes this system is the best possible fit.

First, a twelve-tone system is readily usable; as modern keyboards already utilize the same configuration.

Second, the number twelve (Base$_{60}$ and Base$_{12}$) is part and parcel to the entire geometric thesis and serves as a foundation upon which all manner of successful systems have been traditionally built.

A quick review of chapters one and three may serve as a convenient reminder as to the deep significance of the number twelve in geometric systems.

Third, the resulting system(s) outlined in this work should remain as *compatible as possible* with existing music theory practice without compromising nature and harmony. We would be unable to maintain the terminology or notation of a twelve-tone system should we choose to completely depart from the logic and theory of a twelve-tone system.

Therefore, to provide acceptable convenience and continuity, we will adhere to the twelve tone octave, as developed by Philolaus and other early masters.

This writer approaches the work from a position of not throwing out the baby with the bathwater. The twelve-tone system, interval names and notations are time tested and have evolved and worked perfectly for centuries. The writer's *beef* is not with the twelve-tone theory per-se but, with the actual tones artificially standardized around an equally-imperfect tuning standard... all done without consideration of vitally-important core factors... such as pure and natural harmony.

The perfect twelve-tone, geometric system would dovetail nearly perfectly with most established music theory precepts. This is an important, if secondary objective of this work.

A Micro-tonal Movement
Community, Software, and Hardware for Alternative Tuning

During the research for this book, and somewhat by synchronicity, the author discovered a small-but-vocal community of alternative tuning advocates that call themselves 'Micro-tonal' musicians. *[quotes in no way intended as derogatory]* Microtuning is technically the practice of utilizing methods of dividing the octave into smaller 'pieces' than the usual twelve tones per octave. These adventurous musicians constantly work to find the tones 'between' the tones. It is an interesting and rewarding practice for many who are motivated to do the work, design new instruments and spend tons of money and time in the pursuit of these errant tones.

I found my interactions with these groups fascinating and enlightening, if too often strained by some of the artistic egos involved. The community is fascinating, due to the sheer number of innovative and expanded tuning systems that have been made available within their various on-line repositories. Most of the adherents are also tolerant of and, proficient in alternate twelve-tone tunings as well. This is the reason the writer feels compelled to mention this 'micro-tonal movement.'

During this research, quite a bit of good information was gleaned from online discussions regarding the basics of constructing unique tunings for handmade instruments and the like. Unfortunately, the writer's general confrontation-averse nature was ultimately exhausted by involvement with so many talented yet passive-aggressive artists and personalities; not to mention the writer's strong aversion to the whole concept of the so-called 'social media' environment, which seems to be misunderstood by most in that seems more akin an anti-social media network.

Nevertheless, this author is grateful to have had the opportunity to meet some of these players and to glean some knowledge from the community's more generous members. Subsequently, I have incorporated some of the acquired, or implied knowledge, suggestions, and calculations into this work. And, for that, I wish to formally offer my sincere gratitude to those who were kind enough to help to crystallize this writer's basic understanding of the methods used to design and work with alternate tuning systems.

Thus far, I have learned that most modern instrument manufacturers do not generally support alternative tunings for their products. This, despite the fact that advances in technology, (special shout-out to MIDI) make it so easy to do so. Subsequently, alternative tuning and micro-tonal music remains mostly inaccessible to all but the most knowledgeable, determined, skilled, and dedicated of practitioners.

A few manufacturers of keyboards, mainly analog synthesizers, retain the ability to reprogram their equipment to use alternative, custom tunings. While my research budget has not permitted experimentation with very many of them, I find that Dave Smith Instruments integrates this *re-tune-ability* into most of their 'Prophet' product line. And, while they do not necessarily make it 'easy' to do so, it remains imminently feasible with a USB connection and a couple of inexpensive software titles. For more details on reprogramming a (DSI) synthesizer to alternate tunings, please refer to **Chapter 37 - Modern Sound Production.**

Some of the major DAWs (Digital Audio Workstations), such as Apple's Logic Pro X and Native Instrument's MASSIVE and Kontakt, provide somewhat convoluted but, generally usable configurations for custom tunings on a per-project basis.

There are also specialized software applications such as the 'Universal Tuning Editor' (UTE) published by 'H-pi Instruments,' capable of creating tuning files for a wide variety of applications in several formats.

The 'UTE' software can also interface directly with some imaginative micro-tonal instruments (some of which are also offered by H-pi

Instruments) as well as interfacing with your computer's native MIDI functions.

The tuning files resulting from this research were designed and created using 'Universal Tuning Editor' published by H-pi Instruments.

'Scala' (not the programming language) is another piece of software out there that performs the same functions. However, Scala is apparently only available (natively) for the Windows platform, which this researcher has thus far, preferred not to utilize. Therefore, I cannot comment on specifics regarding its overall usability or functions. However, the software is widely known in the alternative tuning and micro-tonal community and is often recommended by its members.

There may very well be others out there. So, do your research if this world of alternate soundscapes is attractive to you. You too can create your own individualized, tonal experience.

As the practice becomes more common, we hope to find and discuss more musical instrument manufacturers which permit and even actively encourage such tonal experimentation by making alternate tuning easily accessible to even the most complex electronic instruments. The discovery of alternate tune-ability of instruments was such a blessing to this research. It allowed the use of actual musical tones on an actual keyboard rather than a simple tone generator to perform sound trials and to validate the findings.

9

The Case for 432Hz
A More Natural Basis for Healing and Sound Therapy

Modern musicians are able to mimic the concept of the 'ancient sounds', using scalar structures called modes, which exist within the modern even-tempered scale standard. This is possible because the basic patterns used in constructing these modal scales (mostly) survived the ravages of history. There are seven main, approximated ancient modes in contemporary music, generally known as Ionian, Dorian, Phrygian, Lydian, Mixolydian, Aeolian, and Locrian. Each of these modes, have one or more branched modes that provide some additional variation in the tonal palette. These modes are based on minor pentatonic (penta=five, tonic=tone) scales that 'simulate' the colorful, uneven temperament of the earliest modes of western and middle-eastern music, while remaining within the strict confines of the modern even-tempered system and obviously within the 440Hz tuning standard. Therefore, these modes, thus constrained, do not and can never reproduce the actual tones used in ancient times.

Although these modes certainly 'sound' appropriately colorful to our modern ears, the tones cannot be assured to be the same frequencies that would have been used in ancient times. This effect is the result of the compromise inherent in the 440Hz, even-tempered tuning system, as well as the fact that no one can definitively claim to know how to recreate the original, ancient tones themselves.

In the ancient world, musical tones and scales were necessarily based upon their understanding of nature's laws - just like practically everything else in their culture(s).

Equalizing chromatic temperament was not, it seems, the overarching concern for the early practitioners of music theory. The most fundamental understanding of natural law to ancient civilizations was in their math and their philosophy. Therefore, how can we think that ancient cultures did not build their musical constructs upon these same foundations?

Indeed, their music was most certainly based on the geometries that formed the foundation of everything else in their lives? The exact relationships and the resulting musical balance with nature, have largely eluded modern musicians who struggle to create within the confines of equal-temperament tuning.

Of the potential, historically utilized values for A^4 from 430Hz to 453Hz, none of the candidate values correlate in any way to polygonal math. The math of the 432Hz frequency itself, evaluates to an imaginary polygonal object having 4.4 sides. Obviously, such an object is not possible in our three-dimensional, physical reality.

However, none of the other values in our range of possible candidates correspond to geometry either. Even so, none of the candidate values check off so many necessary boxes as the value: 432.

Let's evaluate that statement and see if it holds water: *Table 9.1 - Potential Concert Tuning Standards Between 430Hz and 453Hz,* details all of the possible A^4, whole-number tuning frequencies within that stated range of candidate frequencies.

The preceding statements and subsequent evaluations are made based on our working 'rules' thus far as follows:

- Does the numerical frequency reduce (by the sum of its digits) to nine? (As all pure geometric values must)

- Is the frequency divisible by 3, 6, and/or 9?

- We up the ante a bit to evaluate whether or not the candidate frequency is also divisible by 12 and then 72.

Potential Concert Tuning Standards
Between 430Hz and 453Hz

Frequency	Reduces to	Divisible by?				
Hz	9	3	6	9	12	72
430	X	X	X	X	X	X
431	X	X	X	X	X	X
432	Y	Y	Y	Y	Y	Y
433	X	X	X	X	X	X
434	X	X	X	X	X	X
435	X	Y	X	X	X	X
436	X	X	X	X	X	X
437	X	X	X	X	X	X
438	X	Y	Y	X	X	X
439	X	X	X	X	X	X
440	X	X	X	X	X	X
441	Y	Y	X	Y	X	X
442	X	X	X	X	X	X
443	X	X	X	X	X	X
444	X	Y	Y	X	Y	X
445	X	X	X	X	X	X
446	X	X	X	X	X	X
447	X	Y	X	X	X	X
448	X	X	X	X	X	X
449	X	X	X	X	X	X
450	Y	Y	Y	Y	X	X
451	X	X	X	X	X	X
452	X	X	X	X	X	X
453	X	Y	X	X	X	X

Fig 9.1 - Examining the Various potential tuning fundamentals for compliance with geometric divisibility criteria.

Should the reader concur with the budding thesis thus far, the writer proposes, based upon the current analysis that; of all the potential tunings for the 'A' above middle 'C,' 432Hz is the most logical choice.

This assertion is not voiced due to any exceptional, magical, or otherwise esoteric association with the number itself. Instead, the opinion is well-formed because, 432Hz is the only frequency that makes logical sense based on the constraining mathematical rules of *geometry* and *natural law*; both of which were of such great importance in the ancient world.

There is another proximal number — not included in *Table 9.1*, above, that manages to catch our wandering eyes. That number is 420Hz. In fact, this number pops up from time-to-time in the experimental math while constructing geometric tuning grids.

However, 420Hz doesn't quite meet all of the criteria necessary to beat out 432Hz for the crown. For the simple reason that we will encounter this frequency during our later work, it is worth mentioning here that there are some few difficult situations, which force an uneasy détente with the 420Hz tone. These cases will be encountered in the subsequent sections.

Nevertheless, 420Hz's incomplete compliance with the full range of divisibility criteria render it objectively inferior to the 432Hz value, which we have now seen, meets *all* of the geometric divisibility criteria. No other value examined even comes close.

The value, 450Hz looks like a nice option on paper. However, the tone is just too high to be the tuning standard A^4 in any realistic composition - especially ones requiring vocal work. The tone of 450Hz is a full 70.672¢ above 432Hz.

The coup de grâs for the 450Hz candidate comes at the hands of its non-compliance with the extended criteria. While 450Hz meets most of the divisibility criteria, it fails when tested against the twelve and seventy-two divisors; again rendering it inferior to the 432Hz value.

As the writer has clearly demonstrated via the above analysis, 432Hz as the *only* logical choice for the fundamental tone within our geometric 'healing scale.'

432Hz is the frequency that best relates to ancient geometry and the basic mathematical principles as we have outlined them thus far. Thus, it is definitely the best standard for A^4 to be used in our 'healing tones' systems.

Yes. 432Hz is the tone that we will utilize as the foundational or 'root' tone as well as our mathematical *pivot point*, around which our geometric tuning grids will be constructed.

"There is geometry in the humming of the strings; there is music in the spacing of the spheres! – Pythagoras

So, let's start bringing all of this together into a clear system. Using our basis in geometry, the 432Hz A^4, and some guidance from existing tuning systems, let's start building our geometric 'sound and frequency healing' tuning system.

In case the kind reader missed this point before; we are not attempting to construct an even-tempered scale system that is merely based upon altering the root tone, as so many have done in the past.

At the very least, our systems will not utilize the so-called 'modern' standard of even temperament. In this text, we are setting our sights on a tuning system that allows us to make *reasonable use* of the resulting tonal structures for healing and relaxation. What is meant by reasonable use in part, is that the system can be immediately useful with commonly-available musical equipment, primarily keyboards, which are available to anyone on the musical instrument market.

While this 'reasonable use' is fundamental to the basic mission of this work, the *perfect* outcome would indeed be described as a twelve tone harmonic system that fits within the standard keyboard layout. And, a system that is just as playable as any even-tempered system. We will go wherever the math leads us.

The math for creating modern, even-tempered music is already in place, and functions sufficiently well for most purposes despite the stated, glaring defects of that system. We will use a more natural system to build a more holistic, stable, and harmonically *balanced* tonal standard.

Our primary concern in this text, is with developing a rational basis for tuning systems that:

- Are firmly based in nature, either via Euclidean, Pythagorean, or Platonic geometry and their various correlative mathematics.

- Possess energetic, physiological, human significance and (subjectively) beneficial correlations, both with emotional and human relaxation states.

- Are the most likely tonal structures reproducible by ancient healers and musicians.

- Fit into a recognizable, repeatable, and logical pattern that accommodates a twelve-tone octave without the limitations and compromises inherent in the existing 12-TET system.

- Possess objective physiological correlations that support the human 'relaxation response.' (Will require further research)

Music From Mechanism

"Musicae ex Machina"

In order to develop a mathematical mechanism for our relaxation and healing tuning system(s), we must initially get the lay of the land as far as readily-available, geometric frequencies are concerned. To that end we will begin to arrange the available, purely geometric tones into a logical order.

First, let's nominate some candidates from our geometric analyses. Obviously, we must use the tone frequencies from Plato's five 3D solids. So, let's bring those over now.

Frequencies Derived from Platonic Solids

Resonance	3D Platonic Geometry
720Hz	Tetrahedron
1440Hz	Octahedron
2160Hz	Hexahedron
3600Hz	Icosahedron
6480Hz	Dodecahedron

Table 10.1 – Frequencies derived from Platonic solid resonances

These frequencies are eminently usable, although some are fairly high in the audible registers. The 3600Hz of the Icosahedron and the 6480Hz of the dodecahedron can be very shrill at high amplitude. Therefore, care must be taken when using them in practice.

Yet, even these higher frequencies are wonderful guides in creating our geometric tuning system(s).

The Platonic solid resonance frequencies, above, are also useful for creating the associated lower octave tones by a tried-and-true method of mathematical *octavation*, which the writer will explain in detail, as it is applied at the top of the next chapter.

Next, we need to incorporate some of the relevant Euclidean geometry (The so-named '-gons'), taking care to ensure that we include any frequency that possesses a direct correlation to sacred geometries (The '-hedrons' and compound geometries). Here are just a few of the first ranks of polygonal resonances to get us started.

Euclidean Geometry to Frequency Correlations:

Freq. Hz	Geometry
180Hz	Triangle (3)
360Hz	Square and Circle (4)
540Hz	Pentagon (5)
720Hz	Hexagon (6)
900Hz	Heptagon (7)
1080Hz	Octagon (8)
1260Hz	Nonagon (9)
1440Hz	Decagon (10)
1620Hz	Hendecagon (11)
1800Hz	Dodecagon (12)

Table 10.2 – Frequencies derived from Euclidean (2D geometry) resonances

Now, let's bring them all together into a single list of frequencies from lowest to highest and pair each tone with its closest 432Hz, 12-TET based scale values. This will be our starting point for correlating the notation with the frequencies.

The author has placed these results in *Table 10.3*, side-by-side with the 432Hz, 12TET calculations, in part, to highlight the differences between the proposed 'Geometric' frequencies and the decimal place remainders resulting from even-tempered calculations, which force the tuning into unnatural mathematical patterns and ratios. These values will also serve as a *reality check* of sorts, for new tone values to ensure our note assignments don't stray too far from 'reality.'

Sorted Frequency Correlations:

Geometric Tone	Closest 432Hz (12tet) note	Actual 432Hz (12tet) tone
180Hz	F$^{\#3}$	188.363Hz
360Hz	F$^{\#4}$	363.27Hz
540Hz	C$^{\#5}$	544.29Hz
720Hz	F$^{\#5}$	726.54Hz
900Hz	A$^{\#5}$	915.3801Hz
1080Hz	C$^{\#6}$	1027.48Hz
1260Hz	D$^{\#6}$ or E^6	1221.8878Hz
1440Hz	F$^{\#6}$	1453.08Hz
1620Hz	G$^{\#6}$	1631.03Hz
1800Hz	A$^{\#6}$	1830.7674Hz

Table 10.3 – Frequencies derived from Euclidean (2D geometry) resonances

There is some question regarding the 1260Hz value in the chart above - as the 1260Hz value itself is relatively equidistant from both even-tempered D$^{\#}$ and E frequencies. So, it is not immediately obvious to which note, if any, it should assigned. But, as you will see, the situation sorts out as our expanded tuning system acquires more solidity.

To explain the process here, look at the lowest geometric frequency of 180Hz. This value most closely correlates to an even-tempered F$^{\#3}$ of 188.363Hz. The tonal distance between these two values is 78.62$^{\text{¢}}$.

The discrepancy is little more than a quarter-tone and represents a kind of *'Exhibit A'* to demonstrate how equal-temperament values jeopardize harmonious relationships within the natural world that are inherently preserved in the geometric approach.

The above comparison to the even-tempered F$^{\#}$, demonstrates a starting point for our work, and is presented for explanatory purposes. 180Hz seems to be a perfect choice for F$^{\#}$ on the face of it. This correlation is further supported by other F$^{\#}$ values in our chart, all of which turn out to be *natural harmonics* of 180Hz and also correlate closely to the 432Hz, 12-TET values for F$^{\#}$ within their respective octaves. This fact represents a remarkable correlation for our system; right out of the starting gate.

We will discuss natural harmonics and overtones in greater detail in *Chapter 21 - Harmonics and Overtones.*

OK! Back to our work and our chart of tones:

When we compare the current list of tones above, to an even-tempered scale based on an A^4 fixed to 432Hz; Right away, we can see that we have the following correlates: Two 'A$^#$'s, four 'F$^#$'s, one 'G$^#$,' and two 'C$^#$s. By examining the right column, you will notice that some of these correlations are numerically 'off' from 432Hz, even-tempered tuning by several Hertz. The notational assignments chosen for our geometric tones may have some professional musical purists ready to pounce.

All this writer can say is, "Wait for it!" The resulting math will bolster the thesis. It is of no consequence at any rate. Commercial music is what it is. We are not here to convince anyone to change that. Additionally, the fact that the writer is not steeped in professional 'music theory,' is a bit of an advantage — as the clutter, unintelligible jargon, and convoluted mathematics that generally confuse these discussions will not be an issue, and are decidedly unnecessary in this context.

This work, as presented, is not approaching the study with any preconceptions on how things should be done. Instead, we are merely putting things together as they make logical and mathematical sense and, as they conform to the previously-detailed, mathematical criteria.

Despite the above disclaimer, this writer admits that; it is somewhat encouraging to find ourselves thus far, so closely correlated with the modern, 432Hz even-tempered musical tones. The proximity, to this writer, demonstrates that we are on a correct path to pure tone. Despite the stated thesis that the even-temperament tones are most definitely inappropriate for relaxation and healing work, we will analyze and utilize any reasonably valid correlation that presents itself. Thus, we continue, undaunted in our analysis.

The F$^#$-Major chord contains three sharps: F$^#$, A$^#$, and C$^#$. The completed F$^#$ Major scale, also includes the G$^#$ revealed above. The entire F$^#$ Major scale is constructed as F$^#$, G$^#$, A$^#$, B, C$^#$, D$^#$, and E$^#$ (enharmonic F).

Therefore, relative to standard music 'theory,' we are treading very close to the existing system's established tone class. Again, we are not necessarily here to play by the rules. Nevertheless, This writer is certainly, not above exploiting the existing parameters when they serve a useful purpose, as in relative correlations like this.

Presented in *Table 10.4* below, is the structure of the twelve tone, F#-Major scale. We will definitely see this pattern as a recurring theme in our exploration and construction of tuning grids.

The tones of primary interest for us are the Major 3rd, Perfect 5th, and Major 7th. We already have a starting place for our Major 3rd, which is an A# of 900Hz. And the Perfect 5th, which is C# and, is to be found at a beautiful geometric frequency of 540Hz, which corresponds to the pentagonal resonance.

F# Major Scale Intervals (12-tone Standard)	
Tonic	The 1st note of the scale is F#
Major 2nd	The 2nd note of the scale is G#
Major 3rd	The 3rd note of the scale is A#
Perfect 4th	The 4th note of the scale is B
Perfect 5th	The 5th note of the scale is C#
Major 6th	The 6th note of the scale is D#
Major 7th	The 7th note of the scale is E#/F
Octave (Perf 8th)	The 8th note of the scale is F#

Table 10.4 – Description of the F#-Major scale degrees

We will need to establish a relationship with F#, which will get the ball rolling in regards to uncovering the other tones, and to fill the remaining gaps.

In short, we will eventually, have a real need for a valid, harmonically-balanced interval stack that will measure and establish the relationship between these tones. And, we will get there. For now however, we will continue to look to geometry, wherever possible, for these initial relationships.

The geometry is what will assist us in establishing the natural, geometric tonal relationships prior to the aforementioned mathematical validation. Roll your eyes all you want. It's just so much more fun this way.

Looking at the chart of the sum of internal angles (See: *Appendix VII - Table of Polygonal Frequency Data*), we see that 360Hz fits in as another F#. It is not unreasonable to use the other known tones in this range to begin working on estimates for the adjacent tones.

To accomplish this, it is first necessary to see the 'big picture' to this point.

Toward that end, in the next chapter, we will begin by charting out the octaves of the tones we have located thus far. The resulting table of frequencies will provide a valuable guide to the steps necessary to complete our work, which will continue in the next chapter. But, first, a bit of a background discussion.

While comparing the geometric tones with the equal-temperament tones, one can notice a lot of decimal remainders in the so-called 'equal tempered' tones. The even-tempered F# for example checks in at 188.3629Hz. Really?!?

Do such partial waveform patterns correspond to natural music or tones in any meaningful way? In this writer's opinion, these 'remainder' waveforms are an unfortunate result of the artificial tonal construct called 'equal temperament,' which only serves to violate Galileo's principle of agreeable consonance of tones that are supposedly, "commensurate in number."

There seems to be nothing at all 'commensurate' between tone frequencies possessing wildly disparate decimal values such as those found in the modern, equal-tempered systems. Butchering waveforms up into fragmented frequencies possessing multiple-decimal-place remainders while using 'square roots of 2 and 3' in an effort to 'shoehorn' them into a harmonic structure, in my mind, is merely forcing the proverbial square peg into a round hole.

The writer stipulates that this is common and accepted practice in modern music. However, to the originators of such a system, I ask: Where exists the beauty and balance in such a scenario? Where is the universal harmony of structure in such a seemingly gerrymandered, ad hoc design? And yet, this system is considered perfectly 'normal' in both our musical conservatories and garage bands.

It *may* be 'agreeable' and 'commensurate' to produce wavelengths of some minor fractionation. Perhaps a 'half' wavelength (x.5Hz) - as the waveform is a function of time (in seconds), reflects predictably and resonantly, or simply continues to propagate into another cycle. This writer can even get on-board with two decimal-point remainders such as 0.25 or 0.75, which 'resolve' to whole numbered tones in higher octaves, especially if these tones reside in the lower registers. This is actually beneficial, as lower frequency sound propagates exceptionally well through materials such as earthen or arboreal flooring, and is significantly less 'directional' (for lack of a better term) in its effect. Some may already recognize that lower frequencies are generally, more 'felt' than 'heard.' That effect works perfectly as far as this system's development is concerned.

While the imperfect frequency remainders, commonly utilized anywhere from four or even eight decimal places, are no absolute atrocity to commercial music production, it is simply not possible to resolve them into a resonant, genuinely harmonious, healing setting. Such just happens to be the main objective in this work.

Among the more egregious offenses regarding equal-temperament may be the fact that some (well-intentioned) modern performers have taken to the practice of digitally down-tuning their even-tempered music a'la Karaoke machine, in a terribly misguided effort to somehow come off as unique or cutting-edge by claiming to utilize a 432Hz (or some other) standard.

For some of these artists, I am convinced that this digital re-tuning is some form of copy-protection that ensures a song, or the entire collection, cannot be accurately 'covered' by other performers who will never, legally possess the exact re-tuning algorithm. A few performers who engage in this practice actually target the 'sweet spot' of an A^4 432Hz (12TET). I wonder why that is.

The rationale for such re-tuning, is possibly a belief that the whole piece is 'magically' re-tuned in even-tempered A^4-432Hz. However, what actually occurs as a result of this process is far more horrific.

The practice of electronically down-tuning equal-temperament music demonstrates a complete lack of either; understanding, or concern for the interval relationships, harmonies, and harmonics involved.

All too often, the resulting recordings are little more than structured cacophony to the sensitive ear.

Such music's harmonic relationships were born in equal temperament, and then further, brutally mangled by the forced digital wrangling of its native frequencies. There is no natural or logical reasoning for this practice, once one understands the harmonic compromises involved *and* their implications to the overall wellbeing of the listener - not to mention any desired appeal for the music itself.

Putting the Pieces Together

Octavating the Known Tones

Our next challenge in the process of creating a better healing and wellness tuning system, is to fill in the octaves of each tone revealed in our F# Major scale. These tones should also conform to our geometric theory since Pythagoras and Plato demonstrated that octaves are merely multiples of a base tone existing upward in a 2:1, 3:1, 4:1, etc. ratio or downward in a 1:2, 1:4, etc. ratio.

Specifically, an octave higher than any given tone is equal to that of the frequency multiplied by two. And an octave below is found as *that same* frequency divided by two. This rule is expressed in modern music theory as the octave ratio (2:1 or 1:2) or in our case, simply 'Octavation.' *We don't care if it's not a **real** word. Music theory is literally packed with unintelligible jargon and similar ad-hoc words and phrases. So, we can do it too.*

Logically, all tones within an octave should fit 'commensurately' between the tonal bookends of the root tone and its octave frequency, whether it be divided into twelve tones, twenty-two tones, or any other number of micro-tonal intervals. It all depends upon the concept of 'commensurate' being applied. Some work. Most don't.

Because we intensely desire the resulting system to be as readily useful as possible, we will continue to focus on the twelve-tone system used on most modern keyboards. This structure ensures that composers of relaxation and healing music have a firm foundation for immediately utilizing the concepts developed herein.

To demonstrate this essential 'octavation' operation, we will use our chosen A^4, which, as you will recall, is 432Hz.

By multiplying 432Hz by two, we arrive at the next *higher*, pure octave of 'A,' which is A^5.

$$A_5 = A_4 \times 2 = 432Hz \times 2 = 864Hz$$

Likewise, the next *lower* 'A' is A^3. We can determine the A^3 frequency by dividing the A^4 frequency by two.

$$A_3 = A_4 \div 2 = 432Hz \div 2 = 216Hz$$

It really is that simple.

If we apply this math to each of our known, original geometric tones, we will be able to determine many of the remaining tones in our 'healing' tones chart. But, for now, the completed chart for ten octaves of our tonal 'A' frequencies is presented below.

Tone	Frequency (Hz)	Reduces to 9?	Divisible by...				
			3	6	9	12	72
A^0	27	Y	Y	Y	Y	Y	Y
A^1	54	Y	Y	Y	Y	Y	Y
A^2	108	Y	Y	Y	Y	Y	Y
A^3	216	Y	Y	Y	Y	Y	Y
A^4	432	Y	Y	Y	Y	Y	Y
A^5	864	Y	Y	Y	Y	Y	Y
A^6	1728	Y	Y	Y	Y	Y	Y
A^7	3456	Y	Y	Y	Y	Y	Y
A^8	6912	Y	Y	Y	Y	Y	Y
A^9	13824	Y	Y	Y	Y	Y	Y

Octave Tones of A^4 – Based on A^4 = 432Hz

Table 11.1 – Evaluation of the octavated 'A' tones alongside the applicable 'test conditions' that will be used in validating all tones within the resulting system.

Notice that all of the calculated frequencies fanatically obey the stated rules for healing, geometric tones. Each of the values reduces to '9.' All of them are divisible by 3, 6, and 9 as well as 12 and 72. I relate to this as the 'firm foundation' upon which the whole system is based. 432Hz itself may or may not prove useful as a primary 'healing' tone. And, this is fine and, frankly, a strictly foundational role is *somewhat* expected. (**Spoiler alert:** Despite initial expectations, 432Hz actually turns out to be a very important central tone.)

But, always keep in mind that the foundation doesn't define the entire structure. It merely informs the basic structure. The usefulness of 432Hz itself as a healing tone is yet to be determined. For the moment, it acts as a source and an anchor point for the tuning systems we will soon develop using these concepts and data.

The astute observer will notice that none of these values for our tonal 'A's' directly correspond to any geometric construct. However, our analysis of possible tuning standards above, has brought us to tap 432Hz as our A^4 standard.

As already established, 432Hz possesses no direct correlation to any 2D geometry. Therefore, the resulting octave calculations are but a mathematical extension of that fact. Again, there remains no better candidate for A^4 based on our previously detailed analysis. To review the many justifications for utilizing a 432Hz tuning standard for this work please see: *Chapter 9 - The Case for 432Hz*.

The fact that the number '432' possesses a vast litany of more esoteric justifications is not a fact lost upon this writer. For the most part, these more esoteric aspects will remain largely, beyond the scope of our explorations. Therefore, based only upon the rationale previously outlined, 432Hz remains the perfect choice among all available, candidates for our A^4 foundation.

All that remains is for us to systematically fill in the rest of the tones and see what happens. Let's dive in and start filling in the blanks.

The following *Table 11.2*, is a workspace for one of our octaves of geometric frequencies derived from the process outlined above. The original, *pure-geometry* frequencies as well as our newly calculated 'A' tones are displayed in the 'Geometric' column.

The writer has chosen to elevate (octavate) some of the geometric tones so that we more easily visualize a single (in this case, the seventh) octave of the system in its entirety.

Hereafter, we will octavate our 'discovered' frequencies to fit in the range of A^6 to A^7, to better visualize the system. All other octave tones are just as easily extrapolated using the same octavation method.

Geometric Tuning System Frequencies (Partial)

Tone	12-TET (440Hz)	12TET (432Hz)	Geometric
A^7	3520	3456	3456
$G^{\#7}$	3322.4400	3262.0674	3240
G^7	3135.9681	3078.9806	
$F^{\#7}$	2959.9542	2906.1698	2880
F^7	2793.8322	2743.0581	
E^7	2637.0263	2589.1012	
$D^{\#7}$	2489.0173	2443.7853	*2520?*
D^7	2349.3238	2306.6254	
$C^{\#7}$	2217.4644	2177.1638	2160
C^7	2093.0051	2054.9683	
B^6	1975.5304	1939.6311	
$A^{\#6}$	1864.6534	1830.7674	1800
A^6	1760	1728	1728

Table 11.2 - Comparison of 12-TET standards with Geometric tones determined thus far with questionable 2520Hz indicated

Because many tones are still missing from our geometric explorations, we must devise a compatible method by which we can 'fill in the blanks.' Fortunately, nature has already provided us with our next step, which we will soon explore. But, for now, we will continue to use octavation math upon those frequencies that we have already determined from our pure-geometrical observations.

Just as we have just done with our 'A' frequencies, in *Table 11.1*, we can utilize octavation to determine the octave frequencies of those tones, already confirmed by geometry.

Recall that an octave is either 'half' or 'double' any frequency depending upon which way you are going. If we calculate every octave for the currently available geometric tones, we can fill in as many octaves, above or below, as we wish.

Beginning with the $F^{\#3}$ at 180Hz, finding the correct frequencies for all F#s in our chart is a relatively simple task.

$$F^{\#3} \text{ at } 180Hz \times 2 = F^{\#4} \text{ at } 360Hz$$
$$F^{\#4} \text{ at } 360Hz \times 2 = F^{\#5} \text{ at } 720Hz$$
$$F^{\#5} \text{ at } 720Hz \times 2 = F^{\#6} \text{ at } 1440Hz$$
$$\text{etc ...}$$

Likewise;

$$F^{\#3} \text{ at } 180Hz \,/\, 2 = F^{\#2} \text{ at } 90Hz$$
$$F^{\#2} \text{ at } 90Hz \,/\, 2 = F^{\#1} \text{ at } 45Hz$$

After inserting the known frequencies, as detailed above, we can easily repeat the above process on any candidate frequencies for the 'Pure Geometry' column. So far, we have done this, completing a significant portion of an entire 'sound and frequency healing' tuning chart. But, our process leaves us with a not-inconsiderable handful of standard notation tones still unaccounted for.

The 'B,' 'C,' 'D,' and 'F' are the note positions, which remain absent from our current analysis. Additionally, the 'D#' and the 'E' require more in-depth analysis and perhaps a little 'special' attention.

This is where things get '*mathie*' very quickly. (C'mon! You knew this was coming.) We need to determine valid and harmonically-balanced *interval ratios* that produce candidate values that correlate with our stated 'rules', while remaining usable in our wider system of tone. But, first...

About D# - It's Not You... It's Me

A break-up is coming. What follows, is the whole, sad, torrid story.

To this point, we only see a single instance of any value 'close' to a D# in our geometric number chart. Therefore, D# cannot be pinned-down definitively or nearly as easily as F#.

For this and other reasons, which will become apparent, the 1260Hz value, (corresponding to a nonagon) appearing as an octavated value of 2520Hz in the above 7th octave chart in the D[#] position, has proven to be a 'special needs' case. In most of the sound trials, 1224Hz is a far better tonal fit. To be fair, the 1260Hz provides a tonal texture that works within the major mode of the scale, just not in a D[#] position.

The determination at this juncture is a somewhat subjective one. But, I have decided a break-up, as regrettable as it may seem, is necessary and justified. (I mean, it's not like we were married to a D[#] at 1260Hz. Right?) We will always remain friends.

Not to worry! Our 1260Hz will continue to be an included work-mate. We will see it again later, albeit as a *legitimate* 'E' in the F[#] variation of our tuning system. (We'll get there.)

Later we will explore using *other* fundamental tones in almost magical 'forks' of our tonal healing system. We will discover that tones, especially geometric frequencies, that do not appear in the tuning system based on A[4], often reappear when we change the system's fundamental tone basis. But, this proves to be a double-edged blade, as the intrepid reader will come to understand.

Initially, in our currently-developing system, 1260Hz seems to represent a very large semitone (or 155[¢]) step above the perfect 4th (D). This large discrepancy introduces dissonance into the standard chord structures when placed at the D[#] position (or the E position for that matter). This indicates that a more appropriate position may be found for the value elsewhere. Additionally, a micro-tonal approach could be utilized to include the tone in a more-than-twelve-note octave. Exploring the second possibility is an interesting proposition but is beyond the scope of this particular body of work.

Based on the discussion above, our first adjustment to our tonal assignments, is to nominate 1224Hz to stand in for 1260Hz (our now ex-D[#].)

> **Note:** For now, we are exclusively using geometric correlation in an attempt to validate a basis for simple geometric scales. Later, once we begin looking at actual interval ratios and associated math, we will see exactly where 1260Hz belongs within our systems... Stay tuned.

This newfound partnership with 1224Hz represents a 50¢ tonal difference, which allows the 1224Hz D# to 'fit' snugly as a diminished 5th. It's within 5¢ of a 'Just' dim5th, is an excellent choice for the 'sub dim5th', and turns out later, to be a valid *smaller-half-tone* interval of 104.96¢, relative to the D. But, *again* I am getting ahead of myself.

Additionally, the tone represents the 17th harmonic of the first octave tonic: All-in-all, a pretty good trial fit.

1224Hz fits our rules as it numerically reduces to nine and, is divisible by 3, 6, and 9 as well as 12 and 72. Motion is 'seconded' and passed! 1224Hz is now our D# in the sixth octave.

One octave above 1224Hz is 2448Hz. We will now add this octavated tone to our seventh-octave chart below.

Tone	12-TET (440Hz)	12TET (432Hz)	Geometric
A⁷	3520	3456	3456
G#⁷	3322.4400	3262.0674	3240
G⁷	3135.9681	3078.9806	
F#⁷	2959.9542	2906.1698	2880
F⁷	2793.8322	2743.0581	
E⁷	2637.0263	2589.1012	
D#⁷	2489.0173	2443.7853	**2448**
D⁷	2349.3238	2306.6254	
C#⁷	2217.4644	2177.1638	2160
C⁷	2093.0051	2054.9683	
B⁶	1975.5304	1939.6311	
A#⁶	1864.6534	1830.7674	1800
A⁶	1760	1728	1728

Table 11.3 - Progress is made by incorporating the D# of 2448Hz (1224Hz, octavated) into the seventh octave chart.

The Current Picture

A Quick Overview of Our Progress Thus Far

The following tuning grid chart is a chart of standard piano keys. The partial view of key numbers 40 through 63, presents us with a fairly nice summary of where we are in creating our healing tones tuning system based on A⁴-432Hz. The chart is presented as both a way for the reader to visualize what is happening as well as a tool for following along through the next several steps of building the tuning system.

The truncated chart, representing the theoretical keyboard keys from #40 to #63, is presented in *Table 12.1*. However, and for further reference, the full chart of all keyboard keys (plus eleven higher octave key-tones) can be found in *Appendix III* at the end of this text.

All of our current, validated geometric frequency values are inserted in the 'Pure Geometry' column, properly octavated for the keyboard position indicated. We will begin here as we continue to the next stage of our journey.

From this point onward, not all of our calculated tones will relate directly to an actual geometric shape or resonance. Most will necessarily be calculated by using fixed ratios (demonstrated later.)

We will endeavor to continue making clear distinction between those tones resulting from pure geometry, and those that are calculated based upon the other, validating 'criteria' for geometric tones developed earlier in this text.

The criteria for geometric tones, currently stand as follows:

All geometric tones must meet the criteria as determined by the mathematics of geometry... Namely;

- Reduction to 9 by the sum of digits (required)
- Division by 3, 6, and, or 9 (preferably nine)
- Additional division by 12 and, or 72 (preferably both)
- Decimal remainder values should comply with the 'sum of digits' rule *and* must 'resolve' to whole numbers that comply with all other criteria in their higher octaves

Keyboard Position	Note Assignment	440Hz 12TET	432Hz 12TET	A4 = 432 Geometric
63	B5	987.7652	969.8117	
62	A#5/B♭5	932.3286	915.3801	900
61	A5	880	864	864
60	G#5/A♭5	830.6100	815.5104	810
59	G5	783.9911	769.7390	
58	F#5/G♭5	739.9895	726.5367	720
57	F5	698.4571	685.7591	
56	E5	659.2552	647.2702	
55	D#5/E♭5	622.2543	610.9415	612
54	D5	587.3300	576.6518	
53	C#5/D♭5	554.3661	544.2866	540
52	C5	523.2513	513.7380	
51	B4	493.8835	484.9039	
50	A#4/B♭4	466.1638	457.6882	450
49	A4	440	432	432
48	G#4/A♭4	415.3050	407.7552	405
47	G4	391.9960	384.8695	
46	F#4/G♭4	369.9943	363.2683	360
45	F4	349.2281	342.8795	
44	E4	329.6276	323.6351	
43	D#4/E♭4	311.1276	305.4707	306
42	D4	293.6650	288.3259	
41	C#4/D♭4	277.1831	272.1433	270
40	C4	261.6261	256.8690	

Figure 12.1 - Partial keyboard chart of tones highlighting a comparison of tone values in equal temperament with proposed geometric tones. 12-TET values restricted to four decimal positions for clarity.

At this early stage of our work, we have rediscovered, what this writer considers to be tones that will be counted among our 'pure' geometric frequencies, to be universally utilized in sound healing techniques of varying types.

As the reader can see; using pure geometry alone has enabled us to determine fully half of the tones needed to build a twelve-tone octave. In fact, these tones harmonize very well together and provide a solid basis for determining the remainder of the tones needed.

Additionally, notice that the tones acquired using our pure geometric approach, closely approximate the $F^{\#}$-Major scale, with the notable exception of the still-absent 'F' and 'B' tones. The missing F-tone however, will soon be remedied. Determining the rest of our tones will be accomplished using a combination of geometric constraints, determination of pure intervals, and a bit of trial and error.

In the opinion of the author, the revealed frequencies are tones possessing the purest, most natural, universal frequencies available for relaxation and healing applications. They are based upon, as are most ancient disciplines, the purity of basic mathematics, specifically geometry, which in-turn forms the basis for all chemistry, physical structure, and energy systems of living beings as well as describing the energetic structure of the known universe at the quantum and molecular levels.

The tones uncovered thus far could easily be incorporated into a very relaxing 'sound bath' or healing 'sonarium' setting. But, there is more... *so* much more to be discovered.

We will now continue to fill in the above blanks as far as nature and math permit.

The Riddle of the 'F'

A 'Near Miss' Dramatically Becomes a 'Perfect Fit'

Next in this research, the writer is driven to solve the riddle of the 'spaces between' these geometrically resonant tones. Is it possible to construct an actual, playable, musical tuning system that can be utilized for more than just 'chording' for healing and relaxation? The answer, I believe, based upon experimentation with the current tone list, is a resounding 'Yes!'

To this end, my attention is drawn to the interval between $F^{\#7}$ at 2880Hz and $D^{\#7}$ at 2448Hz. The value, 2880°, corresponds to a polygon having eighteen sides. Our original value for $D^{\#}$ (Before the sad breakup in Chapter 10) was a geometric correlate of 2520Hz. The 2520° value corresponds to a sixteen-sided polygon. But, 2520Hz is harmonically, too far out of range to be our 'F.'

But, there just so happens to be a seventeen-sided polygon in which the internal angles calculate to 2700°, that lies right between these two values. Somewhat coincidentally, 2700Hz corresponds most closely to an even tempered F^7 (when based on $A^4 = 432$Hz). This tone might just be the wedge we need to open up the remaining possibilities in our effort to construct a better tonal system for healing and wellness.

But, how can we test to validate a good, harmonic fit? Well, we have to bring in the math!

In music theory, a semitone (half-step) calculates to a strict 100^{c} when using standard, twelve-tone equal temperament.

However, that same interval is calculated as 111.731$^{\text{¢}}$, a *'Just semitone'*, in a system known as 'Just Intonation.' This is why some claim that the minor 2nd in 12-TET, is approximately 12$^{\text{¢}}$ flat.

There are other intervals, used in various, other systems. But, the Just Intonation system turns out to be a perfect tool for this work.

Therefore, our interval between 2700Hz F^7 and F$^{\#7}$ at 2880Hz should closely approximate this value, *if* the writer's assumption is correct in thinking that F^7 should be assigned the tone of 2700Hz.

The math here is somewhat involved and was therefore, performed by something much more adept than your writer, at mathematics; a calculator. The formula for determining the interval width, in cents, of any two frequencies is:

$$\text{¢} = 1200 \times \log_2 (f_2 / f_1)$$
$$(log_2 = 0.301029995)$$

Where '1200' represents the total number of cents in an octave and f_2, f_1 are the two frequencies for which we want to calculate the interval width in cents($^{\text{¢}}$). In this case, 2700Hz and 2880Hz.

This formula helps us to calculate our semitone intervals relative to the standing system(s) in even temperament *or* 'Just Intonation' tuning. And, remarkably - against all random probabilities, we see that, in the above calculation, our geometric step from F^7 to F$^{\#7}$ calculates to precisely 111.731$^{\text{¢}}$: A perfect semitone according to the 'Just Intonation' system. The frequency ratio multiplier between these two notes, calculates to 1.5625 and demonstrates a 772.627$^{\text{¢}}$ interval width relative to the octave's root tone 'A' of 1728Hz. The latter measurement marks the tone's position in the scale, as a *Just Augmented 5th*. And it is right where it needs to be!

I had hoped that it would be close. But, I certainly did not expect it to be exact. But, there you have it! A perfect match. We may just be on track for creating a somewhat balanced-temperament sound and frequency healing tone system, after all.

The Just Augmented 5th (772.627$^{\text{¢}}$ above the root), is a lovely fit. One that happens to work nicely with the septimal minor 3rd (aka sub-minor 3rd), which will ultimately provide us with our 'C.'

We may have expected this position to calculate out to a *minor 6th* instead of an augmented 5th. But, the minor 6th works out to a value that does not conform to our geometric criteria. Therefore, 2700Hz becomes a perfect addition to the system, even if it is not a textbook *Just minor 6th* of 813.687ᶜ.

To further qualify the decision to use an F⁷ of 2700Hz, Let us see a quick calculation of the interval width represented by our proposed musical fourth of this 2700Hz. This measure compares the F⁷ to our A^{#7}. In modern music's 12-TET tuning, a perfect fourth calculates to 500ᶜ. In 'Just Intonation,' the value is actually 498.045ᶜ. (with a multiplier, between those tones, of 1.3333)

Repeating the above calculation with F⁷ (2700Hz) and A^{#7} (3600Hz) reveals that these two tones are indeed, a *Just Perfect 4th* interval width of 498.045ᶜ. Again, this much-welcomed, confirming precision was not entirely expected. But, the result positions us very well for completing our healing tone system.

As well as being a powerful validation of the thesis for this work, all of these discoveries put us on a course to make significant use of several elements of the aforementioned 'Just Intonation' system in accomplishing our objectives.

No further justification is required. We formally adopt our 2700Hz 'F⁷ and calculate the octave tones of 'F' as displayed in *Table 13.1*, below - and inserted into the developing progress chart in *Table 13.2*.

With F⁷ assigned to 2700Hz, we can now calculate the remaining F-tones in our system by using the octavation method previously described. The chart in *Table 13.1*, is the result and displays the calculated frequencies from F⁰ to F⁸.

Octave Tones of F - Based on an F^7 of 2700Hz

F - Octaves	Frequency (Hz)
F^8	5400
F^7	2700
F^6	1350
F^5	675
F^4	337.50
F^3	168.75
F^2	84.375
F^1	42.1875
F^0	21.09375

Table 13.1 - The octaves of 'F' calculated from our F^7 of 2700Hz.

Notice that the decimals in some of our 'F' tones get a bit crazy in the low frequencies! But, they all reduce to nine and resolve to whole numbers in the higher octaves. Therefore, we 'roll with' the numbers as they are.

As previously observed, some frequencies drop into *non-geometric* territory around 180Hz (180 degrees is the simplest possible regular polygon). Thus, we see decimal remainders at the lower frequencies, where no 2D (or 3D) geometry exists. One interesting aspect of this phenomenon is that; even while descending into decimal remainders, the numerical reduction to nine always remains intact.

Obviously, frequencies with decimal values are not generally divisible by any whole number, such as our 3, 6, 9, 12, 72 test criteria. Therefore; the standard of numerical reducibility to nine will be the standard for inclusion of decimal frequencies — providing, of course, that their upper octave calculations resolve to whole numbers that meet the 'division-by' requirements.

We now have the perfect tools to fill more of the gaps in our tuning system. If we use the available math, as detailed above, this writer has full confidence that we will be able to successfully complete our work and meet our objective to create a new and meaningful tonal system for sound and frequency wellness and healing.

Updating the chart to integrate our new F-2700Hz gives us the following progress report:

Tone	12-TET (440Hz)	12TET (432Hz)	Geometric
A^7	3520	3456	3456
G$^{\#7}$	3322.4400	3262.0674	3240
G^7	3135.9681	3078.9806	
F$^{\#7}$	2959.9542	2906.1698	2880
F^7	**2793.8322**	**2743.0581**	**2700**
E^7	2637.0263	2589.1012	
D$^{\#7}$	2489.0173	2443.7853	2448
D^7	2349.3238	2306.6254	
C$^{\#7}$	2217.4644	2177.1638	2160
C^7	2093.0051	2054.9683	
B^6	1975.5304	1939.6311	
A$^{\#6}$	1864.6534	1830.7674	1800
A^6	1760	1728	1728

Table 13.2 - Our seventh octave chart after incorporating the new F^7 of 2700Hz

14

Regarding Tuning Systems
There Is More Than One Way to Tuna Fish

It turns out (who knew?) that the system of tuning, known as 'Just Intonation' or 'Just Tuning' has been with us even longer than the so-called '12 tone-equal-tempered tuning' that has enjoyed an elevated status and wide use since the late 1800's — as well as sporadic use in some variation, as far back as the 1700's.

The Just Intonation system is characterized by frequency progressions constructed with the use of whole-number ratios (such as 6:5, 5:4 and 4:3) rather then the ham-fisted irrational numbers (powers of two and cube roots, divided by other mystery numbers) that are utilized to artificially force tones into an equally divided pie of 100¢ intervals — thus *forcibly* wedging them into unnatural spacings within the 1200¢ octave.

Note that this criticism of complex math using irrational number values stipulates that the theory, in part originated with the ancient masters. Yet, systems that use this method are not the only systems originated by the masters of ancient civilization(s). In fact, the writer asserts that some of the more complex mathematical theorems developed at that time were just that; theories that they were working on - perhaps in an attempt to unify all of the intervals. Who knows? Many of the original writings are forever, lost to history.

However, their much simpler method of using whole-number ratios to determine tonal intervals is what we will be using exclusively from this point forward.

Granted, the modern, even-tempered system works reasonably well for commercial music applications. But, the tones provided are anything but pure. Just ask those fretless, bowed-instrument players if you want to get an 'ear-full' regarding forced equal-temperament.

This late-developing system (12-TET) is the method of tuning with which the *western* musical world has been saddled since at least the late nineteenth century. 12-TET's origins are rooted in unsavory compromises negotiated between orchestral associations, operatic groups, and instrument (clavier?) manufacturers within Europe and North America. As with all decisions made by committee, this one falls far short of perfect.

For those who recognize that 'equal-temperament' has been used for even longer, in various forms, the writer stipulates that 'something' *called* equal-temperament (or even-temperament) has been used for a few centuries.

However, it has been demonstrated that the keyboard 'tuners' of most venues almost always 'fudged' the tones (up or down) several cents to arrive at a more tonally-accurate palette. Therefore, they were not actually tuning to *equal*-temperament but, some variation of *even*-temperament. This writer's considered opinion is that equal-temperament has been a bane upon music professionals, especially bowed-string instruments, since its inception.

For further enlightenment on the chronic disdain for equal temperament among composers, tuners, and the like, the writer suggests the very well organized and presented material contained in the wonderful book, *How Equal Temperament Ruined Harmony (and Why You Should Care)* by **Ross W. Duffin**. Mr. Duffin's well-researched discussions on early use (and mis-use) of equal-temperament are both amusing and historically enlightening.

For better or for worse, modern, commercial music is apparently 'locked in' to this equal-tempered construct, as well as the flawed A^4-440Hz concert tuning standard; both of which have demonstrated blinding imperfections and inflexibility to such a point that an increasingly large number of knowledgeable creators prefer to opt-out of the system altogether.

Therefore, Just Tuning and to a lesser degree, *Mean Tone* tuning have been thrust back into the limelight as the most-easily accessible, usable, and prescribed remedies.

Any tonal interval, which utilizes the whole-number ratio method of calculating intervals *could* be termed a 'Just interval.' The Just Intonation system itself is an enhancement of Pythagorean and Platonic concepts (if not the actual ratio theory) wherein the primary (Major) intervals were originally determined by dividing a tuned string (possibly using the monochord device). These basic monochord divisions are founded upon whole-numbered intervals as well. Thus, the practice is deeply rooted in the historical origins of modern tuning systems if not directly related to modern methods in wider use.

Latter-day music theorists are fond of correlating the more arcane Pythagorean intervals back to a 'powers-of-two divided by mystery numbers' system. As Pythagoras, et. al., experimented with several differing mathematical models for tuning, it is no surprise that some confusion still exists relative to the various methods exposited.

The resulting modern contrivances are dubbed 'Pythagorean' systems or intervals, despite the appearance that many are actually mathematical constructs of an 'overtone series' that 'describe' a specific *manner* of tonality that is *related* to Pythagoras' mathematical experimentations. Suffice it to say that attempted merging of these so-called, Pythagorean number chains with the equal-temperament mindset has not resulted in any significant improvement relating to the issues and discussions surrounding tuning system standards.

That Pythagoras most certainly recognized that his 3:2 ratio was analogous to the contrived 31... : 22... is obvious. His harmonic series of intervals is an attempt to fill in some 'empty' spaces of his own. In fact, he seems to have played around extensively with these 'irrational math' harmonic sequences. The man was a genius mathematician after all. However, the implementation of whole-number ratios remains the basis for the most (subjectively) harmonic tuning systems.

Yet, for those who prefer that the pie pieces be always sliced perfectly even, 12-TET is for you.

Having previously devised a far simpler, whole numbered solution for tetrads and stacked tetrads (octads?), It is possible that the exercise, with irrational numbers, was purely academic, and an attempt to determine a better balance within a twelve-tone-per-octave system that was eventually developed by Philolaus?

It is entirely possible that albeit quite different from the systems used for twelve tone systems today, it could very well form underpinnings for musical systems with which this writer is currently unfamiliar. The fact remains, however, that we cannot know for sure what Pythagoras had in mind when working on his various sonic theories. In fact, we cannot be certain that the various implementations of Pythagorean systems actually originated with the master himself or perhaps with his students writings.

However, and I could be completely off-base here, this writer does not believe for a single 'beat,' that Pythagorean intervals expressed in relation to musical tunings systems, are appropriate for sound and frequency healing work such as that once-practiced in Pythagorean and Platonic healing schools. And, likely, these systems were not even designed for primary tuning of melodic instruments. It's just too convoluted to be believable that a culture based upon the sheer elegance and simplicity of mathematics — left us with such a intricately, complicated musical legacy. The writer will gladly stand corrected if ever presented with an easily-implemented, harmonically balanced, Pythagorean tuning system that reproduces pure harmonies as readily as the Just systems produced in this work. But, until that time comes...

Simplicity, balance, logic, and the sheer elegance of geometry were the standards by which the ancient masters formulated their various systems. The modern expressions of Pythagorean intervals are, on the face of it, too convoluted to be useful to us in relaxation, healing, and wellness work.

To be sure, implementations of 'useful' Pythagorean tuning hybrids exist. And, they are an interesting academic distraction for the interested musician. This writer's perspective is one of a system that is readily utilized by even the most casual of custom tuners.

Dealing with the inherent complexity of number chains and barely-intelligible jargon conveys no benefit upon the practice of sound and frequency healing. And, no one should be required to invest months of their valuable time to learn the in's and out's of such an intentionally-arcane system — especially when a far simpler and effective system can be forged from the basic maths.

That being said; many will demur as to this perspective. And, that is a personal decision. However, those who wish to actually and immediately engage in composing tracks that are reproducible and playable for a wider audience while using readily-available instruments and musical hardware, will see instant results when using a system such as the following geometrically-based tuning grid(s), for their general composition work.

Therefore, this writer strongly holds that the historical progression of conceptualizing intervals and chromaticity occurred in a direction towards *decreased* complexity (perhaps originating from the more complicated Pythagorean 'number chains' and moving toward simpler implementations) and not in the opposite direction.

Although Greek musical theory possessed a conceptual familiarity with the chromatic progression, the modern chromatic (12TET) scale bears little resemblance to the ancient constructs. Furthermore, many of the ancient constructs were demonstrated to be imperfect, which is why others continued to work on them. Therefore, they logically underwent continued development in subsequent eras, to the extent that the ancient influences are barely unrecognizable in most modern harmonic systems anyway.

The seemingly, unnecessary mathematical complexity inserted into many of our modern tonal systems, serves only to obfuscate the ultimate simplicity of music's natural structures. Musicians want to play. Theoreticians want to tweak. These two facts will never change. But, to which of these the dear reader aspires is a matter of deeply-personal choice.

Just Intonation resolves many of the apparent complexities found in many other systems, and results in subjectively, more tonally-accurate interval structures without all the unnecessary number-crunching required by the several, other systems in increasingly widespread use today by mainstream and micro-tonal musicians.

Other successful tuning systems throughout the centuries include the previously-mentioned 'Mean tone' and its many variants, which date as far back as the 1500's on the western calendar, and EDO, which stands for 'Equal Division of the Octave' of which 12-TET is a close relation. Each of these systems has innumerable variations ranging, in this writer's personal experience, from 9 tone EDO to 61 tone EDO and 31 notes per octave, Mean Tone, etc.

Adventurous musicians have demonstrated that increasingly more notes-per-octave are possible in these systems. One recent composition this writer has seen, claims to have been arranged in 160 tone EDO. Of course at that note density, it becomes extremely difficult for the untrained ear to hear the relative differences between adjacent tones. Additionally, chording becomes a niche art form, and the various melodic structures are a mine-field of dissonances for the inexperienced player.

'Eagle 53' is another popular tuning system, which divides the octave into very small intervals thus, providing the musician with seemingly infinite tonal options. However, the objective for most musicians is to use whichever tuning system provides both the desired tonality while remaining usable on a standard keyboard layout. Such is the objective of this work.

Yes! I'm so glad you asked. It is *quite* possible to customize guitars to these tuning systems as well. Of course, doing so requires 'moving' the fret wires on the guitar's neck (called 're-fretting') to match the custom intervals. Additionally, the individual open-string tunings themselves may necessarily change. But, unlike programmable keyboards, this is very difficult and expensive to achieve and, is of course, a permanent change to the tonality of the instrument.

Just as we strive to create immediately-usable keyboard configurations, we hope to apply this knowledge to the guitar fretboard as well. The objective is to provide compatible tunings that do not require re-learning of the fingering patterns on most instruments. However, one luthier in particular showed your intrepid writer the 'middle finger' when I asked about doing this on one of my own guitars.

I'm still not sure if that was an enthusiastic 'yes' or an insulting 'no.' (Luthiers are very uncommon in the West Pacific rim.)

Given all of the available choices for tuning systems, it is the Just Intonation system which reliably provides exceptional tonality, familiar scale and chord structures (fingerings on the keyboard), and is capable of tones-per-octave in as many ranges as the user wishes. For sheer simplicity and usability, the work in this text adheres to twelve tones to the octave and, strives to remain as close to the tenets of Just Intonation tuning as is possible. This is done for obvious, logical reasons, as well as more esoteric and traditional rationale associated with the number twelve.

That there are several paths to adjacent tonal destinations, the writer will not deny. However, the fact that many of those alternate paths are impossibly arcane to many, very difficult to implement, and generally require specialized, customized (and very expensive) equipment is the ultimate deal-breaker.

To further elaborate upon the writer's growing bias *favoring* Just Tuning, let's take a look at the anecdotal story of how western intervals came into being in the first place. For this, we return to the monochord instrument of the ancient past.

It is widely believed that Pythagoras devised, and Plato et. al., later recreated the basic interval ratios using that device, we today call a 'monochord' (basically meaning "one-string"). The device was designed with a single string of unconfirmed composition, which was tuned to an unknown tonic by applying variable string-tension.

By 'fretting' this string in various locations, the user would elicit differing tones based on the position of the particular fret location. For instance, if one was to 'fret' the string in its exact center position, the string would be effectively halved resulting in two string segments of half the original length, which ring with an identical tone. That tone being an octave above the whole string's fundamental tone. The resulting interval ratio would be an obviously-visible 2:1, which is the universally-recognized interval ratio for an octave above the tonic.

Now, let's fret the string at a position that is one-third the full length. This divides the string into two unequal sections.

117

One section is one-third and the other is two-thirds of the entire length. The resulting pitch of the one-third section is proportional both to the length of the original string, and harmonically balanced with the tone of the two-thirds section. Its resulting interval is 3:2, which describes a perfect 5th above the octave tone described above.

If we continue our little thought experiment by dividing the string into four even sections (by fretting it at three equidistant locations), we arrive at yet another octave above, which is 3:1 over the original tone.

We can arrive at any perfect interval measurement simply by dividing the string at various, proportional (not necessarily equidistant) locations. The interesting thing about this practice is that; no matter where you fret the string, both tones currently represented on that string will harmonize — as both tones are proportional ratios of the whole. The writer found that last part especially fascinating.

Simplicity is the key to everything. These intervals are expressed in simple ratios of whole number composition. Even your writer can do that math.

The resulting system of whole-number interval ratios is simple, effective, and elegant. Why would it be necessary to introduce unnecessary complication to such a system? Well, the obvious answer could be; "To discover more usable tones." And, while that is something this writer can definitely support, it is by no means necessary to increase complexity to achieve this objective.

In addition to the logical expression of intervals, the Just Tuning system has the added benefit of being *less* complicated while remaining arguably *more* accurate — harmonically, with regard to a human's general perception of tonal contrast.

In the end, it will all come down to opinion… Your opinion. And, through the course of producing this text, it has been made abundantly clear to this writer that there are those who have different, entrenched opinions on this topic. However, despite personal choice arguments, there are few who could rationally dispute the veracity of the claims of simplicity and tonal accuracy with regards to the Just Intonation system. It just works.

Just Intonation has been in wide use since (at least) the Middle Ages, in one form or another. That it was eventually superseded by Mean Tone systems in the 1500's is not disputed by this writer.

The appearance of the grand cathedrals' pipe organs were a primary driver behind the adoption of various Mean Tone variants. And, pipe organs around the world, were tuned according to these Mean Tone standards until only recently.

At the time of this writing, in North America, there remain several pipe organs which are still tuned using Mean Tone variants. However, few remain 'in the wild' within Western Europe. The reasons for this remain unclear.

Ultimately, it was Constantine's Universal Church of Rome making the final decisions (dictates) regarding church practice throughout the pertinent historical period(s). Therefore, it is somewhat likely that the migration to (and, then... away from) the Mean Tone standard was executed for reasons other than tonality or ease of use. Who can truly say why such power-and-control structures do anything?

The good news is that many of the intervals utilized in mean tone systems are also applicable in Just Intonation, due to system overlap. Thus, it may be apparent to some that this work's implementation of Just Tuning incorporates some very few of the traditional mean tone (quarter-comma variant) ratios without the need to address the syntonic comma issue... unless you just want to. This writer doesn't care to address it.

If you don't know what all that means, it's perfectly fine. I didn't either. And, once I did learn what it meant... I didn't care. Apologies if that seems dismissive.

Ultimately, the jargon, complicated math, and inscrutable intricacy of most tuning applications are of little consequence or concern to us and the work we are doing here. But, knowing a small bit of the history is important toward understanding why we are here and where we are going.

Charting Our Healing Tones

We're In The Home Stretch Now

Well, it's about time to get back to work and finish our healing tones chart and, our *first* tuning system grid. (Yes. Surprise! There will be more than one.)

Tone	12-TET (440Hz)	12TET (432Hz)	Geometric
A^7	3520	3456	3456
G$^{#7}$	3322.4400	3262.0674	3240
G^7	3135.9681	3078.9806	
F$^{#7}$	2959.9542	2906.1698	2880
F^7	**2793.8322**	**2743.0581**	**2700**
E^7	2637.0263	2589.1012	
D$^{#7}$	2489.0173	2443.7853	2448
D^7	2349.3238	2306.6254	
C$^{#7}$	2217.4644	2177.1638	2160
C^7	2093.0051	2054.9683	
B^6	1975.5304	1939.6311	
A$^{#6}$	1864.6534	1830.7674	1800
A^6	1760	1728	1728

Table 15.1 (13.2) - Our seventh octave chart after incorporating the new F^7 of 2700Hz

When we left off in *Chapter 13*, after a little mathematical drama, we had just settled on the frequency(ies) for our 'F' tones. The seventh octave chart of our current progress is displayed in *Table 15.1*, above.

We have previously, assigned our D$^{\#}$ the frequency of 1224Hz as a preference over the 1260Hz. It's octavated tone of 2448Hz is represented in the chart above, *as is* the new F^7 tone of 2700Hz.

Going forward, we will use the math of semitones and cents to determine what other 'geometric' healing tones are to be revealed to us.

With 'B,' 'C,' 'D,' 'E,' and 'G' all missing, we have our work cut out for us. But, we are now armed with plenty of tools to assist us in locating the best values for these tones.

Finding 'D'

We will first explore possibilities for the D^7 in the chart above. The logic is this: If a semitone in 'Just' tuning is 111.731$^¢$ with a frequency ratio of 1.0666, then running the calculation on C$^{\#7}$ and, targeting that interval width value, should reveal a candidate frequency for D^7, which conforms to our stated rules. Let's see how it pans out.

C$^{\#7}$ is set to 2160Hz. Therefore 2160Hz raised by 111.731$^¢$ should give us a perfect semitone value for D^7. Again, there is no direct conversion from frequency to cents. It has to go into the black hole of the mystery math before a candidate value emerges. This fact means we can throw some educated guesses up and see how the math and frequencies fit or don't fit the pattern.

So, again to the scientific calculator for:

$$¢ = 1200 \times \log_2 (f_2 / f_1)$$
$$(\log_2 = 0.301029995)$$

For 'f_1', we will try the geometric value for a fifteen-sided polygon (f_1) against the C$^{\#}$ of 2160Hz. This gives us a value for f_2, of 2340Hz.

When using 2340Hz, the resulting interval width, is 138.60$^¢$.

The result tells us that the interval width between 2160Hz and 2340Hz is 138.60$^¢$. This interval width is significantly larger than a semitone. So, we can see that the candidate value we are searching for must be less than 2340Hz but greater than 2160Hz.

Taking a quick look at all proximal values that meet the criteria for reduction to nine, we eventually find that our tried-and-true 'guess-timation' method leads us to 2304Hz.

When we substitute this value into the mystery math machine, as f_2 along with the previous f_1 value of C#-2160Hz, we receive a semitone value of exactly 111.731$^¢$. "Yahtzee!" We have a match.

A frequency of 2304Hz conforms to our 'rules' for such values as laid out previously. It numerically reduces to 9, is divisible by 3, 6, and 9, and as a bonus, it is also divisible by 12 *and* 72.

So, calling that a complete 'Win!' We will now add the candidate value of 2304Hz into our chart as D^7. We can now calculate all of our D tones by using the octavation method previously explained. And, so here they are:

Octave Tones of D - Based on D^7 = 2304Hz

D - Octaves	Frequency (Hz)
D^8	4608
D^7	2304
D^6	1152
D^5	576
D^4	288
D^3	144
D^2	72
D^1	36
D^0	18

Table 15.2 - The octaves of 'D' calculated from a D^7 of 2304Hz.

What remains to be determined are the tones for B, C, E, and G. As you will see, this turns out to be entirely do-able. Plus, we receive a lot of help from the 'Just Intonation' tuning system's interval stack.

Additionally, the author is well aware that there are much quicker methods to achieving the same results. The point of this practice is to lay bare the step-wise logic of these creations for everyone. Custom tuning is no longer, to be the exclusive realm of the 'experts.'

So, again we update our seventh-octave chart to reveal our progress. Our new D⁷ has found a home and manifests as a 2304Hz frequency. Will these tones survive sound trials on a real keyboard? The kind reader will have to bear with us to learn the answer to this and many other burning questions.

Tone	12-TET (440Hz)	12TET (432Hz)	Geometric
A⁷	3520	3456	3456
G#⁷	3322.4400	3262.0674	3240
G⁷	3135.9681	3078.9806	
F#⁷	2959.9542	2906.1698	2880
F⁷	2793.8322	2743.0581	2700
E⁷	2637.0263	2589.1012	
D#⁷	2489.0173	2443.7853	2448
D⁷	2349.3238	2306.6254	2304
C#⁷	2217.4644	2177.1638	2160
C⁷	2093.0051	2054.9683	
B⁶	1975.5304	1939.6311	
A#⁶	1864.6534	1830.7674	1800
A⁶	1760	1728	1728

Table 15.3 - Current progress charted with the new D7 of 2304Hz compared to Equal Temperament tones using 440Hz and 432Hz as the A4 fundamental.

We now turn our undivided attention to the next wayward note assignment, that of the 'B' tone.

Determining Our 'B'

There are several interval calculations used in world music. The 111.731¢ metric is but one, which happens to describe a 'Just Intonation' semitone. Another such value is 498.045¢, which represents a 'Just' perfect fourth. Since we are now attempting to pin down B⁶, perhaps it would be a good idea to see how that math may be of further service to our efforts.

Using the same mystery-math formula as above, let us see if we can more closely identify a candidate for our B⁶, utilizing the same methodology.

A whole tone below our B^6 would be A^6, which has already been confirmed as 1728Hz. We need to determine the B^6 frequency that would give us a whole-tone interval close to the JI metric of 203.910$^\text{¢}$, which describes a *whole tone* interval.

Choosing not to belabor the math further than necessary, we will simply observe that:

2160Hz is 386.314$^\text{¢}$ above our 1728Hz 'A,' which is the value in cents that describes a *Just Major Third*. This result however, merely confirms our current value(s) for $C^\#$ and that the logic is sound for locating our lost B^6 at or approximating a value of 203.910$^\text{¢}$.

Looking for the frequency that matches our whole tone interval of 203.910$^\text{¢}$ leads us (algebraically) to discover 1944Hz, which exactly matches all requirements for our B^6.

$$1200 \times \log_2 (1728 \div 1944) = 203.910^\text{¢}$$

1728Hz is our A^6, and 1944Hz is the whole tone above it. This is the B^6 we were looking for!

And again, this value conforms to our 'rules.' It numerically reduces to 9, is divisible by 3, 6, and 9, and as a bonus, it also happens to be divisible by 12 and 72.

We can now include the octave tones for all 'B' tones in our system!

B - Octaves	Frequency (Hz)
B^8	7776
B^7	3888
B^6	1944
B^5	972
B^4	486
B^3	243
B^2	121.5
B^1	60.75
B^0	30.375

Table 15.4 - The octaves of 'B' calculated from a B^6 of 2304Hz.

This happy outcome gives us an updated chart for our seventh octave, including our new B^6 candidate frequency of 1944Hz, that looks like this:

Tone	12-TET (440Hz)	12TET (432Hz)	Geometric
A^7	3520	3456	3456
G$^{\#7}$	3322.4400	3262.0674	3240
G^7	3135.9681	3078.9806	
F$^{\#7}$	2959.9542	2906.1698	2880
F^7	2793.8322	2743.0581	2700
E^7	2637.0263	2589.1012	
D$^{\#7}$	2489.0173	2443.7853	2448
D^7	2349.3238	2306.6254	2304
C$^{\#7}$	2217.4644	2177.1638	2160
C^7	2093.0051	2054.9683	
B^6	1975.5304	1939.6311	1944
A$^{\#6}$	1864.6534	1830.7674	1800
A^6	1760	1728	1728

Table 15.5 - Current progress as of the addition of our B^6 tone of 1944Hz compared to Equal Temperament tones using 440Hz and 432Hz as the A4 fundamental.

Interestingly, we now have a complete tone model for the F$^{\#}$ Major scale and the majority of its constituent chords. Preliminary sound trials reveal that these interim results work nicely on a standard keyboard layout. Somehow, I feel that this is just too *convenient*.

Is the F$^{\#}$ Major scale the most natural result of geometric sound design? It turns out that some few seekers have explored or stumbled upon this question in recent years. Yet, not many have done much that would be considered 'fully-formed' or readily usable with the theory. Your writer hopes to break with that particular trend.

Now, this researcher must add himself to the list of those who are enamored by the natural affinity for harmony provided by our F$^{\#}$-Major tones thus far. It is hoped that the work outlined here will serve to somewhat enhance and promote increased interest in that particular aspect of study. If the F$^{\#}$ series is indeed somehow special, it behooves us, as much as possible, to more deeply understand why that might be.

Pinning Down the 'C'

Next on our list is 'C.' In theory, the interval from A to C is a *minor 3rd*. Checking the 'Just Intonation' intervals, we learn that the perfect minor 3rd *should* yield an interval width of 315.641¢ from the A tone. In this case, that is a frequency of 1728Hz.

A quick check of the math reveals that the frequency at the interval width of 315.641¢ turns out to be 2073.5997Hz. The interval ratio in decimal terms is 1.199976. In the writer's opinion, this result is just messy and too disorderly. Nonetheless, the writer would accept the result if it met the necessary criteria. However, not only is the result a decimal remainder value, but the whole number portion does not align in any way to the other intervals.

Listening to the 'A' and this 'C' makes it painfully evident that this is not the 'C' that fits. Although the digits reduce to six, the value cannot resolve to a whole number in higher octaves. Therefore, I am unwilling to give up on finding a better geometric fit. The reality is that the usual minor 3rd, interval is not what we are looking for here.

Searching and inquiring about other tuning systems in the world of micro-tonal music; a gruff and mysterious on-line presence, directed me to the (JI) interval of 266.871¢ (ratio of 1.1666667. This value would give us what is called a *sub-minor 3rd*. I had not previously known of or utilized this interval, which is a ratio of 7:6 and, turns out to be a very common Just interval, also known as a '*septimal minor 3rd*.'

The math for 266.871¢ yields a value of 2016Hz. The resulting value meets all of our criteria (i.e., 3, 6, 9, 12, 72), and while the tone is a bit quirky, it harmonizes beautifully when played against the 'A' and other significant intervals. As a bonus, a C6 at 2016Hz prevents its lower octave frequencies from devolving into decimal values—all the way down to C1. Thus, 2016Hz turns out to be a magnificent addition to our healing tones! (Many thanks to that 'gruff and mysterious' online presence)

Adopting the sub-minor 3rd or 'septimal' 3rd of 2016Hz gives us the following chart of octave values for all of our 'C' tones:

C - Octaves	Frequency (Hz)
C^8	8064
C^7	4032
C^6	2016
C^5	1008
C^4	504
C^3	252
C^2	126
C^1	63
C^0	31.5

Table 15.6 - The octaves of 'C' calculated from a C^6 of 2016Hz.

And, our updated chart for the entire seventh octave now looks like this:

Tone	12-TET (440Hz)	12TET (432Hz)	Geometric
A^7	3520	3456	3456
$G^{\#7}$	3322.4400	3262.0674	3240
G^7	3135.9681	3078.9806	
$F^{\#7}$	2959.9542	2906.1698	2880
F^7	2793.8322	2743.0581	2700
E^7	2637.0263	2589.1012	
$D^{\#7}$	2489.0173	2443.7853	2448
D^7	2349.3238	2306.6254	2304
$C^{\#7}$	2217.4644	2177.1638	2160
C^7	2093.0051	2054.9683	2016
B^6	1975.5304	1939.6311	1944
$A^{\#6}$	1864.6534	1830.7674	1800
A^6	1760	1728	1728

Table 15.7 - Current progress as of the addition of our C^7 tone of 2016Hz compared to Equal Temperament tones using 440Hz and 432Hz as the A4 fundamental.

Regarding 'C' (*A Brief Detour into Completely Unrelated Related Territory*)

At this point, I want to make a brief side-journey regarding our 'C' tone. (It is hoped that the reader is open to tolerating these little 'side-bars' as they are a common feature of this text.)

Many who have followed the progress of the work this far, may also be familiar with the phenomenon of the 'Schumann Resonance.' For those who are not, the Schumann Resonance is a class of primary frequencies and their harmonics, that constantly propagate within the Earth's *atmosphere*.

These oscillations are caused by atmospheric conditions such as lightning, winds, storms, sonic booms, and other atmospheric events. The Schumann Resonance frequency changes with the intensity of these natural (and sometimes anthropomorphic) events - sometimes resonating in a high range of approximately 16-24Hz or, in the lower ranges, as low as 5.2Hz. Resonances have occasionally, been observed much higher, extending into the range of 26Hz. The boundary values vary depending upon the day and the data source.

The interesting thing here is that one of the more commonly cited, baseline Schumann frequencies is often cited as being very close to 7.83Hz. (Again, depending upon the source.) If you continue reducing 2016Hz down below C^0 , you soon arrive at C^{-2} with a value of 7.875Hz - A close and mildly interesting approximation, which is admittedly, easily relegated to the realm of mathematical coincidence.

It would be interesting if, we were to use this very low octave as an atmospheric tone in any sessions. But, the lowest value generally reproducible by consumer-grade equipment would be in the area of 30Hz. We will re-visit this scenario in a later chapter where we will discuss the Schumann resonance in a bit more detail.

The values of 7.83 and 7.875Hz, both reduce to nine, just as any valid value in our geometric series. This is the primary reason why it caught the writer's eye and imagination when perusing the data. The effect is mathematical, not magical. Yet, remains a somewhat interesting happenstance.

Bringing It Home - Locking in the 'E,' and the 'G'

We are closing in on a complete tuning system for our relaxation and healing tones tuning system. Thus far, our compromises have been minimal in that we have only made a subjectively-motivated change to our choice of frequency for our D# and, accepted a somewhat quirky sub-minor 3rd tone as our candidate for 'C.'

As we consider the remaining empty spaces in our chart, the 'E' and the 'G,' we find that the math leads us directly to our 'E' but requires a bit more imagination for the 'G.' So, let's get to it. Shall we?

Our 'E' represents the *Perfect 5th* position in our system. Our prevalent, Just Intonation interval stack suggests an interval value of 701.955¢ to form a perfect 5th relative to our root 'A.' The interval ratio to accomplish a perfect 5th turns out to be 3:2 or a multiplier of 1.5.

The resulting value for the seventh octave 'E' is revealed as 2592Hz. This value represents precisely 701.955¢ above the 'A.' Additionally, it meets All of the stated 'rules' for our system. As a special treat, all resulting values down to E^2 are whole numbers. All in all, a very nice outcome.

The octave chart for our 'E' tones, now looks this (*Table 15.8.*) And, our updated seventh-octave chart reveals that we have only one note remaining to be determined. The 'G'.

E - Octaves	Frequency (Hz)
E^8	4032
E^7	2592
E^6	1296
E^5	648
E^4	324
E^3	162
E^2	81
E^1	40.50
E^0	20.25

Table 15.8 - The octaves of 'E' calculated from a E^7 of 2592Hz.

Tone	12-TET (440Hz)	12TET (432Hz)	Geometric
A^7	3520	3456	3456
$G^{\#7}$	3322.4400	3262.0674	3240
G^7	3135.9681	3078.9806	
$F^{\#7}$	2959.9542	2906.1698	2880
F^7	2793.8322	2743.0581	2700
E^7	2637.0263	2589.1012	2592
$D^{\#7}$	2489.0173	2443.7853	2448
D^7	2349.3238	2306.6254	2304
$C^{\#7}$	2217.4644	2177.1638	2160
C^7	2093.0051	2054.9683	2016
B^6	1975.5304	1939.6311	1944
$A^{\#6}$	1864.6534	1830.7674	1800
A^6	1760	1728	1728

Table 15.9 - Current progress as of the addition of our E^7 tone of 2592Hz compared to Equal Temperament tones using 440Hz and 432Hz as the A4 fundamental.

Now, for the 'G'

Filling the slot for our 'G' requires a bit more consideration. The G represents the *minor 7th* position. To accomplish a perfect 'Just' minor 7th requires us to set our sites on an interval value of 1017.597¢.

Unfortunately, the usual ratios which would get us close to the perfect value, yield only values riddled with imprecision and decimal values.

The reader may recall that our minor 3rd position required similar mathematical gymnastics until we discovered the magical sub-minor 3rd of 266.871¢, which we adopted, over the 'Just' minor 3rd of 315.641¢. This was because the preferred-fit ratio for the minor 3rd (now our C^6 at 2016Hz) resulted in frequencies with unresolving decimal remainders and was therefore, incompatible with the criteria established for our geometric system.

In the case of the minor 7th, we do a bit of a deeper dive into some music theory. It turns out that the *seventh harmonic* of the fourth octave root, in this case, 432Hz, indicates the frequency which should match the minor 7th, three octaves above it. (Much more on harmonics later.)

The seventh harmonic of 432Hz is 3024Hz. According to the generally accepted rules of harmonics, this fact directly indicates that the seventh octave's minor 7th (G7) should be 3024Hz.

It feels a bit like cheating, doesn't it? To cut through the suspense; Yes! 3024Hz meets all of the requirements and is definitely the correct frequency. It is and will always be 3024Hz for our charted G7.

Working backward now, we can see that this is 968.8264¢ above a tonic of 1728Hz. Since it is paired with the sub-minor 3rd (aka septimal minor 3rd,) Our C tone in this case, it comes as no surprise that the minor 7th in our chart, turns out also to be a sub-minor (or septimal) tone itself. In this case, a *sub-minor 7th* (aka *Septimal m7th*.)

So, we will calculate and check all of our octaves as usual, and take a step back to admire our completed tuning grid chart, including our newly-minted G7 frequency of 3024Hz.

G - Octaves	Frequency (Hz)
G8	6048
G7	3024
G6	1512
G5	756
G4	378
G3	189
G2	94.5
G1	47.25
G0	23.625

Table 15.10 - The octaves of 'G' calculated from a G7 of 3024Hz.

With the completion of this first, *draft* tuning system, it became necessary to learn how to upload the tuning data into an actual MIDI instrument for the purpose of final sound trials, and to determine if any adjustments were necessary. This wasn't as easy as it sounds.

Tone	12-TET (440Hz)	12TET (432Hz)	Geometric
A⁷	3520	3456	3456
G#⁷	3322.4400	3262.0674	3240
G⁷	**3135.9681**	**3078.9806**	**3024**
F#⁷	2959.9542	2906.1698	2880
F⁷	2793.8322	2743.0581	2700
E⁷	2637.0263	2589.1012	2592
D#⁷	2489.0173	2443.7853	2448
D⁷	2349.3238	2306.6254	2304
C#⁷	2217.4644	2177.1638	2160
C⁷	2093.0051	2054.9683	2016
B⁶	1975.5304	1939.6311	1944
A#⁶	1864.6534	1830.7674	1800
A⁶	1760	1728	1728

Table 15.11 - The completed tuning chart as of the addition of our G⁷ tone of 3024Hz compared to Equal Temperament tones using 440Hz and 432Hz as the A4 fundamental reference.

As it turns out, there are several ways to accomplish this. However, the writer chose to take the direct path and create tuning files for a keyboard synthesizer. This allowed a full testing of the tuning system(s) as constructed in this work. We will definitely go into detail regarding this process later in this text.

Suffice it to say that your generally, mild-mannered writer became as giddy as a prom queen when this system was played upon a real keyboard. The system is quirky, but it definitely works! Yet, we have *so* much more work to do before our thesis comfortably resides on Terra Firma.

A Completed Healing Tone System
Some Said it Couldn't (or Shouldn't) be Done

Voila! Our full prototype chart for the entire tuning system is now complete. And, it looks like this:

Tone	12-TET (440Hz)	12-TET (432Hz)	Geometric	Named Interval
A⁷	3520	3456	3456	Octave
G#⁷	3322.4400	3262.0674	3240	Maj 7th
G⁷	3135.9681	3078.9806	3024	Sub m7th
F#⁷	2959.9542	2906.1698	2880	Maj 6th
F⁷	2793.8322	2743.0581	2700	Dim 6th
E⁷	2637.0263	2589.1012	2592	Perf 5th
D#⁷	2489.0173	2443.7853	2448	Dim 5th
D⁷	2349.3238	2306.6254	2304	Perfect 4th
C#⁷	2217.4644	2177.1638	2160	Maj 3rd
C⁷	2093.0051	2054.9683	2016	Sub m3rd
B⁶	1975.5304	1939.6311	1944	Maj 2nd
A#⁶	1864.6534	1830.7674	1800	5-Limit semitone
A⁶	1760	1728	1728	Root

Table 16.1 - Current draft tuning system. In comparison to Equal Temperament tones using both 440Hz and 432Hz, as the A⁴ fundamental reference.

As we progress further, we will see more of the underlying math behind these tones, which will enable anyone to create their own unique tuning system or just verify our work thus far. I am sure some out there will take great joy in looking for places to poke holes in the thesis, and improve the systems contained in this work. Whichever scenario works for you, this writer welcomes it as; the concepts and theory behind this work *should* be closely examined and refined by others.

The primary point I wish to press is this; We should not take the established commercial music narrative so seriously. We are not limited to just eighty-eight pre-determined, pre-programmed, 440Hz, 12-TET tones, pre-loaded on the standard keyboard, and to which every other instrument, despite its specific tonal characteristics and unique potential must nevertheless accommodate.

Try out the herein-proposed tuning system. If you like the tonality and design, or just happen to agree with the thesis, please 'knock yourself out' using it to make your music, sound-based healing practice, and the lives of others more successful, peaceful, and joyful.

Those Despicable Decimals

We have seen that; in several cases our derived frequencies devolve into decimal remainders in the lower octaves. This *devolution* (as I like to call it,) generally occurs close to 180Hz, a value below which no pure geometric resonance exists. This occurs because, 180° corresponds to the most basic of the two-dimensional polygonal shapes, that of a regular triangle. Thus, 180Hz is the lowest possible 'pure geometry' tone. As we have done with all geometric values, octavation allows us to quickly determine both the lower, and upper registers of any tone class. It is seen as inevitable that in these lower frequencies, we would see some degree of devolution, in the form of decimal remainder action in these same lower frequencies.

In our currently-proposed tuning system however, only two tones above 180Hz, $G^{\#2}$ and F^3, possess decimal remainders. Thankfully, these remainders are both 0.50Hz, which we have already accepted as reasonable, due to the fact that they resolve to whole numbers in the next higher octave. Additionally, each of these decimal values demonstrate the *oh-so* critical numerical reduction to nine. Such tones are considered perfectly acceptable by the rules.

Of course, checks for divisibility (3, 6, 9...etc.), are pointless with decimal remainders. Therefore, the <u>numerical reduction to 3, 6, or 9 is the primary validating factor</u> for these 'remainder' tones - this is also contingent upon their higher octave values' compliance with the divisibility rules as stated. Specifically, any decimal value frequencies *must* resolve to whole number frequencies in higher octaves.

Again, lower octave values with decimal remainders are to be *expected*, both between 180Hz and 360Hz but, especially below 180Hz.

Lacking any need for more stringent mathematical criteria nor a more elegant solution, we eagerly accept such values in the current draft of our base tuning system.

Commentary Regarding Decimal Place Remainders

That some frequencies end up with decimal remainders is not, by itself, to be considered an undesired outcome for most tuning systems. However, the system we are trying to build here is one where geometric values and whole number frequencies (in that order) are the most desirable.

Therefore, if one were to construct their own tuning system design from a different, non-geometric tonic value, I consider it very likely that decimal-place frequencies would be common and unresolvable by our criteria. It may therefore, be perfectly acceptable to make use of alternate frequency ratios for those (generally) minor tone values - in commercial music applications. In fact, I propose that they may be easier to work with than the ones presented here.

However, the writer's general aversion to extensive decimal remainders is primarily due to the simple fact their resultant pressure waves do not propagate harmonics in an easily predictable or naturally-reflected manner when utilized for organized music. This is not to mention that they cannot conform to the thesis and stated rules of the game as outlined earlier in this work, because they require 'special handling' as explained above.

We must always keep uppermost in our mind, the intended application of any music produced, *prior* to choosing a tuning system for that production. Healing and relaxation or anti-stress applications, in my opinion, require 'pure' tones, which emulate a somewhat natural (analog) origin, complete with their natural harmonics and overtones.

This is the way of nature, geometry, and universal energy flow.

Commercial and mainstream applications will, of course, utilize any variation of this, or any other systems that produce the desired tonal texture. It is not the writer's intention to amend or replace such systems but, to enhance only the methods of making music and tone for the purpose of uplifting, relaxation and healing purposes.

The Ratios - JUST the Ratios!

It will be evident to any music theoreticians slogging through this treatise that we have moved somewhat 'off the reservation' for conventional scale systems that universally utilize the typical, accepted keyboard logic.

However, the herein produced tonal systems have organically gravitated towards a well-known system known as 'Just Intonation' with very few exceptions. This is good news because the design of 'Just Intonation' has been around for a very long time and is widely respected, utilized, and appreciated as an alternate tuning system amongst both micro-tonal and twelve-tone alternative tuning musicians.

It should also be noted that this coincidental conformity with Just Intonation came as a complete surprise to this researcher. In fact, the depth of knowledge regarding the system, at the onset of this research project was so shallow that the writer was not even aware that the 'Just Intonation' system existed. A problem in need of a better solution had presented itself. It was that solution that we are seeking in this work. Just Intonation is a large part of that solution. That's it.

Fortunately, the background work for this work, included a somewhat lengthy dive into several authoritative textbooks. The writer therein recognized that many of the interval ratios already discovered, matched up with several interval ratios, derived in some earlier prototype systems (read as: "Early failures") and, were referenced within these various texts. The subsequent focus on the 'JI' system made this project much more manageable and coherent.

In fact, it is doubtful that the project could have been successfully completed without the integration of several aspects of the JI system, as the writer understands it today.

The chart below shows where we currently stand in our construction of a geometrically-based tonal system and displays the interval widths in cents, for the entire system. If we use what we have found thus far, we necessarily leave behind many of the conventions of standard tuning theory, and plant both feet firmly the realm of customized tonal systems.

	Tuning Grid Based on A-432Hz (7th Octave)					
Note	Interval	Ratio	Multiplier	Frequency (Hz)	Interval from Root (¢)	Step Interval (¢)
A	Octave	2:1	2	1728.00	1200	111.731
G	Maj 7th	15:8	1.875	1620.00	1088.269	119.443
G	Sept min 7th	7:4	1.75	1512.00	968.826	84.467
F#	Major 6th	5:3	1.666666667	1440.00	884.359	111.731
F	Aug 5th	25:16	1.5625	1350.00	772.627	70.672
E	Perf 5th	3:2	1.5	1296.00	701.955	98.955
D#	dim 5/Aug4	17:12	1.416666667	1224.00	603.000	104.955
D	Perf 4th	4:3	1.333333333	1152.00	498.045	111.731
C#	M 3rd	5:4	1.25	1080.00	386.314	119.443
C	Sept min 3rd	7:6	1.166666667	1008.00	266.871	62.961
B	M 2nd	9:8	1.125	972.00	203.910	133.238
A#	5-Limit Semi	25:24	1.041666667	900.00	70.672	70.672
A	Root	1	1.00	864.00	—	—

Table 16.2 - Tuning grid based on an A⁴ fundamental of 432Hz, showing the seventh octave including interval ratios, semi-tone step width, and full interval width.

This required departure from standard, music theory's norms, means that the usual constructs, such as the Major Triad, the harmonic dyad, and even most of the common chord patterns, will likely, sound *different* to our ears and may not always appear on the standard keyboard, as typically expected.

The writer chooses experimentation as a method for locating the fingering patterns available in our new system. As it turns out, they are not as foreign as one might expect. Most of the standard keyboard logic remains intact. But, there are some areas where one may question the validity of the entire thesis.

This fact especially applies to those who have 12-TET trained pitch recognition and, consider themselves as possessing 'perfect pitch.' For those individuals, acclimating to these systems will require no small degree of patience and perseverance.

In the tuning grid displayed in *Table 16.2,* most values in the 'Interval From Root' column, conform to straight Just Intonation interval values using interval ratio calculations outlined in '*The Just Intonation Primer*' and other related materials. One could justifiably, consider the remaining values as Just ratios due to the simple fact that they arise from whole number ratios, rather than irrational numbers.

The writer considers this system to be a vindication of the evolving thesis and general concept, that has been swirling through his mind now for years. But, the concepts were ones for which the basic knowledge required to create such systems was lacking. It is ultimately satisfying to finally give expression to the sounds and thoughts that have haunted this writer since receiving that first certification as a 'Sound and Frequency' healer more than ten years before this work began.

"But..." Now we must ask ourselves, "What if we can construct a system that uses the more common 'JI' values for *all* of the intervals?"

What if we can build an alternative tuning system that allows us to use the full set of common chord and scale logic or 'fingerings' available on the standard keyboard?

What would such a system look like? Well, I believe it would look a lot like the standard keyboard albeit with completely different, geometric frequency values. Such a structure would allow the use of a standard keyboard and standard keyboard logic for *all* chords and scales.

We will only know, if we try. So, I have a few ideas about that.

Thus far, we have constructed a very nice and eminently usable tuning system based on A-Major and using our 432Hz A^4, as the fundamental tone. If nothing else, this accomplishment serves as a robust proof-of-concept for creating a healing tonal system based on geometric resonances.

But, what would be the result, if we constructed a similar system (or multiple systems) using other known-good geometrically-based tones as our fundamental, or root tone?

In our earlier geometric explorations, every step taken seemed to naturally gravitate towards F#, the F#-Major chords, and the associated scales. So, what if we constructed another tuning system using the same methods, an F# fundamental, and simply tweaked it as necessary and appropriate, using our 'Just Intonation' intervals?

Here's what I propose:

There are ratios that replicate (very nicely, by the way) the standard keyboard's traditional fingerings in Just Intonation. While our <u>A-Major Tuning Grid</u> system works reasonably well, there are some harmonic inconveniences associated with using it for general composition.

The 'geometric' <u>A-Major Tuning Grid,</u> also gives us access to many (but not all) of our 'geometric' tones - as intended. The only 'gotcha' is that we need to relearn (or unlearn) some few, traditional keyboard logic patterns, used for the desired chords and scales. This situation applies primarily, to the usage of minor modes in the system, as the major tones are mathematically, perfectly aligned with JI tuning.

The ultimate objective is to find a way to use the standard keyboard layout and, as many familiar chord and interval fingerings as possible. Wouldn't that be nice?

Because our geometric analysis seems to hold up F# as a critical tone class (180Hz, 360Hz, 720Hz, 1440Hz, etc...), let us now explore creating a new tuning system based on F# that uses the basic interval ratio calculations, available to us in the 'Just Intonation' structure. This method would allow us to meet the two stated objectives;

- Access to most, if not all, geometric tones revealed in our initial analysis while using F# (360Hz) as our tonic frequency.

- Continued use of familiar chording, interval, and scale patterns utilized for modern keyboards. (Standard keyboard logic)

Sound like fun? Let's do it!

Credit Where Credit is Due
A Brief Side Trip - To the Past

When this project began, way back in 2011, your mild-mannered author, had no idea what I was doing. All that I had, was this somewhat vague idea; a belief that there *must* be better system. I admit that carrying a certain typical, stubborn defiance of established dogmatic systems was a driving factor. (No science is *ever* 'settled.')

Inevitably, there will be some who will say that I still don't 'get it.' But it is what it is. My own music theory background in those days, was virtually non-existent. Personally, I just wanted to play! *'fuggetabout'* the details!

But, the tones available in 440Hz-12TET were dissonant and dirty in my head. What's a poor boy to do? I decided to create a better system of tonality… a more balanced harmonic lattice, if you will. As I later discovered, this is not a unique attitude when it comes to modern music. There are many who possess an active disdain for 440Hz-12TET. Yet, to date, I have found no source, which outlines the exact methods proposed in this text. Nor, have I located any method that creates the same or similar results revealed in my work.

Although there is never an end to learning when it comes to music theory, I like to think I have not only come to deeply respect it and those who actually understand the deeper theories of tone and harmony; But, I have also learned quite a lot of tuning related theory during the years of my experimentation and research.

That much of it has been rejected from these systems is not so important as the fact that due diligence was paid and, therefore provided these concepts a fair trial.

I have always had a question. And that question, when given voice, resulted in nothing but strange stares, and no small amount of behind-the-hand derision from my peers. Healers, teachers, musicians, and non-musicians alike, summarily refused to consider the proposition at all. That question was; "What about the 'other' tones?"

You see, I practice holistic wellness care (primarily chiropractic) by education and profession. After two decades of successful practice, I began to indulge my fascination for energy and sound and their obvious healing applications. I was deeply intrigued by the practice and thus, subsequently obtained a dubious certification in the art of sound healing. There were concepts to be studied, learned, and practiced (And, I practiced my keister off.) Many expensive classes, musical bowls, crystal chimes, gongs, drums, and tuning fork sets; even a didgeridoo were purchased; all at great expense. (Some I still use, albeit in a different paradigm than originally intended.)

My mentors taught me that the human body's energy system is based upon electromagnetic frequency and, by extension, sound and color (light frequencies). This basic set of premises remain prime components of my core beliefs. Such beliefs are supported by observed physiological effect, as well as emerging research from within the field of modern quantum energy mechanics. (*Shout out to Nassim Haramein and Torus Labs!*)

However, I did the unthinkable. I directly challenged the use of the standard tones when performing 'sound baths' and 'healing sessions.' And, this implied a modicum of actual criticism toward those who had become *authorities* in the field.

This overtly critical posture had the immediate effect of rendering me a pariah within my small circle of sound and frequency healing professionals. I had tripped over (actually, 'knocked over' would be a better phrase) the unwritten rule; Never… *ever* question the teachers. It wasn't the first time. I don't suppose that it will be the last.

But, (and bear with me here) if we are to practice an ancient and honored technique for the relaxation, wellness, and overall betterment of humanity, then why would we utilize an obviously flawed tonal basis that didn't even exist, prior to the 19th century? It makes no sense to me that so many practitioners doggedly cling to the false premise of modern tuning standards, employed with ancient sound healing techniques. This still baffles me, to this day.

Well, the community of holistic practitioners, certainly has its own dogma and canonical code. The tenets were never to be questioned. Yet, I did question the status-quo and, continue to do so. The *Solfeggio* tonal system was the only notable exception to my disdain. However, Solfeggio tones are not scalar, do not lend themselves well to making actual music, and have been, thus far limited and somewhat inflexible in their applicability... until now! (See: *Chapter 33 - The Solfeggio Tonal System*)

The rationale was simple; How can we profess that 12-TET tones tuned to an A^4 at 440Hz, such as the middle 'C' (commonly utilized for the root chakra, and sounding out at a frequency of 261.6261Hz,) are appropriate and beneficial to human physiology, when the tuning standard that dictates this frequency, known in modern times, as middle 'C', is not based in any historical text, and didn't even exist as middle 'C' until a little over one-hundred years ago?

I was, and remain obsessed with the firm belief that; there must be *more, different, other,* and just... ***better*** tones! Frequencies that are perfect, natural and, are the intended tones that are most beneficial for human relaxation, wellness, and healing. We are looking for tones that are *not* the result of brute-force irrational-number mathematics and the shoe-horn approach to building tuning systems. We *are* looking to construct a system based upon natural phenomena that exert a palpable and positive affect on human energy and physiology.

In the early stages of this work, as mentioned, your writer went so far as to acquire many and various instruments with which to practice this magnificent art form. One of these acquisitions was a full set of customized quartz crystal bowls. Unfortunately, they were tuned to 432Hz, 12TET. This purchase was years before the deluge of '432Hz' healing music started popping up on the Internet.

This particular purchase was also some time before I discovered the many defects inherent in 12-TET systems.

The manufacturer in China, was very resistant to the concept at the time. But, eventually agreed, while simultaneously, not exactly embracing the concept.

Since that time, approximately ten years prior to this writing, very similar (read: 'identical') tunings for the same crystal bowls have coincidentally become the 432Hz standard for that particular production line. I feel much the pioneer. Unfortunately the adoption of these particular crystal bowls is barely, marginally superior to the original 440Hz, 12-TET sets already and widely available, which is to say; they are equally useless.

Obviously, I found the 432Hz equal-temperament tuning to be wholly insufficient for the intended task, as it employs the exact same 'shoe-horn' approach that 440Hz, equal-temperament utilizes. As frustrating as this realization was, it re-energized the search (and research), which led to the work you hold in your hands now.

The circuitous path traveled, has led me to the point where this information has solidified, and will find its way into the hands of those who sincerely wish to use pure methods and pure tonal structures for their work — not to mention those who may be willing and able to improve this work and expand upon it.

Oh! Regarding that original set of custom crystal bowls... Well, at least ONE of them is actually useful... The A-432Hz, of course.

As a result of the years of probing and questioning, your writer no longer claims many friendly contacts in the holistic world of sound and frequency. Mind you, this is not to say that I don't have *any* friends.

> **"Future medicine will be the medicine of frequencies."**
> **- Albert Einstein**

It is this writer's hope that; if given a fair trial, this work may serve as a sort of vindication for these concepts, and as a prototype model for the use of pure sound as a medicinal modality.

It is a long-held, considered opinion that either it was just too much effort for these entrenched practitioners and teachers to explore the question, or they did not sufficiently understand music history and theory to the point of understanding the question's validity.

Hopefully with the formalization of this work's thesis and publication, The point will be made more clearly and, perhaps even adopted and developed fully. On the other hand, perhaps, this work will simply produce new detractors. Who knows? Probably a bit of both.

Our path thus far, has serendipitously led us to an old and venerable tuning system called *Just Intonation*. For a very long time, the writer arrived at these Just intervals for this work, without any idea that this was what was actually happening. The intervals were derived by 'working logically, backwards' as demonstrated in the construction of the initial tuning grid.

Sometime in 2016, an on-line presence pointed out that the derived intervals were in fact, Just intervals. Since that time, a deep appreciation for the Just Intonation system has been forged. While the writer makes no claim of complete understanding of the system's deeper theory, the inherent constructs, patterns, and intervals have been a massive boon to this decade-long effort.

The theory and concepts behind Just Intonation are outlined in the wonderfully complete manual '*The Just Intonation Primer*,' by **David B. Doty**, which is available for purchase on the usual, popular web sites. To anyone wishing to more deeply understand Just Intonation, I highly recommend obtaining a copy of Mr. Doty's primer.

We will not be delving too deeply into the Just Intonation theory and patterns in this work. This fact is mostly due to the high level of complexity as well as the wide variety of tonal variations the system permits. But also, due to several departures that become necessary.

As the writer, I am deeply appreciative of the work that went into and, the availability of the *Just Intonation Primer*. It's existence; as well as the Just Intonation system itself, has perfectly complemented the work thus far accomplished.

The more common Just interval ratios used in this text are summarized in *Appendix VIII - Just Intonation Ratios and Interval Conventions.*

But, what about 'equal' or 'even' temperament?

The equal-temperament issue is most easily addressed by stating that; In this work, we are not the least bit concerned with it; other than as a useful point of reference. And, it *is* a useful tool for reference, commercial music, and entertainment. But, the tones produced from such a system are decidedly imperfect, and the intervals are deeply flawed, making it an altogether, inappropriate tool for relaxation, meditation, and therapeutic applications.

Instead of an even temperament, we will strive for a special kind of natural and *balanced* temperament. And, this writer will unapologetically, do so on his own terms.

The systems we are building here are for relaxation, healing, and meditative purposes for which the modern structure of music is largely insufficient and wholly irrelevant. Therefore, we simply continue to 'follow the math' of geometry and Just Intonation, to see what gems we can dig up.

What's So Special About F#?
Playing Favorites Again, I See

Upon deeper review of the data thus far presented, one may justifiably ask themselves the question; "What's so special about the F#?" The short answer to the question is; In the world of equal-temperament and a 440Hz tuning standard, there's absolutely nothing special about F#, the F#-Major scale, or any of its chords.

The longer, less sar-*caustic* answer is that the label 'F#' is nothing more than that, a label - a simple designation assigned to a specific degree within a tone-class. The singular purpose of which is to differentiate it from others within that scale or tonal system. Such indicators are utilized, merely to imply a distance or interval width to the indicated note position, relative to other notes in the same system. The notation could just as easily have been a 'C'... or 'Y' for that matter. Such notation is entirely system-dependent.

The critical correlation for any viable tuning system is in the ratios of each frequency to its adjacent tones. The perceived 'purity' of those relationships between specific notes, are de*noted* as each tone's specific relationship to the fundamental itself, manifested as the intervals, chords, tones, and harmonics produced by the system.

Additionally, in the world of therapeutic sound and frequency, we concern ourselves not only with how the ear *perceives* tonal relationships, but to how the body, nervous system, and physical matter in-general *reacts* to the various frequencies' compression waves, produced by propagating vibrational energies.

The reference of 'F#' and most importantly for our purposes, the major scale based upon it, possess specific relationships within that are harmonically balanced and *commensurate*. Such relationships depend entirely upon the system's design. This fact allows us to subjectively perceive a harmonious relationship when the right notes, or tones are played together or in series.

This harmonic balance is affected, both subjectively and objectively, by perception and physiological reaction. The F# Major scale and its harmonic structures resulting from this work, are deep and rich in both subjective, physical effect and apparent, emotional power.

This observation is, of course, a somewhat personal observation. However, the observation itself, also extends so far as to place the F# Major tone class above all other systems, explored or created in this work - for the sheer width and breadth of its dynamic ability to affect the listener in myriad positive ways.

All Major scales, in both equal-temperament and Just Tuning, share similar relationships between their various tones. These variable relationships are defined by the system itself, with some variety as to the actual interval relationships designed into them. However, the *relative* relationships of assigned notations remain the constant that allows direct comparison and contrast. An 'A' in any 12-TET system is generally not far away from a same-octave 'A' in a Just Intonation construct. We have used this fact to great advantage thus far, and will continue to do so as we move forward. While there are some exceptions to this truism, it has borne out in the majority of instances.

The main source of all this exciting variety is in the choice of the 'root,' the note and frequency that serves as the fundamental tone from which all others are calculated. This root tone determines the subsequent steps through the twelve-tone system that recreate the same or similar relationships found in each.

Many readers may already know that you can play the same piece of music in different 'keys.' We can recreate any piece of music using music's various key signatures merely by changing the root note while preserving the inherent interval relationships contained within the musical piece itself.

Therefore, the root note, and by direct inference, the chosen key signature is generally a matter of artistic preference.

The alteration of the scale (key signature) utilized however, deeply affects the tonal 'color' of each successive tone in the scale. 'Color' is one of those vague musical descriptors, used to express that which cannot easily or reliably be described as a tonal quality. Yet, most people 'get' it when you use these expressions. This contrast or difference in color between key signatures is one reason why musicians often attribute a certain mood to differing key signatures in music, as well as the various sub-modes expressed within them.

Because ancient music did not (generally) use the same A, B, C... sharp and flat designations as we currently utilize, it is arbitrary at best, to assign any particular significance to the F# Major revealed in the geometric tones under exploration here. However, the mood palette of our F# system is decidedly, if somewhat arguably, special when compared to those of the other systems we will be creating within this text.

The writer understands that this longer explanation is not much clearer than the short version provided in the first paragraph. As we continue to explore the special relationship between geometry and tone; The fact is that the nominal F# just keeps popping up *time and time* again. The natural progression of the 'geometric' tones discovered in this work, inevitably gravitates towards an F#-Major sequence. Any deeper, esoteric meaning to this is left to the philosophers, theoreticians, and historians to determine.

We will explore this apparently special relationship with F# when we create a new tuning grid based on a 360Hz F#. The fundamental of 360Hz is both a perfect, geometric frequency and, is additionally confirmed as an F#, in our recently completed A-Major Tuning Grid, based on A-432Hz. The fundamental frequency, being a 'magical' 360Hz, is a resonance value representing both the circle and the square. Nice way to start don't you think?

Indeed, The F#-Major Tuning Grid (See: *Chapter 20 - Creating an F# Based Tuning Grid*) is the only tuning grid that is absolutely rooted and immersed in pure geometric tones as well as proving to be perfectly playable on a standard keyboard.

The 360Hz itself, octavates downward to 180Hz, 90Hz, 45Hz. These are, all important geometric numbers if not directly corresponding to an actual geometrical figure. Additionally, the same tone series ascends into 720Hz, 1440Hz, and 2880Hz — again, perfect, geometric resonances. Likewise, the inner tones of the F#-based system yield even more geometric, Platonic solid, and sacred geometric tones than any other tuning grid based on this geometric theory and design.

In this writer's opinion, the inevitable conclusion is that the system created upon F# is the most perfect of all of the grid systems created in this work. While this is not an entirely objective assessment, I do believe many who practice the art of sound and frequency healing, would concur with this assessment, if they were to give it a fair trial.

In the next chapter, we will put this belief system to the test as we create a tuning grid system based on a fundamental frequency of 360Hz, the venerable F#.

◈19◈

Variations on a Healing Theme

Pressing Our Luck With Alternate Fundamentals

When we created our original Healing Tone system, we focused primarily on basing the design on a mathematically rationalized foundation of the chosen tuning standard of an A^4 pegged to 432Hz. The system's root was linked to the series of frequencies, which are predominantly related via geometric logic, to that 'A' fundamental.

Because the frequency, 432Hz, is admittedly not a 'pure' geometric tone, some readers might feel a bit uncomfortable with that frequency forming the foundational basis of a 'geometric' tuning system. This reticence is understandable despite the fact that the number is unique in the range of standard A^4 frequencies most commonly used through the centuries. (See: *Chapter 6 - The 432Hz Question,* earlier in this text.)

However, to be fair and somewhat ecumenical, your writer has worked out several alternative scenarios regarding the fundamental 'A' that we will be using here. The fact is, no matter what *other* fundamental standard we use, the frequencies yielded are just as objectionable as any of the 12-TET standard tones. The 432Hz value for A^4 is the only fundamental value that yields the high degree of geometric tonal balance and harmonic symmetry, which will be revealed in the following pages.

We will now explore the concept of altering tonal color and texture by the seemingly simple act of changing the fundamental tone to another of our geometric frequencies.

We will demonstrate several related geometric tuning systems that meet the requirements of our geometric tuning system while, in most cases, but not all, effortlessly and almost magically, preserving the 432Hz tonal basis of the A⁴ position.

Before we begin, it is essential to note that changing the fundamental note also alters each subsequent tone's relationship within the octave. For example, where 'B' was the Major 2ⁿᵈ in our initially-proposed system, based on 'A,' altering the fundamental to F#, causes the 'B' to assume the role of the Perfect 4ᵗʰ.

This ability also presents us with the unique opportunity to tune an instrument in such a way as to prioritize the preferred musical key (as in F#-Major, A-Major, etc.,) while still permitting any desired musical key changes with aplomb.

Using our A-432Hz based system and our geometric relationships as a guide, let's explore what seems to be our geometric system's preferred tone class - That of the F#.

The A-Major tuning system we have created uses a specific non-linear, incremental stepping between tones. Instead of forcing the octave into *absolutely* equal pieces, as in equal-temperament, we used the concepts inherent in 'Just Tuning' aka 'Just Intonation' to create subjectively-better, more balanced harmonic relationships between the tones. For the current system under consideration, we will necessarily review the intervals previously utilized and make any necessary changes based on the system's needs as well as the criteria we have established as our 'rules of the game.'

The intervals and ratios used in our A-432Hz based (Actually; A-432Hz Major biased) tuning system are detailed in *Table 19.1*.

What might be considered the purest of these intervals and their resulting tones, are set in **bold** text in the table. The remaining entries, are intervals that were determined based upon the desired frequencies or by the Just intervals that yielded appropriately harmonic values conforming to our geometric rules.

Common Just Intonation Intervals and Their Widths in Cents

Interval	Ratio	Multiplier	Total ¢
Octave	**2:1**	**2**	**1200.00¢**
Maj7th	**15:8**	**1.875**	**1088.269¢**
Sept min 7th	7:4	1.75	968.826¢
Maj 6th	**5:3**	**1.66666667**	**884.359¢**
Aug 5th	25:16	1.5625	772.627¢
Perf 5th	**3:2**	**1.5**	**701.955¢**
Small dim 5th	17:12	1.41666667	603.000¢
Perf 4th	**4:3**	**1.33333333**	**498.045¢**
Maj 3rd	**5:4**	**1.25**	**386.314¢**
Sept min 3rd	7:6	1.16666667	266.871¢
Maj 2nd	**9:8**	**1.125**	**203.910¢**
Chrom semi	25:24	1.04166667	70.672¢
Unison	**1**	**1**	**0**

Table 19.1 - Just Intonation-derived intervals utilized in creating the A-Major Tuning Grid.

The A-Major system turned out to be eminently playable if a bit quirky in the minor tones. We will see what happens when using F#.

Notice that each of our minor tones; (min semitone, Sept m3rd, dim 5th, and Sept m7th) are a bit 'off' of what might generally be considered *standard* intonation for these intervals. But, take a closer look at the natural pattern that has developed among the **bold**ed entries. The intervals indicated, all conform perfectly to Just Intonation intervals *and* comprise a perfect major scale. Therefore, playing anything in an A Major key would feel exceptionally natural and intonate very well.

Thus far, it appears that the Major mode of our tuning systems are a much more natural fit to the thesis. The minor tones are a bit more challenging to sort out. As we move forward, we will see if, and how this observation holds true.

The pattern for major scales in modern music is a pattern of steps recalled by a kind of mnemonic device, '*WWHWWWH*.'

This simple memory device reminds us that we can create a major scale from any tone by making the indicated whole (W) or half (H) steps in the stated order.

In our <u>A-Major Tuning Grid</u> system, we defined the frequency of our tones and re-defined the inherent intervals for what is perceived as a more balanced and harmonious structure. Despite this apparent wrangling, the standard structures remain largely intact.

The perfect scenario is one that preserves the standard keyboard fingerings as closely as possible. The wonderful part is that Just Intonation's major intervals are thus far getting the job done very cleanly - at least with regards to the major scales and chords.

The major scales and dominant chords in our current system, based on the A-432Hz fundamental tone, all seem to work very well in this regard.

Amazingly, most musicians emerging from 'traditional' schools of music generally, have no idea that this kind of creative flexibility is even possible. This statement excepts the bowed-string players for whom the struggle is very real — as their musicality must deal with the tonal discrepancies any time they play accompanied by a fixed-tuning instrument such as the piano. (Sometimes its $G^\#$ and sometimes its $A\flat$. Other times, it's somewhere in-between.)

But, what if we want to play in a minor pentatonic mode with our A-Major tuning loaded into our keyboard? Well, that is the challenging part. Until the player learns to compensate and develops new ways (patterns) of using the tones, it may create some frustrating moments. (Honestly, it was both challenging and fun.) While the <u>A-Major Tuning Grid</u> (As we now refer to it) works very well. It does require some 'getting used to.' The minor pentatonic tonal sub-classes definitely sound different.

As I 'played around' a bit with the A-Major Tuning Grid, I sometimes felt as if I wanted more tones in the octave to work with. These additional tones per octave are eminently possible with extended micro-tonal tuning but, remain beyond the stated scope of this text.

To those interested in microtonal work, I recommend looking up the XenHarmonic Alliance on major social media platforms as well as their on-line Wiki. The 'Alliance' maintains the wiki with literal *volumes* of excellent information regarding microtuning methods and theory. Be warned however, the micro-tonal world is a rabbit-hole from which the inquisitive are unlikely to re-emerge.

So, let's now refocus and take a look at those ubiquitous F#s, revealed by our initial geometry explorations, and see if we can use the various mathematical 'coincidences' to improve upon the system by using F# as our fundamental or root tone.

Suppose we use an F$^\#$ tone (any one will do nicely) such as 360Hz. In such a case, we can use this tone as our fundamental tone and, begin building a separate, unique tuning system that will both;

- Match our geometric values and favor playing the instrument in the key of F$^\#$-Major, as well as…

- Preserving near-perfect access to other key signatures (using standard fingering patterns.)

We will imaginatively dub this new system our 'F$^\#$-Major Tuning Grid' as our methods here are observed to favor both the F$^\#$ and the F$^\#$ major musical mode.

From the start, it is crucial to understand that the interval ratios may not necessarily be the same as those used in the A-Major system. We do not want to start building a new approach that is burdened by any previous compromises. But, if it works, it works. We start fresh, with the standard JI intervals and just see how it all calculates out.

Just Intonation intervals and published octave 'dissections' are easy to utilize in calculations and are readily available from many sources on-line (in case you forget them or lose this invaluable book.)

Let's enumerate some of the key intervals and their math now. The intervals are intended to be read from bottom to top.

The following *Table 19.2*, lists some of the more common Just Intonation ratios which we will be using going forward. There exist other 'off-chart' intervals that we may need for special situations, in the event that the more common ones just don't work out. The writer will attempt to note any such instances by clearly stating that we are 'going off-chart.'

Common Just Intonation Intervals		
Interval Name	Ratio	Total ¢
Octave	2:1	1,200.000¢
Maj 7th	15:8	1,088.269¢
min 7th	9:5	1,017.597¢
Small min 7th	16:9	996.090¢
Harm minor 7th	7:4	968.826¢
Maj 6th	5:3	884.359¢
min 6th	8:5	813.687¢
Perfect 5th	3:2	701.955¢
Dim 5th	64:45	609.777¢
Aug 4th	7:5	582.512¢
min 5th*	7:5	582.512¢
Perfect 4th	4:3	498.045¢
Maj 3rd	5:4	386.314¢
min 3rd	6:5	315.641¢
Maj 2nd	9:8	203.910¢
minor 2nd tone	10:9	182.404¢
Semitone	16:15	111.731¢
Small semitone	17:16	104.955¢
Unison	1:1	0¢

Table 19.2 - A partial list containing some of the key
Just Intonation intervals

*Our ratio for the minor 5th is often documented as a 'septimal tritone.' According to apparent, standard practice, the label of minor 5th is not always used. Furthermore, that position is often assigned as an Aug4th or dim5th. The 7:5 tritone is a lovely, harmonic tone, which meets the minor 5th position's needs very nicely, although the terminology may not be 'technically' correct. When using a min5th, it is generally considered to be somewhat midway between the tritone and the perfect fifth. Thus the 7:5 ratio is derived.

Now that we are all familiar with more of the players, let's begin our new challenge.

We will first start a new, pristine grid and, enter our starting point of the fundamental F#-360Hz as well as its natural octave of F#-720Hz. This chart will be constructed and read from the bottom to the top. Your most gracious, and humble writer has already entered the desired interval *names* into the chart, although we may find the need for changing a few of those, as we progress.

Tuning Grid Based on F#-360Hz						
Note	Interval	Ratio	Multiplier	Frequency (Hz)	Interval from Root (¢)	Step Interval (¢)
F#	Octave	2:1	2.0	**720.00**	1200	
F	Major 7th					
E	minor 7th					
D#	Major 6th					
D	minor 6th					
C#	Perfect 5th					
C	Major 4th					
B	Perfect 4th					
A#	Major 3rd					
A	minor 3rd					
G#	Major 2nd					
G	Minor 2nd					
F#	Root	1:1	1.0	**360.00**	—	—

Table 19.3 - Skeletal chart of our new F# tuning grid based on a fundamental of 360Hz.

The fundamental tone, F#-360Hz, is automatic and is taken directly from our geometry analyses and the A-Major system (previously detailed). The octave (720Hz) is simple multiplication by two (2:1 octave ratio) - giving us the F# *above* - yet another significant geometric resonance value reflected in our previous work. We will continue uncovering each of the appropriate tones until we have a completed, usable tuning grid.

The first task will be to; locate our desired ratio for the G in our new system. 'G' is the first tone above the tonic, or fundamental of F#. The interval here is usually a semitone that should give us a Just interval of 111.731¢. But, more importantly, we need to validate our resulting tone by the ever-present geometric 'rules,' which we will now reiterate and clarify.

The frequencies we need for all of these tones must:

1. Numerically reduce to 3, 6, and/or 9. While purely geometric tones, and most whole-numbered tones generated, will always reduce to nine; There is no way to build a usable system with only numbers that result directly from interior angle summations of actual polygons or polyhedrons. The numerical gaps between actual geometric shapes (i.e., 180Hz~360Hz) are simply too large for that to be a realistic expectation. Therefore, at minimum, each frequency must reduce to at least one of these three numbers... Preferably '9.'

2. If the results are *not* 'decimal remainder' frequencies, they must be divisible by at least one of 3, 6, 9, 12, and 72. - While all whole number frequencies must meet this criterion, some frequencies will have decimal remainders of 0.25, 0.5, or 0.75. Such decimal-remainder frequencies cannot be validated in this way, therefore;

3. If the resulting frequencies possess decimal remainders, the number value must create an interval of one the specific ratios listed (above,) *and* comply with the requirement for numerical reduction to 3, 6, or 9.

4. If it becomes necessary to utilize an 'off-chart' interval, the resulting frequency, to be considered completely valid, must be a whole number and comply with the absolute letter of rules 1 and 2; above.

With rules of the game understood by all… Let's continue.

Creating an F#-Based Tuning Grid

Could This Be the Universe's Preferred Key Signature?

Assigning F#-360Hz as our fundamental and, working our way 'up' the chromatic scale, brings us to our first challenge, which is to calculate and validate our 'G' frequency. This tone will occupy the position of the *minor 2nd*.

The minor semitone, also known as our minor 2nd... and beyond!

We are looking for our G above the F# Tonic of 360Hz. The proper frequency should conform to the description of; 'semitone' of 111.731ᶜ above the tonic. The only likely ratio to achieve this specific interval width is 16:15.

If we multiply our fundamental, 360Hz by 16:15, we get a result of 384.00Hz.

Note: To make this operation easier to manage, simply multiply by the first number of the ratio and then divide the result by the second number as shown here:

(360 x 16) ÷ 15 = 384.00

We now have a candidate that satisfies the assumed, perfect interval for the position of our minor 2nd. Next, we must validate our candidate value against the remaining criteria. Therefore, we proceed to the numerical reduction test. Recall that any valid geometric candidate must reduce by the sum of its digits, to one of the values 3, 6, and 9, preferably nine *and*, should be wholly-divisible by at least one of our cardinal numbers (3, 6, 9, and *preferably*, at least one of 12 and 72).

The current candidate is 384.00Hz.

To validate this candidate value, we add **3 + 8 + 4 = 15**
The sum of digits is greater than nine. So, another step of numerical reduction is necessary.
The sum 15 further reduces as; **1 + 5 = 6**

Thus, we see that the value 384Hz reduces to '**6**'

Criteria 1 has been met! Now, for the division test.
384 is not divisible by '9.' But, it is divisible by '6' and '12.'

$$384 \div 6 = 64.00$$

Criteria 2 is met!

Our first semitone (the minor 2nd) above F# is a G at **384.00**Hz.

Note	Interval	Ratio	Multiplier	Frequency (Hz)	Interval from Root (¢)	Step Interval (¢)
	Tuning Grid Based on F#-360Hz (draft progress)					
F#	Octave	2:1	2	720.00	1200¢	
F	Major 7th					
E	minor 7th					
D#	Major 6th					
D	minor 6th					
C#	Perfect 5th					
C	Major 4th					
B	Perfect 4th					
A#	Major 3rd					
A	minor 3rd					
G#	Major 2nd					
G	minor 2nd	16:15	1.0666667	384.00	111.731¢	111.731¢
F#	Root	1:1	1	360.00	—	—

Table 20.1a - Adding our first calculated semitone; The minor 2nd

Now that everyone understands how the game is to be played, we will proceed to the lightning round to avoid falling asleep. Each and every frequency must meet the same or superior criteria. For instance, 384Hz reduces to '6.' A superior result would be a value that reduces to '9.' We will check divisibility by '9' first, in each case.

The Major 2nd Position:

G# is our Major 2nd. The likely interval ratio is 9:8.

$$(360 \times 9) \div 8 = 405.00$$

405.00Hz reduces to '9'

$$4 + 0 + 5 = 9$$

Criteria 1... Met!

Divisible by '9.' ?

$$405.00 \div 9 = 45$$

Criteria 2... Met!

The interval value is 203.910^{c} — A Perfect Just Major 2nd.
Our third tone, the Major 2nd, is **405.00**Hz.

We add this tone to our growing progress chart and, set our sights on the minor 3rd position which provides a pleasant surprise.

Note	Interval	Ratio	Multiplier	Frequency (Hz)	Interval from Root (¢)	Step Interval (¢)
	Tuning Grid Based on F#-360Hz (draft progress)					
F#	Octave	2:1	2	720.00	1200^{c}	
F	Major 7th					
E	minor 7th					
D#	Major 6th					
D	minor 6th					
C#	Perfect 5th					
C	Major 4th					
B	Perfect 4th					
A#	Major 3rd					
A	minor 3rd					
G#	Major 2nd	9:8	1.125	405.00	203.910^{c}	92.17872^{c}
G	minor 2nd	16:15	1.0666667	384.00	111.731^{c}	111.731^{c}
F#	Root	1:1	1	360.00	—	—

Table 20.1b - Our Major 2nd turns out to be a perfect fit at 203.910¢

The Minor 3rd Position:

Our 'A' note, in this case, occupies the position of the *minor 3rd* tone.

The likely candidate interval ratio is 6:5 and, the perfect result would provide us with a *Just minor 3rd* candidate with an appropriate interval width of 315.641^c.

$$(360 \times 6) \div 5 = 432.00$$

432Hz (look familiar?) is already, clearly validated in our previous work. Of course, we already know that 432Hz reduces to nine and is divisible by 3, 6, 9, 12, and 72. Thus, No adjustments are necessary!

The interval value is 315.641^c — A Perfect Just minor 3rd!
Our fourth tone, the minor 3rd, turns out to be our pivotal 432.00Hz.

Let's post this tone to our chart and, move on to the Major 3rd.

Note	Interval	Ratio	Multiplier	Frequency (Hz)	Interval from Root (¢)	Step Interval (¢)
F#	Octave	2:1	2	720.00	1200^c	
F	Major 7th					
E	minor 7th					
D#	Major 6th					
D	minor 6th					
C#	Perfect 5th					
C	Major 4th					
B	Perfect 4th					
A#	Major 3rd					
A	minor 3rd	6:5	1.2	432.00	315.641^c	111.731^c
G#	Major 2nd	9:8	1.125	405.00	203.910^c	92.17872^c
G	minor 2nd	16:15	1.0666667	384.00	111.731^c	111.731^c
F#	Root	1:1	1	360.00	—	—

Tuning Grid Based on F#-360Hz (draft progress)

Table 20.1c - Our Minor 2nd math-magically results in a 432Hz 'A.'

Note: A rather (quirky) option for this position would be the Subminor 3rd using a 7:6 ratio, which oddly, gives us a 420Hz frequency. 420Hz meets the minimum requirements despite having several other issues. But, the natural 432Hz that organically pops up here seems perfect just as it is.

The Major 3rd Position:

A# represents the *Major 3rd* position in our growing tuning grid system. The intended interval ratio, according to Just Intonation, is a 5:4.

$$(360 \times 5) \div 4 = 450.00$$

450.00Hz Reduces to '9.'

$$4 + 5 + 0 = 9$$

Criteria 1... Met!

Divisible by '9'?

$$450.00 \div 9 = 50$$

Criteria 2... Met!

The interval value is 386.314¢ — A Perfect Just Major 3rd!

Our fifth tone, the Major 3rd, is 450.00Hz.

We will add it to the chart and start working on the Perfect 4th.

Note	Interval	Ratio	Multiplier	Frequency (Hz)	Interval from Root (¢)	Step Interval (¢)
F#	Octave	2:1	2	720.00	1200¢	
F	Major 7th					
E	minor 7th					
D#	Major 6th					
D	minor 6th					
C#	Perfect 5th					
C	Major 4th					
B	Perfect 4th					
A#	Major 3rd	5:4	1.25	450.00	386.314¢	70.6724¢
A	minor 3rd	6:5	1.2	432.00	315.641¢	111.731¢
G#	Major 2nd	9:8	1.125	405.00	203.910¢	92.17872¢
G	minor 2nd	16:15	1.0666667	384.00	111.731¢	111.731¢
F#	Root	1:1	1	360.00	—	—

Tuning Grid Based on F#-360Hz (draft progress)

Table 20.1d - Our A# calculation results in a perfect 'Just' Major 3rd of 386.314¢

The Perfect 4th Position:

B is in our *Perfect 4th* position. The most likely interval ratio, according to Just Intonation, is 4:3.

$$(360 \times 4) \div 3 = 480.00$$

480.00Hz Reduces to '3.' (We will soon see that 'B' is always a rebel.)

$$4 + 8 + 0 = 12 \ldots 1 + 2 = 3$$

Criteria 1... Met!

Divisible by '9'? No. But, it is divisible by '6' and also '12.'

$$480.00 \div 6 = 80$$

Criteria 2... Met!

The interval value is 498.045¢ — A Perfect... Just Perfect 4th interval! Therefore, our sixth tone, the Perfect 4th, is 480.00Hz.

We'll add this one to the chart and shift our focus to the Major 4th.

	Tuning Grid Based on F#-360Hz (draft progress)					
Note	Interval	Ratio	Multiplier	Frequency (Hz)	Interval from Root (¢)	Step Interval (¢)
F#	Octave	2:1	2	720.00	1200¢	
F	Major 7th					
E	minor 7th					
D#	Major 6th					
D	minor 6th					
C#	Perfect 5th					
C	Major 4th					
B	Perfect 4th	4:3	1.3333333	480.00	498.045¢	111.731¢
A#	Major 3rd	5:4	1.25	450.00	386.314¢	70.6724¢
A	minor 3rd	6:5	1.2	432.00	315.641¢	111.731¢
G#	Major 2nd	9:8	1.125	405.00	203.910¢	92.17872¢
G	minor 2nd	16:15	1.0666667	384.00	111.731¢	111.731¢
F#	Root	1:1	1	360.00	—	—

Table 20.1e - The Perfect 4th calculation results in a 'peachy'... Just Perfect 4th interval width of 498.045¢, with a step interval from A# that measures 111.731¢; a Just semitone.

The Major 4th Position:

C is perched in the 'Major 4th' position. And, this tone tends to be a bit challenging. The term Major 4th turns out to be somewhat of a catch-all phrase for valid tones in this range. You could have a diminished 5th, Augmented 4th or even a crazy Septimal Tritone or pure harmonic in this position. And, it could still be (somewhat inappropriately) referred to as the Major 4th position - as it is used here to indicate a placeholder name rather than an absolute metric.

In equal temperament, the Major 4th sits at exactly 600¢ above the fundamental. It is a vital, transitory tone being wedged right in the middle of the octave. So, its value is often tricky to work out. This is likely one reason why the shoe-horn of equal-temperament math gets it so very wrong. But, our geometric methods get it right!

As was previously observed, the standard (even-temperament) tuning for this position, is considered by many but not all, to be a bit sharp. Therefore, we are looking for a value that is tuned to approximately 15¢ to 18¢ flatter by the math.

A brief search of the Just ratios, leads us somewhat indirectly, to the Augmented 4th at a 7:5 ratio. The writer has focused on this ratio because none of the proximal ratios yielded values that were usable in our current system.

For example, the ratio 179:128 at 580.579¢ yielded 503.3475Hz and, never resolves to a whole-numbered tone. Additionally, the value is closer to 20¢ flat. Not really what we are looking for here.

Other proximal ratios were tested. And, all yielded disappointing results when measured against our stated criteria.

Thus, we happily make use of the Augmented 4th as it is most accommodating with regard to our criteria. In fact, it yields a perfect validation all around.

Our interval ratio for the Augmented 4th, will be 7:5. This tone is also referred to as a '*Septimal Tritone*' in many of the 'JI' charts.

Running the calculation on the *Augmented 4th*, 7:5 ratio, gives us...

$$(360 \times 7) \div 5 = 504.00$$

504.00Hz Reduces *directly* to '9.'

$$5 + 0 + 4 = 9$$

Criteria 1... Met!
Divisible by '9'? Of course.

$$504.00 \div 9 = 56$$

Criteria 2... Met!

The interval width is 582.212$^{\text{¢}}$ — a Just Augmented 4th. That actually works!

It is officially settled. Our seventh tone, the formerly-labeled Major 4th, is now an Augmented 4th at 504.00Hz.

Let's add it to our progress chart and pivot our efforts toward the Perfect 5th position.

Tuning Grid Based on F#-360Hz (draft progress)						
Note	Interval	Ratio	Multiplier	Frequency (Hz)	Interval from Root (¢)	Step Interval (¢)
F#	Octave	2:1	2	720.00	1200$^{\text{¢}}$	
F	Major 7th					
E	minor 7th					
D#	Major 6th					
D	minor 6th					
C#	Perfect 5th					
C	Aug 4th	7:5	1.4	504.00	582.512$^{\text{¢}}$	84.4672$^{\text{¢}}$
B	Perfect 4th	4:3	1.3333333	480.00	498.045$^{\text{¢}}$	111.731$^{\text{¢}}$
A#	Major 3rd	5:4	1.25	450.00	386.314$^{\text{¢}}$	70.6724$^{\text{¢}}$
A	minor 3rd	6:5	1.2	432.00	315.641$^{\text{¢}}$	111.731$^{\text{¢}}$
G#	Major 2nd	9:8	1.125	405.00	203.910$^{\text{¢}}$	92.17872$^{\text{¢}}$
G	minor 2nd	16:15	1.0666667	384.00	111.731$^{\text{¢}}$	111.731$^{\text{¢}}$
F#	Root	1:1	1	360.00	—	—

Table 20.1f - Our 'C' calculations turn out to result in an Augmented 4th of 504.00Hz

The Perfect 5th Position:

C$^\#$ represents the *Perfect 5th* position in our ever-expanding tuning grid system. The *only* interval ratio we want to use for this tone, is a 3:2.

$$(360 \times 3) \div 2 = 540.00$$

540.00Hz Reduces to '9.'

$$5 + 4 + 0 = 9$$

Criteria 1... Met!

Divisible by '9'?

$$540.00 \div 9 = 60$$

Criteria 2... Met!

The interval value is 701.955$^\cent$ — A beautiful Just Perfect 5th.

Our eighth tone, the Perfect 5th, is therefore; 540.00Hz.

We will throw it into the chart and start working on the minor 6th.

Note	Interval	Ratio	Multiplier	Frequency (Hz)	Interval from Root (¢)	Step Interval (¢)
F#	Octave	2:1	2	720.00	1200¢	
F	Major 7th					
E	minor 7th					
D#	Major 6th					
D	minor 6th					
C#	**Perfect 5th**	**3:2**	**1.5**	**540.00**	**701.955¢**	**119.4428¢**
C	Aug 4th	7:5	1.4	504.00	582.512¢	84.4672¢
B	Perfect 4th	4:3	1.3333333	480.00	498.045¢	111.731¢
A#	Major 3rd	5:4	1.25	450.00	386.314¢	70.6724¢
A	minor 3rd	6:5	1.2	432.00	315.641¢	111.731¢
G#	Major 2nd	9:8	1.125	405.00	203.910¢	92.17872¢
G	minor 2nd	16:15	1.0666667	384.00	111.731¢	111.731¢
F#	Root	1:1	1	360.00	—	—

Table 20.1g - Our Perfect5th turns out perfectly as a 540Hz tone. This tone is considered and absolutely critical geometric tone corresponding to the pentagon and pentacle.

The minor 6th Position:

D represents the *minor 6th* position in our growing tuning grid system. The likely interval ratio we want to use for this tone, is a 8:5.

$$(360 \times 8) \div 5 = 576.00$$

576.00Hz Reduces to '9.'

$$5 + 7 + 6 = 18... 1 + 8 = 9$$

Criteria 1... Met!

Divisible by '9'?

$$576.00 \div 9 = 64$$

Criteria 2... Met!

The interval value is 813.686ᶜ — A nice, Just minor 6th.

Our ninth tone, the minor 6th, is therefore; 576.00Hz.

We add it into the chart and get to work on the Major 6th.

Note	Interval	Ratio	Multiplier	Frequency (Hz)	Interval from Root (ᶜ)	Step Interval (ᶜ)
	Tuning Grid Based on F#-360Hz (draft progress)					
F#	Octave	2:1	2	720.00	1200ᶜ	
F	Major 7th					
E	minor 7th					
D#	Major 6th					
D	minor 6th	8:5	1.6	576.00	813.686ᶜ	111.731ᶜ
C#	Perfect 5th	3:2	1.5	540.00	701.955ᶜ	119.4428ᶜ
C	Aug 4th	7:5	1.4	504.00	582.512ᶜ	84.4672ᶜ
B	Perfect 4th	4:3	1.3333333	480.00	498.045ᶜ	111.731ᶜ
A#	Major 3rd	5:4	1.25	450.00	386.314ᶜ	70.6724ᶜ
A	minor 3rd	6:5	1.2	432.00	315.641ᶜ	111.731ᶜ
G#	Major 2nd	9:8	1.125	405.00	203.910ᶜ	92.17872ᶜ
G	minor 2nd	16:15	1.0666667	384.00	111.731ᶜ	111.731ᶜ
F#	Root	1:1	1	360.00	—	—

Table 20.1h - Our minor 6th, does not disappoint. Our 'D' turns out to be a 576Hz tone

The Major 6th Position:

D$^{\#}$ represents the *Major 6th* position in our growing tuning grid system. The likely interval ratio we want to use for this tone, is a 5:3.

$$(360 \times 5) \div 3 = 600.00$$

600.00Hz Reduces to '6.'

$$6 + 0 + 0 = 6$$

Criteria 1... Met!

Divisible by '9'? of course not. But, it is divisible by '6' and '12.'

$$600.00 \div 6 = 100$$

Criteria 2... Met!

The interval value is 884.359$^{¢}$ — A stable Just Major 6th.

Our tenth tone, the Major 6th, is therefore; 600.00Hz.

We add it into the chart and get to work on the minor 7th.

	Tuning Grid Based on F#-360Hz (draft progress)					
Note	Interval	Ratio	Multiplier	Frequency (Hz)	Interval from Root (¢)	Step Interval (¢)
F#	Octave	2:1	2	720.00	1200$^{¢}$	
F	Major 7th					
E	minor 7th					
D#	Major 6th	5:3	1.6666667	600.00	884.359$^{¢}$	70.6724$^{¢}$
D	minor 6th	8:5	1.6	576.00	813.686$^{¢}$	111.731$^{¢}$
C#	Perfect 5th	3:2	1.5	540.00	701.955$^{¢}$	119.4428$^{¢}$
C	Aug 4th	7:5	1.4	504.00	582.512$^{¢}$	84.4672$^{¢}$
B	Perfect 4th	4:3	1.3333333	480.00	498.045$^{¢}$	111.731$^{¢}$
A#	Major 3rd	5:4	1.25	450.00	386.314$^{¢}$	70.6724$^{¢}$
A	minor 3rd	6:5	1.2	432.00	315.641$^{¢}$	111.731$^{¢}$
G#	Major 2nd	9:8	1.125	405.00	203.910$^{¢}$	92.17872$^{¢}$
G	minor 2nd	16:15	1.0666667	384.00	111.731$^{¢}$	111.731$^{¢}$
F#	Root	1:1	1	360.00	—	—

Table 20.1i - Our Major 6th, uses a 5:3 ratio, which results in a 600Hz D$^{\#}$.

The minor 7ᵗʰ Position: (or Sub minor 7ᵗʰ)

E represents the *minor 7ᵗʰ* position in our growing tuning grid system. The likely interval ratio we want to use for this tone, is a 9:5.

$$(360 \times 9) \div 5 = 648.00$$

648.00Hz Reduces to '9.'

$$6 + 4 + 8 = 18... \ 1 + 8 = 9$$

Criteria 1... Met!

Divisible by '9' as well as 12 and 72.

$$648.00 \div 9 = 72$$

Criteria 2... Met!

The interval value is 1017.596ᶜ — A 648.00Hz, Just minor 7ᵗʰ. Definitely works!

However, (and, you *had* to know this was coming.) there is another value we would like to consider here. That value is related to our previous 'breakup' with D#-1260Hz earlier in our work.

Recall that the value of 1260Hz didn't really fit the D# when calculating the original A-Major Tuning Grid. But, I told you we would be seeing it again later. Well, here it is! 1260Hz finally finds a new home — as an 'E.'

1260Hz, actually its next lower octave tone of 630Hz, will also work very well in this position. In fact, The writer would argue that it works every bit as well as 648Hz. It's a tough, subjective call as to which value to adopt. Your ears may need to make the decision in your particular case -- as the writer has already done here.

If we target this Sub-minor 7ᵗʰ for this position, our interval width would be a near-perfect 968.826ᶜ. And, the interval ratio would be 7:4.

Let's take a look at this Sub-minor 7ᵗʰ in the current paradigm.

Running the 7:4 Sub minor 7th ratio calculations gives us...

$$(360 \times 7) \div 4 = 630.00\text{Hz}$$

630Hz Reduces to '9.'

Criteria 1... Met!

Divisible by '9'?

$$630.00 \div 9 = 70$$

Criteria 2... Met!

Again, 630Hz yields a very nice Sub minor 7th. It works nicely.

Thus, our eleventh tone, The minor 7th, is either a 648.00Hz minor 7th or a sub minor 7th at 630Hz. We will allow the sound trials and personal preference to determine which of these is more harmonically appropriate. For now, let's include both options as valid candidates.

	Tuning Grid Based on F#-360Hz (draft progress)					
Note	Interval	Ratio	Multiplier	Frequency (Hz)	Interval from Root (¢)	Step Interval (¢)
F#	Octave	2:1	2	720.00	1200¢	
F	Major 7th					
E	minor 7th	9:5	1.8	648.00	1017.596¢	133.238¢
E*	Sub min 7th	7:4	1.75	630.00	968.826¢	84.4672¢
D#	Major 6th	5:3	1.6666667	600.00	884.359¢	70.6724¢
D	minor 6th	8:5	1.6	576.00	813.686¢	111.731¢
C#	Perfect 5th	3:2	1.5	540.00	701.955¢	119.4428¢
C	Aug 4th	7:5	1.4	504.00	582.512¢	84.4672¢
B	Perfect 4th	4:3	1.3333333	480.00	498.045¢	111.731¢
A#	Major 3rd	5:4	1.25	450.00	386.314¢	70.6724¢
A	minor 3rd	6:5	1.2	432.00	315.641¢	111.731¢
G#	Major 2nd	9:8	1.125	405.00	203.910¢	92.17872¢
G	minor 2nd	16:15	1.0666667	384.00	111.731¢	111.731¢
F#	Root	1:1	1	360.00	—	—

Table 20.1j - Our Minor 7th presents us with an interesting decision, which will ultimately be made by the individual performer. Turns out that either works well

The *Sub minor 7th* (7:4) not only meets our geometric criteria and yields a 630Hz tone. It also uncovers a significant amount of geometry in the octaves above. Some may feel that 630Hz is a better harmonic and geometric fit than the 648Hz Just minor 7th. After hearing the two tones in sound trials, I submit the following:

While providing some interesting color, the Sub minor 7th widens the interval between it and the Major-7th to a seemingly, more appropriate 119.443°. I see no reason not to accept this resulting interval between the 'E' and the 'F' when the values work perfectly within the constraints of the criteria established. However, either frequency choice appears to be a valid option according to the math as well as their subjective tonal quality.

Sound trials have determined that both of these options have their merits and 'work' well within the framework of the tuning. Again, this will remain a personal-preference option for each musician-practitioner to decide. Either choice depends upon one's need to produce as many pure geometric tones as possible. Whether making the choice of a slightly wider interval at the Just Major 7th or sticking with the straight sub minor 7th; either will work well musically.

Specifically, the use of the sub minor 7th opens the system to more 'pure' geometric frequencies while the Just minor 7th uncovers no pure geometric tones at all. This is a consideration for the practitioner to consider.

This writer prefers the sub minor 7th at 630Hz. However, I do stipulate to the attractiveness of the Just minor 7th in certain situations.

This is a really tough call. And, one that I personally resolve by using the Just minor 7th in the lower registers and the sub minor 7th in upper registers. The basic 'difference' between these two tones is 48.77¢ ,which is termed a 'septimal quarter-tone' interval. Using these two different values in the same tuning grid, as described, originally raised a red flag against using them simultaneously in the lower and higher octaves.

However, this writer is again pleasantly surprised to find that they can coexist very well together when utilized in moderation.

174

As always, your mileage may vary. Either method of use is a perfectly solid strategy that meets all of our criteria.

Now, let's finish our work with the F#-Tuning Grid.

The Major 7ᵗʰ Position:

F represents the *Major 7ᵗʰ* position in our nearly-completed tuning grid system. The likely interval ratio we want to use for this tone, is a 15:8, which is the ratio yielding our Just Major 7ᵗʰ.

$$(360 \times 15) \div 8 = 675.00$$

675.00Hz Reduces to '9.'

$$6 + 7 + 5 = 18... \ 1 + 8 = 9$$

Criteria 1... Met!

Divisible by '9'?

$$675.00 \div 9 = 75$$

Criteria 2... Met!

The interval value is 1088.269¢ — This tone is yet another perfect fit. This time as a Just Major 7ᵗʰ.

Our eleventh tone, the Major 7ᵗʰ, is therefore; 675.00Hz.

We add it into the chart (*Table 20.1k*) and finish up with this tuning grid.

Finishing up with **The Major 7th Position:**

Note	Interval	Ratio	Multiplier	Frequency (Hz)	Interval from Root (¢)	Step Interval (¢)
F#	Octave	2:1	2	720.00	1200¢	111.731¢
F	Major 7th	15:8	1.875	675.00	1088.269¢	119.4428¢
E	minor 7th	9:5	1.8	648.00	1017.596¢	133.238¢
E*	Sub min 7th	7:4	1.75	630.00	968.826¢	84.4672¢
D#	Major 6th	5:3	1.6666667	600.00	884.359¢	70.6724¢
D	minor 6th	8:5	1.6	576.00	813.686¢	111.731¢
C#	Perfect 5th	3:2	1.5	540.00	701.955¢	119.4428¢
C	Aug 4th	7:5	1.4	504.00	582.512¢	84.4672¢
B	Perfect 4th	4:3	1.3333333	480.00	498.045¢	111.731¢
A#	Major 3rd	5:4	1.25	450.00	386.314¢	70.6724¢
A	minor 3rd	6:5	1.2	432.00	315.641¢	111.731¢
G#	Major 2nd	9:8	1.125	405.00	203.910¢	92.17872¢
G	minor 2nd	16:15	1.0666667	384.00	111.731¢	111.731¢
F#	Root	1:1	1	360.00	—	—

Tuning Grid Based on F#-360Hz (draft progress)

Table 20.1k - Our Major 7th works out to be a 'Just' Major 7th of 675.00Hz.

As previously stated, the F#-720Hz is our Octave. The interval ratio, as for every proximal octave calculation, is 2:1.

$$(360 \times 2) \div 1 = 720.00$$

Reduces to '9.'

$$7 + 2 + 0 = 9$$

Criteria 1... Met!

Divisible by '3', '6,' '9,' '12,' and '72.'

$$720.00 \div 9 = 80$$

Criteria 2... Met!

The interval value is 1200.00¢. -- Perfect!
Our thirteenth (octave) tone is (of course) 720.00Hz.

The 720Hz value is yet another critical geometric value that corresponds to the tetrahedron and the hexagon.

So... There you have it! It really is that simple… A perfect tuning grid for F#-360Hz.

So, here is our finished chart for our new <u>F#-Major Tuning Grid</u> system;

Tuning Grid Based on F#-360Hz (draft progress)						
Note	Interval	Ratio	Multiplier	Frequency (Hz)	Interval from Root (¢)	Step Interval (¢)
F#	Octave	2:1	2	720.00	1200¢	111.731¢
F	Major 7th	15:8	1.875	675.00	1088.269¢	119.4428¢
E	minor 7th	9:5	1.8	648.00	1017.596¢	133.238¢
E*	Sub min 7th	7:4	1.75	630.00	968.826¢	84.4672¢
D#	Major 6th	5:3	1.6666667	600.00	884.359¢	70.6724¢
D	minor 6th	8:5	1.6	576.00	813.686¢	111.731¢
C#	Perfect 5th	3:2	1.5	540.00	701.955¢	119.4428¢
C	Aug 4th	7:5	1.4	504.00	582.512¢	84.4672¢
B	Perfect 4th	4:3	1.3333333	480.00	498.045¢	111.731¢
A#	Major 3rd	5:4	1.25	450.00	386.314¢	70.6724¢
A	minor 3rd	6:5	1.2	432.00	315.641¢	111.731¢
G#	Major 2nd	9:8	1.125	405.00	203.910¢	92.17872¢
G	minor 2nd	16:15	1.0666667	384.00	111.731¢	111.731¢
F#	Root	1:1	1	360.00	—	—

Table 20.2 - Tuning grid based on an F# fundamental of 360Hz, displaying the fifth octave including interval ratios, semi-tone step width, and full interval width from the root. Optional values for the minor 7th position at 'E' are shown

*Again, the honorable mention for the position of the minor 7th is the ratio 7:4. The 7:4 ratio gives us a sub minor 7th (aka harmonic minor 7th), which is a particularly delightful tone (preferred over the minor 7th by this writer) within the minor pentatonic scale.

The resulting frequency in the chart is 630Hz. This frequency also meets all of the stated requirements and gives the harmonic minor 7th position an interval of 968.826¢. As an additional bonus feature, the 630Hz tone contributes a greater number of geometric tones and is better represented in the natural harmonics.

Always keep one eye on how any desired interval ratio options affect your harmonies and your harmonic values.

If one wishes to play in higher registers, the flatter of any two interval choices may be more appropriate. In the lower registers, the sharper of the two may work better. In either case, honoring the harmonics of the fundamental frequency should be a major criteria when making the decision. Creating a tuning file that incorporates both ratios (one for low keys and the other for high) is an elegant solution if your keyboard or software tuning standard permits and, if your harmonics calculate out properly.

In the F#-Major Tuning Grid system, the author has determined that the best fit; both for harmony and harmonics, is the Sub-minor 7th at 630Hz.

The F#-Major Tuning Grid system plays perfectly, using standard fingering patterns, on the keyboard. It has not been necessary to map any original, complicated chord or scale patterns. It seems that we can literally play music as on any piano keyboard.

Your mild-mannered author admits to a certain irrational sense of relief and accomplishment as this system is now considered to be the perfect tuning system for wellness, relaxation and healing music. Exactly what we were going for with this whole project.

Welcome to a perfect replacement for standard tuning!

When first calculating the tuning charts based on F#, This writer found it difficult to believe that it worked out so perfectly and efficiently. The calculations have been re-visited dozens of times to verify the findings.

Yet, here it is— a wonderfully playable alternative tuning system for sound healing and relaxation therapy. It incorporates our 432Hz 'A,' so naturally that one wonders where this system has been hiding and why it is not widely used today... Or why we actually continue to adhere to the flawed system that *is* in wide-spread use today.

Curiouser and Curiouser...

An unintended effect that appears in this system, made itself evident when casually double-checking the interval values in hertz.

An unexpected and interesting pattern surfaced. And, to be honest, it initially made little sense to the writer. But, the effect was nevertheless just another one of those artifacts of the math.

To explain, we will display a table that lays out this interesting pattern for all to see. The reader may or may not believe that this was never planned or factored in to the initial calculations. The effect was 'discovered' *after* the grid was completely designed. The following *Table 20.3*, uses the 630Hz sub minor 7th and, illustrates the observed phenomenon. Substituting the 648H minor 7th yields similar results.

Note	Frequency (Hz)	Step Interval (Hz)	Reduces to...
F#	720.00	45	9
F	675.00	45	9
E	630.00	30	3
D#	600.00	48	3
D	576.00	36	9
C#	540.00	36	9
C	504.00	24	6
B	480.00	30	3
A#	450.00	18	9
A	432.00	27	9
G#	405.00	21	3
G	384.00	24	6
F#	360.00	—	—

Table 20.3 - A closer look at the intervals, in Hertz, between tones

Yes. You are seeing this correctly. When calculated from root to octave, the interval widths between each tone, in actual hertz, really *do* display a very familiar effect. If you reverse the order, to calculate from top to bottom instead, the results would be similar; every tonal interval is represented by a value, in hertz, that always reduces to three, six, or nine. The circle is complete. (Is this something that would qualify as a 'mic-drop' moment? ...Maybe not.)

What makes this effect even more interesting is when one recalls that the mathematical metric of cycles-per-second (Hertz) is a *modern* unit of measure — having its origins in the 19th century.

How is it that this modern unit matches up perfectly with a system design, based on geometric principles? When both are considered, on the surface they represent two completely unrelated, anachronistic disciplines.

Of course, there is a perfectly rational mathematical explanation. The deed is accomplished, quite practically, by the strict adherence to the criteria of three, six, and nine reduction — both in our interval calculations as well as our geometric tone selections.

But, the writer asks a simple question here; Does that (buzz-kill) fact really dilute the apparent, magical quality of the observed results? One would have to be fairly jaded to not appreciate the systemic, circular balance inherent in such a system.

However, we must in all fairness, acknowledge the fact that this balance is literally built-in at every step, albeit unintentional in this case. Yet, this writer cannot resist yet another dig at modern standardized systems by stating that; 12-TET just can't touch this level of simple, mathematical, and cyclical self-validation.

A few notes about the geometric <u>F#-Major Tuning Grid</u> data;

Many of the calculated tone values are different from those calculated for the same note positions in the <u>A-Major Tuning Grid</u> system. This result is a mathematical effect due to changing the fundamental (In this case to 360Hz) and the working interval ratios. While our <u>F#-Major Tuning Grid</u> system contains a surprisingly extensive array of natural polygonal, platonic solid, and sacred geometry frequencies, it is likely that no known system can include all of them while remaining readily-usable.

Our stated purpose has been to create a system that works well on a standard keyboard layout. This, we have now achieved, as the two systems revealed thus far (A-Major and F#-Major) contain *most* of the significant geometric numbers. (Fruit of Life resonances are only represented in the harmonics.)

And a study of the harmonics of these tones reveals even more significant values to be had in the outer reaches.

The near-perfect proliferation of harmonics and overtones with this work is the prime reasoning why this writer strongly advocates for analog production of tones during performance and recording; since analog techniques are most capable of producing these natural harmonics.

Live instruments, vacuum tube-based instruments, and tube-based pre-amps and amplifiers are invaluable in reproducing these harmonics rather organically. Any recordings made, should additionally be preserved in a lossless format (discussed later) with no digital trimming of top and bottom harmonics. Playback of recorded ambient or background tracks as well as any other supplemental works should, wherever possible, utilize equipment that is based upon analog technology.

At the very least, high-quality analog emulation should be utilized. But, *only* when pure-analog equipment is not available or practical. While this is an imperfect workaround, it is often better than reproduction that lacks harmonic reproduction altogether.

We will explore more regarding (very) basic recording and sound reproduction considerations in the final chapter of this text.

What Have We Really Accomplished Here?

Based upon the thesis of this work, we have sought to achieve multiple objectives, which are summarized as follows:

- Create a tonal system compatible with the history and traditions of healing using music and frequency.
- Formulate the system within the constraints of a twelve-tone octave system, pivoting around a 432Hz A^4 tone standard, in order to make the resulting system tonally coherent and easily accessible using readily available modern instruments. Design the system to conform with the mathematical 'rules' derived from 2D and 3D geometries as detailed in the early chapters of this body of work. These criteria include the 'reduction to 3, 6, 9,' the 'divisibility by 6, 9, 12, and/or 72,' as well as the whole-number preference for resulting tones. (aka, geometric correlations)
- Construct the system to include the widest possible variety of significant geometrically-corresponding frequencies including Platonic geometries as well as the so-called 'sacred' geometries.
- Construct a system that allows for a minimal learning curve when transitioning from 'standard,' 12-TET application, keyboard fingering and theory.
- Provide the basis for extended tunings that have the potential to include a more extensive array of geometric tones by utilizing smaller divisions of the octave resulting in more tones per octave.

The majority of these objectives have been somewhat-loosely based upon historical information relating to the geometry of Pythagoras, Plato, and many others. Based upon the dearth of surviving information on the subject of healing applications of tone, it is nevertheless, clear that the classical Greeks, as well as the more ancient cultures of pre-dynastic Egypt and Sumeria, made extensive use of sound for many esoteric purposes, including comprehensive wellness. A more in-depth examination of these cultural practices is not practical in the current format.

With the writer's discovery of the 'Just Intonation' system, the goal of achieving a readily usable, twelve-tone system, as well as minimizing the learning curve required to adapt the approach to modern keyboards has been remarkably successful.

We now have a tuning system design that can be applied to any programmable keyboard and many existing Digital Audio Workstation (DAW) software packages — with varying degrees of effort.

While the writer holds out hope for certain instrument manufacturers to adopt this tuning system as a standard firmware inclusion, it is foreseen that the various percussive instruments, commonly utilized in relaxation and healing sessions, such as crystal bowls, chimes, tuned drums, and others will necessarily be 'custom order' items for some time to come.

Throughout this entire process, our guiding criteria have been rooted in the geometric correlations with each frequency and a 'pivot' point of the 432Hz A^4. From the beginning, we have included as many 'pure' geometric numbers as possible while maintaining proper intervals and playability. The rationale for the foundational, 432Hz pivot point is discussed extensively in earlier chapters.

Additionally, 'non-geometric' frequencies, calculated to fill the intermediate tones in each system, also conform to the same mathematical criteria as the 'pure' geometric tones.

While there may appear to be exceptions to this rule, especially in the presence of those few tones possessing decimal place remainders, the over-arching principle of numerical reduction to the numbers three, six, or nine always applies. Additionally, such decimal remainders are required to 'resolve' to whole number frequencies in higher octaves; thus conforming to the intent of the stated rules.

Regarding the inclusion of 'as many as possible' pure geometric tones, the author concedes that; None of the proposed systems include *all* of the possible and desirable geometric tones. However, the writer also sees the F#-based tuning system as the crown jewel of all herein-proposed systems. Indeed, the F#-Major Tuning Grid system includes a dizzying array of geometric and traditionally 'sacred' numbers.

A partial list of the geometric healing tones included in the F#-based tuning system is presented in the chart on the following page.

Significant Geometric Resonance Values in the F#-Major Tuning Grid System

Degrees/Hz	Correlations to Geometry and Cultural Significance
45	Primary Angle (8th sub-harmonic of 180 and 360)
90	Right Angle (4th sub-harmonic of 360)
135	3rd Harmonic of 45
180	Triangle (3 sides)
	Semi-circle (crescent)
360	Circle & Square (4 sides)
	Number of days in a Mayan 'tun', Sumerian and Pre-dynastic Egyptian year
540	Pentagon (5 sides)
720	Hexagon (6 sides)
	Tetrahedron (Platonic Solid)
	Vesica Piscis (common version)
900	Heptagon (7 sides)
1080	Octagon (8 sides)
1260	Nonagon (9 sides)
1440	Decagon (10 sides)
	Octahedron (Platonic Solid)
	Number of minutes in a 24-hour day
	Resonance of the three circles inscribing the triquetra
1620	Hendecagon (11 sides)
1800	Dodecagon (12 sides)
2160	**Hexahedron/Cube** (Platonic Solid)
2400	Merkabah
2520	Seed of Life & Egg of Life
2700	Seventeen-sided polygon
2880	Eighteen-sided polygon
	Enclosed Seed of Life (8 circles)
3600	**Icosahedron** (Platonic Solid)
5040	Thirty-sided polygon
5760	Thirty-four-sided polygon
	16 circles as in certain extended sacred geometries
6480	**Dodecahedron** (Platonic Solid)
7200	Flower of Life
	42-sided polygon
	Days in a Mayan 'katun' of twenty, 360-day years
11520	32 Circles (doubled Flower of Life, aka Flower of Infinity)
	66-sided polygon

The writer would like to direct the reader's attention to this chart, so as to notice that the proposed F# tuning system includes all of the first ten geometric frequencies (as well as eleven of the first twelve), the complete harmonic series associated with them, as well as all five Platonic solid resonances and their harmonics.

This comprehensive inclusion of geometric and related tones, reveals a nearly-perfect structure of harmonics over a very wide span of octaves. (We will be discussing harmonics in the next section.)

Also, the writer points out that not all of the existing polygonal geometry correlations are listed in the table. There are simply too many of them to list due to the natural resonances, octavations, and harmonics. This is a very fortuitous and validating outcome, indeed.

Additionally, you can see a wide array of other geometric resonance correlations, including most of the major 'sacred' geometries, present in the F#-Major Tuning Grid system. This system's expansion to an extended octave system; one containing more than twelve tones per octave, would undoubtedly yield an even more comprehensive array of these significant frequencies. But, that is a task for another day, as we have both met and exceeded the objectives detailed from the start of this work. In other words, "We crushed it!"

But, rather than pour a nice glass of single-malt, we will instead make another pot of coffee and continue our efforts to see whether or not this system could be further expanded or further refined.

To that end, let's re-focus our attention to explore the importance of those harmonics we spoke of before.

21

Harmonics and Overtones

Filling the Empty Spaces

Have you ever had the experience, while listening to recorded sounds such as music, voice, or nature recordings - that the sound is so empty and unnatural that it seems artificial... incomplete... hollow? Of course you have. We all have heard 'sterilized' sound before.

How about a synthesized voice, such as Dr. Stephen Hawking or one of those robo-voices in some videos commonly posted on popular websites? Even without visual input, we know that those voices are not natural. But, how do we know this without further evidence? All we know for sure is that 'something' is different — that the sound is not natural.

We all want the highest quality loudspeakers, headphones, or ear pods when listening to music or audio from recorded tracks. So, our preference for 'near perfect' (aka as natural as possible) sound reproduction is not a matter of debate. Yet, some reproductions just seem to be of such poor quality as to be sonically irredeemable. Is it the equipment or the recording? Perhaps both?

Having grown up during the HiFi vinyl recording era where big speakers and huge analog amps were all the rage, The writer is accustomed to 'feeling' as well as hearing music. As a consequence, I am often frustrated by the perceived 'emptiness' of modern, digital recordings. Something is missing in the final reproduction of the sound that is essential to 'experiencing' the sound rather than merely hearing the sterilized data-stream played back.

This is not intended as a commentary on the typical genre of music created today, as the same statement applies to many 'classical' works that have been subsequently converted to digital format.

What's going on here? What are the fundamental differences between a live performance, its transmission over a network, a high-quality recording, or a low-quality recording - all of the same performance?

The answer may seem obvious to many. We intuitively understand that the more technology existing, between us and the actual performance, the greater the compromises, and the poorer the resulting quality of the performance's reproduction becomes. Anyone who ever took a cassette recorder to a concert, back when such was permitted, (Yes. I'm that old) knows that the recording is always inferior to the actual experience... a mere shadow of the performance. But, the issue goes deeper than this. And, many instinctively know it.

The more profound answer involves so much more... It's about the information carried (and propagated) by sound's compression waves traveling through the malleable media of air - creating harmonic eddies of secondary pressure waves and resonant vibrations within the acoustic environment.

We are speaking, specifically, about the audio information that is compromised or lost during network transmission, recording, compression or playback (vs. live sound). Such lost information mainly consists of the harmonics and overtones that simply do not survive the neutering processes involved in the recording, mixing, transmission, and reproduction process. Every step removes (or distorts) some (often critical) information from the sound stream.

Anyone with healthy auditory anatomy and physiology can easily tell the difference between a live performance and a studio recording. This writer cannot name a single performance that does not lose a significant amount of information when reproduced or copied (or 'ripped' in the modern parlance.)

Most studio recordings are supposedly made with the highest quality control standards in place. Unfortunately, any signal processing, whether analog or digital, either introduces unwanted information (interference, flutter, tape noise, electronic hum, etc.) or loses some of what we should hope to preserve (due to subtraction, loss, harmonic distortion, and compression). It's not simply about the quality of the recording equipment used, it's the underlying standards upon which the (digital or analog) reproduction is based.

To illustrate the point; If cost was not an issue, which amp would you prefer to purchase for your home entertainment system, a cheap no-name knockoff with extremely powerful amplification, or a high-end name brand with a slightly lower output power rating? Not a difficult question to answer. Is it?

Standard digital recording and mixing techniques are all based upon an industry standard that by-default trims the signal to 'fit' within the assigned bandwidth and, this process uses 'sampling rates' that omit (ignore) any data that lies *between* the sampling cycles. On the other hand, analog recording and mixing techniques generally only trim audio signals when the right potentiometer is manually set to do so. So, in this example, digital techniques are analogous to the 'cheap, no-name, knock-off' from the above example while analog techniques are basically a 'warts-and-all' production technique that requires actual skill to manipulate successfully.

That there are terrible productions and clear mistakes within the realm of analog music is not in dispute. (See the inset comment below, for one example) The point is made to illustrate that analog production is much more sensitive to error than digital techniques due to built-in error correction technology and variable sampling rates inherent in digital equipment. This is good for commercial, digital music producers. But, it is a difficult situation for experienced analog producers who don't want or need the equipment second guessing and automatically modifying the sound stream.

The one ameliorating factor to this apparent digital production mess of rules and default settings could very well be full-waveform recording using the .wav or other truly 'lossless' recording standard. But, the complexity of such recordings always depends upon the equipment used in capturing the signal.

So, we come full circle to the original assertion. Analog production and recording techniques are best for preserving the full audio field (warts and all).

The ironic twist is that digital recording, mixing, and reproduction techniques were initially hailed as miracle solutions for the added noise(s) introduced by the earlier analog systems. But, in the end, the cure was, arguably, worse than the problem they were originally designed to correct.

You see - since digital recording and reproduction requires vast amounts of data storage to preserve the entire sound field, compromises had to be made.

One example of analog mixing gone terribly wrong is found in Boston's amazing classic rock tune, 'Don't Look Back.' If you listen to the track closely, (just after the bridge, 3min,59sec in) you will notice a sudden, inexplicable volume drop. (I'll wait.) This volume drop was mixed in using analog equipment, presumably to allow overhead for an increase in amplitude that apparently never occurred. I assume the producer felt it was a good call at the time. This was done assuming the full signal with its ringing harmonics would always be there as cover, which on analog media, it is (for the most part). That it was a terrible error depends upon which media type you listen to. So, whether it was good, bad, right, or wrong, is academic. It's part of the track forever now.

This analog artifact is now a permanent, indelible characteristic of the converted, digital master recording. And, those familiar with the track now expect to hear it, as it is considered just part of the tune. In digital reproductions however, this volume drop has been accentuated to the point of absurdity since the analog 'cover' for the volume drop is no longer present on digital copies of the tune. Listen to the analog recording. The volume drop, although present, is far less noticeable.

Storage device capacity at the beginning of the digital era in the early 1980's, was at a high premium. So, a decision to cut the bottom and the top off the signals to make the files smaller was standardized.

The recording industry rationalized this decision by erroneously claiming that these frequency ranges were 'extraneous' and 'not generally audible.' The 'powers that be' reclassified most harmonic resonance as a type of 'distortion' and summarily discarded it (A colossal judgment-error in this writer's opinion.)

These unilateral acts, implemented by the recording industry and manufacturers, (Sony/Phillips) significantly reduced the required storage space so that an entire *album* or production data would fit on a single, laser-read media — whether it were CD, DVD, Digital tape, or Laser Disk format. But, at what price progress?

So much of the crucial harmonic information was literally thrown away in the digital music specifications. Music was essentially 'sterilized.' And, at the time of this writing, two entire generations have now grown to adulthood with the not-insignificant consequences of that unilateral, corporate decision.

Furthermore, in order to compensate for the lack of natural, energetic stimulus in modern music, your writer observes that the popular musical medium has necessarily become more powerfully intrusive and visceral (via sheer wattage,) and consequently less *musical* in order to convey any physical or emotional effect whatsoever. That those emotional and brain-wave effects, driven by lower and lower frequencies at higher and higher output wattages, seem to be of a primarily, depleting quality, is of significant concern, but are ultimately a matter for another discussion.

Modern music's general amplitude levels are much higher, while lower frequencies and subsonic frequencies are featured and enhanced. However, these lower frequencies - driven by extreme (usually digital) amplifier wattage, are not what I would call uplifting influences on the human body and mind. They actually have the ability to do real neurological and physiological harm - and, I'm not just talking about hearing problems.

So, what is the more profound answer to the question asked above? What information is compromised, making a live (analog) performance preferable to even the highest quality of digital recordings?

The answer is, of course, 'natural harmonic information.' Too little preservation of harmonics yields a hollow, thin reproduction. On the other hand, an excess of overtones, reverb, or extraneous vibration delivers a thick, muddy mix. Either of these is of little use to us in the sound and frequency healing field. The solution lies in that old axiom; 'Balance in all things.'

When perceiving any sound, the absence of, or abnormalities within the harmonic spectrum immediately signals whether that sound is or is not a harmonious, natural phenomenon.

191

Imagine hearing a person scream in horror, or sing with joy in a live theater production - versus hearing a general, high fidelity recording of that same performance. It's no contest. You can always tell the difference. And that telling contrast is found in the presence or absence of natural harmonics/overtones.

For our purposes, relaxation therapy and healing, we must allow the harmonics to ring out of the live production as well as any recorded re-production. This fact informs the proper method(s) of performance and reproduction as well as being highly suggestive of the environment(s) in which they are to be delivered.

A completely live performance is exceedingly preferable but not always practical for a single practitioner. Where we can (or must) utilize pre-recorded 'backing tracks,' they must be of impeccable quality and reproduced through the finest equipment possible. Additionally, headphones or ear pods are never going to be adequate to the task of reproducing the air movement (pressure waves) necessary to saturate the environment and the receivers' body with the healing 'vibes.'

Indeed, this writer is no fan whatsoever of the 'ear wear' so common these days. Of course their use in public settings is far preferable to subjecting others to the sounds that generally pass through them. But, in a therapeutic setting, the use of earphones is a very bad joke as the only organs to receive the frequencies are the ears and the brain. In a full body application of the sound bath, the entire body, every organ, and every water molecule is affected by the sound waves. So, yeah. Ear phones or buds will simply never get the job done.

Any sound session, of the type we are discussing, must be transformed into a whole-body experience analogous to attending a live performance. The receiver(s) must be immersed in the full perceptual experience of sound and frequency. Additionally, all of the receiver's senses should be involved in the experience. This concept extends to sight and smell/taste as well as hearing and touch senses.

Even our latest and greatest reproduction equipment introduces unwanted compromises: digital players, obscenely expensive ear-phones, high-quality digital home systems, etc. None of these can reproduce the full color, sound, and sensation of that live performance - especially from a digital copy. They all suffer from the same digital limitations, standardized in the 1980s, intended to reduce cost, minimize storage requirements, and conform to the limited-bandwidth capacity of which all equipment of the time were susceptible. The weak link is… the recording and mixing methods.

Digitally processing a signal of any type using the most readily-available methods, will always compromise the harmonics of the original sound produced. The process leaves gaping voids in the audio signal produced during playback. Much of this is unavoidable as the bulk of the original harmonics propagate from the instruments,

> **If you want to do excellent relaxation and healing work with music and proper tones, you MUST naturally move the air and subsequently vibrate the very water molecules of the client's body with agreeable frequencies… - Author**

performance amplifiers, and the recording environment itself. But, most of the deleterious effects are actually avoidable by utilizing proper analog methods.

It is logical to point out that recently-available technologies that digitally 'rebuild' harmonic profiles during playback are not omniscient, meaning that they cannot recreate the original environment's inherent harmonics, nor those of the venue where the original recording was made. If using an industry-standard digital copy of the performance, the data is simply not there. No so-called advanced system of 'emulation' can possibly put that information back into the track once it is digitally removed.

So what does this have to do with sound and frequency healing and relaxation?

Everything. I repeat; Every… Thing!

As an illustration, let's take a look at our tonic tone for the F#-Major system previously detailed. If I play that F#-360Hz on an acoustic guitar, (I know… just work with me here.) What are we actually 'hearing' in that tone? Well, I'll tell you...

The leading tone that we hear is the actual 360Hz. But, we are also getting tiny pieces of:

- The octave above, which is 720Hz.
- The Perfect 5th from the octave above, which is 1080Hz.
- The third octave tone, which is 1440Hz
- The Major Third from that third octave, which is 1800Hz
- The Perfect 5th of the third octave, which is 2160Hz
- Many more harmonics above, and some below.
- Other harmonics resulting from the instrument's material structure and the environment in which the tone is played.

These harmonics are created (propagated) naturally — acoustically by the compression wave and the resulting air movements (collisions, summations and interference patterns of reproduced wave-fronts), whether driven by the instrument itself, or by environmental effects such as reflections from studio surfaces or the analog amplification of the instrument's full-spectrum sound.

And, we have only specified the first through the sixth harmonics. They are all, in varying degrees, a part of the tone. You do not consciously hear them. But they are there - filling in the gaps to make the struck or plucked tone as full as it can be. Again; natural harmonics are propagated mainly by the pressure waves moving through the air, which are in turn created or triggered by the instrument's and any amplifier's own oscillations - not to mention any speaker systems used. There is no known technology which can precisely recreate that which has been removed from the sound field during the recording process.

Therefore, the obvious solution is; Don't remove anything from the sound field in the first place.

Standard digital recording? … Just say No!

Now, compare the preceding 360Hz example to the same tone if played on a basic electronic keyboard. You know. The kind you can get for cheap at the nearest superstore. Let's assume that F#-360Hz is one of the keys on that plastic contraption (It isn't. But, let's pretend.)

What are we actually hearing in *that* tone?

The correct answer is: 'It's anyone's guess.' But, I will bet you good money that; Even if that keyboard is programmed to simulate harmonics, it will do so digitally, partially, ineffectively, and certainly incompetently. And, just like determining 'Live vs. Recorded,' hearing the difference between the natural (vibrating string) and unnatural (digital-electronic signal pulse) sound is even easier for the human ear. This fact is so self-evident that we rarely even think about it.

So, what are we really talking about here?

I am trying to drive home a vitally-important point for which most born after 1983 (The dark year that the digital recording and playback via Compact Disc technology was introduced) have little-to-no experience. That missing experience is one of the fullness and richer texture of music and sound that has not had the natural harmonics engineered, processed, and compressed out of it.

> **Note: Polyphonic analog synthesizers are especially valuable in overcoming many of these limitations, particularly when utilizing sampled sounds whose sonic envelopes are also analog and, are constructed from the full-spectrum sound. For example, high-quality, lossless sample files.**

This writer will stipulate to the fact that analog recording and playback is considered (mostly) a relic of a bygone era, although the practice and technology seems to be staging a significant comeback. Your mild-mannered writer will also state unequivocally that modern signal processing, merciless frequency clipping, and strong-arm audio compression algorithms (to save storage space on devices and network bandwidth) objectively result in a vastly inferior signal stream.

That poor digital signal has been stripped bare-naked of any natural harmonics that would otherwise fill those vast empty spaces in the music.

As we are concerned with performances (and recordings) for the purposes of relaxation, meditation, and healing applications, we need to understand what is happening in the harmonic realm of our music so that we can ensure a full and robust production for our sound and frequency healing and relaxation performances.

The tuning systems we create in this project are, in the opinion of the author, essential to the future of sound therapy and healing.

And, the inherent harmonic structures themselves are an indispensable, vital part of these tones and cannot be discounted or summarily discarded just for the excuses of convenience or expediency. Nor can anyone be permitted to assert that the generally-filtered and discarded signal portions are somehow extraneous and of no particular benefit.

My bottom line is this; If you want to do good relaxation and healing work with music and proper tones, use digital recording and equipment. However, if you wish to do great relaxation and healing work, you must move the air in the room, and subsequently energize the water molecules in the client's body to activate their own innate ability to re-align frequencies in and around them. To accomplish this, the natural harmonics of the production must be preserved. Again, you cannot accomplish such deep and lasting results with headphones or so-called ear pods — nor can this be done with standard, digitized recordings. Analog is both the past and the future.

So... What are these 'harmonics' and 'overtones?'

Sound engineers and physicists will give different answers to this question because neither usually pay much attention to the difference between the two. In fact, there isn't much difference at all other than nominal classification

Tonal overtones are the overlying (or underlying) 'child' frequencies propagated by a pressure/compression wave in the air.

Frequency harmonics are the overlying (or underlying) wave-forms created by a propagating wave in a conductive medium.

Do you spot the difference there? Neither did I at first.
Apparently, musicians tend to occupy themselves with 'frequencies in the air' while physicist occupy themselves with 'wave-forms in a conductive medium.' Whatever the academic distinction, physicists prefer the term 'harmonics.' Musicians use both terms interchangeably (often in error.) And, therein lies the rub. That which is misunderstood, is often ignored and discounted.

Here is the only difference that matters to us between 'overtones' and 'harmonics;' Harmonics are numbered from the tonic. So, in the above example, 360Hz is both the root and the 1st harmonic.

720Hz is the 2nd harmonic. 1080Hz is the 3rd harmonic, etc.

Physicists calculate harmonics in a *conductive medium*, using the actual wavelength of the initial wave-front. This method would yield similar, if more mathematically complicated, results for musical tone. But, the more straightforward approach for calculating harmonics in music is described in the examples below.

Conversely, overtones begin their numbering *after* the tonic. So, the 360Hz is just the tonic. The 1st overtone is 720Hz. The 2nd overtone is 1080Hz, etc.

That's it! This distinction regarding numbering is the only practical difference in the basic understanding of what overtones and harmonics actually *are*. For our purposes, we will (try to) consistently refer to them as 'harmonics,' thus always including the tonic in our discussion.

So, how do we know what harmonics are propagated from any tone? Thankfully the answer here is 'simple..'. Simple multiplication. (Arm-chair physicists may want to avert your eyes from this section as it is vastly simplified compared to waveform calculations, as we are assuming air as the conductive medium.)

The following examples should clear up any remaining confusion.

Given that the tonic is always the 1st harmonic, each successive harmonic (for sound moving through air) is calculated as follows:

$$(f_1)x = x^{th} \textbf{ Harmonic}$$

Easy. Right?

To illustrate the process;

$$f_1 =$$

$$360Hz = 1^{st} \textbf{ Harmonic}$$
$$360Hz \times 2 = 720Hz = 2^{nd} \textbf{ Harmonic (1}^{st} \textbf{ overtone)}$$
$$360Hz \times 3 = 1080Hz = 3^{rd} \textbf{ Harmonic (2}^{nd} \textbf{ overtone)}$$
$$360Hz \times 4 = 1440Hz = 4^{th} \textbf{ Harmonic (3}^{rd} \textbf{ overtone)}$$
$$...$$

This method gives us a perfect tool for validating our interval calculations too. We outlined this process once before when validating our 'G' in the A-Major Tuning Grid.

One may recall that we calculated the 7th Harmonic of 432Hz to 'cheat' our way to find the minor 7th frequency candidate for the seventh octave.

That success is due to the fact that each pure harmonic has a direct relationship with specific intervals within the tonal system. An ideal twelve-tone per octave tuning system would possess interval frequencies where the harmonics themselves are also present as calculated, primary tone values elsewhere within the system itself.

For example;

The 3rd harmonic represents a Perfect 5th above the octave tone. In this case, 1080Hz. And, 1080Hz is indeed our Perfect 5th above the 720Hz octave relative to 360Hz. Our 2nd harmonic tone of 1080Hz is a natural harmonic of the root tone (360Hz.) This is what we mean by self-validating frequencies. And, while not all tones in a system will derive and self-validate in this manner, the main tones should.

These relationships are explained and detailed in more depth, in the Appendix of this text. See the section; *Appendix IX - Harmonics and Interval Validation.*

So, what if my calculated Perfect 5th tone is not 1080Hz? Is my tuning system design doomed?

Well, I wouldn't say it was 'doomed' per se. But, if the Perfect 5th tone is not 'consonant' or 'resonant' on a very real level with the calculated harmonic; Then it is likely not the best value for your perfect 5th. Playing such a Perfect 5th against the root tone would introduce some dissonance (excessive 'beating') in the harmonic realm.

The best case is for the harmonics, to the highest extent possible, to reflect the actual tones present and being played, in the tuning system itself. And, I will stipulate that this is not always possible or practical. But, in most cases, it is definitely do-able.

The second best case is for the harmonic frequency to appear 'somewhere' in the tuning system's table of natural harmonics. We see this sometimes with sub-minor tones. The harmonics are sometimes 'associated' via the overtones of other notes within the tuning.

What happens when this level of validation cannot be achieved? In that case, testing both tones for *any* harmonic compatibility is the only remaining option outside of choosing an interval for your tone other than 'Perfect 5th', which yields a proper value as shown in your harmonic calculations. Sometimes, the value for your chosen interval class just doesn't appear in the harmonic charts. At that point, it is important to reconsider either the fundamental or the chosen interval class for that note.

The point is; introducing dissonance between the tonic and the Perfect 5th (or any interval) is not an ideal situation in any case. Validated harmonics are the key to maximizing purest tonality throughout relaxation and healing sessions. The work we are engaged in relies upon eliciting rich harmonics. (Think: 'singing' a metal or crystal bowl.)

However, if a known-good tone just doesn't appear in the harmonics. We either have to choose a different interval class for that tone, or simply move on and accept it.

Minor tones are a bit more resilient (perhaps 'flexible' is a better word) in this regard than are the major tones.

> **Again, please understand that we are doing our utmost to provide 'pure' tone and 'pure' harmonics in our relaxation and healing sessions. This concept may have little to nothing to do with any specific, modern, and commercial applications of music.**

However, as the saying goes, 'Your mileage may vary.'

Because major key signatures are the most commonly used and desirable for healing and relaxation music, this writer suggests perhaps, using minor tones and modes primarily for 'passing' or transitional phrases.

We can use perfect harmonic relationships to leverage a bit more precision in our tonal system while providing some much needed validation for our tuning system's design. But, don't let this concept become a block to adding perfectly valid and nice tones to your system when a better alternative just doesn't present itself.

While not every labeled tone will derive from an identical harmonic value appearing in the primary tuning grid, this validation method serves as a useful tool for building more harmonious tonal systems, which will sparkle with 'harmonic' energy. I suggest for every tonal system design, that a table of harmonics also be prepared. A properly-prepared dynamic table such as in a spreadsheet, will provide valuable guidance during the design phase of your system.

Spreadsheet applications are ideal for managing the design of a custom tuning system. A few hours of preparing a spreadsheet saves tons of time during the design process. All harmonics can be laid out and recalculated immediately upon changing any pertinent value, such as interval ratio or tonic. This practice has been of great assistance on the journey outlined in this text.

To some readers, this chapter on harmonics and overtones and in fact, most of this text, will have been a greatly over-simplified introduction to which many will no doubt, take exception. And, that is as it should be. This text was not written for expert music theorists. It was written to provide the novice as well as many sound and frequency healing practitioners, with enough information to get the best possible results without suffering sensory overload.

What About Other Key Signatures?

Now We Are Really Pressing Our Luck

Thus far, we have created working tuning systems based upon two fundamental tones; A-432Hz and F#-360Hz. The resulting tuning grids, which work especially well in the major modes, are now dubbed the <u>A-Major Tuning Grid</u> and the <u>F#-Major Tuning Grid</u>, as they both, to different degrees, prefer or favor the major key designation of the tone in which they are rooted.

The major modes of the system rooted on 'A-432Hz' are entirely playable, and the minor tones are colorful and distinctive - if in places, somewhat quirky to play using standard keyboard fingerings. All-in-all, it is a very nice system to work with if you are open to experimentation with the various harmonies involved.

The tuning system based on F#-360Hz, is eminently playable and harmonious. In fact, I would say it is nearly perfect as it is. It is a joy to play tunes in standard notation, especially those played in the key of F#-Major.

Therefore, this writer considers our little experiment a complete success. We have accomplished all of the heretofore, stated goals of this work, provided ample support to the thesis outlined in the outset, and, have presented a reasonably articulate, and not entirely humorless proof of concept for the systems presented.

Yet, there are other possibilities that entice us to push farther. Buckle up, 'cause things are about to get weird.

Sure! F# is 'nearly perfect' for relaxation and healing sessions. But, *what if* a different fundamental yields an even better system? I cannot let this question go unexplored and unevaluated. And, I think the inquisitive reader would also like to know the answer.

Certainly, if you don't like the way an A Major scale sounds when playing on a keyboard that is tuned to the F#-Major standard, then perhaps the 'native' A-Major Tuning Grid will play better for you. Isn't this type of flexibility and creativity what music is all about anyway? If you subscribe to the stated premise, then why not tune to a standard that is designed to accentuate the key signature being played? Seems logical. But, does it actually work that way?

In the beginning, we started with 'A.' And, the geometric math led us directly to F#, which yielded surpassingly successful results. But, let us now explore the possibilities in using other of our derived fundamentals as the basis for more variant tuning systems.

Before beginning, the kind reader must allow for the possibility of a few compromises in terms of the interval ratios to be used. While we do not wish to pound 'square pegs into round holes', we will be making full use of the Just Intonation system's interval library. Some of these interval ratios will yield somewhat... *colorful* results, which is why we want to explore these alternate tuning systems in the first place.

Additionally, we will, in several situations, be forced to go somewhat 'off chart' for interval ratios as we explore ways of creating reasonably versatile designs from the various fundamental tones. If nothing else, this exercise may drive home the point that the previous F#-Major Tuning Grid system is nearly perfect - out of the box. That questionable statement is exactly why the following, time-sucking exercise must be completed.

To completely explore the extant possibilities, we will go through the same process, as previously detailed, with every possible fundamental tone for the purpose of fully-exploring any and all possibilities. The reader need not be concerned. The writer will not subject you to every thrust and parry in this exercise. But, will instead, provide a lively commentary from the highlight reels.

We will begin by attempting to build a new tuning system based upon A$^\#$. And, our first not-so-tortuous decision will be; which A$^\#$ do we use?

Shall we use the one from our A-Major tuning system? Or... Should we grant preference to an A$^\#$ from the F$^\#$-Major Tuning Grid system?

To the writer's surprise and, against all projected odds, the first discovery is that the A$^\#$ in both systems is, coincidentally, the same frequency!

That frequency is 450Hz. So, armed with this fortuitous information, let us now see if such luck holds true as we build a new tuning system based on the fundamental tone of A$^\#$-450Hz.

Tuning Grid Based Upon A#

Turns Out to be a 'Sharp' Edged One

In order to complete the A# tuning grid, it was necessary to get a bit creative. In that regard, our previous methods using the same interval ratios as those in the A-Major Tuning Grid were not entirely sufficient to the task of creating a system that adheres to our desired criteria. Although this researcher was very confident that a workable A# system was possible from the beginning. It took some time to tweak it into existence. Eventually, a *good* (not great) design emerged from the math through a process of trial and error.

The A# system was ironed out using some off-the-chart ratios from the extended Just Intonation interval charts. (Available in many texts and on several web sites) Typical divisions of the 1200¢ octave using the JI system include a Major 2nd of 203.910¢ and a Major 7th of 1088.269¢. In order to (barely) balance the system and achieve usable values that adhere to our stated criteria, it was necessary to tap intervals that would not typically appear in a 'Just' twelve-tone octave.

This result is the most convincing argument thus far of a system that would more appropriately be created in an extended-octave micro-tonal system consisting of several more tones than we are currently striving to achieve. I propose that a twenty-four-tone scale might be a 'sound' option in this regard. Perhaps we will explore this in some later work. But, I refuse to give up on this twelve-tone version until every avenue has been explored.

To obtain our coveted 432Hz 'A,' it was necessary to use an 'off-chart' interval of 48:25 (*classic diminished octave*). This ratio provides a much larger interval between the minor 7th and the Major 7th, coincidentally making that interval a classic semitone of 111.731¢ above the minor 7th. Due to this fact, the interval between the Major 7th and the octave is a *classic chromatic tone* of just 70.672¢. Thus, the usual relationship between the octave and the Major 7th position is somewhat... askew, making for some unexpected yet, interesting tonal variation.

One interesting point about the interval between the A (Major 7th) and the A[#] (octave) is that a similar relationship naturally exists between the same two notes in the F[#] tuning system. That relationship being 111.731¢ to the A, from the minor below it, and 70.672¢ from the A to the A[#]. These observations helped the writer to stay the course and remain on-mission; assuring me that this was a good call to make.

The sharp-eyed mathematician among us will, no doubt, spot the elephant in the room regarding the derivation of 'A-432Hz' in the above exercise. If a 432Hz 'A' is so natural then why did it need to be 'forced' with a strange interval ratio that so widens the interval between the minor 7th and the major 7th positions? Shouldn't it naturally appear?

The writer shares this thinking and, while having no clear rationalization at this time, we can confirm that this is not the only time we will be forced to ask the same question. What follows, is the somewhat hedged answer I have found, and the fuzzy logic behind it.

If we use the same interval ratio for the major 7th position that was used in both the A-Major and F[#]-Major grids, we are targeting a 'Just major 7th' (1088.269¢ above the fundamental) with a 15:8 ratio. The math yields a frequency of 421.875Hz, practically a full semitone off from the desired 432Hz and barely acceptable by our stated criteria.

A due-diligence search for frequencies matching our criteria leads us first to 420.00Hz for the 'A.' Doing the calculations reveals that this is equivalent to a 28:15 ratio.

Furthermore, the 420Hz tone is 1080.557¢ above the fundamental making it a good choice for an 'A' tone in this grid - being a little more than 8¢ off from a Just Major 7th.

Isn't it great to live in a universe of choices? While 420Hz is far too low to be the actual 'A' tone in most cases, as it is 49ᶜ off from our 432Hz, the math makes the 420Hz a closer match for the minor 7th to major 7th interval previously observed and verified in the F#-Major Tuning Grid.

There is no dogma or doctrine implied within this work. Therefore, the choice is on the individual practitioner as to which is more critical in any application. The 420Hz number reduces to six and is divisible by six, and twelve. In fact, it is the only other number even close to 432 that meets the basic criteria. Therefore, it technically meets the *minimum* criteria while remaining a subjectively inferior option to the 432Hz value, which is divisible by 3, 6, 9, 12, and 72. However, because 420Hz works harmonically, it is *very grudgingly* proposed as an option for this tuning grid. Albeit one that I, personally, do not wish to employ to any degree. As for me, I will stick with the quirkiness of the A-432Hz in this position for all the reasons previously outlined.

By 'borrowing' the off-chart interval ratio of 48:25 for the Major 7th position, from our Just Intonation system, we gain our 432Hz 'A', which calls for an asterisk at the Major 7th position. All of the other intervals thus far, remain the same as those found in the F# tuning system's design. Thus, the remaining tones maintain their anticipated relationships with each other.

In this system, we also accept a Major 3rd and a Perfect 5th, which yield remainders of 0.25 and 0.50 as well as some fairly large remainders in the very lowest octaves. As discussed earlier, the rules of the game accept decimal remainders, as long as they meet the 'reduction to nine' criteria and resolve to whole numbers in higher octaves.

Next on our list, the Major Whole Tone of 63.28125Hz, way down at C⁰ is, so far, the largest decimal remainder encountered in this work. Although the value is perfectly valid, the writer reluctantly rejects it (and therefore the interval ratio of 9:8) in favor of the 63.00Hz value.

The writer does so because, the 28:25 interval also gives us a perfect 252Hz 'C' in that position of the grid. The 63.28125Hz value passes the reduction-to-nine test and, it resolves to a whole number in the upper octaves. This makes the 9:8 ratio perfectly acceptable by the stated rules.

But, for the writer, a preference for the *natural* 252Hz 'C' is the stronger instinctive course. This is the sole reasoning behind the 9:8 interval value not being included in this grid. Again, personal choice is a factor here. If the 9:8 result of 63.28125Hz is acceptable and preferable, then by all means experiment with it.

This writer will be the first to concede that the Major 7th 'A' in this A# system is an eccentric bit to play on the keyboard. The harmonies and fingering patterns in the range of the minor 7th through the octave tone, while challenging to spot, are, in this writer's subjective opinion, strangely pleasing. However, standard keyboard patterns for this range will necessarily change.

Additionally, these choices for the 'inverted' ratios at the top end provide for some compelling challenges to the player as well as some interesting variations. With this single exception, this is a fairly harmonic and well organized grid. Temperament was never our primary intention. The point is that it works well but, is a bit inflexible.

For those who choose to utilize this tuning for relaxation and healing applications, know that the distribution of pure geometric tones as well as Platonic solid resonances are present but, not nearly as extensive as those found in the F#-Major Tuning Grid. We definitely have the usual 180, 360, 540, 720, 1080 tones and similar, related progressions. However, many geometries are simply not represented. For applications where these A# Major tones are specifically desired, this would make the A#-Major Tuning Grid an acceptable-yet-challenging choice.

With all that said, here is the chart for our tuning system based on the A# fundamental. This one is a 'win' despite the interesting mathematical acrobatics at the minor 7th and Major 7th positions.

But, we will included the alternate, *small Major 7th* as an option for those who wishing to use it or whoever may simply prefer it.

The writer would be the first to agree that this grid could have turned out better. But, it could also have turned out much worse. The system as-designed, definitely works. The compliance of the desired intervals to the established, geometric criteria is the real rub.

The reason why some fundamentals are extremely compliant while others seem to actively fight the system may just have something to do with the geometric system's F# tonal preference that was touched upon in the earlier chapters.

Tuning Grid Based on A#-225Hz						
Note	Interval	Ratio	Multiplier	Frequency (Hz)	Interval from Root (¢)	Step Interval (¢)
A#	Octave	2:1	2	450.00	1200	70.672
A	class. dim 8ve	48:25	1.92	432.00	1129.328	111.731
*A	sm. M 7th	28:15	1.8666667	420.00	1080.557	62.961
G#	m7th	9:5	1.8	405.00	1017.596	133.238
G	M 6th	5:3	1.66666667	375.00	884.359	70.672
F#	m 6th	8:5	1.6	360.00	813.686	111.731
F	Perf 5th	3:2	1.5	337.50	701.955	119.442
E	m 5th	7:5	1.4	315.00	582.512	84.467
D#	Perf 4th	4:3	1.33333333	300.00	498.045	111.731
D	M 3rd	5:4	1.25	281.25	386.314	70.672
C#	m 3rd	6:5	1.2	270.00	315.641	119.442
C	middle M 2nd	28:25	1.12	252.00	196.198	84.467
B	Semitone	16:15	1.06666667	240.00	111.731	111.731
A#	Root	1:1	1	225.00	—	—

Table 23.1 - Tuning grid based on an A#3 fundamental of 225Hz, showing the fourth octave including interval ratios, semi-tone step width, and full interval width.

Is there something about geometry and the universe that just prefers the F#-360 basis for musical systems? As demented as that question may seem to some, we will necessarily revisit this question as we progress chromatically, through the remaining possibilities for fundamental, root tones.

The writer chooses to keep and open mind in this matter until all of the possible root tones have been challenged and 'gridded.'

Tuning Grid Based Upon B

Let's B'gin

As with all things in life, we need a starting point. In this case, we are looking for a good, solid 'B' tone to serve as a firm foundation. Unlike our previous A# tuning grid, this one presents us with a tough choice.

In our original tuning grid, based on A-432Hz, the fifth octave 'B' tone is set to 486Hz. However, due to choices previously made, the F#-360Hz tuning grid gives us a 'B' tone of 480Hz. We will need to make a decision as to which one to use and, the only way I know to do that is to begin working the grid out both ways to see which one dovetails with our existing systems. Don't worry. I won't burden you with both trial runs.

First, let us see what we can do about our minor semitone, the 'C.' If we can get that one worked out, it may give us a clue as to how to proceed. And, indeed it does.

When using 243Hz (one octave down from 486Hz) as the fundamental tone, we have a few choices as to the ratio. The first possibility is our venerated 25:24 *'Classic Chromatic Semitone'* which we made use of in the A-432Hz tuning grid.

This ratio yields a frequency of 253.125Hz, which at first glance, stands no chance whatsoever of meeting our criteria. However, the number's digits do reduce to nine as required, and is a decimal frequency which resolves to a whole number in the octaves above.

But, based on the interval width produced (70.642$^\text{¢}$), which is basically, a large quarter-tone, the ratio of 25:24 may not be an appropriate ratio for this tone. We will keep it *'in our pocket'* as we explore other, perhaps more harmonic options.

Our next possibility is the 17:16 'Smaller Semitone' weighing in at 104.956$^\text{¢}$. This ratio is a common feature in many of the tuning grids outlined in this work, several yet to be revealed. Again, this ratio when applied to our fundamental of 243Hz, yields a frequency of 258.1875Hz which is also reducible to nine. And, it has a decimal remainder which technically meets the resolution to whole number criteria. So, 17:16 is a possibility. We will also put a pin in that for now.

The reason we don't jump on this is because 243Hz forces an unreasonable compromise, as we look into the 'A' tone above. So, in this case, it's not the 17:16 that doesn't work so much as the other compromises required by the 243Hz tonic if we choose to use it.

Our last, *reasonable* opportunity is the 16:15 'Just Semitone' at 111.731$^\text{¢}$. On the face, this seems like the perfect choice. Alas, the resulting value of 259.20Hz is yet another decimal remainder which doesn't resolve to a whole number in higher octaves.

As flexible as these tuning systems are, they do present some very strict constraints upon the fundamental frequency. The above exercise is enough to demonstrate that the 'B' frequency of 243Hz from the A-432Hz tuning grid dies not appear to be the fundamental needed for this grid.

Therefore, we turn our attention to the 240Hz (an octave down from B-480Hz) from our F$^\#$ tuning grid. Hopefully, it will be a better fit for our fundamental 'B.'

When working with our 'C' tone, we find that the same interval ratios used above, yield similar results. The 16:15 'Just Semitone' calculates to 256.00Hz. At first glance this appears to be a good result. However, 256 reduces to four. Additionally, it does not pass the 'divisible by' test. Therefore, what appeared to be a perfectly nice 111.731$^\text{¢}$ semitone must be discarded.

Similarly, the 25:24 ratio used previously fails to meet muster. Sadly, this ratio yields 250Hz, which reduces to seven and does not pass the 'reduction to' test. It also is therefore, rejected.

To the rescue is the 17:16 'Smaller Semitone' which yields a 255Hz value. I don't feel it is actually 'perfect.' But, 255Hz numerically reduces to three and is therefore divisible by the same. So, it meets the absolute-minimum requirements for inclusion.

While not initially pleased with the 17:16, small semitone in this position, subsequent work reveals that the interval is very useful and appropriately colorful - once you get accustomed to it. And, in later work, we will be seeing this interval ratio at work again.

Going back to the table of Just ratios, we discover another possibility for the position of 'C.' The one that stood out to me is called a 'Septimal Semitone' or 'Sub-minor 2nd.' The ratio for this one is 21:20 and it yields a frequency of 252Hz with an interval of 70.672¢. While 252.00Hz would be a nice solution for the 'C' position, this value widens the interval between the 'C' and the 'C# ,' which effectively reverses the mathematical relationship between these tones as well as with the fundamental. It is usable. But, chord structures would necessarily need to take this into account, making the 17:16 (smaller semitone) the better of two difficult options.

Conflicting impressions on what is the proper option for the 'minor second' position were difficult to resolve. However, the widening of the interval between 'C' and 'C#' was too much to accept. Therefore, we adopt the 17:16 'small semitone' as our 'C' with an honorable-mention to the 21:20, septimal semitone.

This will not be the last time this 'B-Major' tuning grid produces headaches of this nature. Jumping ahead, I will reveal that the Perfect 4th position required similar wrangling to arrive at a workable tone. This required tapping an unnamed 27:20 interval at 519.551¢ in order to meet our needs. The resulting tone is 324Hz.

The 324Hz tone rests 133.238¢ above the Major 3rd making it closer to a *Super Major 4th*. We will simply label it a '*Large Major 4th*.'

Once we had adopted the 240Hz 'B' from our F$^#$ tuning grid and dealt with these two stubborn positions in the grid, the remainder of this version of our 'B Tuning Grid' fell into place quite easily using interval ratios that we have seen before.

While the small semitone at 'C' and the large major 4th at 'E' are like unruly children in this tuning, they do reveal themselves to be of some use and possessing not-inconsiderable tonal color.

However, the two tones 'bear no fruit' - meaning that none of the produced tones at 'C' or 'E' are of 'geometric' significance. Despite this fact, there do exist some validation in the harmonics, both values meet the stated rules, and both are sufficiently harmonious. Thus, they are considered useful if only for some harmonic variation. And, while music theory experts are now pulling their hair out over the methods presented here, this writer will concede that, in this case, the resulting tuning system is *not* an optimal configuration.

I had hoped for a bit more based on the effort and prior successes. But, the B-Major Tuning Grid draft, currently exists with the specified limitations.

Not to be deterred, I loaded this tuning into my synthesizer and gave it a good test. And, while I am not enamored with it in any way, it doesn't entirely lack in redeeming qualities; once one learns to avoid the pot-holes at the 'C' and 'E' positions. If one carefully chooses their moments with these positions, they do have their rightful place - just not the *usual* place one might expect when approaching a standard keyboard layout. However, the writer will point out that playing in F$^#$-Major works nicely using this grid.

The Japanese have an interesting expression that I feel applies here. The translated saying goes something like this: "Ask nine people, hear ten opinions."

九人十色 (ku nin, tou iro) - lit: Nine people, ten colors (opinions)

Some may not only find a good use for these wayward tones but will find some love of their inherent stubborn and rebellious nature. I return to this one from time to time and enjoy 'noodling' with it's off-natured and untempered qualities — all the while searching for a way to resolve the issues inherent in the grid. Too often, I come back to this grid, and recalculate looking for better interval fits. However, this one has proven to be stubbornly resistant to conformity per our criteria. Perhaps that is why the writer refuses to give up on it.

Whatever your considered opinion, there are many useful relaxation and healing tones in this tuning grid. There are many pure-geometric tones and Platonic solid resonances as well; although not nearly as many as contained in our previous efforts such as the now venerable F#-Major Tuning Grid. The writer's advice: Just use the F# Major Tuning Grid, and avoid the pot-holes.

In any case, presented below, is the *draft* B-Major Tuning Grid:

Tuning Grid Based on B-240Hz (4th Octave)						
Note	Interval	Ratio	Multiplier	Frequency (Hz)	Interval from Root (¢)	Step Interval (¢)
B	Octave	2:1	2	480.00	1200	111.731
A#	M 7th	15:8	1.875	450.00	1088.269	70.672
A	Sub min 7th	9:5	1.8	432.00	1017.596	48.770
G#	M 6th	7:4	1.75	420.00	968.826	155.140
G	m 6th	8:5	1.6	384.00	813.686	111.731
F#	Perfect 5th	3:2	1.5	360.00	701.955	119.443
F	dim 5th	7:5	1.4	336.00	582.512	62.961
E	Lg. M 4th	27:20	1.35	324.00	519.551	133.238
D#	M 3rd	5:4	1.25	300.00	386.314	70.672
D	5 limit m 3rd	6:5	1.2	288.00	315.641	111.731
C#	M 2nd	9:8	1.125	270.00	203.910	98.955
C	Sm Semitone	17:16	1.0625	255.00	104.955	104.955
B	Root	1	1.00	240.00	—	—

Table 24.1 - Tuning grid based on an B⁴ fundamental of 240Hz, showing the fourth octave, interval ratios, semi-tone step width, and full interval width.

Tuning Grid Based Upon C

It Could'a Been a Contender. But It Isn't

From the very beginning of our construction of the tuning grid based on 'C', we are faced with the same choice encountered when starting the tuning grid based on 'B.'

The completed tuning grids that are based on 'A', 'A#', and 'F#' indicate a frequency of 252Hz for our 'C' fundamental, while the 'B' grid system derives a frequency of 255Hz for the 'C.' However, we will cut to the chase and reveal that 252Hz is the far better choice. Hours of working with 255Hz was an exercise in sheer futility while 252Hz was more forgiving; If only by a small degree.

I will also note for the curious, that while 255Hz reduces to three and is only divisible by three, 252Hz reduces directly to nine and is divisible by 3, 6, 9, and 12. Does this somehow make it a better 'C'? Or, are we just seeing more mathematical coincidences?

As keyboardists, we are the most familiar with the key of C-Major. Everyone starts with the 'C', diatonic scale when first learning to navigate the keyboard. It is just the easiest key signature to play because generally, if you stay to the white keys all is well. Perhaps it is due to this indoctrination that I expected the tuning grid based on 'C' to be no more difficult to construct than any other.

The truth is that I don't consider the finished grid to be usable to any significant degree. And, this is after hours upon hours working with it to achieve the best fits possible that comply with the stated geometric rules and methods as they apply to these tuning systems.

As stated, we use a 252Hz fundamental tone to anchor the system. But, in terms of the intervals and ratios utilized, this 'C-based' system is way off-chart in many respects.

For one thing, it is naturally (and decidedly) lacking in pure geometric tones. In order to achieve for example, a geometric 540Hz C#, it was necessary to tap a 15:14 interval ratio. This gives us 199.443¢ width between 'C' and 'C#.' This is far too wide to be considered musically useful as it basically represents a whole-tone interval.

As a result of this extra-wide interval, the Major 2nd consequently receives a haircut of about 8¢ lower than if we were able to use a 111.731¢ semitone. This is not a complete deal-breaker. But, there is yet more to challenge us.

Similar acrobatics were needed to achieve a geometric 360Hz F# in the position normally occupied by an aug 4th or dim 5th. The required interval ratio turns out to be a septimal tritone of 10:7, which is 617.488¢ above the fundamental. This gives us a larger semitone interval of 119.443¢ between F# and G, which is not a complete disaster because, the F# tuning grid also yields this interval width at the same degree of the scale (in that grid, the interval is from C to C#.)

Next, our minor 3rd, optimally a 6:5 ratio at 315.641¢ gives a frequency of 302.40Hz. According to the criteria, this is an unusable tone as the value will never resolve to a whole number value in higher octaves. This fact forces us to look for options. So, we call upon our old friend, the 7:6 sub minor 3rd to save the day. Again, a sub minor 3rd is 266.871¢ above the fundamental.

Finally, our Major 6th simply would not play nicely at all. It has been so pleasant to see 432Hz (mostly) naturally work out for our 'A' tones. However, in this case, not only was it necessary to 'fudge' the minor 6th with a 45:28 interval at 821.398¢, it was also required to use a septimal major 6th of 12:7 at 933.129¢ to achieve a 432Hz 'A.'

In the writer's attempts to normalize the whole mess, it became clear that there were just too many compromises. Either we need a better fundamental tone for 'C', or we need a completely different approach.

To continue the litany of difficulties with the 'C' tuning grid, Our 'A' tone at the preferred Major 6th position (5:3 ratio) most naturally works out to 420Hz. Since this is technically a valid tone which meets our criteria, I offer it as an option.

However, I find myself unable to allow 420Hz to substitute for the familiar A-432Hz despite the relative ease of use afforded by the 5:3 Major 6th interval. The 432Hz value, for the most part, has effortlessly appeared in successful tuning grids. This time, however, the result can only be achieved by forcing it with the 12:7 detailed above.

> Ironically, 420Hz has popped up several times in the preliminary work with these geometric grids. But, usually there is an better, more harmonic solution to be found within the usual interval ratios. Up until now, that option has always resulted in a 432Hz value for 'A.'

The writer chooses to leave both of these options (420Hz or 432Hz) open for discussion and personal choice unless a clearer option presents itself. We would much rather have a usable tuning system than to continue forcing more 'expected' results into it. Although, with *much* easier-to-use options already well documented, (F$^{#}$-Major Tuning Grid) it is unclear why anyone would choose to struggle with this one.

We have expanded our experiment beyond its originally-successful scope to explore the possibility that there may be, perhaps, a tuning standard, based upon our geometric principles, that can stand as an equal or superior system to the F$^{#}$ system previously explored.

Thus far, we have demonstrated that; while usable and even interesting tuning grids *can* be constructed from other fundamental note values; thus far nothing approaching the level of balance, found in the F$^{#}$ tuning grid system, has been revealed. What we *have* encountered is clearly evidence of a heretofore, unidentified, and built-in bias that favors construction upon the tones of the F$^{#}$ Major tone class.

Although we now have a C-Major Tuning Grid (of sorts), it turns out to be far too light in 'good' tones and very challenging to use musically.

So, as disappointing as it may be, we will leave it as-is and move on to greener pastures.

Perhaps on some reflection, we can revisit this one to see if more acceptable solutions present themselves. Despite the difficulties with this grid, I am heartened by the successes we have enjoyed thus far.

Even these *failed* grids provide a certain validation to the previous successful grids designed in this text — as being unique and valuable. And, we will note for the record, that the fundamental tones of the more successful tuning grids are starting to look as if there is definitely a systemic *preference for the F#-Major tone class* to which 'C' incidentally, is *not* a member.

Tuning Grid Based on C-252Hz (4th Octave)						
Note	Interval	Ratio	Multiplier	Frequency (Hz)	Interval from Root (¢)	Step Interval (¢)
C	Octave	2:1	2	504.00	1200	111.731
B	M 7th	15:8	1.875	472.50	1088.269	119.443
A#	Sub min 7th	7:4	1.75	441.00	968.826	35.697
A	Sept M 6th	12:7	1.714285714	432.00	933.129	111.731
*A	M 6th	5:3	1.66666667	420.00	884.359	62.647
G#	Large m 6th	45:28	1.607142857	405.00	821.398	119.443
G	Perfect 5th	3:2	1.5	378.00	701.955	84.467
F#	Sept Tritone	10:7	1.42857143	360.00	617.488	119.443
F	Perf 4th	4:3	1.33333333	336.00	498.045	111.731
E	M 3rd	5:4	1.25	315.00	386.314	119.443
D#	Sub m 3rd	7:6	1.16666667	294.00	266.871	62.961
D	M 2nd	9:8	1.125	283.50	203.910	84.467
C#	Just halftone	15:14	1.07142857	270.00	119.443	119.443
C	Root	1	1.00	252.00	—	—

Table 25.1 - Tuning grid based on an C³ fundamental of 252Hz, showing the fourth octave including interval ratios, semi-tone step width, and full interval width.

26

Tuning Grid Based Upon C#

Another 'Sharp' One

Considering how resistant the 'C' tuning grid was to our mathematical seductions, it is a personally validating experience to once again work on a tuning grid that 'just works.' A quick shout-out to the F#-Major tone class. C# is a big player in the key of F#-Major as it represents the Perfect 5th of the F#-Major scale. And, the emerging theory that F# is a preferred tonal class for our particular system design, looks to have received a bit more validation.

To make a short story…shorter, The required ratios to create a perfect Geometric tuning grid based on C# required almost no work at all. That statement fairly sums up this entire (brief) chapter.

The C# grid uses the exact same ratio stack as the F#-Major Tuning Grid. All that was necessary was to select a fundamental tone, 270Hz (**540Hz ÷ 2**) from our F# tuning grid and, it all fell into place with no further work required.

The 432Hz 'A' appeared naturally - once again demonstrating that it is the perfect 'pivot' tone for our relaxation and healing tuning systems.

This C# tuning grid is rich with 'pure' geometric tones, Platonic solids, and sacred geometry resonances although, not quite as rich as the F# tuning grid. This one is definitely a winner! It is easy to play, very harmonic, and will drive any detractors of this text's thesis crazy.

After all the effort and angst necessary to coax anything of worth out of the previous grid, based upon C-252Hz, this one was a pleasure.

It required only the use of ratios already proven in the F#-Major Tuning Grid plus an additional 'bonus' of an optional choice for D#.

Again, I am nearly convinced that there is a very special relationship with the tones of the F#-Major tone class that explains this apparent ease of fit? I certainly do not have sufficient evidence for an absolute validation of this theory, especially since the 'B' grid remains problematic. But, after exploring the concept of geometric tone and working with the information for several years now, I am convinced there is something, much deeper than simple math, going on with these numbers and tones.

Presented here for your entertainment, is the C#-Major Tuning Grid.

	Tuning Grid Based on C#-270Hz (4th Octave)					
Note	Interval	Ratio	Multiplier	Frequency (Hz)	Interval from Root (¢)	Step Interval (¢)
C#	Octave	2:1	2	540.00	1200	111.731
C	M 7th	15:8	1.875	506.25	1088.269	70.62
B	min 7th	9:5	1.8	486.00	1017.596	133.238
A#	M 6th	5:3	1.66666667	450.00	884.359	70.672
A	m 6th	8:5	1.6	432.00	813.686	111.731
G#	Perfect 5th	3:2	1.607142857	405.00	701.955	119.443
G	dim 5th	7:5	1.5	378.00	582.512	84.467
F#	Perf 4th	4:3	1.4	360.00	498.045	111.731
F	M 3rd	5:4	1.33333333	337.50	386.314	70.672
E	m 3rd	6:5	1.25	324.00	315.641	133.238
D#	JI Maj 2nd	9:8	1.2	303.75	203.910	92.179
D#	Small M 2nd	10:9	1.125	300.00	182.404	70.672
D	JI semitone	16:15	1.1111111	288.00	111.731	111.731
C#	Root	1	1.00	270.00	—	—

Table 26.1 - Tuning grid based on an C#3 fundamental of 270Hz, showing the fourth octave including interval ratios, semi-tone step width, and full interval width. A bonus, optional tuning for D# is also indicated.

Tuning Grid Based Upon D

Deez Ds…Gotta Love 'em!

One has to love the ease and simplicity of this system of tuning. When turning our attention to the 'D' tuning grid, a theory, which has been previously discussed, caused some initial concern over this grid.

The theory is; since the system, under construction in this work, has repeatedly shown an affinity for F$^{\#}$ and particularly the tones of the F$^{\#}$-Major scale, it might explain why tuning grids based on tones not included in F$^{\#}$-Major have thus far been so stubborn to conform.

Thus far, the A$^{\#}$, C$^{\#}$, and F$^{\#}$ grids have been 'cooperative' to varying degrees and, have worked out with minimal difficulty while all attempts at creating a C tuning grid turned out to be a fruitless chore (The C tuning grid being essentially useless for our purposes.) Of course, A$^{\#}$, C$^{\#}$ and F$^{\#}$ are all members of the F$^{\#}$-Major tone class. Yet, our current subject, the 'D', holds no place in that particular class of tones.

"Well," you might say. "What about the 'B?'" Yes. 'B' is a member of the F$^{\#}$-Major tone class. And, while the grid required some special attention, in the end it worked out to a *somewhat* usable - if not a particularly harmonic or tone-rich system.

Anyway, it's still just a working theory. Now, it is time to work out the 'D' Tuning grid system.

The A-Major and F$^{\#}$-Major systems both indicate a fundamental tone of 288Hz for our root 'D.'

From previous experience, we will not dispute this agreement between systems unless given sufficient cause. Therefore, 288Hz will be the fundamental upon which we build our tuning grid based on 'D.'

For our minor semitone above 'D,' I would like to use the same 16:15 ratio that was previously such a hit. However, 16:15 while providing the usual 111.731¢ interval, yields a decimal frequency of 307.20Hz. The resulting value reduces to three but the decimal remainder cannot resolve to a whole number tone using simple octavation. Therefore, our 16:15 ratio is not what we are looking for here.

While searching for a likely tone value, the frequency of 306Hz seemed to be the closest best fit for this position. The interval between 288Hz and 306Hz calculates to 104.955¢. The resulting interval ratio turns out to be 17:16, a small semitone or *'overtone half-step.'* This interval is 'slightly' smaller than a *Just semitone*. But, we have used it previously to our advantage. Therefore, we will add it to the possibilities while we continue to look for a better option.

What to do? Well, let's use our math skills to find out what our options may be.

Between the 16:15 semitone and the 17:12 overtone half-step, we have 50:47 (107.121¢), 33/31 (108.237¢), 49:46 (109.307¢), and 81:76 (110.307¢).

Testing for each of these interval ratios yielded nothing but unacceptable choices due to the unresolvable decimal remainders.

Therefore, it appears that there is little choice but, to make the call and adopt the 17:12 ratio yielding 603.00¢ (at least that number reduces to nine.) The unnamed interval will be identified as a *'pseudo-dim 5th'* in our chart. The frequency, of course, will be 408Hz.

Additionally, we find that the 6:5 ratio for our minor 3rd gives us another unresolving decimal remainder. Yet, our trusty *Sub minor 3rd* comes to the rescue with a 7:6 ratio and a resulting tone of 336.00Hz.

The major 2nd and the Perfect 4th worked out nicely with common ratios that we have seen several times before. But, the augmented 4th/ diminished 5th position did not work out well with the preferred 7:5 ratio; yielding yet another unresolvable decimal frequency of 403.20Hz.

Utterly undaunted, the 17:12 was tested giving us a value of 408Hz which meets our criteria. But, it leaves us with an interval that is a bit wide for that particular position, (again 104.955ᶜ) between the G and the G#.

Thankfully, the perfect 5th which is our 'A' in this tuning grid works out perfectly using the preferred 3:2 ratio - yielding our now-familiar, 432Hz 'A' tone. But, we again run into issues with the A#, which does not work out with the 8:5 ratio we would prefer. The resulting value is 460.80Hz.

This tone value is yet-another unresolvable and unacceptable decimal remainder. So, thinking all the way back to our original A-Major tuning grid, we pull a 25:16 ratio that yields a 450Hz frequency (772.627¢). The 450Hz A# gives us a 70.672ᶜ width between A and A#. A bit narrow. But, an acceptable contrast at the position.

The remainder of the tones in this grid make use of the more common interval ratios which are utilized in other successful grids. All are detailed in the chart below.

The unresolvable decimal remainders in this workup were strange in that they seemed to follow pattern of .20, .40, .60, and .80. Additionally, they always seemed to occur in the minor tone positions. Notice that there were very few issues with the major scale tones in this grid... only the minor tones made trouble for us.

Well, a little addendum to this narrative is that; this pattern will be seen repeatedly in the minor tones. It's relevance is unclear. But, we do know that the resulting tones are perfectly harmonious - even though they do not cooperate with the geometric mathematics. All of the major-scale tones in this grid make use of the more common interval ratios which are utilized in the other successful grids. Yes. It seems that minor tone values are the problem child of these systems. And, the math may be the reason why the major tone structures seem to be somehow, preferred.

You can see for yourself in the table below.

While the relative ease in preparing this particular grid would seem to contradict the theory outlined earlier, regarding a certain difficulties with tones that are not part of the F#-Major tone class, the tuning itself is not without its rebellious points. It is eminently playable on a standard keyboard although it does fall under the writer's 'quirky' classification of tunings. Minor tones are a real...challenge.

Additionally, the 'D' tuning grid system does have a significant population of pure geometric and platonic tones.

Tuning Grid Based on D-288Hz (4th Octave)						
Note	Interval	Ratio	Multiplier	Frequency (Hz)	Interval from Root (¢)	Step Interval (¢)
D	Octave	2:1	2	576.00	1200	111.731
C#	M 7th	15:8	1.875	540.00	1088.269	119.443
C	min 7th	7:4	1.75	504.00	968.826	84.467
B	M 6th	5:3	1.66666667	480.00	884.359	111.731
A#	Aug 5th	25:16	1.5625	450.00	772.627	70.672
A	Perfect 5th	3:2	1.5	432.00	701.955	98.955
G#	Pseudo dim5th	17:12	1.416666667	408.00	603.000	104.955
G	Perf 4th	4:3	1.33333333	384.00	498.045	111.731
F#	M 3rd	5:4	1.5	360.00	386.314	119.443
F	Sub m 3rd	7:6	1.166666667	336.00	266.871	62.961
E	Maj 2nd	9:8	1.125	324.00	203.910	98.954
D#	sm. semitone	17:16	1.0625	306.00	104.955	104.955
D	Root	1	1.00	288.00	—	—

Table 27.1 - Tuning grid based on an D3 fundamental of 288Hz, showing the fourth octave including interval ratios, semi-tone step width, and full interval width.

I suspect that we will 'catch another break' so to speak as we proceed to creating the next grid on our list - the D# tuning grid. Since D# is a member of the F#-Major tone class, I am expecting a rather easy go of it.

Tuning Grid Based Upon D#
Deez Sharps Are Driving Me Mad!

Expectations are funny, unpredictable beasts. They rarely lead directly to the desired outcome. This D# grid turned out to be a real 'bear' to deal with.

The initial problem with the D# grid is deciding upon the fundamental frequency. Our A-Major and D-Major tuning grids indicate a 306Hz value. But, our A# tuning grid as well as our venerable F# chart indicate a (somewhat odd-ball) 300Hz frequency.

Not to be so easily forgotten, our 'B' tuning grid as well as the 'C#' tuning grid both indicate 303.75Hz as a candidate. But, to add even more confusion to the mix, we see a 294Hz D# appear in the problem-child, 'C-Major' tuning grid.

In retrospect, this did not bode well for the expected ease in designing a D#- based tuning grid.

So, we have to decide between 294Hz, 300Hz, 306Hz, 315Hz and 303.75Hz. OK... So, where to start? Well, the F#-Major chart's tone makes the most sense, in my opinion. But, it isn't going to be quite that easy for us. This statement is being made after hours of tortuous testing for which the kind reader will be spared the sordid details.

Two of our candidate fundamentals reveal harmonically-workable grids; the 300Hz and the 306Hz. So, either the inexplicable weirdness of a 300Hz or the safe-haven of the 306Hz fundamental is our potential reality now.

Both values actually turn out to work fairly well harmonically. But, the musical sweetness of our 360Hz F# and the 540Hz C# naturally appear in the appropriate positions when utilizing the 300Hz fundamental. When testing with the 306Hz fundamental, these 'magical' values were unobtainable.

Following this somewhat criteria-biased-yet-logical line of thinking, we adopt the 300Hz frequency as our fundamental D# in this tuning grid. The reader may recall that this value was originally pulled from the ever-useful F#-Major Tuning Grid. Therefore, these two systems remain linked by utilizing the 300Hz D#. This fact alone is a welcome piece of validation for the method(s) under development.

The most glaring problem with the 300Hz grid relates to our venerated 432Hz 'A' tone, which should be present in the minor 5th position. It's just not there! What we do have is that occasionally-recurring phenomenon of the natural A-420Hz that keeps popping up from time to time in our work.

The significance of this continues to intrigue this writer. Although, there is a theory under consideration that our mathematical preference towards numbers that comply with the stated 'geometric' criteria, naturally affects our math so that the next possible, compliant value for 'A', the 420Hz value, naturally pops up in the results. Better mathematicians than I would be needed to shed more light on the phenomenon. Yet, the writer is 90% certain that its appearance is a mathematical artifact of the required geometric criteria for our numbers.

To be sure, the 'A' tone can be fixed. All it would require is using a 36:25 diminished 5th ratio (instead of our preferred 7:5). Unfortunately, this move rewards us by completely, obliterating any usefulness of the minor 5th position by inflating the interval between the G# and the A to a whopping 133.237ᶜ. Fortunately, by using a 27:20 ratio at the G# position we can bring the situation back into a semblance of balance. The resulting G# becomes 405Hz and restores the minor 5th position to a reasonable interval width of 111.731ᶜ, A Just semitone.

As it turns out, with the adjustment to achieve our coveted 432Hz tone, our draft D#-Major Tuning Grid falls into place with relative ease compared to the work done on the C# grid.

It works but, not without some compromise. You will notice that while several of the interval ratios are identical to the F# grid. There are three significant departures due to our geometric 'tempering' efforts.

The occasional appearance of 420Hz is also what initially lead the writer to re-visit the 'C' tuning grid just to make sure the best fit was achieved. Indeed, the 420Hz 'A' is a mathematical match there as well. But, due to other issues, it doesn't spare the 'C' tuning grid from my eternal scorn. 420Hz is just another unacceptable compromise in any of our grids. If you choose to use the C-Major Tuning Grid, consider the 420Hz a harmonically-appropriate option. But, certainly not for sonic therapy, relaxation, or healing sessions.

The main reason for these adjustments is a strange pattern within the progression of tones that initially seemed unresolvable with the basic criteria this work demands. This original pattern reveals frequencies of 300Hz, 400Hz, 500Hz, and 600Hz in the fourth octave chart. While it skips 700Hz, it continues up the octaves as 800Hz, 900Hz, 1000Hz, and 1200Hz.

The issues most apparent in the grid are with the 400Hz in the 'Perfect 4th' position as well as the 500Hz in the 'Major 6th' position. These values appear to closely mimic the more 'even-tempered' intervals, which in itself, is not a high crime. However, both of these values violate our 'numerical reduction' rule and, the 500Hz is not divisible by any of the targeted divisors. Therefore, these values needed to be re-assessed.

The closest 'valid' tone for the G# in the fourth position is 396Hz (33:25). It actually works well and meets our criteria. But, it widens the interval between the G# an the A to 150.638^{c}. The higher choice (due to our 432Hz 'A') would be 405Hz. Applying the interval ratio of 27:20 (519.512^{c}) in this situation, makes the G to G# interval a large whole-tone at 133.234^{c}. Therefore, we settle for the more reasonable interval and use the 27:20 ratio. We will label it, according to 'Just' intervals, a *Harmonic 4th*.

Likewise for the Major 6th, the original value of which was 500Hz, the closest valid value is 504Hz. Looking through the possible intervals, there is a 42:25 ratio which gives us this workable value. The original Major 6th interval width of 884.359^{c} gets raised to 898.153^{c} (504Hz) and is also a 'quasi' tone, which we will call a *'quasi Major 6th.'*

There is another option at this position; A 14:9 would give us a 506.25Hz value. However, for the adjustments required in the interval widths, this writer ultimately opted for the 504Hz value.

The first tuning chart, below, is the way the grid originally worked out with the 420Hz 'A.' This draft chart is not adopted due to the many deviations from our criteria, which have been detailed above.

The grid works out passably well for certain applications. But, can never become an accepted tuning class within our relaxation and healing tones system. The objectionable tones are indicated by bold text in the chart below. The intervals themselves are not objectionable so much as the values they yield.

Tuning Grid Based on D#-300Hz (Draft - Orphaned)

Note	Interval	Ratio	Multiplier	Frequency (Hz)	Interval from Root (¢)	Step Interval (¢)
D#	Octave	2:1	2	600.00	1200	111.731
D	Maj 7th	15:8	1.875	562.50	1088.269	119.443
C#	Lg min 7th	9:5	1.8	540.00	1017.596	133.238
C	Quasi M6th	42:25	1.68	504.00	898.153	84.467
C	**Major 6th**	**5:3**	**1.666666667**	**500.00**	**884.359**	**70.672**
B	min 6th	8:5	1.6	480.00	813.686	111.731
A#	Perf 5th	3:2	1.5	450.00	701.955	119.443
A	**sept Tritone**	**7:5**	**1.4**	**420.00**	**582.512**	**84.467**
G#	**Perf 4th**	**4:3**	**1.333333333**	**400.00**	**498.045**	**111.731**
G	M 3rd	5:4	1.25	375.00	386.314	70.672
F#	min 3rd	6:5	1.2	360.00	315.641	111.731
F	M 2nd	9:8	1.125	337.50	203.910	92.179
E	**semitone**	**16:15**	**1.066666667**	**320.00**	**111.731**	**111.73**
D#	Unison	1:1	1	300.00	—	—

Table 28.1 - Draft tuning grid based on an D# fundamental of 300Hz, showing the fourth octave including interval ratios, semi-tone step width, and full interval width. This draft is rejected for the multiple, stated reasons.

The following tuning grid chart outlines the D#-Major Tuning Grid as a 'best-fit' addition to our tuning grids — allowing for adjustments to the previously-offending tones using intervals we have already seen. It does not include the 420Hz 'A' discussed above. Instead, the diminished 5th resulting in the coveted 432Hz has been applied. Additionally, this draft grid does possess some rather interesting choices for the major tones. For example, the harmonic 4th in place of the perfect 4th is a particularly ear-catching result that it is 21¢ above the usual perfect 4th.

It is not an entirely objectionable system while at the same time, not being a particularly useful system for general music — especially when contrasted with the wonderfully balanced F#-Major tuning Grid, previously completed. But, when 'chording' with this tuning, the writer finds the tonal texture surprisingly... intriguing and mysteriously interesting. The adventurous player will find some fairly strange note combinations that should not work academically-speaking yet, actually yield interesting and colorful effects.

This writer actually enjoys this one personally, but must again concede as to its obvious defects. And, again we sing the praises of the F#-Major Tuning Grid; the one that 'just works' without compromise.

Tuning Grid Based on D#-300Hz (4th Octave)						
Note	Interval	Ratio	Multiplier	Frequency (Hz)	Interval from Root (¢)	Step Interval (¢)
D#	Octave	2:1	2	600.00	1200	111.731
D	Maj 7th	15:8	1.875	562.50	1088.269	70.672
C#	Lg min 7th	9:5	1.8	540.00	1017.596	111.731
C	Pyth. M6th	27:16	1.6875	506.25	905.865	91.179
B	min 6th	8:5	1.6	480.00	813.686	111.731
A#	Perf 5th	3:2	1.5	450.00	701.955	119.443
A	Dim 5th	36:25	1.44	432.00	631.286	111.731
G#	harmonic 4th	27:20	1.35	405.00	519.551	133.238
G	M 3rd	5:4	1.25	375.00	386.314	70.672
F#	min 3rd	6:5	1.2	360.00	315.641	111.731
F	M 2nd	9:8	1.125	337.50	203.910	98.95859
E	sm. semitone	17:16	1.0625	318.75	104.955	104.9554
D#	Unison	1:1	1	300.00	—	—

Table 28.2 - Tuning grid based on an D#3 fundamental of 300Hz, showing the fourth octave including interval ratios, semi-tone step width, and full interval width.

This D#-Major Tuning Grid reveals a surprising number of geometric tones. But, again, it cannot compare to the F#-Major system's proliferation of pure geometry in its frequency distribution.

The interval ratio acrobatics required to include the 432Hz, as well as the 540Hz tones makes this one a marginal success at-best.

The F#-based system of tones continues to be the undefeated champion of this work. No other grid thus far has worked so well 'out of the box' while retaining near-perfect playability.

Even as we apply the same methods and thesis to these other grids, they simply have not worked out as well as the venerable F#-Major Tuning Grid.

As for the theory regarding a preference for the F#-Major tone class, we definitely see some evidence of just such a preference. But, the preference evidently does not extend *equally* to all tones contained in the F#-Major tone class. We will continue to evaluate this theory as we continue with the last four draft, grid systems.

Tuning Grid Based Upon E

'E'ezy Does It Now

Our choices for the fundamental tone are 315Hz or 324Hz. The majority of our tuning grids thus far completed, suggest the 324Hz value. The C-Major and A#-Major Tuning Grids are the only two systems suggesting a 315Hz fundamental for our E Tuning Grid's fundamental.

When considering the utter disdain for the initial results in the C-Major Tuning Grid and the, earlier, documented, difficulties in constructing the A# grid, I am leaning toward 324Hz as our 'E.' Who could blame me?

To decide between these two candidates, one only needs to see the preliminary results using the now-familiar F#-Major grid's collection of ratios in action.

I look to three tones to determine the basic viability of the fundamentals; The value for the A, the C#, and the F#. When using the 315Hz value as a fundamental, the 4:3 ratio for the Perfect 4th yields 420Hz. (There it is again!) The 5:3 ratio for the Major 5th results in a value of 525Hz (262.5Hz is the next octave down) for C#.

Conversely, if we test the 324Hz fundamental against the same ratios, the A immediately pops up as 432Hz and, the C# is a perfect 540Hz. Our F# works out nicely but, not completely naturally, to a perfect 360Hz... We need to pull out a commonly-used 10:9 ratio to make that happen.

All of these are critical geometric tones. Thus, if they don't work, the draft of the grid is not able to produce basic geometric resonances and our primary objectives. (We strive to balance C$^\#$ at 540Hz and F$^\#$ at 360Hz in all of these grids. Just as we prefer the A-432Hz.)

The above comparison makes the choice a clear one. 324Hz is the fundamental tone for the tuning grid based upon 'E.'

There are other challenges to overcome however. The first of these is again the position of the first semitone, which is 'F.' We find that the 16:15 (111.731¢) interval ratio that we would prefer to use gives us a nasty result of 345.60Hz. (This is part of that same 0.2, 0.4, 0.6, 0.8 minor tone pattern previously discussed.) The digits do sum to nine. But, that decimal remainder of 0.6, cannot resolve to a whole number in higher octaves. So, we look to our backup ratio for a small halftone at 17:16 (104.955¢), for a possible solution. We then find ourselves with a tone of 344.25Hz whose digits also sum to nine. And, this decimal value resolves to 1377Hz in higher octaves.

So, apparently, we are using 17:16 for our 'F' tone in the 'minor 2nd' position. The 17:16 ratio by the way, is labeled as an *overtone half-step* or *small semitone* depending upon which table of intervals you stumble upon.

As mentioned above, we have selected the familiar 10:9 (182.404¢) over the 9:8 (203.910¢) interval to give us a geometrically-perfect 360Hz F$^\#$ in the Major 2nd position. And, just like that, we move on to the final challenge(s).

The final two issues are very similar in that they involve the Aug 4th/dim 5th (minor 5th) and Aug 5th/dim 6th (minor 6th) positions respectively. For the Aug 4th position, we would like to use 7:5 as it has performed so admirably for us in the past.

We can only arrive at the 'desired' 450Hz A$^\#$ by using the standard 'Just Augmented 4th' ratio of 25:18 (568.717¢) and, for the Aug 5th position, we likewise are compelled to use the Just Augmented 5th ratio of 25:16 (772.627¢) to obtain 506.25Hz as our 'C.'

Again, just as we saw in the D$^\#$ grid, we have a choice between 504Hz (14:9) and the above 506.25Hz. And again, the choice was made to preserve the best possible interval widths. However, in this case, the preferred tone was the 506.25Hz.

The 506.25Hz frequency reduces to nine and resolves to a whole number in higher octaves. I don't consider these intervals and tones to be compromises at all. The tones are well-balanced when playing and complement each other very nicely. That they are certainly a departure from previous results is not surprising. Quite the contrary. It makes the <u>E-Major Tuning Grid</u> a pleasure to work with. This writer only wishes that it were richer in pure-geometric tones — a feature, which is sadly lacking. The grid presents us with a smattering of the desired geometry but alas, not nearly the proliferation we have seen with *certain* other grids in this work.

However, for a tone that is not a member of the F#-Major tone class, the 324Hz 'E' has served us well. We now have another very nice, hypothesis-clarifying, tuning grid based on our theoretical work. Without further ado, I present the <u>E-Major Tuning Grid</u> for your consideration and experimental pleasure.

Note	Interval	Ratio	Multiplier	Frequency (Hz)	Interval from Root (¢)	Step Interval (¢)
E	Octave	2:1	2	648.00	1200	111.731
D#	Maj 7th	15:8	1.875	607.50	1088.269	119.443
D	min 7th	7:4	1.75	567.00	968.826	84.467
C#	Major 6th	5:3	1.666666667	540.00	884.359	111.731
C	Aug 5th	25:16	1.5625	506.25	772.627	70.672
B	Perf 5th	3:2	1.5	486.00	701.955	133.238
A#	Aug 4th	25:18	1.388888889	450.00	568.717	70.672
A	Perf 4th	4:3	1.333333333	432.00	498.045	111.731
G#	M 3rd	5:4	1.25	405.00	386.314	119.443
G	sub min 3rd	7:6	1.166666667	378.00	266.871	62.961
F#	M 2nd	10:9	1.1111111	360.00	182.404	77.448
F	sm. semitone	17:16	1.0625	344.25	104.955	104.955
E	Unison	1:1	1	324.00	—	—

Table 29.1 - Tuning grid based on an E³ fundamental of 324Hz, showing the fourth octave including interval ratios, semi-tone step width, and full interval width.

Tuning Grid Based Upon F

Watch the F-Bombs?

W e now turn our attention to our next tuning grid. This time using a fundamental foundation of 'F.' This tone happens to be a member of the F#-Major tone class (enharmonic E#). Thus, it is anticipated that it should work fairly well as a geometric tuning grid.

As is our customary procedure and, hoping for a clear consensus, we search out the best fundamental tone from among the tuning grids thus far completed.

Unsurprisingly, we find ourselves with a choice. However, since we have now completed a significant number of these tuning grids, we are able to draw from previous experience to make the best decisions with more ease and confidence.

The A, A#, C#, D#, F# grids as well as the soon to be revealed G# tuning grid, all indicate a 675Hz fundamental 'F' tone for our chart. Most of the 'white keys' (B, C, D and the not yet completed G grids) indicate 672Hz while the E tuning grid suggests 688.50Hz but, it was always an oddball anyway.

Due diligence with some preliminary work confirms this writer's initial instincts that the 675Hz (337.50Hz one octave down) value is the proper fundamental tone for this grid — based on our criteria and desired results. However, this preliminary testing did not turn out to be as clear-cut as initially expected.

To briefly explain, the 672Hz fundamental yielded a somewhat useful grid albeit with that stubborn 420Hz 'A' tone in the major 3rd position. However, using this lower fundamental tone does not tap into the 'geometric' tones in any way. Neither the coveted F$^{\#}$-360Hz nor the C$^{\#}$-540Hz are uncovered. Therefore all of those sweet geometric resonances and their harmonics were completely missing — instead leaving us with disappointing tone values of 357Hz and 528Hz respectively.

Conversely, when using the 675Hz value for our 'F' (calculating from the lower octave tone of 337.5Hz,) the magic is back. The F$^{\#}$-360Hz, C$^{\#}$-540Hz and our prized F$^{\#}$ tone series all appear organically when using some (now) very familiar interval ratios. As for the A-432Hz, a diminished 4th ratio (32:25) brings it right out for us.

It was not all rainbows and unicorns however. The major 7th required a bit of work in that we pulled a familiar 28:15 interval ratio (1080.557¢) from our back pocket to arrive at a beautiful 630.00Hz for the 'E' tone. This seems low to this writer. But, it works well in the context of this grid system.

Additionally, we have grown somewhat accustomed to the major 4th being one of the more well-mannered positions on these tuning grids. This time, it required a bit of attention in that the aforementioned 32:25 diminished 4th (427.373¢) is required to give us our desired 432.00Hz 'A' value.

For the major 2nd, a value of 378Hz was the gift of a 28:25 interval ratio, which gives us a *mid-major 2nd* (at a F to G interval width of 196.798¢.)

The resulting F-Major Tuning Grid is a relatively solid piece of work. The tonality provided is obviously quite a bit different from that of the F$^{\#}$-Major Tuning Grid against which the writer will always judge the other systems outlined in this work. This grid's qualities have me reaching for a synonym for 'quirky', which this writer realizes has been a much-used adjective in this work.

The grid itself reveals a rich assortment of pure geometric tones and some of the Platonic solids resonances in a tuning that provides a decidedly different tonal palette than that of the other grids presented.

Perhaps that is the point. After all, our thesis insists that confining music in a 440Hz, 12-TET cage is exactly what is wrong with it. Options… It's all about options. And, here is yet another.

Note	Interval	Ratio	Multiplier	Frequency (Hz)	Interval from Root (¢)	Step Interval (¢)
	Tuning Grid Based on F-337.50Hz (4th Octave)					
F	Octave	2:1	2	675.00	1200	119.443
E	Grave M 7th	28:15	1.866666667	630.00	1080.557	62.961
D#	min 7th	9:5	1.8	607.50	1017.596	133.238
D	Just Major 6th	5:3	1.666666667	562.50	884.359	70.672
C#	Just min 6th	8:5	1.6	540.00	813.686	111.731
C	Just Perf 5th	3:2	1.5	506.25	701.955	119.443
B	Aug 4th	7:5	1.4	472.50	582.512	84.467
A#	Just Perf 4th	4:3	1.333333333	450.00	498.045	70.672
A	dim 4th	32:25	1.28	432.00	427.373	111.731
G#	Just min 3rd	6:5	1.2	405.00	315.641	119.443
G	mid M 2nd	28:25	1.12	378.00	196.198	84.467
F#	Semitone	16:15	1.066666667	360.00	111.731	111.731
F	Unison	1:1	1	337.50	—	—

Table 30.1 - Tuning grid based on an F3 fundamental of 337.50Hz, showing the fourth octave including interval ratios, semi-tone step width, and full interval width.

Because our completed work on the F#-Major Tuning Grid has been extensively detailed earlier in this work, we will next skip, chromatically, to the Tuning Grid based on 'G.'

Tuning Grid Based Upon G

G-eez! Are We There Yet?

Inexplicably, your eternally-optimistic writer continues to expect that each grid calculated will become easier than previous works.

However, the G-based tuning grid proves that expectation both naive and futile. The choices for our 'G' fundamental are significantly more difficult than those preceding. And, even when making what is believed to be, the best possible choice for the fundamental tone, this grid refuses to play nice. But, as a critical part of the validation process of this work and, for the primary tuning system it promotes, all grids must be completed as a best-effort production. So, here we go.

For this G-based tuning grid, the A$^\#$ and D$^\#$ grids suggest a 375.00Hz fundamental while the A, C$^\#$, E, and F tuning grids suggest 378.00Hz. The grids based on B, D, and F point to a 'G' that is 384.00Hz while the C and (yet unrevealed) G$^\#$ grids suggest 382.50Hz. The F$^\#$ tuning system, however, concurs with a 384.00Hz value.

In preliminary testing, 375.00Hz showed early promise with the same interval ratios used in the F$^\#$-Major Tuning Grid. Unfortunately, closer examination revealed tones such as 400Hz, 500Hz, and 800Hz. (A pattern we have wrestled before) And, while it is interesting that such a progression of numbers appears, yet again, in the data blocks, they are not usable based upon our criteria. To 'fix' them in this case throws any semblance of usability, not to mention the entire thesis, out the proverbial window.

So, rather than pummel that particular deceased equine any further, we will instead, jettison the 375.00Hz fundamental value.

When testing the 378Hz fundamental 'G', the work progressed a bit further. But, the 'A' turned out to be irreparable at 420Hz. And, the C# and F# were completely off the charts. Your somewhat fatigued writer had grown accustomed to the 540Hz C# and the 360Hz F# tones, nestling fairly naturally within the pattern. This time however, they did not appear until coaxed out of the aether with some alternate, way-off-chart interval ratios. This had the overall effect of completely wrecking the relationships with the adjacent tones. Therefore, 375.00Hz doesn't appear to be our magic fundamental tone.

Warning: Compromises Ahead!

Well, it really is a universe of compromise. The trick is to find those compromise(s) that you can live with. And, while for the writer, this is not necessarily one of them, I feel it is my responsibility to point out that it is one that others may be perfectly happy with. The spoiler here is that a perfectly harmonic G-Major Tuning Grid can be produced using our basic criteria. But, the best result does not produce a *purely* geometric tuning grid. Instead, we find ourselves having the following discussion:

In many of the preliminary grids that were prepared for this research and, some discussed in previous sections, the writer repeatedly encountered a strange numerical phenomenon in the 'minor' tones of several preliminary grids. In these cases, the Major scale tones would settle nicely into the usual math (generally derived from the F#-Major Tuning Grid). However, the minor tones would display decimal remainders in a fixed pattern of 0.2, 0.4, 0.6, and 0.8.

> To be specific; By 'minor tones' in this context, we are speaking of the first semitone above the fundamental (minor 2nd) as well as the minor 3rd, Aug 4th/dim 5th, minor 6th, and the minor 7th.

As irritating as the numerical issue eventually became, these grids were musically harmonic — although the minor tone values revealed could never meet the stated criteria of the geometric systems. Additionally, accepting these tones eliminated any possibility of pure geometric resonances resulting in the minor tones' or their harmonic series.

But, again, the tones themselves actually play very well in this odd-ball configuration.

The two 'bad-boy' grids thus far proving to be non-compliant with the geometric-grid criteria are 'C' and now, the 'G.' The writer asserts that this cannot be simple coincidence. 'C' and 'G' comprise the diatonic *perfect fifth*. Arguably, the first harmonies that are discovered by beginners noodling at a keyboard. The C-E-G, C-Major triad is about as universal as it gets for beginners.

And, guess what? The other grid that turned out to be a rebel was, in fact, the <u>E-Major Tuning Grid</u> — Although it did eventually turn out to be a fairly-workable system, it also displayed this strange numerical pattern. These non-F#-Major, diatonic fundamentals seem to share some common quality that makes them stubbornly non-compliant with our geometric system. But, it appears that adapting the system to allow for these minor-tone anomalies, actually permits harmonious systems to be created. Again, within this system, there seems to exist a preference for the F#-Major tone class. Perhaps the math of geometry doesn't extend equally to tone classes other than F#-Major.

The reader will see this particular theory come to life when we again, break all-reasonable convention and, begin 'messing around' with the sacrosanct, Solfeggio tonal system in *Chapter 33 - The Solfeggio Tonal System.*

At any rate, the 'C' note and the diatonic key of C-Major, are designations that have been the default starting point for teaching music since the lettering system was first established. And, while the significance of the above-described numerical phenomenon is unclear, the fact that it does exist is unavoidable.

When we look ahead a bit to *Chapter 33 - The Solfeggio Tonal System,* this phenomenon is present in every one of the resulting grids, except one. And, they too are eminently playable and very harmonic. But, the 'minor' tone designations do not comply with geometric resonances as we have defined them, in this text.

In fact, with the exception of a Super Major 2nd at the 'A' position (8:7 and 231.174$^{¢}$), the <u>G-Major Tuning Grid</u> also works out beautifully *if* one allows for the numerically odd-ball minor tones (which the writer certainly does *not* in the present F#, geometry-centric context).

It seems that, for whatever reason, in these particular non-F#-Major grids, the fundamental notes, being complete 'outsiders' with reference to the F#-Major tone class; their minor tones simply do not comply with the geometric criteria as developed in this text. In fact, every effort to wrestle the values into compliance results in a completely broken harmonic relationship with other tones.

However, our target in every grid developed in this work, has always been focused on the major scale tones. They are the true 'gold' within the geometric systems. And, the gold mine itself, remains the F#-Major Tuning Grid, previously detailed. That system provides results, which supply a completely playable scale system that was the initial and, remains the ultimate objective of this text. However, there was no way to predict a mathematical preference for a certain tone class until it was demonstrated in the subsequent tuning system designs.

It is true that minor tones have given us a fair yield of geometric tones in the past. But, the major tones have always been where the action is concentrated. Apparently, minor tone tuning has always proved to be a special challenge to musicians engaged in creating alternate tuning systems. So, our geometric system is in good company in being no exception to that general observation.

In an effort to demonstrate to the kind reader what is happening here, The G-378Hz grid is presented in *Table 31.1* — as it appears when using the standard, 'expected' intervals derived from the F#-Major grid.

The only deviation from the 'standard' intervals, is in the super-Major 2nd (8:7) tapped to achieve 432Hz as our 'A' or I suppose one could even tap the 10:9 ratio which gives us a better interval width, and results in the familiar, if somewhat obnoxious, 420Hz value. The resulting tuning grid is presented on the facing page as *Table 31.1*.

So, here we are presented with… A beautifully melodic system by any account. One that is nicely balanced and even somewhat 'geometric' in the Major mode. But, it is a system where every minor interval reveals a pesky non-resolving, non-geometric decimal remainder in the pattern of .20, .40, .60, or .80 in the resulting frequencies.

Note	Interval	Ratio	Multiplier	Frequency (Hz)	Interval from Root (¢)	Step Interval (¢)
Tuning Grid Based on G-378.00Hz (Draft A – decimal pattern in the minor tones)						
G	Octave	2:1	2	756.00	1200	111.731
F#	Just M7th	15:8	1.875	708.75	1088.269	70.672
F	Classic m7th	9:5	1.8	680.40	1017.596	133.238
E	Just M 6th	5:3	1.666666667	630.00	884.359	70.672
D#	Just m6th	8:5	1.6	604.80	813.686	111.731
D	Just Perf 5th	3:2	1.5	567.00	701.955	119.443
C#	Aug 4th	7:5	1.4	529.20	582.512	84.467
C	Just Perf 4th	4:3	1.333333333	504.00	498.045	111.731
B	Just Maj 3rd	5:4	1.25	472.50	386.314	70.672
A#	Just min 3rd	6:5	1.2	453.60	315.641	84.467
A	Sup M 2nd	8:7	1.142857143	432.00	231.174	119.443
*A	Whole Tone	10:9	1.111111111	420.00	182.404	40.672
G#	Just Semi	16:15	1.066666667	403.20	111.731	111.731
G	Unison	1:1	1	378.00	—	—

Table 31.1 - Draft A Tuning grid based on an G³ fundamental of 378.00Hz with a curious and repetitive remainder pattern in the minor degrees.

I cannot help but to be fascinated by the phenomenon, which has been encountered several times in the prepared grids; especially those possessing fundamentals that are not part of the F#-Major tone class.

Yet, at the same time, these tones are completely unacceptable to the developed criteria of our geometric tuning systems. Their presence actually 'blocks' certain geometric frequencies from appearing at all, which dilutes the perceived, theoretical effectiveness of the tuning as a whole.

That this effect is a simple mathematical artifact is obvious. But, it certainly makes life a bit more interesting for our geometric tuning system design.

To adjust for these apparent discrepancies and, still allow a playable minor tone series, requires a literal handful of off-the-chart interval ratios as demonstrated in this 'Draft B' grid for the fundamental of 'G.' None of them seem to improve the grid's harmonic balance to any extent. And, all of them compromise the physical playability of the system using standard keyboard patterns. But, in the grand scheme, it's what we are left with when attempting 'G-378' as our fundamental tone.

What's the deal those minor tone remainders anyway?

To be sure, the G-Major Tuning Grid is usable. Of course, the Major tones are very balanced using the Just Intonation ratios. The addition of Super Major 2nd and Acute major 7th being the obvious exceptions to normality.

But, again, why would one choose such a challenging system to work

Tuning Grid Based on G-378.00Hz (Draft B – decimal pattern adjusted out)						
Note	Interval	Ratio	Multiplier	Frequency (Hz)	Interval from Root (¢)	Step Interval (¢)
G	Octave	2:1	2	756.00	1200	111.731
F$^{\#}$	Acute Maj 7th	40:21	1.9047619	720.00	1115.533	146.707
F	Acute Maj 7th	14:8	1.75	661.50	968.826	84.467
E	Just Maj 6th	5:3	1.666666667	630.00	884.359	101.867
D$^{\#}$	Sub m 6th	11:7	1.571428571	594.00	782.492	80.537
D	Just Perf 5th	3:2	1.5	567.00	701.955	84.467
C$^{\#}$	dim 5th	10:7	1.428571429	540.00	617.488	119.443
C	Just Perf 4th	4:3	1.333333333	504.00	498.045	111.731
B	Just Maj 3rd	5:4	1.25	472.50	386.314	119.443
A$^{\#}$	Sub min 3rd	7:6	1.166666667	441.00	266.871	35.697
A	Sup Maj 2nd	8:7	1.142857143	432.00	231.174	126.219
G$^{\#}$	Sm. Semitone	17:16	1.0625	401.625	104.955	104.956
G	Unison	1:1	1	378.00	—	—

Table 31.2 - Draft B Tuning grid based on an G^3 fundamental of 378.00Hz with the repetitive remainder pattern adjusted out using some familiar and a couple of off-chart intervals.

with when we have the amazing F$^{\#}$-Major Tuning Grid available to us. There is little in the way of additional geometry naturally-appearing in this system. Even the C$^{\#}$ and F$^{\#}$ tones are coerced into geometric compliance.

Having made every effort to resolve the issues with the G-378Hz fundamental, the best possible solution is applicable to the Major scale tones only, which again, work well. The minor tones are the real glitch in the system. And, despite our valiant efforts, it just doesn't work with this fundamental tone.

As you can see, this system has but, few redeeming qualities. The 'A' initially turns out to be 420Hz but can be adjusted to 432Hz with the 8:7 interval ratio. And, the all-so-important C$^{\#}$ and F$^{\#}$ are both cobbled into the rest with some barely-acceptable interval relationships as a sour reward.

Even for one such as myself who is completely unconcerned with the constraints of temperament, this one appears to be destined for the rubbish bin. I have included it both as an interesting study on the over-arching importance of the correct fundamental-to-interval relationships in creating these systems — as well as another 'exception that proves the rule' that the F#-Major Tuning Grid is both special and perfect as an example of perfect *geometric temperament*.

What we have learned is that;

1. With fundamentals present in the F#-Major tone class, Major tones are very compliant with our geometric constraints.
2. With fundamentals present in the F#-Major tone class, minor tones are *generally* very compliant with geometric constraints.
3. With fundamentals that are not members of the F#-Major tone class, minor tones are generally non-compliant with our geometric constraints.

And...

4. The F#-Major Tuning Grid is (hands-down) the most elegant, harmonically balanced, and playable grid thus far produced by our geometric criteria.

Moving on to a fundamental of 382.50Hz reveals more disappointment. There appears no 432.00Hz or even 420.00Hz in this one. There are no geometric correlations in any of the tones produced using our tried and true intervals.

This draft system has quickly earned its place in the growing dumpster fire that is the G-Major Tuning Grid. This writer will not even justify its existence by including the draft grid.

Our lone, last candidate is 384.00Hz. Keep in mind that the G-384Hz value is derived from the F#-Major Tuning Grid. Fortunately, this tone works as our fundamental 'G' tone… with a bit of help from the math.

The primary issue with this fundamental is that it leaves us a 4:3, Perfect 4th of 512.00Hz. This value seems perfectly fine at first glance.

But, it unfortunately reduces to eight and is therefore unacceptable by our criteria.

Compounding this problem, is the realization that the 'proper' value should be 513.00Hz — a mere 1.0Hz away. The ratio 171:128 (501.423¢) is a valid though off-chart interval for our system. Additionally, the ratio is *far* removed from the set of previously utilized Just ratios, which have provided the backbone of the system design. The resulting tone is simply labeled as a 'harmonic' tone. And, while it meets all criteria for a valid tone in our geometric system, it stretches the interval between the Major 3rd and (what was) the Perfect 4th to 115.11¢. This is not, by itself, a stake in the heart.

But, the hits keep coming. We eventually wind up with a *marginally* acceptable tuning grid based on the 384Hz 'G' fundamental. This writer will never make the claim that it is pretty or even particularly orderly. The chart is included as 'Draft C' in *Table 31.3*.

After a long run of reasonable successes, Your mild-mannered writer confesses that this G-Major Tuning Grid is very limited and incompatible with the strict geometric criteria that have been applied.

This particular (Draft C) tuning grid is further confirmation that not all our fundamental tones will conform to our twelve-tone geometric tweaking methods. The only previous system to so-completely disappoint in this regard was the C-Major Tuning Grid. And, just like the that horridly un-harmonic tuning, it will remain orphaned until perhaps an alternative solution reveals itself.

Table 31.3 is the G-Major Tuning Grid (alternate draft), based on 384Hz, in its current, imperfect form. While it is not quite as repulsive as the other 'G' grid variants, it still is not something anyone would consider 'playable' or even useful. Of course, geometric frequencies are revealed in this system. But, again, the main geometric series consisting of 360Hz, 540Hz… etc. utilize off-chart ratios and are therefore forced into an unholy alliance of off-chart-tonality.

In point of fact, the 'Draft A' tuning grid found in *Table 31.1* (above) is by far the more playable G-based grid. That its minor tones possess a strangely interesting pattern of non-conforming decimal remainders is an uncomfortable issue that renders the system incompatible with the goals of this text.

But, it is a mathematical phenomenon that we will see again in our further explorations. Therefore, it is necessarily included in our current study.

Note	Interval	Ratio	Multiplier	Frequency (Hz)	Interval from Root (¢)	Step Interval (¢)
G	Octave	2:1	2	768.00	1200	111.731
F#	Grave M7th	15:8	1.875	720.00	1088.269	119.443
F	Sub min 7th	14:8	1.75	672.00	968.826	62.961
E	Pyth M6th	27:16	1.6875	648.00	905.865	65.337
D#	Aug 5th	25:16	1.5625	600.00	772.627	70.672
D	Just Perf 5th	3:2	1.5	576.00	701.955	111.731
C#	Diat. Tritone	45:32	1.40625	540.00	590.224	88.800
C	harmonic	171:128	1.3359375	513.00	501.423	115.109
B	Just Maj 3rd	5:4	1.25	480.00	386.314	111.731
A#	dim m3rd	75:64	1.171875	450.00	274.582	70.672
A	M 2nd	9:8	1.125	432.00	203.910	98.955
G#	sm. Half step	17:16	1.0625	408.00	104.955	104.955
G	Unison	1:1	1	384.00	—	—

Title row above table: **Tuning Grid Based on G-378.00Hz (Draft C - Orphaned)**

Table 31.3 - Draft C (best effort) Tuning grid based on an G³ fundamental of 384.00Hz adjusted using some familiar and a few of off-chart intervals.

Additionally, the major tones of the 'Draft A' grid are well-balanced and eminently usable. As always, the minor degrees seem to be the source of most of our headaches when working with these picky, twelve-tone systems.

32

Tuning Grid Based Upon G#
'G'ee! I'm Running Out of Puns!

This researcher has now been thrice-bloodied in his quest to validate a novel thesis of the close relationship between geometry and healing tones. But, out of eleven fundamentals (so far), we have created eight useful and harmonic tuning grids. One could consider the whole experiment a rousing success if referring only to the <u>F# Major Tuning Grid</u>.

The C-based and G-based grid systems proved that there is no room for the weak-of-will in this project. The 'E' grid, although workable, is quite challenging to utilize and is therefore, counted among these failed systems. So far, the C, E, and G grids have been, each to varying degrees, radical non-conformists to our geometric system's tweaking methods. But, eight of our tuning grids have thus far, worked out well to *varying degrees*, as each possess certain qualities of balance, harmonious tones and usefulness.

Ironically, the C-E-G triad is probably the most familiar diatonic structure in western music. None of these notes, however, are part of the F#-Major tone class. There seems to be the underlying basis for the myriad issues encountered with the grids' design

I suspect that an imaginative mathematician will one day see a way to unify these tones with the other grids. But, we have the several very nice tuning grids, which are perfectly playable and contain tons of geometric tones and platonic resonances to solidify the thesis of this work.

Primary among the grids is the F#-Major Tuning Grid, which in addition to being quite useful, harmonious and compatible with standard keyboard layout, is also exceedingly rich in the very geometric resonances that this researcher was seeking for use in relaxation, meditation, and healing applications.

Additionally, other grids constructed on fundamentals that are part of the F#-Major tone class, have worked out *fairly* well using the geometric criteria and system of design. But, again, none work out nearly as well as the F#-Major Tuning Grid system.

But, we are not quite done yet. The G# fundamental remains to be explored. And, G# is definitely part of the F#-Major tone class. So, we face this final challenge with something akin to wide-eyed optimism.

In the face of the issues with the rebellious fundamentals (C, E, and G), it is a great comfort, validation, and relief to end on a high note with the G#-Major Tuning Grid.

Yes, I am the king of 'spoilers.' The G#-Major Tuning Grid returns us to the good graces of the universe. It works out very well with interval ratios that have best carried us the whole way on this journey of discovery, towards a truly rich, diverse, and harmonic set of tuning systems for relaxation and healing music.

Although previous systems present a few options for the fundamental tone, there really is no other choice but 405Hz for the G# fundamental tone. It is found in *all* of our 'known good' tuning grids. The more problematic grids suggest values of 408Hz or even that strange little 420Hz. At this point, we all know where the good tones come from. And, that is from grids associated with the F#-Major Tuning Grid system and the F#-Major Tone class.

Proceeding as each time before, we calculate the G# grid using 405Hz as our chosen, fundamental tone. Immediately upon inserting the list of interval ratios from the F#-Major system, nearly every value simply falls, perfectly into place.

Only one of the intervals need to be tweaked with a now-familiar ratio. That ratio is the minor 7th position, now labeled as a 'small minor 7th.'

This adjustment was necessary to pull out the geometric series associated with F# (i.e. the 360Hz, and 720Hz). Thus, we tapped the familiar 16:9 ratio in that position, which gives us a perfect 720Hz at 996.090¢ above the fundamental.

The end result is an eminently-playable tuning grid system, not so unlike the F#-Major system, where every tone value reduces to nine and all decimal-remainder frequencies (there are four in this octave) ultimately resolve to whole numbers in the higher octaves. Two of our gridded frequencies resolve in very high octaves indeed. The 'G' resolves to 6075Hz and the 'A#' to 3645Hz.

And, with these systems, we now have all the geometric tones we would ever need for perfect relaxation and healing sessions.

Note	Interval	Ratio	Multiplier	Frequency (Hz)	Interval from Root (¢)	Step Interval (¢)
G#	Octave	2:1	2	810.00	1200	111.731
G	M 7th	15:8	1.875	759.375	1088.269	92.179
F#	small m 7th	16:9	1.777777778	720.00	996.090	111.731
F	M 6th	5:3	1.666666667	675.00	884.359	70.672
E	m 6th	8:5	1.6	648.00	813.686	111.731
D#	Perf 5th	3:2	1.5	607.50	701.955	119.443
D	m 5th	7:5	1.4	567.00	582.512	84.467
C#	Perf 4th	4:3	1.333333333	540.00	498.045	111.731
C	M 3rd	5:4	1.25	506.25	386.314	70.672
B	m 3rd	6:5	1.2	486.00	315.641	111.731
A#	M 2nd	9:8	1.125	455.625	203.910	92.179
A	Semitone	16:15	1.066666667	432.00	111.731	111.731
G#	Unison	1:1	1	405.00	—	—

Tuning Grid Based on G#-405.00Hz (5th Octave)

Table 32.1 - Draft G# Tuning grid based on an G#4 fundamental of 405.00Hz and displaying the fifth octave.

Here we have it! The eminently playable, <u>G#-Major Tuning Grid</u>:

The <u>G#-Major Tuning Grid</u> is a perfect way to end this experiment on a 'high note.' The major points of our thesis have been well-validated and documented; if perhaps, adjusted to account for an observed preference for the F# tone class.

All of the resulting data has been presented in its totality (warts-and-all). The successful results, if somewhat tempered by certain unexpected complications and discoveries, have proven to be nothing short of spectacularly validating with regards to the stated objective.

With the conclusion of our experimentations and discoveries, we will now address some of the loose ends. Certain phenomena we have encountered have raised questions that need to be explored and answered, if at all possible.

One of this writer's unanswered questions is "What the heck is with the decimal remainder series of 0.2, 0.4, 0.6 and 0.8 in many of the draft versions of these tuning grids?"

Well, we may never have a perfect answer for the question itself. But, I have definitely determined a system in which we can certainly take advantage of the phenomena, for the greater good.

You are invited to join your long-winded writer for an exploration of existing systems of sound and frequency healing theory.

We will gently apply some of our geometric theories to these systems while attempting to learn more about their bases, origins, and applications.

Our first stop on this side-quest is; The Solfeggio series of tones.

The Solfeggio Tonal System
Buckle Up and Settle In. This Will Take a While

In the amazing world of sound and frequency healing, any practitioner that's been around for any time at all will have some recognition of, and familiarity with the class of tones known by the moniker of 'Solfeggio' tones. Six of these tones are considered 'original', while three latter-day additions to the series are the so-called 're-discovered' tones.

Solfeggio tones (often, somewhat erroneously, referred to as the Solfeggio scale), are arranged in three 'sets' of tones which utilize a skein (a sequential numerical pattern in which the result of one calculation is inserted back into the original math) associated with the number 111 and additionally, creating tones that correspond to the 'reduction to 3, 6, 9' theoretical model.

The skein as it applies to the Solfeggio series could be illustrated as:

$$\text{freq}_a + 111 = \text{freq}_b \text{ ... then re-assign freq}_a = \text{freq}_b$$
... repeat

The skein itself is reminiscent of the mathematical structure of fractal forms. The math of a fractal construct also reassigns a mathematical result into a subsequent iteration of the initial formula. This is the over-arching reason why the writer's attention was initially drawn to the Solfeggio series of tones, as their structure closely reflects the theoretical, holographic, fractal structure of the known universe.

The following table lays out the Solfeggio tones, the skein by which they are apparently structured, as well as the traditional applications.

Also, notice that harmonic information is included for each tone. The reasons for this will soon become apparent.

The tones are arranged, for convenience, into three series, which are imaginatively indicated as series 'A', 'B', or 'C.' The *original* six tones are thought to have originated with a Benedictine monk by the name of Guido d'Arezzo in the 11th century.

Frequency	Numerical Reduction	Therapeutic Application(s)	Noted Skein
Series A		**Pain Relief, Grounding & Negative Energy Release**	
* 174Hz	3	Pain management and anesthetic	—
* 285Hz	6	Wound healing and restoration	Equal to 174 + 111
396Hz	9	Liberation from fear and guilt	Equal to 285 + 111
Series B		**Change, Repair, Transformation, & Heart Connections**	
417Hz	3	Release the Past, Initiates Positive Change	—
528Hz	6	Transformation, Healing, Miracles, DNA	Equal to 417 + 111
639Hz	9	Personal Connections & Relationships	Equal to 528 + 111
Series C		**Awakening, Intuition, Transcendence, & Ascendence**	
741Hz	3	Expressing Solutions, Opening, Sharing	—
852Hz	6	Achieving/Return to Spiritual Order	Equal to 741 + 111
* 963Hz	9	Awakening, Transcendence, Ascendence	Equal to 852 + 111

*Indicate 'rediscovered' Solfeggio tones per Drs. Leonard Horowitz and Joseph Puleo, <u>Healing Codes for the Biological Apocalypse</u>, Along with the commonly-purported esoteric application(s) for each.

Table 33.1 - The nine canonical tones of the Solfeggio tonal system with numerical reduction, generally-accepted therapeutic application and numerical skein data.

Brother d'Arezzo was working to devise a method for teaching the melodies and the very few required harmonies to monastic musicians of the period.

One of these ingenious methods made use of what is called the 'Guidonian Hand' (*Fig 33.1*) in which specific notes were associated with the finger joints and tips of each finger. A choir leader only had to indicate a location on his hand in order to instruct the choir members on which note or harmony to vocalize.

Brother Guido's original musical notations, which he also developed as part of his teaching program, were based upon the six original Solfeggio tones and labeled 'UT, RE, MI, FA, SOL, and LA.'

These syllables were adapted from the first syllables of each pseudo-line of the "*Hymn to Saint John the Baptist*" This very popular Benedictine hymn of the period, was itself, adapted from an even more ancient work written by the 8th century Roman poet, Horace.

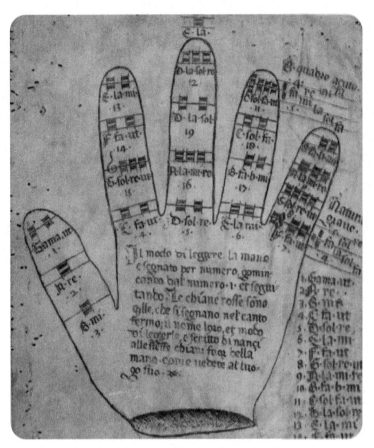

Fig. 33.1 - The Guidonian hand mnemonic device as it appears on an ancient Benedictine manuscript.

The moniker of 'Solfeggio' was given to d'Arrezio's method for teaching and notating pitch in monastic music. Later, the syllable 'UT' in Guido's system became 'DO.' Eventually, adding upon the original system, the modern diatonic scale adopted the typical 'DO, RE, MI...' teaching method, which is still used to this day.

The six original tones, of monastic music and taught by Brother d'Arrezio became what we know today, as the Solfeggio series of tones.

Whether the modern understanding of the exact frequencies are the same as those used in the 11th century remains open to some debate.

The original Solfeggio tones form the basis for those hauntingly-intoned Gregorian chants, which became the staple of monastic music practice for hundreds of years. It is postulated that the musical use of the original six tones was mysteriously discontinued or was simply 'lost' at some point during the tumultuous Middle Ages of civilization.

The six original Solfeggio tones received some much-needed, independent validation in the 1970's with the publication of the book; *__Healing codes for the Biological Apocalypse__* by Dr. Leonard Horowitz in collaboration with Dr. Joseph Puleo. The text itself, is no longer in print and, physical copies can only be acquired at great cost from used book sellers.

However, as the story goes, Dr. Puleo was inspired to utilize some Pythagorean mystery math, which according to the story, revealed a series of codes purportedly concealed in the scriptural book of Numbers; part of the Torah and the biblical Pentateuch. (The research was derived primarily from *Numbers 7:12-83*)

These 'hidden' codes, identified by Puleo and Horowitz, are purported to possess a strong correlation with the original six original Solfeggio tones. For any who wish to dive deeper into this trek of discovery, the text is available in electronic book format at a much reduced cost. However, at the time of this writing, the abysmal quality of the available digital copies in the Portable Document Format (PDF), render them essentially unreadable.

In addition to the original six tones, three other frequencies were reportedly discovered through this 'de-coding' work. Common lore suggests these 'new' tones, 174Hz, 285Hz, and 963Hz are not part of the original Solfeggio series but, were discovered in modern times by the extended work of Dr. Joseph Puleo in his collaboration with Dr. Leonard Horowitz.

In more recent times, there have appeared some adventurous practitioners that throw the 432Hz tone in with the Solfeggio series. This writer offers no judgment as to being right, wrong, good, or bad. Yet, ...432Hz is also, *not technically* a part of the Solfeggio series of tones. It is more properly considered part of the *'Natural'* series of tones which we will reveal (but, will not be discussing in any real depth) later in this chapter.

The Solfeggio tones do not construct, nor do they inform a commonly recognizable scale. Consequently, they relate directly to no common use tuning standard or system. At best, they may constitute a series of significant harmonic intervals based upon some variation of the Pythagorean systems. As such, their actual derivations are quite the mystery.

However, it should be noted that many practitioners acknowledge some strong correlations to Just Intonation that are present in the tonal series. Some go so far as to (mistakenly) dub the Solfeggio series of tones as 'Just Intonation' itself despite the fact that none of the tones form a single interval which could be identified as anything more than 'harmonics in series.'

Arguments could be made on both points. However, for now we will proceed on the basic assumption that; Solfeggio and Just Intonation are two, possibly related but, entirely separate entities.

Whatever the case may be, various customary, therapeutic usages for the Solfeggio series (indicated in *Table 33.1.* above) can serve us as a guide toward a tonal series of equal or superior value within the relaxation and healing systems already discovered in this work.

What is proposed is an integrative system which can act as a kind of musical bridge between the Solfeggio tones and our healing tone tuning systems. One that allows us to dig more deeply into the intent of those who originated such an arcane system in the first place. While this proposal is based entirely upon theory, It is the writer's hope that you, the kind reader and practitioner, may find the hypothesis at least sufficiently compelling to explore.

To construct such an integrative system based on the Solfeggio series, we must first seek out any correlations, commonalities or other 'hooks' that these tones may have to playable scales and the pertinent mathematics of geometry. We can thereafter explore the tonal possibilities inherent in the Solfeggio series as they may (or may not) apply to our extended tuning theory.

Exploration:

Each series of Solfeggio tones is constructed in such a way that the digits 1 through 9 are orderly arranged in a specific sequence within the columns of each series. For example, when looking at the Series A, notice that the first column contains the 1, 2, and 3. The third column is 4, 5, and 6 while the middle column is comprised of 7, 8, and 9.

The number sequence of 1-3 begins with the first column in the first series, the second column in the second series, and the third column in the third series. Basically, each column moves one position to the 'right' in each successive series with the last column in any series becoming the first column of the next. This understanding means that you only need to remember one number, 174, in order to reconstruct the entire series. That's easy enough. Right?

This little memory device is exactly how this writer memorized the Solfeggio series when first studying them long ago. And, while it is a somewhat unique pattern, it never dawned on this writer to question the explicit order until the conceptual and historical significance of '3, 6, 9' progressions and reductions rose to my awareness through the research for the several relaxation and healing tuning grids previously outlined in this text.

Digging Deeper:

The first tone in each series always contains the numbers 1, 4, and 7. Therefore the first tones of each series are 174, 417, and 741 respectively. Again, the last number in one tone becomes the first digit of the next series' initial tone.

When considering the intervals between each series' three tones, we learn only a bit more about this simple sequence of frequencies.

Continuing this basic exploration with the second and third series of Solfeggio tones reveals an identical pattern that carries throughout the system.

The second tone in each series always contains the digits 2, 5, and 8 while the third number in the series uses the 3, 6, and 9. The second and third tones are, as before, derived by the addition of '111' to the previous tone. The origin of the first tone of each series continues to present a bit of a mystery.

Series A	Pain Relief, Grounding & Negative Energy Release
174Hz → 285Hz	A difference of 111Hz & Interval width of 854.250$^\mathfrak{c}$ (inharmonic tone)
285Hz → 396Hz	A difference of 111Hz & Interval width of 569.446$^\mathfrak{c}$ (89th Harmonic)
174Hz → 396Hz	Interval width of 1423.696$^\mathfrak{c}$ (inharmonic tone)

Table 33.2 - Solfeggio tones of Series A. note that 174 + 111 =285 and 285 + 111 = 396

Notice the skein in the above tones... For example:

$$174 + 111 = 285 \text{ and } 285 + 111 = 396$$

There is a basic skein associated with each of the Solfeggio series; one in which '111' is added to each tone in order to arrive at the next tone in that series. Therefore, the interval is not measured in cents, but in *actual Hertz* (cycles per second). This is an amazing feat for an 11th century monk; Don't you think?

Again, it seems we are missing a common denominator, a common fundamental tone to tie them all together.

Series B	Change, Repair, Transformation, & Heart Connections
417Hz → 528Hz	A difference of 111Hz & Interval width of 408.589$^\mathfrak{c}$ (inharmonic tone)
528Hz → 639Hz	A difference of 111Hz & Interval width of 330.333$^\mathfrak{c}$ (155th Harmonic)
417Hz → 639Hz	Interval width of 738.922$^\mathfrak{c}$ (inharmonic tone)

Table 33.3 - Solfeggio tones of Series B. Note that 417 + 111 = 528 and 528 + 111 = 639

Series C	Awakening, Intuition, Transcendence, & Ascendence
741Hz → 528Hz	A difference of 111Hz & Interval width of 241.656$^\mathfrak{c}$ (inharmonic tone)
852Hz → 963Hz	A difference of 111Hz & Interval width of 212.020$^\mathfrak{c}$ (144th Harmonic)
741Hz → 963Hz	Interval width of 453.675$^\mathfrak{c}$ (inharmonic tone)

Table 33.4 - Solfeggio tones of Series C. Note that 741 + 111 = 852 and 852 + 111 = 963

What do we learn from this exercise?

Only that none of the calculated interval-width values suggest a connection to any common tonal progressions And, in fact, form no readily recognizable musical harmonies (intervals,) even in the Just Intonation or Mean Tone systems.

There seems to exist no fundamental basis for any connection between these tones outside of the skein related to '111.' No common origin story, if you will. And, after all this work, we are still no closer to reliably determining the actual natural or mathematical origins of the tones in each series based on any of the identified math.

We will therefore shift focus and take a brief few pages to explore some of the commonly purported origins of the Solfeggio series too see if anything holds up to scrutiny.

All practitioners need to have an answer to the clients' inevitable question(s); "What is the basis for these tones?", "What are they supposed to do for me?", or "Where do these tones come from?" The honest answer that my clients have thus far received is "No one really knows for sure."

However, there are some practitioners out there (like your writer, for instance) for whom that answer is wholly unsatisfactory. What follows are a few of the erroneous answers which have been commonly promulgated regarding the origins of these tones. We will also explore the reasoning behind exactly why the more commonly-used explanations are incorrect.

We may not learn much that is new but, we can certainly make pointed observations. For instance; Why is the middle tone in each series a clearly identifiable harmonic while the first and third tones appear to be completely off-the-charts, *unidentified inharmonic* intervals?

There is a deeper pattern here. But, again; We need to understand the basis or attempt to determine the fundamental for the series before any real conclusions can emerge. And, so far, the Solfeggio series are not giving up those particular secrets.

Schumann Resonance:

There does exist a common trope that the originators of this system are said to have somehow, based them on earth's Schumann resonances.

Could these tones somehow reflect the harmonics of the average Schumann resonance? If so, what is the Schumann resonance frequency upon which such basis was formed? And, more importantly; What the heck is a Schumann resonance anyway? Let's start with that last question as it is the easiest to answer.

What the heck is Schumann resonance anyway?

Schumann resonance(s) are naturally-occurring atmospheric and electromagnetic standing waves that occur due to the weather (lightning, wind, rain, etc.) as well as from human activity (war, demolitions and other explosive human acts in particular.) These oscillatory pressure waves propagate throughout the atmospheric region between the planet's surface and the ionospheric boundaries, which region acts as a natural, physical 'wave-guide.'

The phenomenon was first postulated by Winfried Otto Schumann circa 1952 and later verified by physicists; once sufficiently-sensitive equipment was available. The timing of the Solfeggio origins in the 11th century CE, are the first clue that the discovery of these Schumann resonances in 1952 is unlikely to have been the source of inspiration for Solfeggio series tones. Yet, we continue.

These Schumann oscillations are verifiable and regularly monitored by specialized reporting stations, which are primarily operated by governmental organizations (Such as NASA, ESA, USGS, Japan's JMA and others) and are located around the globe. Therefore, the phenomenon known as Schumann Resonance is an actual, verified atmospheric effect.

Nevertheless, there are at least, two significant problems with the Solfeggio-Schumann correlation theory.

The first of these problems is that the Schumann resonance is not fixed and therefore varies widely over time. A quick look at any of the reporting station data for atmospheric resonance (NASA, ESA, USGS, JMA), reveals harmonics and primary oscillations as low as 5Hz and as resonance waves as high as 45Hz, with other harmonics rising both below and beyond.

Therefore, *if* the Solfeggio frequencies are indeed 'harmonics' of the Schumann resonance, what base frequency would one propose be used to calculate the tones? There are literally thousands of choices of which none hold any more significance than any other.

The second problem with the Schumann resonance correlation theory is that none of the customarily utilized 'average' frequencies, for Schumann resonance, possess subharmonics of the values indicated by the Solfeggio tones themselves. This can easily be verified by doing the very simple math on each tone to 'reverse-engineer' the sub-harmonic charts for each tone — which should help determine the 'fundamental' upon which the actual tone series is based. This brings us right back to our first and second questions:

Could Solfeggio tones somehow reflect the harmonics of the average Schumann resonance?

And… If so, what is the Schumann resonance frequency upon which such basis was formed?

The commonly held idea (in some holistic circles) that the vibrational frequency of the Earth itself is 7.83Hz (The commonly cited Schumann tone) is demonstrably false. This confusion arises from a lack of understanding of the difference between atmospheric and geologic phenomena. After all, most of us don't hold degrees in earth sciences.

Schumann resonances are exclusively, an atmospheric phenomenon; being measured as atmospheric disturbances (pressure waves) although usually observed and measured at surface level.

The frequency of the Earth itself is an altogether different phenomenon and arises from the movements of crustal, mantle and molten core materials, which creates electromagnetic waves including the electromagnetic shields surrounding our planet and which protect the Earth from cosmic radiation.

While the Earth's ever-changing, electromagnetic frequency does affect the Schumann resonance to some degree, the assumption that the converse is also true, is not verifiable.

Therefore the entire, common misconception that directly correlates global resonance (electromagnetic) and Schumann resonance (atmospheric pressure wave) is simply not supported by the available scientific facts.

If the entire series is based upon a single (Schumann resonance) reference tone, then the fundamental tone should be a common sub-harmonic to each of the Solfeggio frequencies.

Alas, no such common fundamental frequency appears in the harmonic math.

To further explain how to work out the sub-harmonics, let's consider the F#-Major Tuning Grid taken from our previous work. The F# fundamental tone upon which we based that tuning grid is 360Hz. The lower (sub)harmonics of 360Hz are derived by simple division. To illustrate, in *Table 33.4* below, we illustrate the first fifteen (sub)harmonics of 360Hz.

The identical method can easily be applied to calculate the subharmonics of any tone.

If we use the same procedure to derive the sub-harmonics of our Solfeggio frequencies, there should be a common (significant) harmonic frequency, correlating to the Schumann resonance, that ties them all together. Yet, calculating the sub-harmonics for each Solfeggio tone all the way down to 0.00Hz, fails to reveal such a common frequency. Disappointing as this is, it was not an entirely unexpected result.

There are a few 'common-use' Schumann reference frequencies in use depending upon which source you consult. One of the most common of these is 7.83Hz. Another commonly-used Schumann Resonance tone is 7.3Hz.

Alas, after running the math all the way down to the 113th sub-harmonic for each tone, This writer can identify no such correlation to 7.3Hz or 7.83Hz in the math of Solfeggio tone harmonics.

While there are some tantalizingly close sub-harmonic frequencies, such as 7.87, 7.70Hz and 7.92Hz, nothing in the harmonic charts for each Solfeggio tone reveals a consistent, universal, or fundamental correlation to the Schumann frequencies. Moreover, none of the correlations, commonly implied by many teachers and practitioners.

Lower (sub)Harmonics of 360Hz			
360 ÷ 1 =	360Hz	1st harmonic	—
360 ÷ 2 =	180Hz	2nd sub-harmonic	1st undertone
360 ÷ 3 =	120Hz	3rd sub-harmonic	2nd undertone
360 ÷ 4 =	90Hz	4th sub-harmonic	3rd undertone
360 ÷ 5 =	72Hz	5th sub-harmonic	4th undertone
360 ÷ 6 =	60Hz	6th sub-harmonic	5th undertone
360 ÷ 7 =	51.42Hz	7th sub-harmonic	6th undertone
360 ÷ 8 =	45Hz	8th sub-harmonic	7th undertone
360 ÷ 9 =	40Hz	9th sub-harmonic	8th undertone
360 ÷ 10 =	36Hz	10th sub-harmonic	9th undertone
360 ÷ 11 =	32.73Hz	11th sub-harmonic	10th undertone
360 ÷ 12 =	30Hz	12th sub-harmonic	11th undertone
360 ÷ 13 =	27.7Hz	13th sub-harmonic	12th undertone
360 ÷ 14 =	25.71Hz	14th sub-harmonic	13th undertone
360 ÷ 15 =	24Hz	15th sub-harmonic	14th undertone

Table 33.5 - Lower harmonics of the 360Hz tone indicating harmonic level and undertone designation.

Within each Solfeggio tonal series, we see a single 'harmonic' tone that is sandwiched between two *inharmonic* tones. (*See: Tables 33.2 - 33.4*) The harmonic tones (89th, 155th, and 144th in each series, respectively) seem to point towards fundamental tones that are far too dissimilar to serve as a common thread between the series.

For example; the 396Hz tone from Series A is a 569.446¢ interval width from 174Hz. This points to the 89th harmonic. But, 89th harmonic of what? Well, if we run the math backward ($f_1 = f_2 \div x$) to find the tone upon which the harmonic is based, then we come up with 4.45Hz.

However, each of our harmonic tones of each series, points to a different tone in this regard. And, none of them appear to be part of the same harmonic series. Thus, again we fail to locate any common thread through dissection of the harmonics.

It occurred to me, and so I will mention that the Schumann Resonance has been on the increase over the decades corresponding to increased human activity of all types. So, it stands to reason that this 'atmospheric pulse' would have been lower and more stable in the pre-industrial and pre-military-industrial past — perhaps even in the time that the Solfeggio tonal series were developed, which is thought to have been sometime in the 11th century.

Therefore, in all due diligence to uncover a possible connection, the possibility of correlations with 4.0Hz, 5.0Hz, 6.0Hz and 7.0Hz were included in the harmonic deep search. The question arises in my mind as to how accurately Schumann Resonance might have been measured in 1957 (or the Middle Ages for that matter) and how the resonances might have been affected by the tremendous, explosive violence of the first half of the twentieth century.

Although I *believe* that the effects upon the Schumann resonance would be significant, from the many nuclear detonations alone, this writer has no actual answers to these questions. Thus, the issue of the base-line pulse of the Earth, the vibrational nature of its atmosphere, and any relationship to Solfeggio tones awaits better data and sharper minds. The writer will note for the record however, that such a correlative link is unlikely to be uncovered.

What about the 432Hz connection?

Some practitioners postulate a direct connection between the Solfeggio tones and the venerated 432Hz frequency. The only connection this writer can fathom would be (again) one of a connection found within a harmonic series, (aka, the harmonics).

When comparing the sub-harmonics of 432Hz (from the fundamental to the 113th sub-harmonic) with those of the Solfeggio tones, we do indeed find 8.0Hz, 7.855Hz, and various other random proximal values listed as harmonics under 432Hz. However, as much as I would like to find a solid connection, this imprecise correlation is tenuous, at best.

The only truly-validating finding would be to see the same Solfeggio root harmonics for every tone, in the constructed harmonic tables. And, that would only valid if we could reliably determine what reference Schumann harmonic night have been utilized in the first place. Again, a futile quest.

Yet, in the harmonics for 432Hz, we see no 174Hz, 285Hz, 396Hz, or 417Hz. This we already knew from previous work. Yet, it bears pointing out that the observation was made.

To reiterate the most important point here, Schumann resonance was 'discovered' in 1952. Solfeggio series tones (the original six tones) arose around the 11th century C.E. Therefore, the claim that Schumann resonance may have provided inspiration for a tonal series developed ten centuries prior to its discovery, is simply an anachronistic concept, and as such, is too much for this researcher to accept.

 The number 432 is nonetheless, a very interesting inclusion. If we apply the '111 skein' to 432, we see a quite different pattern emerge. 432 + 111 = 543. 543 + 111 = 654. 654 + 111 = 765. 765 + 111 = 876. Each sum displays a descending digital sequence (5, 4, 3, … 6, 5, 4… 7, 6, 5). And, each series reduces to three, six or nine accordingly - exactly like the actual Solfeggio values.

However, such a system would exclude frequencies containing the number '1' altogether, and be quite different tonally if Solfeggio were in any way, inclusive of the 432 value or some common harmonic. In this case, the series would lose a great deal of its inherent elegance.

Instead, this particular result, regarding 432Hz, partially corresponds to what is called the 'Natural Series B' of tones (*Table 33.6*) also shown, in context, later in this chapter within *Table 33.17*.

These series are the result of simply counting from one to nine in a top-down pattern. The number on the bottom of any column gets carried to the top of the next column. Additionally, we skip the number ten (as it reduces to 'one' anyway) and simply use one as the next number.

If you apply this pattern from top-to-bottom and left-to-right, you will see the 'Natural' series of tones as follows:

Natural Series A - Does NOT correspond to the skein of '111' addition	
198Hz	198 + 111 = **309** (non-compliant)
219Hz	219 + 111 = **330** (non-compliant)
321Hz	321 + 111 = **432**

Natural Series B - Corresponds to the skein of '111' addition	
432Hz	432 + 111 = **543**
543Hz	543 + 111 = **654**
654Hz	654 + 111 = **765**

Natural Series C - Corresponds to the skein of '111' addition	
765Hz	765 + 111 = **876**
876Hz	876 + 111 = **987**
987Hz	987 + 111 = 1098 (Next tone?)

Table 33.6 - A closer look at the 'Natural' Series of tones and its relationship to the 432Hz tone. Notice that the first two tones are non compliant with the skein of 111 addition while subsequent tones are easily derived by adding 111 to the previous value.

An interesting aspect of this exercise is, as indicated above; the first two tones do not conform to the skein of '111' addition. For example, adding '111' to the first tone of 198 yields a value of 309, not 219, which is the actual second value in the series. Adding '111' to 219 does not yield 321Hz, instead resulting in 330Hz. Yet, without any systemic modifications whatsoever, the subsequent numbers, beginning with 321Hz of Series A, onward through series B and C, conform perfectly to the skein of '111' addition.

This is yet another interesting mathematical conundrum for the kind reader's consideration. The writer can offer no explanation for the numerical discrepancies.

If we were to work backwards from 321Hz and subtract 111, we would arrive at a value of 210Hz, which correctly reduces to three. Further backwards application of the '111' skein from 210Hz would give us an initial value of 99Hz, which correctly reduces to nine. The reason for the 'Natural Series' of tones not being constructed with

99Hz and 210Hz as the initial values is not completely clear but, may have something to do with this series' place in the chart of the various 'sacred' tonal constructs that we will be looking at later in this chapter and illustrated in *Table 33.17*.

Unfortunately, it appears as if the current values may have been 'shoe horned' in, to fit a pre-existing thesis. If the writer is correct in the implied assumption, then the entire system could simply be nothing more than a gerrymandered application of some interesting mathematics.

The purpose of the present exercise was originally intended to demonstrate that; While 432Hz is an extremely important frequency, it is not a 'Solfeggio' tone. Nor, does it present in any manner identifiable as derivative of the Solfeggio tones' origins. It's immense value in human wellness and sound healing is such that it stands apart as the basis, or *foundational* tone for a more 'natural' series of tones as laid out in *Table 33.17*, titled <u>Sacred Series Based on a Fixed 111 Interval</u> later in this chapter and, partially outlined above. Thus, this exercise also stands as some further validation for a 432Hz tuning basis in the practice of sound and frequency healing work, but alas, does nothing whatsoever to assist in our quest for the actual, mathematical origins of the Solfeggio series of tones.

What About the Golden Ratio?

The Golden Ratio, also known as phi and notated by the lower-case Greek letter 'Φ' is a mathematical constant that is rendered, ubiquitously in nature and other fractal environments.

> **The point of the journey, is not just to arrive.**
> **- Neal Peart**

The value of the Φ constant is 1.61803398875. The phi constant is liberally applied in art, architecture, music and other disciplines and represents a kind of optimum symmetry in nature, which is perceptually pleasing to the mammalian brain in various ways.

It makes sense to take just a quick moment to briefly test the Solfeggio tones against the Golden Ratio to see if any important correlations are immediately obvious.

Therefore, let's take a moment to multiply, and then divide each Solfeggio tone by the ubiquitous phi constant to see what we might uncover.

Aside from a somewhat eye-catching result of identical decimal remainders between the products for each tone (no mystery whatsoever,) this writer immediately sees no obvious correlations within these admittedly superficial testing results. Nothing in the harmonics, the phi ratio calculations, or even their presence in the 432Hz (12-TET and Geometric) tunings is immediately apparent to indicate any special relationship between phi and Solfeggio tones.

Series A	
174 x Φ = 281.538	174 ÷ Φ = 107.538
285 x Φ = 461.140	285 ÷ Φ = 176.140
396 x Φ = 640.741	396 ÷ Φ = 244.741

Series B	
417 x Φ = 674.720	417 ÷ Φ = 257.720
528 x Φ = 854.322	528 ÷ Φ = 326.322
639 x Φ = 1033.924	639 ÷ Φ = 394.924

Series C	
741 x Φ = 1198.963	741 ÷ Φ = 457.963
852 x Φ = 1378.565	852 ÷ Φ = 526.565
963 x Φ = 1558.167	963 ÷ Φ = 595.167

Table 33.7 - A cursory glance at the results of multiplication and division by the ubiquitous Phi constant.

Other researchers have performed more detailed phi constant and Fibonacci analyses with this tonal series. And, to this writer's knowledge, none have come up with nothing more significant in this regard, than our admittedly-cursory analysis reveals.

Based on the disappointing but frankly, expected results of these analyses, it is increasingly unclear to this writer where the Solfeggio tones derive their luster and popularity in the relaxation and healing 'world.' That good results are widely achieved and reported is not in question. As to whether the results are due to the tones themselves or the practitioners' energy of 'intention' is perhaps the more pertinent question.

Notwithstanding the fact that research in the area of consciousness and quantum mechanics have indicated some interesting results tangential to the Solfeggio frequencies, we are left at this time with little actual, mathematical or scientific validation as to the significance or relevance of the Solfeggio tone series to human wellness. To the extent that the 3, 6, 9 mathematics and the anagram-like digital transpositions (within and between each series) may be significant, this writer concurs. However, thus far, a laundry list of proofs (some of them, above) reveal little of the mathematical, specifically geometric magick often attributed to the Solfeggio tonal series.

Frustrated but, not to be easily deterred, we shall press on with our exploration… deeper into the useful significance of these tones. We have learned a lot about what Solfeggio is not at this point. But, we have gleaned little actual data explaining their mathematical origins or what the tones actually are.

Honestly, we may never have a clear explanation. But, that fact will never dissuade us from exploring the very real opportunities that the series represents.

Cymatics and Solfeggio Tones:

Modern technology that explores the actual 'shape' of sound has been dubbed 'cymatics.' Current cymatics research is based upon the early work of Ernst Flores Friedrich Chladni, in the 1700s, and later work by Dr. Hans Jenny as well as others working in the field.

Chladni, a German musician and physicist wrote one of the first authoritative treatises on the physics of sound. To over-simplify the matter, in his research, he discovered that sound waves have a particular shape which can be 'seen' using a simple metal plate covered in fine sand. A string instrument's bow was used to 'play' the metal plate by running the bow across the edge of the metal plate at various locations. The resulting vibrations, which created tones from the metal plate, caused the sand on the plate to shift position and form complex geometries.

Later, in the later years of the 1960s, Dr. Jenny refined this technique with an electronic oscillator, which was used to vibrate the metal plate using air-conductance of sound.

Dr. Jenny found that different tones were able to create different complex geometries, which were consistent and repeatable. Dr. Jenny went on to research many different methods of sound creation and, his work in 'cymatics' resulted in an increased modern understanding of sonic geometries.

Recently, a group of researchers at SomaEnergetics under the guidance of John Stuart Reid, the developer of the CymaScope device and, mentioned earlier in this text for his resonance work in the Giza pyramids, utilized advanced cymatic techniques to test six of the existing Solfeggio tones created from specific tuning forks, with the objective to visualize and analyze their sonic geometries.

Not only did this work produce some very interesting still images of the Solfeggio tones' geometry but, the researchers were also able to gather detailed geometric waveform data from the resulting data. The specific data related to the 'nodes' and 'anti-nodes' revealed in the cymatic images is fascinating and worthy of further scrutiny.

Requests for permission to reproduce the images and data here, in this text, apparently did not warrant a response from SomaEnergetics or CymaScope. Nor have our inquiries regarding obtaining cymatic images for specific frequencies received attention. However, as of this writing, some of the data and images are publicly available on the SomaEnergetics website.

While none of the data provides any earthshaking insights regarding our current investigation vis-a-vis Solfeggio tones, it is intriguing to consider the implications of such geometrically-organized waveforms within the traditional practices of music and human wellness.

In fact, for hundreds of years, the human species have, somewhat ironically, been applying advances in technology to slowly-but-increasingly reach back toward our more ancient musical and indigenous healing traditions. Fortunately, there are those researchers out there who understand that modern technology can be a powerful, validating force in the human race's quest for recovering the significant, sonic wellness techniques that were first developed and utilized by our not-so-primitive ancestors.

This writer is, personally encouraged by the current progress of cymatics research and hopes to see it reach the level of a truly validating modality in the near future. However, at this time these technologies are financially inaccessible to many of the researchers doing the actual work in the real world. Until this situation significantly changes for the better, cymatics will continue to be relegated to the realm of expensive, 'novelty' technology.

A Solfeggio Tuning Standard Arises!

The author proposes a thesis; that the Solfeggio tones are not only beneficial, single tones within a numerical skein; nor are they necessarily best-utilized as single tone modalities… Instead, they are perhaps, more expansively viewed as reference frequencies (fundamental tones in, and of themselves), which can be utilized in tuning systems much like the ones previously designed.

Furthermore, and based upon the various analyses above, they may very well be useful tuning standards resulting in harmonic series and *could* even prove to be subsets of the previous F#-Major Tuning Grid.

The inclusion of every Solfeggio frequency in a single tonal series, would necessarily require more than the usual twelve tones per octave. But, individually, they should also be able to stand as the basis for unique, playable, and harmonic twelve tone chromatic series. This could be interesting.

The whole theory behind Solfeggio tones and almost every discussion this author has ever had about the tonal series itself, always circles back to various musical scales and tuning systems. And, this is where most practitioners can easily become mired because, few practitioners of sound and frequency therapies, possess the knowledge, spare time, and expertise to re-tune and re-engineer their sessions in such a complex manner. Therefore, this writer resolves to outline this process in order to make it easily accessible to anyone wishing to work with these 'extended' Solfeggio tuning systems.

Notwithstanding the previous analyses and discussion, it still should come as no great surprise that the Solfeggio tones can be applied to tuning systems such as our humble, twelve tone tuning grids that we have repeatedly developed in this work. The concept is simple in that any tone can serve as the fundamental in a tuning system. But, the selection of the right fundamental is the key point to achieving desirable results. The math would be the same no matter what root frequency is utilized. But, a truly ordered and harmonic relaxation and healing system can only result from the best fundamental tones. Therefore, why not use Solfeggio tones as our fundamental tones and, see what happens?

So, what if these tones are actually more useful as tuning references in and of themselves? It is the writer's assertion that it would make a very significant difference in the way sound and frequency are utilized in the pursuit of human wellness and relaxation. And, again I say that we put it to the test straight away.

We are going to attempt creating a healing tuning grid based on each Solfeggio tone. For the reason that, in common application, each Solfeggio tone has a healing or energetic target; we can somewhat readily create an entire tuning system rooted within each primary tone and, therefore enhance the tonal spectrum by 'expanding' it into an actual musical system... and therefore, also make use of the entirety those luscious harmonics.

At the outset, your writer harbored serious doubts that any resulting *minor* tones would adhere to any of our previous, strict rules in such a system. But, even in that, there is no shortage of surprises.

Minor tones are cast in the role of 'problem-child' in many a tuning system. Therefore, we will take a page from the ancient masters and first, attempt to create major tone scales appropriate for building such structures as triads, tetrads, etc. and therefore, access simple major-chord structures to enhance the Solfeggio tones effectiveness. If we manage to somehow, work in appropriate minor tones, we will simply celebrate and make use of them as well.

Let's try it out!

Solfeggio 'Just' Tempered Tuning Grids?

We are again, jumping into the 'deep end.' But, we have tons of experience behind us. So, we can definitely do this!

First, we will attempt a Solfeggio tuning grid for the Major 2nd, Major 3rd, Perfect 4th, Major 5th, Major 6th, and the Major 7th. We will include the minor tones in the calculations. But, the primary goal is to create two stackable tetrachord-*esque* structures that work well, harmonically. Our first grid will be based on the Series A-174Hz tone.

Just for kicks, (and, because I've already tried it) let's use the most successful interval ratio series we have thus far encountered. That interval series arises from our F$^{#}$-Major Tuning Grid developed earlier in this work.

And, here is where we see a Solfeggio tonal series spring to life. The first Solfeggio grid, *Solfeggio174*, falls into place perfectly and, is a surprisingly useful and playable tuning system... even the minor tones have a wonderful and welcome surprise for us!

If one includes the minor tones, you could easily play this keyboard tuning just as you might play a standard keyboard or if using the F$^{#}$-Major Tuning Grid. (Note that with these Solfeggio tuning grids, we are not overly concerned with the 3, 6, 9 reductions or the decimal remainders consistently present, in the minor tone slots.

But, we will attempt to keep the 'major' tones as compliant to our universal criteria as possible — as well as deferring to those decimal remainders that resolve to whole numbers in higher octaves.

As it turns out, such initial doubts were wholly-unfounded. As you will see below, the entire library of major tones work out as very compliant to the 3, 6, 9 reduction skein. It required no effort or adjustments whatsoever. The progression just fell into place as if finally 'coming home.'

The following grid contains the Series-A tone of 174Hz (as the fundamental), its octave tone, and its harmonics in a Just Intonation version of a Solfeggio tuning grid.

As expected, the minor tones work out to unresolving decimals. Yet, they are surprisingly orderly and, *strikingly* familiar — naturally constraining themselves to single decimal place values only, as well as, in some strange case of déjà vu, occurring in a certain orderly pattern that we have seen a few times before.

The observed pattern of the decimal remainders in the minor tone slots, is one which was previously noted in earlier versions of our geometric tuning grids, and outlined in some detail in previous sections of this work. The observed pattern, consists of the repeating decimal series of 0.2, 0.4, 0.6, and 0.8 remainders. The only exception to this interesting decimal-series, is the grid based upon 285Hz where, *every one* of the calculated minor tones naturally resolves to a whole-number value. Additionally, in that 285Hz-based grid, as in *all* of the prepared grids, each tone reduces to 3, 6, or 9 whether a remainder is observed or not.

The consistent and tonally useful results gained from utilizing 'Just Intonation' intervals continues to be a source of constant, gratification.

The resulting tuning grid system is surprisingly versatile. The targeted 'tetrachord-esque' (major tonal) structures are displayed in *Table 33.8* as bold type entries and, consist of a complete major scale resulting from the system's fundamental tone. The fact that these can be effortlessly 'stacked' (with no limma or comma issues) and utilized as-is, provides us with a surprisingly fortunate outcome indeed.

Not one to be satisfied with a single validation, This researcher is driven to fully press the thesis and continue through *all* of the Solfeggio series by creating a tuning grid for each Solfeggio tone (each energetic humor) of the three separate series... if for no other reason than to explore the possibilities and to see what happens. Therefore, let's see what the next fundamental tone, 285Hz, has to offer using the same 'geometric' progression.

For the Series-A 285Hz grid, (*Table 33.9*) we immediately see a few things that appear to be in need of a bit of cleaning up if possible.

The first of these issues is at the Major 2nd position. Using what has become our 'standard' interval ratio (9:8) for this position initially yields a 320.63Hz value, which appears, at first glance, to be unresolvable to a whole number.

However, by increasing the decimal resolution on the spreadsheet application (Really should have thought of that before.), we can see that this is nothing more than a rounding issue and that the actual value is 320.625Hz. Not exactly a perfect outcome. But, definitely compliant with the criteria and, as it turns out, very appropriate and pleasant, harmonically.

Note	Interval	Ratio	Multiplier	Frequency (Hz)	Interval from Root (¢)	Step Interval (¢)
	Tuning Grid Based on Solfeggio SERIES-A 174Hz					
F	Octave	2:1	2	348.00	1200	111.731
E	Major 7th	15:8	1.875	326.25	1088.269	70.672
D#	minor 7th	9:5	1.8	313.20	1017.596	133.237
D	Major 6th	5:3	1.666666667	290.00	884.359	70.672
C#	minor 6	8:5	1.6	278.40	813.686	111.731
C	Perfect 5th	3:2	1.5	261.00	701.955	119.443
B	Aug 4th	7:5	1.4	243.60	582.512	84.467
A#	Perfect 4th	4:3	1.333333333	232.00	498.045	111.731
A	Major 3rd	5:4	1.25	217.50	386.314	70.672
G#	minor 3rd	6:5	1.2	208.80	315.641	111.731
G	Major 2nd	9:8	1.125	195.75	203.910	92.179
F#	minor 2nd	16:15	1.066666667	185.60	111.731	111.731
F	Root	1:1	1	174.00	—	—

Table 33.8 - Proposed tuning system grid upon the 174Hz Solfeggio tone. The most proximal correlate to 174Hz in the F#-Major Tuning Grid was used to derive the root note assignment of 'F.' When creating MIDI hardware tuning files to these specifications, the use of a 435.00Hz A4 fundamental is recommended.

Your writer, not being a particularly talented mathematician, received the first clue of this, when noticing that the first octave tone, above the 320.625Hz turned out to be a perfectly acceptable 641.25Hz. Therefore, simply increasing the resolution to three decimal places demonstrates that the value for the Major 2nd - while appearing to be an oddball, is actually a 'perfect' value for the grid as the decimal remainder resolves upward to a whole number value, and the initial value reduces perfectly to nine.

We run into the same issue with the value for the 7th. The value of 534.38Hz is actually 534.375. The former doesn't appear to be a value we might hope for in any 'geometric' tuning grid. However, with the increased decimal resolution, the value turns out to be technically valid. And, the next higher octave tone is revealed to be 1068.75Hz. That value resolves to a whole number two more octaves higher.

So far we have constructed two perfectly playable tunings based on Solfeggio fundamental tones. The interval ratios have also shown themselves to be a very close reflection of the F#-Major Tuning Grid previously designed in this work.

The full 285Hz-based grid is presented in all its glory, below:
Just Intonation's ratio interval stack, has again, proven to be an invaluable tool for the creation of our relaxation and healing tones systems.

Tuning Grid Based on Solfeggio SERIES-A 285Hz						
Note	Interval	Ratio	Multiplier	Frequency (Hz)	Interval from Root (¢)	Step Interval (¢)
D	Octave	2:1	2	570.00	1200	111.731
C#	Major 7th	15:8	1.875	534.375	1088.269	70.672
C	minor 7th	9:5	1.8	513.00	1017.596	133.237
B	Major 6th	5:3	1.666666667	475.00	884.359	70.672
A#	minor 6	8:5	1.6	456.00	813.686	111.731
A	Perfect 5th	3:2	1.5	427.50	701.955	119.443
G#	Aug 4th	7:5	1.4	399.00	582.512	84.467
G	Perfect 4th	4:3	1.333333333	380.00	498.045	111.731
F#	Major 3rd	5:4	1.25	356.25	386.314	70.672
F	minor 3rd	6:5	1.2	342.00	315.641	111.731
E	Major 2nd	9:8	1.125	320.625	203.910	92.179
D#	minor 2nd	16:15	1.066666667	304.00	111.731	111.731
D	Root	1:1	1	285.00	—	—

Table 33.9 - Proposed tuning system grid upon the 285Hz Solfeggio tone. The closest correlate to 285Hz in the F#-Major Tuning Grid was used to derive the root note assignment of 'D.'

Now, let's turn our attention to the final Solfeggio tone of Series-A; 396Hz. The grid is presented below (*Table 33.10*) with few comments as the identical math has yielded identically beautiful results using the 396Hz fundamental tone.

Again we see that curious decimal sequence in the minor tones. The repeating .20, .40, .60, .80 sequence continues to have this writer somewhat intrigued. Yet, it seems to be the logical result of the symmetrical interval ratios as they are applied to a three-six-nine divisible fundamental frequency as well as our over-arching three-six-nine digit-reduction scheme.

This mathematical factoid however, does not diminish this writer's fascination regarding the consistency and symmetry of the decimal frequencies, and the fact that the effect appears in every tuning grid based on the Solfeggio series, with the sole exception of the aforementioned 285Hz grid.

The major tones, again, all work out to be perfectly valid, harmonious tones as each of them turn out to be reducible to the 3, 6, 9 values (A definite bonus.) While this reducibility criteria was not intentionally applied to all tones within the Solfeggio tuning grids, it is nevertheless satisfying to the overall thesis.

Note	Interval	Ratio	Multiplier	Frequency (Hz)	Interval from Root (¢)	Step Interval (¢)

Note	Interval	Ratio	Multiplier	Frequency (Hz)	Interval from Root (¢)	Step Interval (¢)
G	Octave	2:1	2	792.00	1200	111.731
F#	Major 7th	15:8	1.875	742.50	1088.269	70.672
F	minor 7th	9:5	1.8	712.80	1017.596	133.237
E	Major 6th	5:3	1.666666667	660.00	884.359	70.672
D#	minor 6	8:5	1.6	633.60	813.686	111.731
D	Perfect 5th	3:2	1.5	594.00	701.955	119.443
C#	Aug 4th	7:5	1.4	554.40	582.512	84.467
C	Perfect 4th	4:3	1.333333333	528.00	498.045	111.731
B	Major 3rd	5:4	1.25	495.00	386.314	70.672
A#	minor 3rd	6:5	1.2	475.20	315.641	111.731
A	Major 2nd	9:8	1.125	445.50	203.910	92.179
G#	minor 2nd	16:15	1.066666667	422.40	111.731	111.731
G	Root	1:1	1	396.00	—	—

Table 33.10 - Proposed tuning system grid upon the 396Hz Solfeggio tone. The closest correlate to 396Hz in the F#-Major Tuning Grid was used to derive the root note assignment of 'G.'

Also, note that the compliance itself, is directly related to the specific interval ratios (derived from the F#-Major Tuning Grid) being applied to a fundamental tone which is, in itself, reducible to — and divisible by nine. The only magic here is in the math.

Next, we move on to the Solfeggio-B Series of 417Hz, 528Hz, and 639Hz. The identical math is applied to these tones as fundamentals of their own tuning grids. The results are essentially identical to the Series-A grids.

Each of these systems works very nicely and provides a perfect way to perform relaxation and healing sessions with much more depth than would be achieved using just the single tones.

Again, in deriving these grids, few adjustments were necessary to our basic math derived from the F#-Major Tuning Grid's Just intervals. The system 'Just' works.

Presented next, are the Solfeggio Series-B tuning grids for each tone-as-fundamental. No commentary is required. Each grid appears to be perfectly balanced with no changes in the math.

Onward to the Solfeggio Series-C tones of 741Hz, 852Hz, and 963Hz. As expected, these tuning grids work out just as melodically as the Series-A and Series-B tones have.

> **Every figure, every row of numbers and every assemblage of harmonious sounds, and the accordance of the cycles of the celestial bodies and the One as an analogy for all which is manifesting itself must become exceedingly clear to him who is searching in the right manner. — Plato**

We now have a method for utilizing Solfeggio-based scales in a relaxation and healing methodology using the standard keyboard layout. The possibilities represented by these systems, as well as the original A-Major and F#-Major Tuning grids are seemingly limitless.

As a sound and frequency healing practitioner, Your mild-mannered writer is both overjoyed to share this information with fellow practitioners and, to open-handedly offer it to a world full of musicians who could now, run for the exits and, leave 440Hz, 12-TET systems behind... Perhaps forever.

Note: In the final draft version of the prototype F#-Major Tuning Grid, we opted for a sub-minor 7th of 7:4 (968.826¢) to bring out certain resonances. The original ratio of 9:5 (1017.596¢) is eminently valid and, is the ratio used in all of our Solfeggio tuning grids as it gives us our 'classic' minor 7th. Depending upon one's tonal preference, the 7:4 sub-minor 7th works equally-well harmonically, as it does in the F#-Major system. The math also works out equally-well in either case.

Note	Interval	Ratio	Multiplier	Frequency (Hz)	Interval from Root (¢)	Step Interval (¢)
Tuning Grid Based on Solfeggio SERIES-B 417Hz						
G#	Octave	2:1	2	834.00	1200	111.731
G	Major 7th	15:8	1.875	781.875	1088.269	70.672
F#	minor 7th	9:5	1.8	750.60	1017.596	133.237
F	Major 6th	5:3	1.666666667	695.00	884.359	70.672
E	minor 6	8:5	1.6	667.20	813.686	111.731
D#	Perfect 5th	3:2	1.5	625.50	701.955	119.443
D	Aug 4th	7:5	1.4	583.80	582.512	84.467
C#	Perfect 4th	4:3	1.333333333	556.00	498.045	111.731
C	Major 3rd	5:4	1.25	521.25	386.314	70.672
B	minor 3rd	6:5	1.2	500.40	315.641	111.731
A#	Major 2nd	9:8	1.125	469.125	203.910	92.179
A	minor 2nd	16:15	1.066666667	444.80	111.731	111.731
G#	Root	1:1	1	417.00	—	—

Table 33.11 - Proposed tuning system grid upon the 417Hz Solfeggio tone. The closest correlate to 417Hz in the F#-Major Tuning Grid was used to derive the root note assignment of 'G#.'

Note	Interval	Ratio	Multiplier	Frequency (Hz)	Interval from Root (¢)	Step Interval (¢)
Tuning Grid Based on Solfeggio SERIES-B 528Hz						
C#	Octave	2:1	2	1056.00	1200	111.731
C	Major 7th	15:8	1.875	990.00	1088.269	70.672
B	minor 7th	9:5	1.8	950.40	1017.596	133.237
A#	Major 6th	5:3	1.666666667	880.00	884.359	70.672
A	minor 6	8:5	1.6	844.80	813.686	111.731
G#	Perfect 5th	3:2	1.5	792.00	701.955	119.443
G	Aug 4th	7:5	1.4	739.20	582.512	84.467
F#	Perfect 4th	4:3	1.333333333	704.00	498.045	111.731
F	Major 3rd	5:4	1.25	660.00	386.314	70.672
E	minor 3rd	6:5	1.2	633.60	315.641	111.731
D#	Major 2nd	9:8	1.125	594.00	203.910	92.179
D	minor 2nd	16:15	1.066666667	563.20	111.731	111.731
C#	Root	1:1	1	528.00	—	—

Table 33.12 - Proposed tuning system grid upon the 528Hz Solfeggio tone. The closest correlate to 528Hz in the F#-Major Tuning Grid was used to derive the root note assignment of 'C#.' When creating MIDI hardware tuning files to these specifications, the use of a 422.40Hz A[4] fundamental is recommended.

Note	Interval	Ratio	Multiplier	Frequency (Hz)	Interval from Root (¢)	Step Interval (¢)
E	Octave	2:1	2	**1278.00**	1200	111.731
D#	Major 7th	15:8	1.875	**1198.125**	**1088.269**	**70.672**
D	minor 7th	9:5	1.8	1150.20	1017.596	133.237
C#	Major 6th	5:3	1.666666667	**1065.00**	**884.359**	**70.672**
C	minor 6	8:5	1.6	1022.40	813.686	111.731
B	Perfect 5th	3:2	1.5	**958.50**	**701.955**	**119.443**
A#	Aug 4th	7:5	1.4	894.60	582.512	84.467
A	Perfect 4th	4:3	1.333333333	**852.00**	**498.045**	**111.731**
G#	Major 3rd	5:4	1.25	**798.75**	**386.314**	**70.672**
G	minor 3rd	6:5	1.2	766.80	315.641	111.731
F#	Major 2nd	9:8	1.125	**718.875**	**203.910**	**92.179**
F	minor 2nd	16:15	1.066666667	681.60	111.731	111.731
E	Root	1:1	1	**639.00**	—	—

Tuning Grid Based on Solfeggio SERIES-B 639Hz

Table 33.13 - Proposed tuning system grid upon the 639Hz Solfeggio tone. The closest correlate to 639Hz in the F#-Major Tuning Grid was used to derive the root note assignment of 'E.' When creating MIDI hardware tuning files to these specifications, the use of a 426.00Hz A⁴ fundamental is recommended.

Tuning Grid Based on Solfeggio SERIES-C 741Hz

Note	Interval	Ratio	Multiplier	Frequency (Hz)	Interval from Root (¢)	Step Interval (¢)
F#	Octave	2:1	2	1482.00	1200	111.731
F	Major 7th	15:8	1.875	1389.375	1088.269	70.672
E	minor 7th	9:5	1.8	1333.80	1017.596	133.237
D#	Major 6th	5:3	1.666666667	1235.00	884.359	70.672
D	minor 6	8:5	1.6	1185.60	813.686	111.731
C#	Perfect 5th	3:2	1.5	1111.50	701.955	119.443
C	Aug 4th	7:5	1.4	1037.40	582.512	84.467
B	Perfect 4th	4:3	1.333333333	988.00	498.045	111.731
A#	Major 3rd	5:4	1.25	926.25	386.314	70.672
A	minor 3rd	6:5	1.2	889.20	315.641	111.731
G#	Major 2nd	9:8	1.125	833.625	203.910	92.179
G	minor 2nd	16:15	1.066666667	790.40	111.731	111.731
F#	Root	1:1	1	741.00	—	—

Table 33.14 - Proposed tuning system grid upon the 741Hz Solfeggio tone. The closest correlate to 741Hz in the F#-Major Tuning Grid was used to derive the root note assignment of 'F#.' When creating MIDI hardware tuning files to these specifications, the use of a 444.60Hz A⁴ fundamental is recommended.

Tuning Grid Based on Solfeggio SERIES-C 852Hz

Note	Interval	Ratio	Multiplier	Frequency (Hz)	Interval from Root (¢)	Step Interval (¢)
A	Octave	2:1	2	1704.00	1200	111.731
G#	Major 7th	15:8	1.875	1597.50	1088.269	70.672
G	minor 7th	9:5	1.8	1533.60	1017.596	133.237
F#	Major 6th	5:3	1.666666667	1420.00	884.359	70.672
F	minor 6	8:5	1.6	1363.20	813.686	111.731
E	Perfect 5th	3:2	1.5	1278.00	701.955	119.443
D#	Aug 4th	7:5	1.4	1192.80	582.512	84.467
D	Perfect 4th	4:3	1.333333333	1136.00	498.045	111.731
C#	Major 3rd	5:4	1.25	1065.00	386.314	70.672
C	minor 3rd	6:5	1.2	1022.40	315.641	111.731
B	Major 2nd	9:8	1.125	958.50	203.910	92.179
A#	minor 2nd	16:15	1.066666667	908.80	111.731	111.731
A	Root	1:1	1	852.00	—	—

Table 33.15 - Proposed tuning system grid upon the 852Hz Solfeggio tone. The closest correlate to 852Hz in the F#-Major Tuning Grid was used to derive the root note assignment of 'A.' When creating MIDI hardware tuning files to these specifications, the use of a 426.00Hz A⁴ fundamental is recommended.

Note	Interval	Ratio	Multiplier	Frequency (Hz)	Interval from Root (¢)	Step Interval (¢)
Tuning Grid Based on Solfeggio SERIES-C 963Hz						
B	Octave	2:1	2	1926.00	1200	111.731
A#	Major 7th	15:8	1.875	1805.625	1088.269	70.672
A	minor 7th	9:5	1.8	1733.40	1017.596	133.237
G#	Major 6th	5:3	1.666666667	1605.00	884.359	70.672
G	minor 6	8:5	1.6	1540.80	813.686	111.731
F#	Perfect 5th	3:2	1.5	1444.50	701.955	119.443
F	Aug 4th	7:5	1.4	1348.20	582.512	84.467
E	Perfect 4th	4:3	1.333333333	1284.00	498.045	111.731
D#	Major 3rd	5:4	1.25	1203.75	386.314	70.672
D	minor 3rd	6:5	1.2	1155.60	315.641	111.731
C#	Major 2nd	9:8	1.125	1083.375	203.910	92.179
C	minor 2nd	16:15	1.066666667	1027.20	111.731	111.731
B	Root	1:1	1	963.00	—	—

Table 33.16 - Proposed tuning system grid upon the 963Hz Solfeggio tone. The closest correlate to 963Hz in the F#-Major Tuning Grid was used to derive the root note assignment of 'B.' When creating MIDI hardware tuning files to these specifications, the use of a 433.35Hz A⁴ fundamental is recommended.

Wow! What a series of beautiful tunings, based upon the Solfeggio tonal series. This writer is deeply heartened by the fact that these grids are now available for every sound and frequency practitioner to experiment with them. None of these Solfeggio tuning systems contain significant geometric resonances or sacred geometry reference tones. However, with the Solfeggio grids, this was never an objective.

Each tuning grid conforms to the basic geometric criteria vis-a-vis 3, 6, 9, 12 and 72, that was previously used in all geometric tuning grids outlined and constructed in earlier chapters. However, in this case, the Solfeggio resonances and *their* harmonics are what has been deemed critical.

The construction of the tuning grids, on its own, may not provide an explanation as to why these tones have become so revered. But, they do make a significantly expanded usage and versatility possible for any practitioner who chooses to compose with, or simply utilize them for ambient chording during relaxation and healing sessions. The benefits are as significant as they are mysterious in their origins.

Yet Another Perspective Circulating Around the Internet

Another analysis of the Solfeggio series, which has circulated around some on-line sources – too various to cite, is based upon the grid (*Table 33.17*) displayed on the facing page.

In each column of this tone grid, is found a certain 'sacred' scale which is based upon the Pythagorean concept of numerical reduction (or progression) called a 'skein.' We have actually been using various skeins all along in our work here. And, this one will seem very familiar, yet is actually applied quite differently, in that each tone of the scales (the columns) is incremented by a constant 111Hz. Each tone across the 'rows' are separated by a constant 12Hz, except curiously, the specific values in columns 'E' and 'F', displayed in bolded-white on a dark-grey background. I have yet discovered no explanation for this apparent discrepancy.

> **Musick has Charms to sooth a savage breast,**
> **To soften Rocks, or bend a knotted oak.**
> **- *The Mourning Bride*, poem by**
> **William Congreve, 1697**

Notice that the Solfeggio series' tones are perfectly reproduced as the 'G' column which is associated with the 'Sacred Scales' as the 'Earth Series' pseudo-scale. (Thus it was decided to include this data in the current chapter.) What all of this means to the reader is open to individual or deeper, esoteric interpretation. But, while it is a very interesting numerical exercise, this grid does not answer the outstanding questions regarding validation of the nature-of and purported function-of each tone or scale. It seems as if these things simply 'materialize' into consciousness with no documented precedent.

For the record, this writer enjoys the experience of vocalizing these pseudo-scales with the assistance of a tuned keyboard/controller and is in no way a detractor of the perceived benefits of the Solfeggio series. However, I do prefer outside validation for my experiences whenever possible. Thus far, we have discovered precious little in that regard. However, we have made some significant, interesting, and tangentially-related discoveries and correlations along the way.

The specific *vocal intonations* listed here, in the far right column, are generally-accepted as some of the chanting sounds applicable to the Solfeggio tones as well as to the corresponding tone in each column on that row. The other (non-bolded) vocalization sounds were obtained by the writer, over the years from various esoteric traditions. The writer makes no claim as to being the originator of the following tonal series sets nor the vocalization guidance contained. I'm just the messenger.

Sacred Series Based on a General 111Hz Interval

	A	B	C	D	E	F	G	H	I	VOCALIZATION
Karmic Frequencies	111	123	135	147	159	162	174	186	198	OM/AUM
Remembering	222	234	246	258	261	273	285	297	219	KI/KEEM
Opening	333	345	357	369	372	384	396	318	321	UT/OOT
Change	444	456	468	471	483	495	417	429	432	REY/REYM
DNA Related	555	567	579	582	594	516	528	531	543	MI/MEEM
Connection	666	678	681	693	615	627	639	642	654	FA/FAHM
Awakening	777	789	792	714	726	738	741	753	765	SO/SOHM (SOL)
Transcendence	888	891	813	825	837	849	852	864	876	LA/LAHM
Ascendence	999	912	924	936	948	951	963	975	987	SI/SHEEM

COLUMNS →	A – Angelic Series	D – Quaternary Scale	G – Earth Series (Solfege)
	B – Secondary Scale	E – Universal Scale	G – Divine Series
	C – Tertiary Scale	F – Senary Scale	I – Natural Series

Table 33.17 - Each of the 'pseudo-scales' in the Sacred Series of tonal structures. Featured is column 'G', corresponding to the Solfeggio series as well as the initial tones of the 'Universal Scale' and 'Senary Scale', which appear to break the mathematical pattern of twelve addition.

So what?

"Why does any of this matter?" You may ask. Honestly, it may not matter at all – depending upon your unique perspective. We are simply exploring the myriad possibilities. After all, there must be millions of tones out there with which to perform or compose relaxation and healing music. Likewise, there are almost certainly specific tones, which carry more powerful and positive effects for some, than others. The answers for this seeker lie in a combination of tradition, history, personal experience, and observed/reported, anecdotal results.

We know without a shred of doubt, that the ancient practitioners utilized sound and frequency for the purpose of wellness and healing.

We also clearly see from the few, extant writings that they were utilizing specific, proven, and time-tested sonic 'treatment' methods.

The evidence of history shows us that they used specific tonal or scalar structures. And, we also know that at least some of these ancient 'masters' of healing music were so deeply-revered for their healing skills that they were remembered, long after their deaths — some rare few, were even deified. All of this, thus validates their lives' work.

The logical assumption is that; there must be something deeply significant in the practice of sound and frequency modalities and their noted, positive affects upon the human condition that is worth exploring, rediscovering, and preserving.

Therefore, it behooves us to glean as much as possible from the

Sound will be the medicine of the future. — Edgar Cayce

theory and methods of those revered ancients. Personally, I deeply enjoy Solfeggio work. It is relaxing, rewarding, and the vocalizations are a great aid to any meditational practice. While the dearth of hard validation may seem to indicate otherwise, it is important to note that there is also a dearth of invalidating data. And, even in today's generally-hostile culture, it *remains impossible to prove a negative*. Thus, I suggest that we leave each to their own conscience, opinions, and choices.

In practice, the Solfeggio series, as well as some of the various derivations, are powerful and subjectively effective tools for any sound and frequency practice.

Having performed the previous exercises in exploring and analyzing the Solfeggio series, this writer has somewhat ironically, developed a much deeper appreciation for what these tones may represent to the world of sound and frequency healing.

The various numerical associations are intriguing — to say the least. And, the anecdotal correlations to associated physiological benefits, taught in several holistic disciplines, is compelling. In personal use, I find the series to be both relaxing and beneficial on several levels. Track your own mileage. It may vary. But, seriously. Try them out.

One final word before moving on: Authoritative works, such as by *Dr. Leonard Horowitz* collaborating with *Dr. Joseph Puleo* in their book, **Healing Codes for the Biological Apocalypse** , somewhat convincingly connect Solfeggio tones to a 'code' unearthed in the biblical book of Numbers.

Notwithstanding the fascinating and compelling narrative as well as the connections proposed, Ultimately, this writer finds it difficult to credit such specific information to a period of history when there was no known, documented standard by which to measure sound in the modern cycles-per-second (Hz), which is after all, a unit of measure that didn't even exist until the late 19th century.

The absence of solid 'scientifically' rigorous validation does not automatically render an observed truth irrelevant. Very often, experience alone is the highest possible form of validation
- Author

The writer will stipulate that the temporal unit known as the 'second' has been standardized since antiquity (always as one-sixtieth of a minute). Yet, the ability to measure pressure waves and accurately time their rate of travel, is not among the things this writer is prepared to attribute to the specific, ancient cultures in question.

Despite personal skepticism and several unanswered questions, Dr. Horowitz's work remains a very interesting read and makes some challenging assertions which should perhaps be carefully considered when working with, explaining, or teaching the usage of the Solfeggio tonal series.

Now For Something Completely Different...

Out of nothing more than curiosity, the author took a deeper look at where these tones lie within our venerable F#-Major Tuning Grid.

The Solfeggio tone of 174Hz does not appear in any of our tuning grids. In fact, all of the Solfeggio tones are conspicuously absent from the geometric tuning grids despite their strict adherence to 3, 6, 9 geometric progressions. This should not really, come as any surprise since the Solfeggio tones are not actually a geometrically-based construct.

However, there may be more than just the one obvious explanation for their absence. One possibility to consider is that since the Solfeggio tones could be seen as a 'harmonic series,' these tones are quite possibly the (intra-harmonic) tones 'between' the tones. I'll call them 'blue-tones' — those tones that we can use to reach between two frequencies with positive effect towards the hidden energies lying between. It's a sort of 'bluesy' theory. Micro-tonal musicians will know what I mean here, if not appreciating the terminology chosen.

What we can clearly observe is that the Solfeggio tones occupy the space between some of our most important tones within the F#-Major tone class.

For example, the 174Hz frequency lies between our F-168.75Hz and the all-important F#-180Hz. In fact, it is almost equidistant between the two tones, being 5.25Hz above the F and 6.00Hz below the F#. This would make it analogous to a quarter-tone interval.

The interval for 174Hz from the F at 168.25Hz, is 53.039¢ (5.25Hz) wide, which is the equivalent of a '33rd Harmonic' of the fundamental tone within the series. (Notice 3+3rd harmonic.) Two of these intervals (106.078¢) gives us a very close approximation to our *'overtone half-step'* or *'small semitone'* (104.955¢) that was periodically utilized in our geometric tuning grids as the minor 2nd interval. 174Hz is the in-between (hidden?) quarter-tone in this case.

Just for fun and polite conversation, the following chart demonstrates how each Solfeggio tone is inserted between the two adjacent notes in the F#-Major Tuning Grid that was constructed earlier in this work.

Notice that the tones of each series share a particular affinity for certain significant notes within that system — particularly but, not exclusively the tones of the F#-Major tone class. Additionally, the complete set of Solfeggio tones fall within a two-and-a-half octave range that is generally, the most used or 'utilized' sections of the standard keyboard for general playing – or admittedly, for vocalization, which was the original intent of the Solfeggio.

In *Table 33.18* below, we have outlined the adjacent notes and chosen a correlate tone based upon either the 'closest' tone value (in Hertz) or the tone which produces an interval of exactly 12Hz.

The rationale for the latter will become clearer when one considers we are borrowing from the pattern of 12Hz inter-scalar intervals in the 'Sacred Series' of tones detailed above. (See! There *was* a purpose for that.) The validated correlate tone is the basis for the Solfeggio tuning grids' fundamental note assignments.

Notice how each Solfeggio tone sits neatly, between the significant major-minor degrees of the F#-Major Tuning Grid system.

Tone	Found Between (Hz)	Closest Correlate's Reduction Validation
174	F - **168.75** and F# - 180	168.75 - 174 = 5.25... 5 + 2 + 5 = 12... 1 + 2 = 3
285	C#- 270 and D - **288**	288 - 285 = 3
396	G - **384** and G# - 405	384 - 396 = 12... 1+ 2 = 3
417	G# - **405** and A - 432	405 - 417 = 12... 1 + 2 = 3
528	C - 504 and C#- **540**	540 - 528 = 12... 1 + 2 = 3
639	E - **630** and F - 675	630 - 639 = -9... = 9
741	F#- **720** and G - 768.	768 - 720 = 21... 2 + 1 = 3
852	G#- 810 and A - **864**	864 - 852 = 12... 1 + 2 = 3
963	B - **960** and C - 1008	960 - 963 = -3... = 3

Table 33.18 - Each Solfeggio tone lies between specific tones within the F#-Major Tuning Grid. The closest correlate, based upon proximity in Hertz or the interval yielding a 12Hz interval is selected and validated against the numerical reduction criteria. Bolded frequencies indicate the validated, proximal correlate tone and subsequently, the note assignment, in the tuning grids, for the original tone.

Additionally, take special note that the difference between each of the closest correlate tones and the reference Solfeggio tone, is a number that also reduces to three or nine.

If our calculations were even a fraction of a hertz up or down, this effect could not be observed. However, since both the Solfeggio and our F#-Major Tuning Grid adhere to the principle of 3, 6, 9 reduction, it is no surprise that the difference between any two significant frequencies would also reduce in the same manner. Symmetry? Yes. Useful? Very likely. Magick? Probably not.

We can also observe how Series A ends with a G# and Series B begins with the same G# as an associated neighbor. Likewise, Series B ends with an F that is a very close 'neighbor' to the F# with which Series C begins. It's not precise. But, it is close enough to cause a briefly-raised eyebrow. There is a certain, fascinating cohesion between these systems, mathematical and audible, that while clearly observable, remains frustratingly unquantifiable using current methods.

Can all of these effects be mere coincidence? If not, then why are the ultimate answers so elusive? Is this writer just seeing these mathematical 'coincidences' through rose-colored glasses? Well, anything is possible, I suppose. However, having approached this work with an intentionally skeptical bent, this writer believes such suspicions should be somewhat tempered.

This exercise is presented merely to document a possibly-significant observation. To date, this researcher has only the theory that the Solfeggio tones are inherently complementary to the adjacent F#-Major, geometric tones of the F#-Major Tuning Grid in some meaningful way.

A Summary of Sorts:

Most of the constructs we have reviewed here, vis-a-vis the Solfeggio series, are various dissimilar mathematical constructs. Admittedly, some may even appear somewhat contrived after-the-fact, despite the interesting mathematical structures involved. Most of the constructs reviewed here possess some association with the skein of 3, 6, 9 reduction or other 'historically significant' numerical links such as '12' and '111.' Some of the constructs work well in theory as well as practice, while others may not appear to work at all — or at best, stretch the limits of credibility.

Among the herein detailed systems, the specific, charted analysis of the various 'Sacred Series' scales based on a 111Hz skein is especially intriguing in this writer's opinion. Such system possesses a clear and orderly mathematical pattern (even though apparently broken in a couple of instances) that is pleasant to experience and somewhat reassuring in its simplicity and clarity. However, it is not a musical system which lends itself to be easily played upon—or even transferred to the modern keyboard. Such a useful characteristic has always been one of the primary objectives for the systems presented in this work.

Have we proven the basis for, or validated the right-of-existence of the Solfeggio series? Certainly not. And, such was never the author's actual intention. Instead your devious author sought to examine what Solfeggio is *not* as well as suggest what it *might be*.

Therefore, it is the author's fervent hope that some misconceptions have been clarified as to what Solfeggio is not, while simultaneously offering some hopefully stimulating discussion on what it may be in *your* relaxation and healing practice.

Yet, are not these foundational concepts that we have discussed throughout this work, exactly what the universe is based upon - geometry, energy, and frequency?

Combined, these attributes are the lingua franca of the entire world, galaxy, and the underpinnings of the entire universe itself. Therefore, as alluded to in the earliest stages of this work; Why would it not stand to reason that the structure, harmony, symmetry, and perfection of therapeutic and healing music be intimately linked to the pure math upon which everything else in our civilization is based? (Specifically geometry)

The whole numbers, universally-significant numbers, and the universal mathematical constants inform every aspect of our civilization's development to-date. Yet, our art, music, and wellness practices all seem to have taken some deviant detour towards overly-complicated, technologically-bewildering, physiologically incompatible, psychologically disruptive, and mathematically-questionable contrivances – to arrive at someone else's idea of structure, balance and 'originality.'

Well, spending just a few minutes of honestly listening to modern music on a local streaming service should disabuse anyone of any illusion that modern culture might actually hold a valid claim to the 'high ground' in that particular regard, or even that; we as a civilization, are in-fact doing right by our fellow humans by following in such blind adherence *to*, and continued propagation *of* such an intrinsically-flawed sound and frequency system as that found in 'equal temperament' constructs based on a 440Hz concert pitch.

That these unnatural constructs created by unknown-committee, have been, and continue to be used in the practice of sound and frequency modalities is the real tragedy of the standard tuning model.

The knower of the mystery of sound [*also*] **knows the mystery of the whole universe. — Hazrat Inayat Kahn**

Chanting and Humming

Make a Joyful Noise! (Psalms: 100)

In any traditional yoga, meditation, or sound therapy practice, there is almost always an aspect of vocalizing or chanting. After all, improving one's wellness status is never a one-dimensional exercise. Whether the focus be toward mantra (words of power) or specific tonal structures (sounds of power), the practice of intoning sound is both common and highly-beneficial — knowing no spiritual or religious boundaries.

For those readers who 'didn't sign up' with the intent to receive esoteric musical information, be warned that in this chapter, we inevitably encounter the unknowable, and travel down a path that leads to destinations not readily acknowledged by mainstream science. As your writer, I enthusiastically, embark on just such a journey. If this type of day-trip is not your cup of tea, feel free to skip ahead to the next chapter where we will put our feet back on slightly firmer ground.

Intoning sound induces the vibrational energy within the targeted emotion, esoteric energy pattern, specific chakra vortex, or endocrine region. The resonances directly excite and energize these areas leading to subjectively enhanced function, which in turn leads to improved balance, elevated energy levels, and improved overall wellness status.

These vibrations provide the mechanical stimulation required to elicit bio-electrical energy, via induction, from the body's crystalline structures, which are comprised of human DNA, various crystalline minerals, and molecular structures including water.

The science behind this assertion is called piezo-electric induction. Simply put: If one applies a mechanical energy (vibration, pressure, etc.) to a crystal, that crystal produces electrical energy. Conversely, putting electrical energy into a crystal causes a reverse piezo-electric effect, producing mechanical energy (generally vibration and sound.) The piezo-electric effect is the basis for quartz-movement timepieces, ultrasound, and many therapeutic protocols (i.e. phonophoresis and iontophoresis). The science is also utilized in more depleting practices, such as sound-based technologies recently developed by humankind's various governments in order to do physical harm to one another.

Let us digress a bit, in order to illustrate the fundamental point;

In 2017, dozens of American officials stationed in the newly-reopened U.S. Embassy in Havana, Cuba began hearing odd cracks and humming in their ears. These episodes were accompanied by bouts of extreme nausea, headaches, visual disturbances, memory loss, disequilibrium, and lethargy – taken together, these symptoms are pathognomonic indicators of traumatic brain injury or 'TBI.'

The cause of this 'Havana Syndrome' was determined to be actual attacks on the building's occupants using *sonic weapon technology*, which is still under development in several countries around the world.

Further reports emerged in subsequent weeks suggesting that the potential sonic attacks against American representatives might be far more common than what was then, publicly known.

In turn, more eyes are now looking toward nation-states seen as hostile to the United States, as being behind the veritable global barrage of sonic attacks. (*Fox News on-line, Holly McKay, October 22, 2020 - https://www.foxnews.com/world/us-officials-were-targeted-across-the-world-including-american-soil-by-seeming-sonic-attacks*)

In 2019, The *Los Angeles Times* reported that extensive MRI examinations of these same victims of the sustained 'sonic attack' upon the U.S. Embassy in Havana, clearly demonstrated that the affected individuals mysteriously **"had less white matter than a comparison group of healthy people…"**. The *Times* further reported that; *"Other structural differences were found as well."* (*Los Angeles Times, Science* section, Lindsey Tanner, July 23, 2019 - *https://www.latimes.com/science/* *story/2019-07-23/havana-embassy-sonic-attack-brain-scans*).

The victims of these sonic attacks very literally, suffered traumatic brain damage (TBI) as a result of a sustained sonic energy attack on the embassy. This fact alone, is confirmation that specific sonic frequencies, at specific amplitudes, are *known to cause changes in human anatomy,* thus negatively affecting wellbeing.

If specific, sonic frequencies are known (and regularly utilized) to negatively affect human wellbeing, why is it then so difficult for many to accept that other sound frequencies can support human wellness?

If one accepts these reports as fact, does it not also stand to reason that the opposite might also be true?

If some frequencies at amplitude do very real, physical harm, might we not expect other frequencies of certain amplitudes to both heal and support wellness?

$$\sim\!\!\smile\!\!\sim$$

The practice of chanting (or *intonation*, if you prefer), is as old as consciousness itself. There exist two basic forms of tonal chanting; *Vowel sound intonation* and *Mantra chanting*. Both practices extend back for thousands of years. And, both practices are known to enhance human wellness.

Vowel sound intonation uses basic vowel sounds at certain frequencies or ranges of frequencies, to create the desired vibrations within the body as well as the immediate surroundings. The intonations themselves usually have no literal meaning. Their basic function is to provide a vehicle for creating and transmitting the created, mechanical vibrations to the body and general environment.

The second variation of verbal intonation, is Mantra chanting. This method uses very specific, powerful *words or phrases*, which carry either literal or allegorical meaning, and convey power in association with the chosen tones themselves.

The tonal vibrations infuse the mantra phrase with mechanical 'energy', which is intended to activate and carry the power of the words within, without, and to higher planes associated with the particular frequency(ies) used. We can associate the practice of Gregorian chants or singing hymns in temple worship, as examples of this type of intonation within the western spiritual practices.

To the dedicated skeptic, we could emphasize the point that even in our so-called modern era, singing or chanting as a method of spiritual observance, remains a very common practice in every church, mosque, synagogue, shul, ashram, and temple. Chanting and intonation are the universal connection across our many, spiritual practices as well as our treasured indigenous traditions — These can serve as a bridge across which the Self can transcend the illusion we call 'reality', even if only temporarily.

As far in the past as recorded history is able to inform us, vocalization and 'words of power' have been an integral part of every spiritual and healing practice known to human-kind. Even the more depleting incarnations of spiritual practice are imbued with their own chants, incantations, and sounds of power. Yet, many remain stubbornly resistant to the simple, practical use of vocal intonation in an uplifting practice even when such practice is shown to be beneficial to health, wellbeing, and vitality.

This writer is personally familiar with this form of stubborn resistance — having once been of the mind that singing or chanting was a purely theatrical, temple or evangelical practice, performed primarily by the hierophants and their attendants. The basic thinking was that; such a practice is not intended for everyday people or common use. However, such thinking could not be farther from the actual truth of the matter.

Any tone can be used to chant any word, phrase or utterance. While there do not seem to be many strict rules, there are common practices, of which tonality is apparently, the only constraint.

It is the tone (frequency at amplitude) which 'carries' the intent and the energy. If the tone is inaccurately produced, the intent could be misdirected or not properly transmitted to the 'Self' as intended. We will attempt to explain these somewhat malleable 'rules of the game' as we progress in our discussion.

Coincidentally, in some western practices, the traditional chanting tones have become closely associated with the original, six Solfeggio tones. However, tones utilized in other, similar systems vary widely depending upon the specific teacher, the individual's instincts, as well as the energy of intent. There are many practices which place their 'trust' in the inner Self to guide one to the correct frequency or tone, if you prefer. This is a surprisingly easy and effective skill to learn. Once you actually feel a positive reaction in your physical body, the rest falls into place quite naturally.

Within the practice of Solfeggio intonation, each tone has an associated vowel sound that is prescribed to accompany it's intonation — in order to imbue the physical body, subtle body, and one's immediate environment with the intended energy pattern(s).

Basic Vocalization Series – Based upon the Six Original Solfege Tones	
Frequency	Vocalization
396Hz	"UT" or "OOT"
417Hz	"RAE" or "REY"
528Hz	"MI" or "MEE."
639Hz	"FA" or "FAH"
741Hz	"SO" or "SOH."
852Hz	"LA" or "LAH"

Table 34.1 - The six original tones of the Solfeggio tonal system with commonly accepted vocalization patterns.

With specific regard to the original six Solfeggio tones; the Solfeggio intonations, described in *Table 34.1* (above,) while not universal, are widely accepted as helpful in eliciting the power of the tones. Feel free to experiment with these using positive intentions towards the *most benevolent outcome*. As with the original usage of these tones, the writer feels strongly that intent is key to success when using the Solfeggio systems.

Intonations using original Solfeggio tones (Pattern A):

396Hz utilizes the "UT" or "OOT" vocalization. This sound loosely correlates to the typical musical "DOH" used to teach children the sounds of the scales, or for vocalists to use during warm-up and practice. The original six Solfeggio tones continue this obvious pattern, ending at "LA".

The basic teaching series, based on the expanded Solfeggio system, continued with "SI" or "SHI" which is often transliterated into "TI" or "TEE" in some chanting traditions. (See: Table 34.2. Below)

And, to amplify or sustain the physical vibrations, many practitioners suggest adding the "M" to the end of each vocalization to stretch it for the full exhalation. (e.g. LAH+M) This practice however, requires significantly more breath control and practice.

In addition to the original Solfeggio tones, we have the three latter-day additions of: 174Hz which seems to closely correlate to the "OM" or "AUM" chant, (See: note under *Table 34.2*, below.)

The next 'rediscovered' tone is 285Hz, which often uses the sound of "KI" or "KEE," and the highest tone of 963Hz, utilizes the "SI" or "SHEE" tone in many practices. As previously mentioned, there are those who use the "TI" or "TEE" vocalization instead of "SI" with this tone. The writer, having studied in Japan, recognizes that certain languages utilize different phonetic strings and, subsequently may use different dominant sounds when chanting.

It is worth mentioning at this point that these are nowhere carved in stone. There potentially exist as many teaching patterns as there are teachers. Therefore, it behooves the individual to work with other extant vocalization patterns to determine which, if any, system is most appropriate for their particular constitution and energy patterns. The slightly variant chanting forms noted in *Table 33.17* of *Chapter 33 - The Solfeggio Tonal System*, are also widely used and represent some interesting and perhaps, useful variation.

Intonations Using an Alternate Vocalization Pattern (Pattern B):

Another of this writer's favorite intonation patterns is charted below alongside 'Pattern A' and, is indicated as 'Pattern B.' This variable pattern was first encountered at a meditation retreat in Thailand in the late 1990's and quickly became a treasured personal favorite.

The writer is not convinced that those leading the meditation sessions were aware that they seemed to naturally gravitate towards certain frequencies. But, they were remarkably, tonally consistent between sessions. So much so that it became a tacitly accepted fact that certain vocalizations were to be chanted at these specific tones. To quote one of my favorite science fiction heroes, "Fascinating."

For simplicity, I will associate the vocalizations in this "Pattern B" with the same Solfeggio tones outlined above. This is by no means intended as a 'rule' for any practice. In fact, although the writer *suggests* the tonal structures outlined in this text, any scales (whether outlined in this text or not) could easily work just as well. These patterns are merely suggested guidelines to familiarize oneself with the patterns and the tones associated with chanting and intonation work.

The point of the additional 'humming' pattern of chanting is to stretch the first half of the compound intonation to half of your exhale and the remainder of your breath is used to magnify the 'MM' sound to create and feel the vibrations it causes in the physical body.

These vibrations are intended to integrate the energy of these "sounds of power" within the physical body and eventually project, or radiate them, as energy, outward into the etheric body. Additionally, it pleasantly tickles… just a little bit.

Common Vocalization Patterns Utilizing Modern Solfeggio Tones		
Frequency	Vocal Pattern A	Vocal Pattern B
174Hz*	OM/AUM	O-UM or OM
285Hz	KI/KEEM	MAH-OOM
396Hz	UT/OOT	OO-OOM
417Hz	RAE/REYM	REY-OOM or RAH-OOM
528Hz	MI/MEEM	MEE-OOM or MAI-OOM
639Hz	FA/FAHM	FAH-OOM
741Hz	SO/SOHM	SAH-OOM
852Hz	LA/LAHM	LAH-OOM
963Hz	SI/SHEEM	HAH-OOM, HUH-OOM or AUM

Table 34.2 - The nine modern tones of the Solfeggio tonal system with some common vocalization patterns.

Note: *The generally practiced frequency for 'OM' in many worldwide, teaching practices seems to be closer to 192Hz, (coincidentally, an interval of 18Hz and 170.423^c upwards) often intoned as its lower octave of 96Hz called "Earth-OM" in some practices. Both of these frequencies, are coincidentally included in the F#-Major Tuning Grid as the G^3 and G^2.

Whatever chanting style, pattern or sequence one chooses to work with, one thing is guaranteed; The more one works with the tones and chanting, the better, stronger, accurate and clearer their chanting will become.

Consequently, the benefits of regular intonation practice will begin to manifest in proportion to the practice. The physical body will always master skills that are practiced for the benefit of the whole.

So, how does one begin practicing with intonation? Easy! Pick a method, teacher, or on-line resource and learn what they have to offer. Then all that is required is practice, practice, practice.

Mantra Chanting

The practice of chanting phrases or words of power is as ancient as history is able to reveal. There is quite literally, no culture of which we are currently aware, that does not or has not practiced the tradition of chanting and singing for spiritual purposes.

That being said, it is the ancient Hindu and more recent (to western culture) Buddhist practice of mantra chanting with which most people associate the practice.

Mantra in the Sanskrit simply means; '*Sacred utterance.*' A mantra can be a sound (such as vowel sounds), a single word, groups of words, or a phrase. These are intended as activation tools for innate spiritual powers, healing, or blessings. Some mantra have literal meanings such as the well-known "*Aum (Om) mane padme hum*" casually translated as "The sacred pearl in the lotus."

Other mantra, such as the "*Om Tare Tuttare Ture Soha*" mantra, also known as the 'Green Tara Mantra', have such ambiguity in their translations that they are intended for deeper introspection on the myriad hidden meanings.

While the actual meaning of any mantra may seem simple, it is strongly suggested to reflect upon the deeper implications and meditate upon them while chanting. Thus, we come to the main difference between vowel intonation and mantra chanting, which is one of deeper meaning.

When chanting mantra, there exists not only the aspects of tone and pronouncing the words or phrases properly but, also the aspect of infusing the chant with *conscious* understanding — either obtained from spiritual insight or from teachers who can help convey some of the deeper meanings. The realization of truth within the words and, the purpose of that truth in your waking life, completes the energetic cycle associated with meditative chanting practice.

In the case of the 'Om mane...' mantra and, most Sanskrit mantras, meaning is derived from the deeply ancient Vedic texts of the <u>Mahayana Sutra</u>, which contains the original teachings. In Tibetan Buddhism, the current incarnation of the Dalai Llama further breaks down each syllable of the 'Om mane...' mantra, as symbolizing the aspects of Self, from the imperfect body and mind to the transformation into pure spirit.

However, I digress... Yet again.

There are very likely, just as many mantras as there are Vedic texts, which is to say 'thousands.' Those mantra, considered most powerful and therefore the most common, are easily accessed through Buddhist meditation classes and several existing texts.

For those particularly interested in the Buddhist methods, may I suggest searching out and navigating to the '<u>Tibetan Nuns Project</u>' where the seeker will find a wealth of information and references for helping you to develop your understanding and practice. While there are many sources of information on the topic, this one happens to be the writer's personal favorite.

Now, let's get back to tone

It is well-understood that tone and frequency play a pivotal part in intonation practice. Those who practice for any time will acknowledge that certain tones seem to resonate more deeply than others. This straight-forward observation should not surprise – especially since each of you kind readers have now invested hours in reading about the Geometric and Solfeggio-based tuning systems.

Nevertheless, all of this discussion leads us inevitably, back to the 'elephant in the room.' How do we determine the exact frequencies to use in our tonal practice?

303

Another way of asking this question is; How does the author know the exact frequencies to use?

As we attempt to explain all of this, the writer's first bit of advice is to completely ignore the standardized frequencies suggested in most on-line sources. Almost without exception, these will be based upon modern (440Hz, 12-TET) tuning systems, which do not and can not reflect natural tones; much less tones which actually honor historical and geometric structure.

For example, many sites will tell you that the tone for 'OM' is a C#... That's it! That's all you get. An actual frequency usually cannot be found, because those writing these articles... Don't know the answer or, do not realize that C# is an arbitrary assignment to a note within a tone class. They erroneously assume a C# based in 440Hz, 12-TET tuning, which hopefully, the reader now understands simply cannot be true.

There must be some method for identifying and validating correct and useful frequencies. Otherwise, what are we doing here?

The good news is that there *is* such a fool-proof system. One that works for every seeker. And, all it requires is dedicated practice.

Yes. When working with tone and vocalization, your body will 'tell' you when a vibrational frequency is right for you. The practitioner will feel a change take place somewhere in their body (the aforementioned 'tickle' perhaps.)

If that feeling is uplifting and pleasant, then that frequency is beneficial for that individual and that energetic level (chakra). Chances are, if you are able to measure the frequency, it will be a geometric tone. Even if it isn't, it will very likely not be any tone found on the modern keyboard. (I.e., not a 440Hz, 12-TET tone)

At the end of the day, each physical being is an individual consciousness, residing within the Whole. F#-180Hz intonations may feel effective at a certain level, or not at all. 174Hz might work better for you... in the beginning.

The suggestion here is this; if your optimum vocalization frequency seems to be 174Hz, or any other non-geometric frequency, then start there. And then, try moving your intonations from that lower frequency (up) to the more natural, 180Hz mile stone. (Take your time! Rushing may trigger some unpleasant reactions.) You can 'elevate' your 'Self' by raising and normalizing your internal vibrations to reflect the more natural frequencies, some found in this text, others in the wider, natural universe.

The theory is that the human body becomes detuned or entrained over time due to prolonged exposure to sounds, frequencies, and energies common in the individual's everyday life. You can then theoretically re-tune the body to no small extent, by normalizing these resonances through the practice of chanting and intonation. This concept is the whole objective of sound and frequency wellness practice. And, when an individual engages in a sonic session, such as a sound-bath or sonic-detox, this re-tuning is exactly what the practitioner is attempting, albeit on a deeper level.

However, as a native part of wholeness, our purpose is reunification with that Whole — to become in-tune with everything that is. Therefore, any individual dissonance must eventually resolve to consonance. This means that there are universally precise frequencies to which we can re-tune our conscious and subconscious Self. The entire purpose of this chapter is to propose a structure wherein this re-tuning of Self, and the Whole, might be better understood and more easily and efficiently accomplished.

Work with tone and chanting to discover those frequencies which trigger a palpable, positive effect and 'go with that' in the beginning. Your subconscious (Self) is very capable of informing the rest. The universe is a mysterious place but, nothing is hidden to those who seek truth with heart-felt dedication.

In the next chapter, we will delve into another tonal construct that has become very popular over the last few decades. We will attempt to dissect its parts and see what, if anything, we can learn from it. That system is one developed by Hans Cousto and, is called '*The Cosmic Octave*' or in some cases, '*Planetary Frequencies*.'

The Cosmic Octave

The Music of our Stellar Home?

As the story goes, a Swiss mathematician by the name of Hans Cousto, discovered a numerical relationship between sound, frequency and the movements of the orbiting objects within our solar system. These relationships were the subject of dynamic calculations, which Cousto theorized might correlate with audible sound, once octavated into the audible range, and may therefore, constitute a literal 'Music of the Spheres.'

The tones were calculated by reducing the orbital frequencies of the celestial bodies to seconds. This fractional reduction value, thus became the single-orbit frequency of the body in question. Of course such long wavelengths would be surpassingly inaudible. Therefore, in order to bring them into audible range, these orbital frequencies were octavated twenty-four fold or more, to resolve them into the audible tones represented in the series. This concept is expressed as;

(Orbital Frequency in seconds) x 2^n = Result (in Hz)

Notably, the 'n' in the formula is whatever 'doubling' is necessary to octavate the rendered tone into the audible frequency range. The resulting frequency was assigned to whatever orbital frequency dynamics were used. If it was Earth's rotational periodicity, then the frequency is labeled 'Earth - Day' or in the case of revolutional (orbital) periodicity, 'Earth - Year', etc.

Accordingly, the group of octavated tones (calculated for many members of our Solar system,) were collectively dubbed the '*Cosmic Octave*' by Cousto and his associates. Seven of these tones were subsequently assigned as 'chakra' tones relative to the planetary tones that were calculated for certain of the solar objects (Sun, Earth, Luna, Venus, Mercury, etc). These chakra tones, which were deemed to correlate the human chakra with major orbital periods and other phenomena, are outlined in the chart below. This writer has heretofore identified no deeper rationale for these assignments other than Cousto's assertion that this is right and proper.

Chakra	Chakra Name (Sanskrit)	Cosmic Tone Name	Cosmic Frequency	Cosmic Note	F#-Based Geometric Frequency	F#-Based Correlate	Variation (cents)
7th	Crown (Sahasrara)	Platonic Year	172.06Hz	F	168.75Hz	F	-33.63¢
6th	Third Eye (Ajna)	Venus	221.23Hz	A	225Hz	A#	-31.05¢
5th	Throat (Vishudda)	Mercury	141.27Hz	C#	144Hz	D	-33.14¢
4th	Heart (Anahata)	Earth year	*136.10Hz	C#	135Hz	C#	+14.05¢
3rd	Solar Plexus (Manipura)	Solar Body	126.22Hz	C	126Hz	C	+3.02¢
2nd	Sex (Svadisthana)	Synodic Moon	210.42Hz	G#	202.5Hz	G#	-66.42¢
1st	Root (Muladhara)	Earth day	194.18Hz	G	192Hz	G	+19.54¢

Table 35.1 - The Cosmic Octave chakra tones contrasted to their closest correlate in the F#-Major, Geometric tuning system. Current 'Planetary' tone data is derived from Meinl's Planetary Tuning Fork data set.

Note: *136.10Hz Cosmic Octave value carries reference to an entry, which simply states "440Hz -31.4¢ " This math seems to directly imply a 432Hz reference.

Notwithstanding several niggling questions regarding the origins of the 'Cosmic Octave,' its use in sound and frequency healing has seen significant adoption rates by practitioners in the field. And, if you look to the chart above, you can observe a very close correlation with the Geometric System's F#-Major Tuning Grid. In fact, most of the tones only differ from their closest Geometric correlate, by an interval that is in the neighborhood of a quarter tone (often significantly less). In the case of the 'Solar Body' (Sun) tone, the difference is a mere 3.02¢.

This close correlation is the primary reason why we are exploring the 'Cosmic Octave' system in this text.

That this system's adoption by practitioners is often taken on faith, without the slightest suspicion that deeper questions are even pertinent to the subject — Certain questions must nevertheless, be addressed. One such question involves the tonal basis (fundamental basis) that was used to assign tone labels (notational names) to the frequencies.

Tonal assignment for the 'Cosmic Octave' initially, seems to be relative to the 440Hz, 12-TET common standard, which we have already discussed. It is an imperfectly contrived standard that is demonstrably not conducive to perfect harmony at any rate. Nor is it in any way, physiologically beneficial within the practice of sound and frequency wellness work. (For those who are 'in the know', please, wait for it.)

The tonal equivalence of the fourth chakra (*Anahata*) in the 'Cosmic Octave' system for instance, is set at a harmonic representing the 'Earth-Year' orbital calculation. The frequency given is 136.10Hz and is assigned the note 'C#', which is the closest correlate in the 440Hz, 12-TET system. The actual 'C#' in 440Hz, 12-TET is located at a frequency of 138.5911Hz.

The primary 'Cosmic' tone of 136.1Hz is referenced, in the data itself, to a mysterious notation that reads; "440Hz minus 31.4¢". While the notation makes little sense in context of the actual frequency calculation, the inclusion of this reference would, at first glance, seem to place the reference for the 'Cosmic Octave' within the 440Hz tuning paradigm.

But, wait! Take another look. What exactly is 440Hz minus 31.4¢? Well, that tone actually calculates to be 432Hz (plus or minus 0.1¢.)

So, is the actual notational reference for the Cosmic tones based upon a 432Hz, even-tempered standard? That certainly appears to be the case, based upon this mysterious reference in the data.

Yet, the current custodians of the system seem to provide just enough transparency to support the various premises associated with the tonal system and, do not provide much more data that could be used to further investigate the findings.

This fact makes verification and honest evaluation difficult, due to the absence of authoritative sources of and rationale for the validation *of* the originating data.

To be fair, that data may exist, *somewhere* in the public domain. However, our actual objective here is not to validate (or invalidate) someone else's work. Instead, we look for any useful correlations within any body of work as-presented. And, this objective has now been accomplished.

Most systems today, adhere to similar levels of obfuscation for the purpose of protecting what is considered proprietary or intellectual property. However, this writer proposes that this mindset is not at all appropriate for a holistic healing and wellness system that is offered to the world as a healing modality.

The practice of selective, systematic obfuscation, makes verification difficult if not impossible, gives rise to the proliferation of fabricated rationales to students and clients, completely blocks customization where warranted and desired, and is a reflection of everything that is wrong with the mainstream scientific community at-large.

In this work, the writer has made a painfully-conscious effort to simplify, and lay out the entire thought process as well as demonstrating each and every step of the processes described herein (often pedantically so). Sure! It requires a lot of words and charts. But, the reader can clearly see the complete thought process at every step. Whether the readers agree or disagree with the premise and methods is a completely separate issue.

Fair enough. We have just encountered yet another instance of 432Hz being useful as either a reference or foundational basis for tonal systems. The difference between 136.1 and 138.5911 in the 440Hz system is statistically significant (2.4911Hz or 31.4¢). And, to be fair, this fact is noted, if somewhat cryptically, on the official website, *planetware.de*. But, what happens when we attempt to 'realign' the assignment of 'Cosmic' tones with the 432Hz standard, instead of the 440Hz standard? The results should be interesting to say the least.

In the completed F#-Major Tuning Grid, the C# in question (The Cosmic 136.1Hz) resolves to a geometric, proximate of 135.00Hz.

Furthermore, the geometric magic of this frequency gives us a perfect 540Hz two octaves 'up.' 540Hz is a critical geometric value representing the pentagonal resonance as well as the Pentacle of Protection. Such precise correlation is not viewed as mere coincidence.

Moving up another octave, this series also yields a perfect 1080Hz, a number representing the octagonal resonance. When referencing the 432Hz tuning standard, the 'Cosmic Octave' suddenly takes on a bit more relevance to us, as its values *closely* reflect some of the most powerful of our geometric frequencies.

Aside from the tuning standard question, the next issue with the 'Cosmic Octave' is this; Why use orbital and rotational dynamics as a basis at all? There exist no inherent radiation of electromagnetic or piezo-electric effects in the planetary orbits themselves. Furthermore, orbital bodies' interactions with gravity and the solar 'winds' are the primary factor affecting their movements through the aether and maintaining their orbital positions against gravity. Shouldn't these be variable over time?

Should not these orbital movements undergo inevitable alterations through the ensuing eons? Are orbiting bodies somehow immune to Newtonian physics? Doesn't Earth's rotation slow or speed up due to impacts, acquisition of mass (system debris increases the Earth's mass up to 40,000 tons every year) and, even the occasional polar shifts?

These are all serious questions. Our own venerable moon, 'Luna' is said to be slowly propelling itself away from its orbit with Earth. Does this not set the precedent for orbital and rotational changes over time? Does it alter the Cosmic tones for Lunar correlates?

Add to all of these questions, the presumption that there are several other relevant geological effects that *should* result in changes in the normal planetary and solar system physics.

The point of these questions and observations is this; Logically, planetary orbital and rotational periods should be far from a constant phenomenon in the vast spans of universal time. Therefore as a basis for the 'Cosmic Octave', the premise seems suspect although, it does seem to produce tone values that are very close to those in our F# geometric tuning system.

Could these discrepancies represent small orbital and rotational changes over time? Could we backtrack these as a basis for explaining these subtle deviations? Again, all serious questions — to which the writer has found few answers. And, short of finding an astrophysicist with way too much time on their hands, we would be satisfied to simply leave it there.

However, and much to this writer's surprise, we learn from modern cosmology that; despite the expectations and predictions of Newtonian physics, cosmologists in their studies of orbital dynamics and paleo-astronomy, also seem to be scratching their heads over the observed, and apparent fact that the planets' momentums and inertias are evidently *not* variable in their orbits and orbital paths. At least, change is not occurring to any degree that might be predicted by the usual Newtonian calculations. Curious.

This cosmological truth points to some kind of unseen force that has yet to be quantified and studied. In fact, the orbital paths and periods seem to be remaining remarkably consistent for extremely long periods of time despite changes in the mass that occur naturally and, would... should warrant some alterations over time. Therefore, the suspect nature of basing the 'Cosmic Octave' upon planetary orbital data may not be... as far-fetched as first presumed.

The 'Cosmic Octave' calculations are said to be based upon these orbital physics and their straight-forward math alone. We will demonstrate this by recreating some of the actual math below.

However, it seems that the very basic physics of 'increased mass multiplied by acceleration' would necessarily be accounted for in said math. Again, these slight alterations in mass and momentum would require massive amounts of time. And, even though cosmologists now tell us that something mysterious maintains the celestial bodies in a constant inertial state of orbital and rotational velocities, there are still unaccounted-for assumptions inherent in the calculations which are in need of some clarification. However, these complicated factors would again, be the realm of the cosmologist.

Despite all of the theory and alternative math, the set of apparently self-evident facts point *at least,* to a certain acceptable margin of error. To that end, this writer assigns a higher margin of error on the Cousto calculations than many would be willing to allow. In fact, the small discrepancies existing between the Geometric tones and the Cosmic Octave tones falls *well within* any margin of error for Cousto's work as well as the geometric proposals contained herein. Your writer is not entirely oblivious to the apparent contradiction and intellectual irony contained in these statements. But, there you have it.

If in fact, Force = mass x acceleration (**F=ma**), then any increase in the Earth's mass (remember, that's 40,000 tons per year) should imply an inverse mathematical relationship with angular acceleration (assuming Force is unchanged in the equation.) Would not such a relationship cause *some* alteration in acceleration? That this affect would be evidenced in rotational as well as angular (orbital) momentum is a fact of Newtonian physics. But, again, modern cosmological observation does not seem to confirm these expected effects. Any physicists out there want to clarify this for us?

Whatever the actual situation, the writer stipulates that even over long periods of time, noticeable changes in orbital dynamics would be difficult to notice and nearly impossible to predict; much less to measure with the absolute precision. Therefore, the small differences between 'Cosmological ' and 'Geometric' tones should fall well within any margin of acceptable standard deviation. That this provides a validating opinion to both systems under discussion, is also, not a fact that is entirely lost upon this writer.

In recent cosmological developments, it has become increasingly obvious that each planet has its own electromagnetic signature. Such emanations would qualify as 'cosmic' or 'planetary' frequencies.

At the very least, *actual* electromagnetic frequencies emanating from a celestial body would seem to be far more significant signature value than the orbital period of that same body, which may or may not, change over geological spans of time.

Unfortunately, we find that the electromagnetic emanations of our home planet actually *are* extremely variable.

This variability is much more than a planet (say, Mars) that has no magnetosphere and extremely thin atmosphere.

As intriguing as it may be to reconstruct a cosmic scale based on actual planetary 'EM' field measurements, the details of such electromagnetic data for members of our solar system would be significantly variable as well, and therefore in constant need of adjustment. Additionally, such cosmological data sets, if even available, have apparently, not yet made it into the public domain. However, the constant variability alone would be a huge obstacle to creating a system with sufficient precision as to reflect the ever-changing emanations from our planetary neighbors.

At the very least, we can indulge ourselves with a deeper look into the intriguing ideas and calculations of Hans Cousto to understand some of his thought process behind the 'Cosmic Octave.'

To that end, let's first take the latest data from NASA (The U.S. National Aeronautics and Space Administration) and see how we can recreate the calculation for the frequency of the 'Sidereal Year' for Earth.

According to *nasa.fandom.com*, a sidereal orbital period is a *"regular, temporal cycle in which a celestial object makes one full orbit of another, specified celestial object."* This is independent of any other axis of motion or frame of reference.

According to the published data from NASA, Earth's sidereal period referencing the solar body, is 365.25636 days. Some sources quote the value as 365.24219 days, which is a more historical measurement called a 'Tropical year.'

Let's examine the results from both of these values to see what pertinent data (if any) is revealed.

For the astrological value of 365.25636 days, we calculate a value in seconds of 31,558,150 seconds.

1 ÷ 31,558,000 seconds = 0.000000031687536Hz
(This is how Hans Cousto derived the initial frequency.)

Next, we 'pull' the frequency into the audible range by octavating it the necessary number of times. In this case a thirty-two-fold doubling seems to have been used.

$$0.000000031687686Hz \times 2^{32} = 136.099Hz$$

Gently rounded, that gives us 136.1Hz (+/- .03Hz)

So, for the standard year, we arrive at the exact value that Cousto originally calculated as the Earth's Sidereal Frequency. Consequently, it is becoming more difficult to maintain a basic, healthy skepticism.

To continue; For the Tropical Year value of 365.24219 days, we calculate a value of 31,556,925 seconds.

Again, we pull the frequency into the audible range by octavating it the same thirty-two-fold doubling that was previously used.

$$0.000000031556925Hz \times 232 = 136.097Hz$$

Gently rounded, that gives us 135.53Hz (+/- .03Hz)

Therefore, we get somewhere between 135.53Hz to 136.10Hz — depending upon which measurement of a year is used. (Thus, the aforementioned, margin of error)

The former result is exactly that of the 'official' Cosmic Octave value for Earth's sidereal year (136.1Hz). It is not surprising at all, given that the officially-recognized length of the solar year has changed, if at all, very slightly within the short span of decades or even centuries of observation, depending upon who does the measuring and with what technology they perform the required measurements.

The result for the Tropical Year calculation (135.53Hz) brings us to a shockingly precise correlation with the geometric value of 135Hz, which value is only 0.53Hz (6.78ᶜ) away from our geometric frequency calculation for the C# previously and further discussed below.

Please note that the former result of 136.1Hz, is *also* a mere 1.1Hz Hertz (14.05ᶜ) away from our F# geometric tuning system's value for the C# in the same octave (135Hz).

Therefore, we see that both calculations are incredibly proximal to the same C# frequency.

These two calculations, not only raise the issue of minuscule, mathematical margin of error, but seemingly provide additional validation and prestige to the calculated value of the C# tone as presented in the F#-Major system itself. Additionally, the process provides no small, critical confirmation and validation to the 'Cosmic Octave' calculations themselves, since two completely different paths (techniques) have effectively led to the same destination.

As for the premise of the tone's useful application(s) in human wellness, there can be no doubt that the *esoteric* reasonings behind the 'Cosmic Octave' are currently, beyond any ability to validate with satisfactory scientific rigor or certainty. However, the same could be said for the F# Geometric system to which it is herein compared. Taken together however, the Cosmic tone's universally-close proximity to the correlate, geometric tones, as observed above, proves difficult to simply dismiss out-of-hand.

We have noted that the frequency for our 'geometric' C# of the same octave is 135Hz. These frequencies (135.00Hz, 135.53Hz and 136.1Hz) would be practically identical to the untrained human ear. And, considering the minute deviations and margins of error inherent in planetary calculations versus the absolute results gained from geometric methods, these two calculations just may represent imperfect reflections of the same esoteric principles and, serve as expressions of the symmetry of our universe.

The geometric tones are thus theorized by this researcher, to be well within any reasonable margin of error vis-a-vis the 'Cosmic' tones. In fact, they may just reflect the same concepts in different terms.

In order for the sidereal year calculations of Earth to result in an exact 135.00Hz, a few days would necessarily be removed from the solar year. And, while we know for a fact that the measurement and observational data of the solar year has changed over recorded history, we currently have no basis to justify any claim that up to five days have somehow disappeared over the ensuing millennia.

However, we do know that in early calendars, this same five-day discrepancy was a significant challenge to the calendar makers of

Sumerian, Babylonia, and Egypt of which cultures opted for a 360-day calendar with various systemic adjustments made periodically. There was always some type of 'fudge factor' involved in solar calendars of the period — as there is today. Thus, we make the seemingly preposterous suggestion that the Cosmic Octave closely reflects the concepts proposed in this very text, pertaining to strict Geometric tuning.

Notwithstanding the more esoteric details, the above result and the incredibly close proximity of the derived tones (i.e. 135.53Hz and 136.1Hz), are surpassingly difficult to dismiss as mere coincidence. In actuality everything about the 'Cosmic Octave' leads us back to the same math and verified results exposed by Hans Cousto earlier in this chapter, in comparison to the Geometric system, proposed.

In the considered opinion of this writer, a value of 135Hz would have been the superior 'perfect' result. But, a universe constantly hurtling headlong towards entropy rarely yields the precision that may be (in the moment) considered 'perfect' results. Cousto's calculations, given an acceptable margin of error in the planetary orbital numbers are just as valid as any purely, geometric values in this regard.

Let's now take some time to compare the Cosmic Octave calculations with the F#-Major Geometric Tuning system to closely observe the very small differences between the calculated tones in each system. The Cosmic Octave tones in this chapter are taken from the researcher's personal set of **Meinl** 'Planetary' tuning forks and confirmed through the documentation located on the 'Cosmic Octave' website at *planetware.de*. The Cosmic Octave values are displayed in descending order, sorted by frequenc. If differing frequencies have been made publicly available, the writer is unaware of them at the time of this writing.

Other than the obvious difference in the methods used to arrive at these two tonal systems and some conspicuously absent 'E' or 'B' tones in the above subset of 'Cosmic Octave' tones, the two subsets are remarkably similar to one another.

The 'Cosmic Octave' and the 'Geometric' system reveal results for each tone, most of which are not even a quarter-tone (@36^e) in disparity.

In fact, in just as many of the cited cases, the difference between these associated tones is barely distinguishable by the untrained ear. However, again the writer stipulates that this fact is no excuse for imprecision.

	Cosmic Octave		F#-Major Geometric			
Note	Tone Name	Cosmic Frequency	Correlate Note	Geometric Frequency	Deviation (cents)	Chakra Assignment
A#	Moon	227.43	A#	225.00	-18.6¢	
A	Venus	221.23	A#	225.00	+29.3¢	6th
G#	Neptune	211.44	A	216.00	+37¢	
G#	Synodic moon	210.42	A	216.00	+45.3¢	2nd
G#	Uranus	207.36	G#	202.50	-41¢	
G	Earth (Day)	194.18	G	192.00	-19¢	1st
F#	Jupiter	183.58	F#	180.00	-34.1¢	
F	Platonic Year	172.06	F	168.75	-33.6¢	7th
D	Saturn	147.85	D	150.00	+25¢	
D	Mars	144.72	D	144.00	-8.6¢	
C#	Mercury	141.27	C#	144.00	-33.4¢	5th
C#	Pluto	140.64	C#	144.00	+41¢	
C#	Sidereal Year	136.10	C#	135.00	-14.05¢	4th
C	Sun	126.22	C	126.00	-3.01¢	3rd

Table 35.2 - The Cosmic Octave 'Planetary' tones contrasted to their closest correlate in the F#-Major, Geometric tuning system. Current 'Planetary' tone data is derived from Meinl's Planetary Tuning Fork data. Chakra assignments included for easy cross-reference.

Author's Note: There are additional Cosmic Octave Series frequencies related to other large solar objects such as asteroids and planetisimals. Those tones listed above are those considered to be the 'Planetary' Series of frequencies.

The chakra frequencies indicated in Table 35.2, are those suggested by 'The Cosmic Octave' documentation on www.planetware.de. The author does not necessarily concur with the suggested chakra correlations and, therefore does not endorse the structures as-presented. All Cosmic Octave data are presented only as references to the Cosmic Octave system as presented in the publicly-available, Cosmic Octave literature.

The 'C' tone for the Sun frequency is especially notable for being a remarkably close match — a mere $3.01^¢$ (0.22Hz) in difference. Again, the writer views these values as well within any reasonable margin of error and, therefore seizes upon the suggestion that these two systems are very closely-related despite having been derived from completely different methodologies.

Perhaps the 'Cosmic Octave' and our geometric system are not so different as initially assumed. After all, utilizing two very different, independent methods related to the laws of the universe, we find a surprising degree of precision in the exposed correlations. Indeed, the demonstrated, close proximity between the 'Cosmic' and 'Geometric' tones is compelling.

The main difference between these two systems seems to be that; Here, with our 'Geometric' tuning grid systems, we are revealing every step of the process, openly — warts and all. However, the caretakers of the Cosmic Octave seem to prefer more of a 'closed source' paradigm. What other, original data exists behind proprietary barriers, that might reveal the deeper significance, and permit a more vigorous validation of the Cosmic Octave data? We may never know.
However, it is nevertheless, an intriguing question to this seeker.

While your writer *still* finds it difficult to qualify the premise that orbital periods, especially of far-distant objects, bear any special significance within wellness and human healing, the premise is nevertheless an interpretation of accepted cosmological truths, reflected in the common language of mathematics... and astrology, if one is to be perfectly honest.

Your author will be happy indeed, to see the day come when such inherent skepticism is proven to be unfounded. as this study of the Cosmic Octave has raised some intriguing questions that I would very much like to see studied in-depth, and ultimately answered.

And, while the premise of the Cosmic Octave's effects upon human physiology is lacking any concrete scientific basis, it can join our own Geometric systems, and a very long list of common, beneficial practices which share that same unfortunate and dubious distinction.

Whatever position one takes, the correlations identified between the Cosmic Octave and the Geometric tuning systems herein illustrated, seem to indicate some deeper kinship, worthy of the effort required to explore them more carefully.

In all candor, this writer came to the 'Cosmic Octave' with a significant bias against its basic premise and ultimately, its validity - a position which has been mollified to no small extent by examining the tonal series in some depth.

And, while I have pursued this exercise with intent towards being completely open to possible correlations and revelations, I still cannot quite find my way towards fully embracing the system's usage vis-a-vis the proposed chakra correlations, in any practice-specific way.

A surprising, if somewhat grudging respect for the system is the best the writer can currently muster, until such time as the *complete* research and developmental methodology for the Cosmic Octave are made publicly-clear.

I do so love a good mystery.

Chakra Sonic Geometry

The Shape of Sounds to Come?

From the beginnings of this project, the discovery of the most relaxing and healing pure tones possible has been the overarching objective. That it became necessary to explore a few related systems was due to the fact that the author wished to firmly establish the parameters for what is now to become a novel tonal system, for working with the human bio-field, or etheric energy system, if you prefer. This goal is to be accomplished by focusing upon the traditional energy centers described in the Upanishads and Vedas of the most ancient healing systems of which modern humanity remains aware — that of the Indus Valley civilizations.

Having approached the subject of human energy resonances from this alternate perspective, it is clear that previous arguments against the use of the modern (A-440Hz, 12-TET) system for relaxation and healing purposes are not only valid, but are logical, indisputable facts of music history.

However, many practitioners, through no fault of their own, daily utilize an erroneous tonal interpretation of the 'seven chakra' system for no other reason than that they are fully unaware that other options exist — or that other, more traditional systems are available. They... We! Are 'healers', not professional music historians and theoreticians. This researcher has fallen squarely into this non-technical category. To this very day, your writer continues to struggle with balancing these two vital aspects of the work. And, I can tell you from experience, you can't really be both at the same time.

Most sound and frequency practitioners and, many other musically-inclined individuals, know only what they were taught. Few, have the time or deeper interest in the 'why', to dissect their work through music theory and ancient history. That's why this text has been produced; to perhaps, shine a critical light on the high points of tonal systems used in healing work. And, to improve such systems for the benefit of humankind.

As with most practitioners, many of our revered teachers seem to cling to the established systems in order to avoid some illusory onus of their life's work being, somehow diminished. Instead, both (teachers and practitioners) should recognize that our work has thus far, been based upon the best information available to us, at the time. And, we should be able to move on with better information as it comes available. It is this writer's hope that the reader will find the information and proposals contained herein to be sufficiently compelling, effective, and practicable.

In the previous chapter and without significant discussion, we revealed the chakra frequencies proposed by the Cousto formulas, which yield the *'Cosmic Octave.'* Additionally, we have previously touched upon the significance of the same within the Solfeggio series. Regardless of the writer's personal feelings toward their basis and origin, there are far too many correlations between those systems and the herein proposed, and independently-developed 'Geometric' system to simply ignore.

Several of these cross-system, near-hit correlations are to be found in the 'Cosmic Octave' chakra frequencies and their proximate, corresponding tones found in the Geometric series. Likewise, the Solfeggio tones provide some degree of correlation as well. But, we will start from the beginning as, neither chakra-related system tracks to the most commonly-used tonal systems. Nor, should they.

Therefore, we will delve into these chakra frequencies in an attempt to build an effective and cohesive system intended for use with the geometric frequencies contained in the $F^{\#}$-Major Tuning Grid revealed in our earlier work. We will begin this exploration by looking at, what might well be, the most widely espoused chakra frequency system taught in western cultures.

That system of course, is the seven-tone system based on the 440Hz, 12-TET, C-Major. (You see what's coming now, don't you?)

In this system (Let's call it the 'Seven Chakra System based upon C-Major'), the first chakra is assigned a tone corresponding to middle-C (278.4375Hz) on the western keyboard. That value of course, corresponds to the A440Hz, 12-TET system's C^3. None of the readily-available data delves into any actual frequencies as the originators appear to *assume* the use of 440Hz, 12-TET tuning.

Seven Chakra System – Based on 440Hz (12-TET)			
Chakra	**Name**	**Note**	**Frequencies**
7th	Crown (Sahasrara)	B	246.942Hz, 493.8835Hz
6th	Third Eye (Ajna)	A	*220Hz, 440Hz, 880Hz
5th	Throat (Vishuddha)	G	195.998Hz, 391.996Hz
4th	Heart (Anahata)	F	174.614Hz, 349.228Hz
3rd	Solar Plexus (Manipura)	E	164.814Hz, 329.627Hz
2nd	Sacral (Svadisthana)	D	146.832Hz, 293.665Hz
1st	Root (Muladhara)	C	130.812Hz, 261.626Hz

Table 36.1 - An example of a seven-tone chakra system based on a theory utilizing the standardized, diatonic tones of 440Hz, even-temperament.

*The 220Hz and 440Hz values at the 6th chakra are the dead-giveaway that the system is locked to the A440Hz, 12-TET standard. Realistically, this convenient, unimaginative arrangement can reasonably and immediately dismissed as patently false.

Thereafter, this seven-chakra system (*Table 36.1*) simply runs, unimaginatively, through the rest of the western C-Major scale assigning the next diatonic 'note' to each successive chakra.

In an apparent quest for organization and simplicity — not only does this system base itself in a completely modern tonal paradigm that did not even exist until the later 18th century, it displays a shockingly blatant lack of imagination, and 'zero' respect to history. That it is limited to only seven chakra would be considered sufficient violation even if the tonal system *was* based on a more historically relevant tonal system.

However, disastrously assuming that Muladhara, and thus the remaining energy centers, are tuned to a modern, western C-Major scale, so conveniently beginning with 'C' at the Root, is more than sufficient disinformation to dismiss the premise out of hand.

And, 'dismissing it' is exactly what many knowledgeable practitioners have done. Either from experience, intuition, or both, many sound and frequency practitioners have thus rejected this system for any practical usage. It's just too conveniently 'modern' to be factual. Thus, the more experienced practitioners continue to search. But, in the searching, we are often following in the footsteps of others who know little more than we do (before reading this text,) and thus, are counting upon other *authorities'* findings, impressions, and opinions for their answers.

One such chakra 'grid' that has been developed takes a step in the right direction and, then for whatever reason, the developers just stopped looking any farther — evidently thinking that the ultimate answers had been found. The system in question is actually based on a 432Hz tuning system.

Seven Chakra System – Based on 432Hz (12-TET)			
Chakra	Name	Note	Frequencies
7th	Crown (Sahasrara)	B	242.452Hz, 484.904Hz
6th	Third Eye (Ajna)	A	*216Hz, 432Hz, 864Hz
5th	Throat (Vishuddha)	G	195.998Hz, 384.87Hz
4th	Heart (Anahata)	F	177.791Hz, 685.76Hz
3rd	Solar Plexus (Manipura)	E	167.812Hz, 323.635Hz
2nd	Sacral (Svadisthana)	D	149.504Hz, 288.326Hz
1st	Root (Muladhara)	C	133.192Hz, 256.87Hz

Table 36.2 - An example of a seven-tone chakra system based on a theory utilizing diatonic tones within 432Hz, even-temperament.

*The 'A' continues to be assigned to the 6th chakra level. However, this time we are using a 432Hz fundamental. Unfortunately, the developer(s) of the system doubled-down on *unintentional* misinformation by using the equal-temperament system built upon the 432Hz fundamental.

Unfortunately, that tuning system is mired in the same 'even-tempered' tuning upon which the previous C-Major Chakra system was based. The fundamental tone has been rightly adjusted, but not the proper interval ratios. Thus we find ourselves with another 'swing and a miss.'

Although a slight improvement is observed by basing the seven tone system on a 432Hz standard, it again appears as if whoever developed the system just stopped seeking. We again encounter that simple, C-Major scale based on even-tempered spacing; beginning somewhat conveniently and arbitrarily, with 'C' at the root chakra. Nowhere has this writer been able to find any Vedic source which adequately supports this placement of tones. Yet, here it is again.

It would be an amazing coincidence indeed, if the imperfectly contrived standard of common, modern tuning were to magically coincide with the chakra mapping system, which wasn't even widely known, much less acknowledged to any real extent in the west until the mid-twentieth century.

Like so many wondrous things transplanted to the west, the beneficiaries of the masters' teachings, apparently decided they were thus, sufficiently enlightened and, could do as well or better than the masters.

Some immediately began expanding, changing and even copyrighting (read: monetizing) their proprietary practices for various purposes. Some of the materials we receive from their teachings are compromises based upon a lack of deeper understanding.

As noted above, this particular aspect of the (western) healing practices does not appear to have been particularly well-thought out. The unhappy result is that many of the core practices and values taught by the true masters, have been diluted and monetized to the point of being essentially useless.

The system of energy work, meditation, and Indus spiritual tradition was brought into the western consciousness by some few masters who traveled from the Indus regions to England, Canada, Australia and the US — eventually establishing their own wisdom schools in those countries. Therefore, this writer finds it beyond ludicrous to assign modern tone systems to these ancient practices.

As we delve into the more innovative and imaginative systems, we encounter a surprise development.

Another Seven Chakra System – Based on branched 432Hz (12-TET)			
Chakra	Name	Note	Frequencies
7th	Crown (Sahasrara)	A	*108Hz, 216Hz, 432Hz
6th	Third Eye (Ajna)	D	144Hz, 288.33Hz, 576Hz
5th	Throat (Vishuddha)	G	192.66Hz, 384.66Hz 768.99Hz
4th	Heart (Anahata)	C	128.33Hz, 257Hz, 514Hz
3rd	Solar Plexus (Manipura)	F#	181.66Hz, 363.66Hz, 726.66Hz
2nd	Sacral (Svadisthana)	E♭	152.66Hz, 305.33Hz, 611.33Hz
1st	Root (Muladhara)	B♭	114.33Hz, 229Hz, 457.33Hz

Table 36.3 - An example of a seven-tone chakra system based on a theory utilizing tones within a variant branch of 432Hz, even-temperament.

*This time, the 'A' is assigned to the 7th chakra level. We are still using a 432Hz fundamental. But, here also the developers of the system miss the mark by using a variation of equal-temperament built upon the same 432Hz fundamental. The writer considers this a misstep in the right direction.

The above system is still based upon seven chakra. But, has managed to hit upon the fact that 'root chakra' does not necessarily mean that the root tone must be 'C.'

Unfortunately, the system utilizes nothing more than a branched, 12-TET *variation* of the 432Hz tuning standard. And, is therefore plagued with the unavoidable defects inherent in any forced equal-temperament system.

The basis for this particular system seems to be a kind of 'skein' that requires the frequencies to have decimal remainders of 0, .33, .66, or .99. This is actually a pretty neat trick if pulled off perfectly. Unfortunately, it is not accompanied by any rationale as to how these tones were derived or validated. This lack of in-depth background information is the greatest obstacle to believability.

Assuming that the skein is attempting to construct a coherent chakra 'scale,' let's see if we can figure out any pertinent interval widths in order to reconstruct this system. (See: *Table 36.4*)

Existing Tone List	
216Hz	0ᶜ
229Hz	101.2ᶜ
No tone	
257Hz	300.9ᶜ
No tone	
288.33Hz	500ᶜ
305.33Hz	599.2ᶜ
No tone	
No tone	
363.66Hz	901.9ᶜ
384.66Hz	999.1ᶜ

Table 36.4 - Tone list using second-octave values from table 36.3.

First we will arrange the tones in ascending order. Let's use the second octave from the chart in *Table 36.3*. We can then calculate and reveal the interval widths in cents. From there, we will be able to see more clearly what was done to create this system.

Based on this analysis, which simply calculates the intervals, in cents, from the indicated fundamental tone of 216Hz, we can now see and compare the values to standard systems. From the arrangement of the tones, it appears as if the 'scale' was created using something very close to equal-temperament. Notice that the intervals are essentially 100ᶜ wide, with some of the scalar frequency values omitted, for reasons undisclosed. We could easily backtrack the math to reveal the complete system. But, such would be pointless as the interval widths tell the whole story.

But, we insert the 'omitted' tones, (shown below in *Table 36.5*, in bold italic) we see what is obviously an even-tempered system based on 100ᶜ to the half-step interval — with a fudge-factor of plus or minus a couple of cents to suit the particular desire for the unique decimal remainders. It seems the originator of this system preferred the remainders of 0, .33, .66, or .99. Again, the reasoning for this is thus far, unknown. One could theorize that some variant of a 3, 6, 9 reduction skein was the objective. However, several of the resulting tones themselves do *not* reduce to 3, 6, or 9. To belabour a cliche' even further; yet another swing and a miss.

The octave frequency numbers of 216Hz and 432Hz represent the 'clincher' demonstrating exactly what was done in developing this system. Apparently, the originator(s) concluded that the 432Hz *even-tempered* scale was appropriate for use with the chakra system.

Completed Tone List		
216Hz	0ᶜ	
229Hz	101.2ᶜ	(100ᶜ)
242.66	198.9ᶜ	(200ᶜ)
257Hz	300.9ᶜ	
272.00	399ᶜ	(400ᶜ)
288.33Hz	500ᶜ	
305.33Hz	599.2ᶜ	(500ᶜ)
323.66	700ᶜ	
342.99	800.6ᶜ	(800ᶜ)
363.66Hz	901.9ᶜ	
384.66Hz	999.1ᶜ	(1000ᶜ)
407.66	1099.6ᶜ	(1100ᶜ)
432Hz	1200ᶜ	

Table 36.5 - Tone list using third-octave values from table 36.3. The 'missing' tones to complete the octave, have been added to more-easily visualize the 12-TET variation as applied in this system. Additionally, note that the usual 12-TET interval widths are included to clarify the scheme utilized.
Interestingly, the original skein remains intact.

There's no real mystery here. It's someone's idea of a variation we will call '432Hz - pseudo even temperament.'

Then, they simply used the variant system to express that belief without the indispensable knowledge regarding the origins and defects inherent in equal-temperament.

Fair enough, I suppose. For over fifty years, this writer didn't know better either. However, the manipulation to arrive at frequencies with manageable, predictable remainders of .33, .66, and .99 was an interesting variation. But, again with no validating rationale attached, it's just a neat numbers trick. So, we move on.

We have discussed the limitations and inherent problems with equal-temperament, ad-nauseam in earlier chapters. So, the kind reader will likely appreciate that we don't get into that again, here.

However, I cannot resist one more dig; In this writer's considered opinion, modern, even temperament's application to ancient practices and wisdom is questionable on every conceivable level.

Ultimately, whether this practice is acceptable, right, wrong, good, or bad is up to the individual practitioner... and their clients. In this demonstration, the writer simply wishes to point out the obvious defect(s) for consideration.

Continuing in this vein, the writer wishes to 'parse out' some of this existing information. The purpose is; to propose a coherent system, applicable to chakra vortex frequencies, that meshes well with the order and symmetry of geometry. Knowing that we already have the frequencies and note assignments calculated, this should be a surpassingly simple task. Thus, we proceed.

First, it is proposed that we acknowledge fully, fourteen etheric energy centers within the human chakra vortex systems. We know there are dozens of energetic vortices inherent within and surrounding the human body. Some of these vortices are useful in interactions with matter and its transmutation (manifestation), while others are useful in interfacing with the energy fields of other living creatures, including humans. Still other etheric vortices are suited to more esoteric purpose such as inner sight, outer sight, and remote sight (as examples). Please note that this is not a complete listing of chakra energy attributions.

While we will not delve deeply into the application and effects, it is imperative that each practitioner understand that there are many more chakra vortices with which we *could* concern ourselves. Such study is impractical in the current format. But, *will* be the topic of future works under this imprint.

From top to bottom, we will list fourteen of the main (common seven chakra system) and accessory chakra centers applicable to the human etheric field and energy centers. This is by no means a comprehensive or even particularly detailed listing.

The purpose of the detail is to assist the reader in following the author's logic and thought processes as they are being presented and discussed.

Fourteen Chakra and Etheric Vortices Related to the Human Bio-Field

- **Higher Realms** - Beyond and Above the 'personal' chakra system, Clairvoyance, Unity with the All, part of the visible aura reported by many practitioners.
- **Soul Star** (Located 'above' the crown chakra and extends upward and outward into other-dimensional realms. Interface with Universal, Transcendence), Extension of the Crown vortex cross-dimensional
- **Crown** (Ascendant energies and Spiritual Enlightenment)
- **Third Eye** (Deep Intuition, Empathy and Inner-sight)
- **Throat** (Expression, Understanding, Being Understood)
- **Greater-Heart** (Higher Love, Wisdom, True Purpose, and Direction)
- **Heart** (Compassion, Appreciation, Seat of the True Self, BE-ing)
- **Palm of the Right Hand** (Giving, Generosity, Delivering to higher purpose, Helping others)
- **Palm of the Left Hand** (Receiving, Acceptance, Possessing, Balancing the same)
- **Solar Plexus** (Main Energy Production and Assimilation - The Furnace or Dynamo)
- **Sacral** (Self Image, Sexual Identity and Reproductive energy)
- **Root** (Boundaries, Confidence, Material manifestation [down-flow], Seat of Physical Identity and Projection of same [up flow])
- **Knees** (Grounding, Balance - Right is forward, Left is backward)
- **Earth Star** (Depths of grounding and connection in the Earth's energies)

'Higher Realms' is included in our final listing. But, it is not specifically a chakra center. Instead, it is a toroidal vortex to/from higher connection. While technically an other-dimensional energy and frequency range, it is helpful in visualizing the raising of energetic consciousness above the typical range of the dense, limited three-dimensional plane.

To be sure, other significant energy vortices exist within the human etheric field and beyond. For instance, some teachers focus on the vortices behind and through each knee or in the shoulders. There is no practical way to explicitly incorporate all of the known vortices into a single wellness session. Therefore we focus upon those that promise the most enlivening effects to the entire system. However, when a practitioner perceives the need to do so, these 'other' vortices can easily be incorporated into a cohesive system by simply drawing upon the appropriate geometric frequencies and progressions.

Now, for the proposed frequencies and ranges for each of the fourteen chakra vortices listed above… the following practical *prototype* grid has been produced for developmental purposes and has thus far shown significant promise.

Chakra Tone Correlations Based Upon Geometric Tuning Grid			
Energy Vortex (Chakra)	Note	Applicable Frequencies	Low Freq. Carrier (LFC)
Higher Realms (Unity)	G#	1620, 3240, 12960Hz	50.625, 101.25Hz
Soul Star (Transcendence)	F#	1440 & 2880Hz	45, 22.5Hz
Crown (7th)	F	675, 1350, & 2700Hz	42.1875, 84.375Hz
Third Eye (6th)	D#	600, & 1200Hz	37.5Hz
Throat (5th)	C#	270 & 540Hz	33.75, 67.5Hz
Right Hand (giving)	E	315 & 630Hz	39.375Hz
Left hand (receiving)	E	315 & 630Hz	39.375Hz
Higher Heart (Hi-Four)	A#	450, & 900Hz	28.125Hz
Heart (4th)	A	432, 864Hz	27, 54Hz
Solar Plexus (3rd)	G#	405 & 810Hz	25.3125, 50.625Hz
Sacral (2nd)	G	192 & 384Hz	24, 48Hz
Root (1st)	F#	180 & 360Hz	22.5, 45Hz
Right Knee (front)	C	252 & 504Hz	31.5, 63Hz
Left Knee (back)	C	126 & 252Hz	31.5, 63Hz
Earth Star (Grounding)	F	84.375 & 168.75Hz	42.1875Hz

Table 36.6 - Proposed chakra tone correlations based upon the geometric tonal system using F#-180Hz standardized tuning grid designed in earlier chapters. The correlates are based upon experiential data and is considered a prototype draft system.

Many of the base or, carrier frequencies in *Table 36.6*, are below the capacity of most consumer sub-woofers to reproduce and, many mainstream amps also may not reproduce signals below 27-31Hz. In such cases, either omit the carrier altogether or octavate it to the lowest frequency that can be handled by your sound reproduction equipment (shielded, analog of course). Appropriate harmonics can be used as well as the recommended Low Frequency Carrier (LFC.)

For those practitioners desiring to work only the main seven chakra vortices as taught in many contemporary traditions, Here is a clarified version based only upon those vortex energies with the secondary frequencies omitted for ease of reference.

Seven-Chakra System Tone Correlations			
Energy Vortex (Chakra)	Note	Primary Frequencies	Low Freq. Carrier (LFC)
Crown (7th)	F	675, 1350, & 2700Hz	42.1875, 84.375Hz
Third Eye (6th)	D#	600, & 1200Hz	37.5Hz
Throat (5th)	C#	270 & 540Hz	33.75, 67.5Hz
Heart (4th)	A	432, 864Hz	27, 54Hz
Solar Plexus (3rd)	G#	405 & 810Hz	25.3125, 50.625Hz
Sacral (2nd)	G	192 & 384Hz	24, 48Hz
Root (1st)	F#	180 & 360Hz	22.5, 45Hz

Table 36.7 - Proposed seven-chakra system tone correlations based upon the geometric tonal system using the F#-180Hz Geometric tuning system designed in earlier chapters. The correlates are based upon experiential data and are collectively, considered a prototype draft system.

What's With the 'A' at the Heart Chakra?

Our reference tone of 432Hz is conspicuously positioned at the 4th chakra vortex position listed above. Many may recoil at this obvious and somewhat presumptious reclassification. The writer completely understands the reticence in accepting the proposal that our much-vaunted A-432Hz fundamental is not an appropriate resonance for the 6th or 7th chakra, to which it is generally assigned.

432Hz is *actually* fundamental to linking the upper and lower chakra system vortices as a kind of transitional or unifying tone.

The upper chakra vortices and the lower chakra vortices meet in proximity at the upper 'knot', which is located just above the 4th chakra vortex. Using the foundational, universal 432Hz tone, brings these two vortices closer *in-sync* (for lack of a better term). Once properly prepared, raising that frequency to the A# tones indicated as the 'Higher Heart' serves to elevate and press higher energy against that knot; loosening it in preparation for upper-chakra work beginning for instance, with the C# of the 5th chakra.

As I am fond of saying, *"Everything is Heart. All uplifting intention begins with Appreciation, grows into deep Gratitude, then matures into Compassion and, ultimately continues in Love."*

This personal quote seems a fitting description of the overriding role of the Heart energies such as *gratitude* and *compassion,* in human spiritual growth, as well as in general health and wellness. This illustrates well, the central role of heart energies in achieving our individual goals, connecting the material (lower chakras) to the ethereal (upper chakras), and using the heart-force as the great amplifying unifier. Thus, it is fitting that the heart chakra be resonant with the essential, pivotal, and unifying frequency of 432Hz. This is most humbling realization that this writer has discovered, thusfar.

Additionally, in our tuning grids, recall that the 'A' reference tone was just that; a reference point, or seed value, around which we unified our geometric system. 432Hz's origins are not at all geometric but its geometric-*esque* characteristics enabled us to build a geometric system upon its resonance; as a unifying foundation. Every successful geometric tuning grid we have built in this work was based in some way, upon the uniqueness and ineffable power of the 432Hz resonance.

To review or refresh your understanding as to why this proposal uses a 432Hz fundamental pivot tone, please refer back to: *Chapter 6 - The 432Hz Question and Chapter 9 - The Case for 432Hz.*

The A-432Hz may not be the player we may have expected. It is 'foundational' and, exists more as a unifying force that joins two parts of the whole into a cohesive One-ness. Think of it as a universal, unifying and connecting component within the entire system, that brings together and 'binds' the upper and lower chakra energies.

Can we use the A-Major tonal series in other ways in healing sessions? Absolutely! We not only enjoy its use in other sections but, highly recommend it. So how does that concept work? Just remember; *"Everything is Heart..."* and must be initiated with heart.

The writer tends to think of the A-Major tonal series (within the F# tuning system) as being similar to punctuation in grammar. In other words, it can be used to indicate when a section is ending, a new section is beginning, and when the whole session is complete. The A-Major tonal series is a baseline series that is appropriately used before, between, and after each *section* of a 'performance' or session. Its use always brings us back to the core or *heart* of any energetic situation.

As your client(s) are entering the space and settling in, your session should have already begun; with light and harmonious chords and phrases keyed in Geometric A-Major, one should fill the space with its heart-based, calming, and expansive resonance — preparing the client(s), performer(s), and the space itself for the coming session.

A-432Hz is the tuning standard for our *higher purposes*. Before any conventional musical group begins a performance, all of the instruments must first warm-up and then tune themselves in order to perform harmoniously.

This warm-up is the first and most important usage of the Geometric A-Major tonal class. By extension, the clients and the space itself, are integral 'instruments' in the work being done. Therefore, we can think of this 'prelude' portion as analogous to the orchestra tuning up. Always encourage your participants to begin their preliminary grounding work during this time... Silently.

The second application for the A-Major key change is as brief interludes, bridges or transitions, if you prefer, between the different sections of the session. Let's say you just completed a ten-minute grounding (Root/Muladhara) series. You now wish to move your focus to the chief resonances of the sacral chakra (Swadhisthana) energies. The frequencies of root grounding should be gently faded out. But, one shouldn't necessarily move directly into the new energetic frequencies of the sacral vortex.

The current 'energy' needs to circulate for a time, before we move onward and upward, so to speak. Some may regard this process as 'sealing' or 'closing' the section with *Heart*. And, it amounts to nothing more or less than a brief change of musical key to A-Major followed by the main key change to the next proper musical signature.

The Geometric A-Major series is perfect for such brief interludes between the energetic *divisions* of your sessions. It is pure, heart-based tone, is non-disruptive, and supports the settling and integration of energies before moving on. It also serves as an audible bookmark to inform the gathering that 'we are now moving on' to the next energetic level.

Utilizing the A-Major key of the Geometric F#-Major Tuning system follows this basic logic and theoretically has similar effect(s).

Finally, we come to the end of the session. As the final tonal series is gently allowed to fade, in we come with the 'binding' and 'foundational' energy of the Geometric A-Major tone class.

This allows a graceful method for ending the session by energetically binding the energies and thus, 'sealing' and integrating the session's energies - with heartfelt gratitude. This 'coda' portion of the session should continue until all participants have returned to full awareness and have *silently* exited the main session space.

That's your writer's opinion anyway.

Creating Our Geometric Sound Field

Natural items are always the best sound sources. This goes without saying. But, to obtain natural instruments that can reliably create the Geometric Tuning System's unique tones is… difficult (and expensive as they would most likely be custom instruments.)

Thus, to detractors of the use of technology in sound and frequency work, the writer asserts that there is absolutely nothing wrong with embracing appropriate technology and bending it to our will.

Generally, technology and the big tech companies bend us and our habits to their will. Contrary to popular thinking, the right technology with the correct application methods will yield amazing results. Results that the client is ready and open to receive. Available technology can also deliver the depth of potential that the practitioner channels with their *intention*. We will superficially discuss this topic in a bit more in-depth fashion in the next chapter, *'Chapter 37 - Modern Sound production.'*

Basic Methodology (Suggested Application)

When utilizing programmable keyboard instruments such as analog synthesizers or similar technology, expansion of any single-tone application is possible by utilizing the notes which make up the Major Triad for the base note indicated.

Just as an Example; When chording on the keyboard, use a C#-540Hz, gently add in the Major 3rd and the Perfect 5th. Within our geometric F# Major tuning, this would give us C#-540Hz, F-675Hz, and G#-810Hz. When gently added, one note upon on another, this triad figuratively 'fills the heart' with tone and encourages the energy to move 'upward.' The magic is in the root tone (In this case, C#-540Hz) and its harmonics, of which the Major triad tones are active participants. Make sure the root tone continuously rings as the dominant (anchor) frequency. You can also reinforce the root tone's effect by reaching down an octave (or three) to incorporate its lower frequencies or even the carrier (LFC) vibe for just a few seconds.

Of course, other instruments and sounds would be incorporated as desired.

Depending on the session's objective, one could move the Major triad an octave up to work toward the *Higher Heart* resonances before transitioning the key signature to the 'D', (with a brief sealing passage using A-Major intervening,) of the *Throat Chakra* resonance. This can serve to incorporate and connect the two. If great sadness, loss, or lack of compassion is in play, move the triad's Major 3rd down a half step and then work back up from this minor triad back into the major to 'uplift' the Heart resonances. The minor triad moves the F-675Hz down to a E-648Hz. Again, these are just examples and, not any kind of strict guideline. As always, consider the A-Major key to close and seal the Heart region before moving to the next section.

336

Note: When using the F#-Major Geometric Tuning Grid, the harmonies for any triad mode will naturally be in-tune. That's the beauty of using that particular Geometric grid system.

Conclusion

In this chapter we have explored a few of the many existing strategies used for addressing human chakra bio-resonance (and etheric resonance) in a therapeutic manner, using the F#-Major Tuning Grid. A strong rationale against utilizing modern tuning systems, especially even-tempered constructs, has been laid out earlier in and throughout this text to the best of this writer's ability.

Additionally, the writer's strong aversion to the use of even-tempered systems, including the 440Hz tuning standard, have been reiterated yet again, in this chapter.

To this point, among the more common and popular bio-resonance systems, there has thus far been revealed no coherent system which does not rely upon the 440Hz even-tempered standard, 432Hz equal-temperament, or a hybrid even temper of variegated rationale. Thus, the author's intended premise has been made abundantly clear.

Furthermore, the implications of said premise are even more transparent. To wit; we in western culture have gotten everything regarding the tunings for sound and frequency healing, completely, disastrously wrong thus far. It is now high time we fixed it.

A proposed system utilizing the theoretical F#-Major Geometric Tuning Grid constructed earlier in this book, has been put forward as a prototype system showing both incredible flexibility and great promise in supplanting the deficient tonal systems in common use today.

That the proposed theoretical system may be subjectively imperfect to some is an accepted outcome. However, the presented system represents a conscientious, (quite literally) inspired, best-effort approach to remedy the litany of imperfections and misconceptions inherent in current, standard sound and frequency, wellness practice. If one were to take exception to the proposals outlined herein, please accept the writer's open invitation to improve upon them.

It is hoped that those in the sound and frequency healing community, around the world may embrace, enhance, and ultimately perfect the system for the greatest, benevolent outcome for humankind.

The writer would like to sincerely thank you, the kind reader for picking up this text and giving its concepts and theoretical constructs a 'fair trial.' Those of us with *Available Light* in the US and Japan, would eagerly embrace and freely disseminate any beneficial, *constructive* communication as well as technical developments that may be discovered while working with these systems and concepts.

We are all in this life together. And, no one gets out without first learning something new and, leaving lots of love behind.

NAMASTE!

For our final challenge, we will *attempt* to assist the novice in creating their very own, powerful, and unique sound system to safely and energetically uplift our client(s), and to assist them on their unique and rewarding journey through life and wellness.

Join your somewhat fatigued writer *one more time*, in **Chapter 37 - Modern Sound Production**, to discover just a few of the basics of building a modern sound studio for delivering massively-powerful sonic sessions.

The writer does not consider himself to be a technical, sound production professional. And, continues to struggle with the parameters of this particular aspect of practice. However, I will do my best to convey that, which has been learned while walking upon this particular path.

Modern Sound Production

"All This Machinery Making Modern Music"

In this, our final chapter, we will superficially explore the tools of sound production and recording with some of the more common technology currently available at the time of this writing.

The information, herein, is intended for the *novice* as it contains what the writer feels to be, some of the most pertinent start-up information that was found to be very difficult or nearly-impossible to locate when beginning this project. It is not intended as a complete nor authoritative walk-through or tutorial.

It's true! When originally beginning this quest, several years ago, there apparently existed no centralized source of information for learning the absolute basics of electronic, computer and MIDI music creation… at least prior to making an equipment purchase. But, if you don't know what to do or even how to do it, how can you decide on a major purchase such as a piece of expensive sound equipment?

Even at the time of writing, there remains a dearth of extant sources for the most basic information intended for the novice on the topic of computer production of audio (and video). It often seems as if those who have it all figured out, are expressly unwilling to share their knowledge and skills with others — seemingly determined to keep the most fundamental knowledge from reaching the newbies who are interested in building their own personal studio.

And, yes! Taking a web-based course on this subject is a fine idea. But, for the gut-it-out yourself type like me, the only way to learn is by doing.

Therefore, the information in this chapter is geared towards those who are just beginning their explorations into the world of MIDI sound, synthesizers and computer-based sound production.

While this is not by any means a comprehensive technical walk-through, it will provide an overview of much of the concepts, software, and necessary connections to begin working with sound and frequency healing from a technological standpoint.

Neither is this his information all-inclusive as far as available equipment is concerned. But, it should provide the beginner with a wealth of information that will prevent falling into that whole "You gotta buy one before you can see how it works" paradigm. Take it from me; money wasted on mistaken musical purchases is a leading cause of marital strife.

For those already versed in the use of MIDI instruments and sound, this will be very basic information indeed. However, for those of us who find ourselves utterly confused by all the components and jargon, this is a good place to make a start.

For instance, if one wished to learn how to use a midi keyboard with their computer, most available information would mostly talk all over the topic or speak in such complex terms that the beginner would be completely lost at the outset.

Of course, there is always the user manual. But, this generally assumes that you already purchased the equipment in question. The available *external* sources of information and guidance, never actually tell you how the process is accomplished beyond connecting the correct cables.

Fortunately, it really isn't that difficult to grasp. But, buying equipment without a clear, prior understanding of how it works and fits in to your system is unnecessarily stressful and costly.

So, in this chapter, the writer will share basic, hard-won information on the three most important facets of starting down the path of turning an average sound bath session into an all-immersive healing experience using (gasp!) technology that supports and enhances any acoustic instruments one may additionally utilize.

These three major concerns (in no particular order) are

- What exactly do I need?
- What equipment will work as intended? And…
- How do you make all this stuff work together anyway?

All of these questions are fair but, complicated to answer. And, the answers often depend upon the practitioner's experience with computers, music, their specific vision, and the budget for a sound and frequency therapy studio setup. However, we will endeavor to provide the most useful, (and basic) guidance possible to get you acquainted with the methodology.

The Heart of the Sound System - A Keyboard Synthesizer

Arguably, the most important and flexible piece of equipment in our entire system would be an analog synthesizer. And, since these beasts come in so many different configurations, allow me to save the kind reader, who may know nothing about these machines, a lot of nail-biting and frustration.

The particular synthesizer necessary for our custom tuning paradigm and to create sound and frequency healing applications, would necessarily meet several specific criteria. Otherwise, the practitioner may find themselves with a piece of equipment that simply cannot do what is needed.

First, The proper synthesizer must be, or possess, analog processing and output circuitry. This cannot be stressed enough and, simply means that the signal is processed and created without the use of digital computer processing. Instead, the signal is produced by capacitors, oscillators, and other solid-state, analog hardware circuits that hand off their respective signal to the next 'link' in the circuitry — and not to a silicon processor. This may be oversimplified but, it is the basic point. Most analog synthesizers will bill themselves as such in their basic marketing.

To be sure, modern analog synthesizers will likely still have digital aspects to their control systems; such as displays, data storage banks, and certain other technology which allows it to interface with computers and other devices. But, the sound signal itself is rendered by passing variable, generated signals through the solid-state circuitry. Additionally, this means that the full signal, warts and all, is sent to the output without any digitizing, clipping, or other computerized curation of the signal.

Next, the synthesizer must allow for complete re-tuning, either by direct manual programming using an included interface, or via the uploading of completed tuning files (using something called the MIDI Transport System or 'MTS'). Such systems must also provide for the permanent, internal storage and manual selection of the desired tuning standard that we have created and loaded. (More on creating tuning files later.) This point is absolutely imperative. And, while many manufacturers seem to have little interest in providing this useful feature in their products, the writer happily found one veteran manufacturer who consistently and reliably incorporates programmable tuning functions into practically every synthesizer produced. That manufacturer is Dave Smith Instruments (DSI) out of San Francisco, California. This company has made analog 'synths' since the earliest days of their use. (The author is in no way affiliated with DSI.)

It should be noted that synthesizers are sold in two basic hardware configurations: console synths and keyboard synths. The difference is that a console synth requires a separate 'midi controller' usually a keyboard while the keyboard synth actually has one built-in. Otherwise, within the same model series, they are the same machine. Either type will work for our purposes providing it meets the other stated criteria.

If you choose a console synth, be very clear with the maker's customer support community as to which controllers are best, most popular, and or recommended for the synth model you choose.

The tuning grids and the various supplemental charts contained in this book were all tested and tweaked using a DSI *'Prophet REV2'* keyboard synthesizer with 16-voice polyphony (sixteen voice polyphony is an amazing, recent development at the time of this writing). DSI, aka;

Dave Smith Instruments, manufactures several other analog synth variations which serve the needs of this sound and frequency healing work very well.

Other manufacturers have, and continue to, periodically produce programmable-tuning synthesizers. However, none to this writer's knowledge, have demonstrated quite the commitment to the custom-tuning feature found in the DSI product lineup. Even the most recognized synth-giants still manufacture much of their product line, either locked into 'standard' tuning or requiring a persistent computer-software interface for playing in alternate tunings. To be fair, Moog systems with which the writer is familiar and that do support alternate tunings are excellent and very useful products.

Ultimately, when selecting a synthesizer, an intuitive interface is the next most important physical component. Some prefer Moog's interface while others will prefer DSI, or some other manufacturer. As long as the synth has true analog sound production, appropriate polyphony, and supports custom user tunings, you will quickly be on your way to creating sound and frequency sessions that your peers can only dream of. (Note: the 'after-touch' feature is also a very useful feature that is common but, not universal to modern synthesizers.)

If you are new to synthesizer keyboard work, any interface, with myriad controls, sliders, oscillators, and potentiometers will be equally daunting. And, while some study is necessary to understand how they work, it is not really as complicated as it first appears. You could be creating custom sounds in no time with just a little persistence.

For those who like to jump right in; Most of the currently-available analog synths come packed with extensive factory default 'sound banks' some of which contain hundreds of pre-programmed sound 'envelopes' for immediate use. You might find your perfect sound without even learning the difference between 'additive' and 'subtractive' synthesis. But, in this writer's opinion, it is so much fun to play around with the oscillators and discover unique sounds with a well-made synthesizer.

Additionally, there are several synthesizer 'cookbooks' on the market which generally skip, or at least gloss over, all the complicated technical language and just show you how different classes of sounds are produced. These are invaluable tools in that they save huge amounts of time and, foster a 'learn as you do' approach.

Sound Output - Basic Monitor Speakers (For Starters)

Synthesizers are just one component of your setup — meaning that it is only one part of an intricate system. There are several more components necessary to complete your system. One of the things conspicuously missing thus far, is a method of actually hearing the sound that is produced. Namely, the speaker output.

> Note: Sounds contained in a synthesizer's sound banks are not linked to any particular tuning standard. They are actually just the logical 'envelope' in which your selected tones are packaged for playback.
> While a sound envelope (MIDI envelope) contains the data instructions on *how* the note will sound, they are agnostic as to the actual tonal frequency fed into them.
> Therefore, they do not require any specific tuning standard to operate correctly. You can definitely make use of the cornucopia of pre-programmed sounds with any custom tunings.

When starting simple or just learning a tune, the best and easiest way to hear what you play would be to connect some studio 'monitor' speakers directly to the outputs of your chosen synth. Most synths will have right and left phono-type outputs that can connect directly to your monitor(s). Make sure you obtain the proper cables for your output connector type as there are a few variations.

Studio monitor speakers are generally small but powerful loud-speaker units that usually look like bookshelf speakers but, have their own crossover and amplifier built in. This way, the pre-amplified output from the synth, is sent directly to the monitor's amplifier, and is reproduced by the actual speaker.

Monitors can serve multiple purposes for various systems. But in this case, are intended merely to hear the sounds produced directly from the synth. Note that wireless monitor speakers (Bluetooth or other wirelessly-transmitted signal) suffer from the same deficiencies as most digital sound devices; i.e. to conserve bandwidth, signal loss is inevitable. As messy as things can get with a wired system, the writer recommends always using a cabled connection as this provides you with the purest possible signal with no detectable delay in the sound reproduction.

Granted, monitor speakers are not an absolutely critical element except for practice and session design. But, they make things so much more convenient. Generally, monitor speakers are not used when actually performing sound and frequency wellness sessions. They are recommended as a quick and simple way of using the keyboard without having to 'fire up' the entire studio sound system just to work by yourself. This setup is also a bare-bones method for exploring the world of sound and frequency therapy without going all-in and going all-broke at the same time. So far, your investment in the system should be somewhere between US$2000 - $2700 (at 2021 US Dollar currency values).

We will discuss more on main sound output amplification and speaker systems as we continue our discussion.

Data Storage and Creation Platform - Dedicated Computer System

For your creation platform, It should come as no surprise that a computer system is required if you truly wish to enter the world of alternate tuning systems. You will need to have a method of design, storage and output as well as a device responsible for being the 'master MIDI clock' of your entire system (optional).

Such a system is easy to acquire but, has a few options of which the less initiated may need to be made aware.

Many software music creation systems utilize what is called 'core threading' of certain tasks. Multi-track music creation is definitely one of those situations that benefits significantly from a system whose main processor (CPU) is equipped with multiple processing 'cores' which can hand off tasks in a process to several different logical processing threads. There currently exists a wide selection of main processors (CPUs) to meet such needs — from four core processors all the up to 26 core processors. However, at this time, anything more than six cores in an otherwise speedy CPU is likely to be overkill in our general-use production work-flow.

The next consideration is available memory. Again, there are several options for system memory (RAM) capacity. To be brief; with current technology, Thirty-two gigabytes of system memory is more than sufficient in all but the most extreme cases. Sixteen gigabytes is a happy medium for most situations.

Both scenarios will provide plenty of 'overhead' for running multiple applications and even checking your social media feed without compromising your system performance. (Seriously though, don't use this system as a general purpose system. Doing so can lead to tears.) The writer recommends a strictly-dedicated system — for production work only.

Permanent data storage (aka hard drives) on your computer system should be very generous. Music files stored on your system can be quite large. The actual lossless recordings for playback will be huge! Since we will be recording our various tracks in the most 'lossless' formats available, the word 'huge' may not quite cover it. For example, if a three-minute lossless track requires 250 megabytes of data, imagine the storage that sixty minutes of audio will require on your system. A quick calculation at only a 192kHz 'bit sampling rate' in two-channel stereo, puts a sixty minute track at a whopping 4.2 gigabytes! This is in addition to all the software and instrument files otherwise needed. Therefore, the writer recommends at least one terabyte of main system storage (system and main data storage) in the form of a 'high-speed' *solid state drive* (or SSD), as well as another two terabyte (2TB) of storage on a separate (internal or external) device for backups and less-used data.

If you plan on producing ambient visuals to accompany some sessions, the video files will require even more storage space. Adjust accordingly depending on your specific needs.

Unless you plan on producing video presentations to go with your sessions (some practitioners have done this to great effect), your graphics processing hardware (aka your GPU) should not require much attention. Any graphics adapter that is compatible with your system and video monitor should serve you well. So, at least that decision should be a bit easier. For those who do plan for video presentations, a good graphics subsystem, (aka a discrete GPU) with at least four gigabytes (4GB) of on-board video memory (VRAM) should do the trick for playback performance.

The one thing I would stress regarding graphics adapters, is that some retail system sellers use cheaper graphics adapters with very little video memory (VRAM) installed on the adapter itself. Also, many CPUs are now equipped with integrated graphics capability.

In the latter case, there may not be a separate (discrete) video adapter in your brand new computer system at all. This is because the CPU handles that function via a built-in or 'integrated' graphics processor. These types of systems usually take (allocate) a chunk of your system memory in order to operate properly.

In the writer's experience, this extra step in processing the video signal through multiple data channels, slows the system down somewhat. For example, avid gamers would never settle for a system that uses in integrated GPU — it would just be too slow.

Therefore, one might consider a separate or 'discrete' GPU that has sufficient VRAM installed on the adapter itself. Your graphics processing will then provide less of a load on the CPU and RAM installations because, the adapter can handle video processing on its own.

> If you produce your own video, the rendering or converting of video tracks will generally require significantly more VRAM. But, again, for simple playback, the stated recommendation of four gigabytes will generally be sufficient.

Additionally, if you now already know that you prefer a 'discrete' video adapter, you could opt to forego the added expense of paying for a CPU with integrated graphics capability.

Musical Instrument Digital Interface (USB-MIDI)

Here is where the rubber meets the road regarding audio/video production. If you play any instrument, then how do you 'record' that music onto your computer?

The short answer is "By way of MIDI." The longer answer requires us to seek out a new understanding of how music is created.

Without going into the whole backstory and structure of the MIDI standard, we just want to know how to make it work with our instrument(s). And, that is exactly what we will explore next.

Remember the synthesizer and computer we discussed before? Well, thanks to modern technology, there is a very easy way for them to communicate with each other. That method is the good ole' USB connection.

Most keyboards and synthesizers sold today, have a USB-MIDI connection. Additionally, this writer hasn't seen a computer without a USB connection since 1995. And, that is our 'in' for this part of the system... At least in the beginning. Later on, the kind reader will understand why the USB connection 'alone' is simply not enough for all purposes. And, again, this issue circles around a problem with digital bandwidth or at least the synchronization between different devices. But, for now, the ubiquitous USB port will be more than sufficient to get us going in the right direction.

Truth be told, traditional, five-pin MIDI connections are the 'bomb' when compared to USB-MIDI. The standard is so capable and flexible

> For the purposes of this discussion, we are not yet talking about the live recording of tracks. Recording is a whole other world from playing live through your monitor speakers.

that once understood, it becomes obvious how standard MIDI connections just make life with multiple devices so much easier compared to dealing with the unavoidable latencies (timing delays) inherent in multiple USB connections.

The deeper technical details are beyond our need to fully explore in this work. But, since we will eventually be working to maximize our sound field with possibly multiple MIDI instruments, it makes sense to use MIDI cable connections, rather than USB-MIDI, for our main tracks — especially when linking several devices to the 'chain.'

Don't get me wrong. The USB connection is imperative as it is the connection with which we will 'communicate' our intentions and settings to and from the synthesizer hardware. In some cases, this connection is utilized to synchronize data between two or more devices using the MIDI timestamp that circulates with all MIDI data within a system. However, a MIDI cable connection is a more bullet-proof option in this regard.

All of this is not to mention certain device administration and programming functions, such as re-tuning the instrument, which generally requires a USB connection (depending upon the instrument and the software used).

Using the provisions of the USB-MIDI protocol standards, we can, with the aid of specialized software applications, re-program the synthesizer, on the fly, with any new parameters needed — such as the all-important tuning specification data. Additionally, the alternate tuning issue is the main reason why we absolutely must use a USB connection.

Additionally, there are alternative methods that use this USB connection in order to make use of specialized software, which allows one to directly control a synthesizer's performance settings directly from a video interface using a mouse or touch-pad. This is a very helpful function in more than just a few instances. Please note that these software-driven synthesizer interfaces are separate (optional) software applications requiring their own purchase license.

Also, many Digital Audio Workstation (DAW) packages, not to mention the various Virtual Studio Technology (VST) software-instrument (plugins) often require a USB connection in order to maintain communication with the external instrument.

Lastly, the USB connection to your computer is very important for your instruments to be recognized and automatically configured as a system device in modern operating systems.

The 'class compliant' category of devices allows modern operating systems to instantly recognize hundreds of MIDI devices, eliminating the need for installing specialized device drivers for each instrument or MIDI accessory. The writer's impression is that one would be hard-pressed to find a MIDI-compliant device that is not immediately recognized by up-to-date operating systems.

Once the physical connection is made, your computer and your DAW should automatically recognize the external synthesizer and configure it for use. The methods for 'loading' the new 'external instrument' as it is now known, into your chosen DAW 'project' is dependent upon which DAW software is being used. Fortunately, the manual for your DAW software covers this process.

Musical Instrument Digital Interface (Standard MIDI)

As the astute reader may have already concluded, this writer prefers MIDI cable connections over USB-MIDI whenever possible. This is basically a bias driven by a need to easily visualize the data flows as well as having the ability to quickly and easily change them, without interfering with the computer software's connection (via USB) to the device in question.

> DAW (Digital Audio Workstation) is any software such as Logic Pro X, Ableton, FL Studio, ProTools, Komplete, and many others that provide the overall framework for producing, editing, and recording your audio tracks.
>
> VST (Virtual Studio Technology) audio plugins that are actually various software interfaces that integrate with (i.e. plug into) the DAW software and which enable or modify certain functions, effects, special instruments, or synthesis methods. Most VST plugins provide their own visual interface which can be controlled from within the DAW software itself. Others can be a bit more cryptic in their operation.

To more easily visualize your MIDI data flow, this writer has developed a preference for using what is called a MIDI 'hub' (aka MIDI Interface). A hub is a central location where all of your instruments connect via MIDI cable connections, to a common device while that device serves as the main USB connection to the computer. The MIDI hub itself, optionally acts as the master clock for all MIDI signals to avoid various instruments straying out of sync.

The clock function of an 'active' MIDI hub (as opposed to a 'passive' hub) allows you to set all of your instruments' clock modes to 'external' or 'slave' thus relying upon the timestamps created by the hub; subsequently never having issues with signal sync or remembering which device has been assigned as the 'master clock' on the system.

The MIDI hub connects to your computer via its own USB connection. Since the (active) hub handles timings, the USB connection receives data that is already synchronized and, this fact eliminates the problem with manually synchronizing multiple USB connections over several instruments. The writer highly recommends an active MIDI hub when using multiple MIDI instruments. It has been a blessing while trying to learn all of this.

After the hub is connected and recognized by your computer system (usually automatically), each instrument is then connected to the hub via MIDI cable interface. On the hub, you have MIDI-In and MIDI-out connections. But, in the beginning, MIDI-In will be the only necessary connection as we will not be setting up any 'MIDI-Through' connections in this discussion. Your synced MIDI signal will be routed via USB-MIDI to the computer and of course thereon to your DAW software.

An added benefit to the beginner, is that the MIDI hub pretty much guarantees that you will not have any problems due to the dreaded MIDI loop error. MIDI loop errors are when one device is accidentally cabled to both send to and receive from the same device(s) on another part of the 'chain.' This problem often occurs when adding a new instrument to the MIDI workflow. So, yeah. For us novices, this is an easy mistake to make with multiple-instrument setups.

Audio Output - The Studio Monitor Controller

An audio hub (aka Studio Monitor Controller) is another essential asset to your system. Like the MIDI hub, it provides a central connection — in this case, for your audio output(s). This audio can subsequently, be routed to your wider system of loudspeakers or, in some models, to a main amplifier or pre-main amplifier (always make sure the audio output is pre-amp level). This is subsequently connected to your loudspeakers. You can also connect your studio monitor speakers to this hub so that all audio is immediately available for listening.

Some manufacturers' audio hubs also provide the connections for a small number of microphones (e.g. PreSonus) to be connected to your ever-expanding system. This comes in handy when adding non-instrumental sounds, such as vocalizations and chanting to your 'mix.'

As the audio hub is also connected to the computer via a USB connection, it becomes available as an audio output for your entire computer system. Therefore any sound generated by the computer is time-synced and output to the audio hub and thereafter to whatever speaker systems you have connected to it. Advice; turn off system sounds or the occasional beep or notification sound will become part of your current sound field.

Why is an audio hub a necessity? Well, it may not be depending on the individual needs of the user. However, having a centralized and computer-selectable audio output device makes subsequent additions of equipment and additional monitor speakers much more convenient. It is also the best way to point your DAW to the correct audio channel.

The addition of the audio hub completes the (very) basic integration of every device in your system with the MIDI and audio output systems. You should now be ready to play! Whatever you hear coming from your speakers should also be audio that is being received by the computer. And, that fact sets you up pretty well to begin setting up and recording sound from within your chosen DAW.

There are many types of audio hubs (or Studio Monitor Controllers) on the market. Do some market research and decide which one(s) have the capabilities that fit your desired setup.

> Adding input devices such as microphones will require a slight re-thinking on the purpose and connections of the audio hub as these models offer input as well as output capability.
> This provides an additional input path for raw (aka non-MIDI) audio, which must be manually synced with the signal(s) flowing through the MIDI hub. The seemingly logical solution; connecting the MIDI-OUT from the audio hub to a MIDI-IN on the MIDI hub, is likely to create a MIDI-loop error. Therefore, it is recommended to use the default (USB) configuration described above or consult your particular products "Getting Started" manual for additional strategies.

A Word Regarding Recording and File Formats

The writer has previously mentioned the importance of recording and presenting your recorded performances in a lossless format. Fortunately, most DAWs allow you to select your recording format from a list of user settings. You will see various options for sampling rate, bit depth, channels and other variables on most settings pages. However, generally speaking, we literally want to crank any available recording settings to the maximum available. Yes. The files will be huge. But, that is because none (or at least a bare minimum) of the sound information is filtered out.

The *.wav* format is the defacto standard file format for audio. However, in recent years, other entities have instituted their own proprietary lossless standards. For instance, *AIFF* is Apple's lossless challenger to Microsoft's *WAV* format. Another standard used by Apple Corporation is the *CAF* format, which is readily found in Logic Pro X as the default format for sound loops. You probably won't have much use for *CAF* unless you are in the groove where you create multiple sound loops for your sessions. Therefore, most of us really only have to make a choice between *AIFF* and *WAV* when using Logic Pro X.

The AIFF format has a maximum time limit of three hours. WAV's own time limit is thirteen hours, and CAF files are not time-limited in any way. Most of us will never come close to pegging these limits in a single track.

Generally speaking, you should encounter few, if any, problems in the event that you choose recording in AIFF format, which is the Logic Pro X default. However, for exporting, it is recommended to use *.wav* files since they are still the industry standard and maximize compatibility across platforms and various DAW systems. And, AIFF format can (currently) only be played back on Apple devices. Other DAWs offer a few other formats or allow for 'plugins' which can offer more lossless alternatives. Some that you may see are *ALAC* and *FLAC*. While both of these are very high quality 'lossless' codecs, the former is again, only compatible with Apple Corporation products and the latter, while widely supported, is by no means a universal fit.

Therefore, if the reader comes to the same conclusion as this writer, a preference for preserving the complete sound field as well as the widest possible compatibility leads us inexorably, to Microsoft's venerable *.wav* recording format.

Creating Custom Tuning 'Files'

One of the most difficult tasks in our production system is also the most critical. Loading the keyboard with whichever alternate tuning scheme we have chosen. The thought of doing so begs the question; Loading what? To where?

The data that we load to re-tune our synthesizer is in a file that needs to be 'uploaded' to the device using something called the MIDI Transport System. (Details not pertinent at this time) And, while this process is not difficult to understand, it must be noted that there is not a single software tool that accomplishes every step in the process.

Therefore, we must assemble a system which will accomplish the following tasks:

- Enable us to construct (and test) the tuning grid
- Export that tuning data to a 'SysEx' MIDI file
- Edit the SysEx file to make it compatible with our device
- Upload the file to the device

So, we have an inconvenient mnemonic of 'Construct, Export, Edit, Upload.' ("CEE-U" … Yeah. I know. But, it's the best I could do.)

Constructing a Tuning File

Depending upon the platform in use (Windows, Linux, or MacOS) you will find differing options for software which enables the creation of tuning files (generally speaking, *.tun* files)

The author settled on a helpful software package developed by **H-π** (pronounced H-Pi) Instruments named '*Universal Tuning Editor*' (UTE). The package supports Windows and Apple operating systems. More information is available at: *https://hpi.zentral.zone/ute*

The software, which is full-featured and very well-maintained by the developer, allows us to input our required parameters and fine tune the system in a 'project format' that can be saved for future editing in **H-π**'s proprietary *.ute* file format.

None of the software evaluated by the author is particularly intuitive. However, UTE is fairly obvious about what data goes where if not how to get it 'in' the interface. But, there is a comprehensive on-line manual, which I suggest familiarizing yourself with. Plus, there is a handy little feature which allows you to click on each 'note' to monitor your work as you go. Although it will require some initial trial and error, you can learn to quickly create your tuning systems, and safely save them to your hard drive.

Exporting the Tuning File

This is another reason why the author chose UTE for the construction of tuning files. In recent updates, the developer has graced us with the ability to export our tuning directly to MIDI SysEx format. This saves us from a bit of software acrobatics — for which we are forever grateful.

Where once it was necessary to navigate to a specific web site, upload your tuning file (in .tun or .kyb format) and allow the site to process the data to create your SysEx (.mts) file, now UTE can accomplish this critical step within their UTE application. Additionally, the chosen file name and therefore the tuning system name will be embedded automatically in the SysEx file. This saves us the need to edit this information in the following step.

Editing the Tuning File

OK, so now we have our SysEx tuning file. Can't we just upload it to the synth and be done?

Well, actually... no. Sure. Your SysEx tuning file is complete in regards to tuning information. But, at this point, there is only generic device information in the file. If you are using Universal Tuning Editor to create your SysEx file, the display name of the tuning system (16 characters max) will have already been encoded to the data. But, We still need to prepare the file with some specific data which relates to the specific device.

Not to worry, it is not a complicated procedure. But, it will require you to obtain yet another piece of software. In this case, a binary/hexadecimal editor (HEX editor).

We will not belabor the details here. But, for those unfamiliar, a HEX Editor is able to read the machine-language file we have created, display the contents on the screen, and allow us to change specific 'bits' of information. Once done, the file can be saved with the edits and remain perfectly readable by the system.

There are many HEX editor software packages available — both free and for sale. Generally, the 'for sale' versions are higher quality with more features. But, for this general purpose, almost any of them will accomplish what is required here.

When you load a SysEx file into your Hex Editor, you will notice a screen full of letters and numbers. Generally, they will be grouped into 'octets' which are eight values with each value containing two characters (numbers, letters or both) like this; (not an actual hex value)

00 f1 f2 33 <u>f4</u> 55 f6 f7 ...

For this example of editing, we will refer to the DSI Prophet REV2, which the author primarily uses in this work.

The SysEx tuning file for the REV2 only needs only one bit changed because, the display *'name'* of the tuning standard was added to the data by UTE's exporter. What we need to change is the first bit of the second octet… or nine places into the file. So, move your cursor (or tab) over to the first (bit) pair of characters in the second octet (underlined in the example above).

Replace the value in that space with the BANK NUMBER in which you want to load this particular tuning. On the REV2, you have sixteen slots of which the first (slot 00) is not editable. Therefore, your choices are '01 through 15.'

Once you enter the correct bank number slot, you can now save the file. It is now ready for uploading to the synth.

Uploading the Tuning Data to Your Instrument

Well, in order to upload our newly-minted tuning file to the synth, we must download still another piece of software. In this case, the writer has chosen 'SysEx Librarian' for the task. The web site can be found at: *www.snoize.com/sysexlibrarian/*

We will remind the kind reader that it is critical to use a USB connection from your computer to the synth or SysEx Librarian will be unable to communicate with your device. Sending SysEx messages out to the entire MIDI chain may have unexpected and inconvenient results. Make sure your destination device is connected properly and selected in the SysEx Librarian main window as the active device.

Once the software has recognized your synth, you can select it from the drop-down list at the top of the screen — to make it the active device. You can then add your Sysex tuning file to the 'library' within the SysEx Librarian window. Usually, a simple drag and drop from the file explorer window works fine.

When the correct device is selected and the correct file(s) appear in the software window, select/highlight the desired tuning file(s) and click 'PLAY.' The data will be sent (played like a regular MIDI file) to your synth. If all has gone according to plan, your new tuning will be available in the alternate tunings menu on your instrument and, in the memory bank slot you chose in the previous step.

That's the basic rundown on how to create and upload alternate tunings into most of the currently-existing, DSI Prophet series synthesizer models. Your chosen synth may be slightly different or may perhaps require different edits to the SysEx tuning file itself. However, what you have here is information that required weeks of digging through on-line sources for this writer to obtain.

Sometime afterwards, the DSI community site for Prophet series users posted a similar walk-through with images on their forum.

At the time of this writing, that walk-through was still available for review on the DSI community pages.

> **Make sure to use SysEx Librarian (or similar) to 'backup' all of your factory tuning files to your hard drive before attempting any changes. The procedure is straightforward to 'download' the data from your synth. Keep the default tuning data files in a safe place on your hard drive in the event that you need to restore all defaults. Once deleted or overwritten, the synthesizer generally has no backup of the default data to restore.**

What about EM interference from all of this equipment?

OK. Now this section may cause some eye-rolling amongst the natural skeptics out there. But, bear with me while we discuss EM (electro-magnetic) shielding for equipment and session spaces.

When working with electronic equipment such as computers, amplifiers and magnetic coils such as those found in speakers, it is important to take into account their inherent EM field generation or 'induction' fields.

EM fields of all types have been demonstrated to be detrimental to human thought processes, physiological function, and overall wellness. And, while most of those identified are extremely high-frequency transmissions such as WiFi, Bluetooth, 4G, and 5G signals, this is simply where the extant studies have been focused. Very little attention has been directed to other sources of 'EM smog' created by common-use technology.

Thus, is behooves us to eliminate as much of the 'stray' EM energies as possible from the space in which such sessions are delivered to clients. Why? Well, firstly because they are unnecessary in our application(s). Secondly, because we really have no proof that these signals are altogether harmless.
In fact, much evidence points toward the opposite conclusion. Thus, eliminating these unnecessary signals also eliminates any potential harm as well as any unintentional interference to the delivery of the intended signals.

Therefore, the implementation of two mitigating strategies is recommended; distance and shielding. Both are imperative to the quality of any sessions that include electronic equipment in proximity to practitioner or recipient.

It is recommended that large EM field-generating devices such as amplifiers be separated by distance, *and* enclosed in a Faraday cage.

A neighboring 'safe' room would be sufficient towards this goal especially if the equipment does not occupy a common wall with the session space.

Additionally, an enclosure, which incorporates copper mesh material to completely enclose the equipment and, which is externally-grounded by standard electrical means is recommended.

All wiring to and from electronic equipment should be enclosed in a type of conduit or similar non-metallic tube, which is itself, enclosed or wrapped in copper mesh material and separately grounded, perhaps to the Faraday cage itself. It is highly advisable to keep powered cables and signal transmission cables separated into two different cabling solutions as high power conduction creates inductive interference in the immediate area.

It is usually unavoidable to have the main musical equipment, computer, and monitor(s) in the session's delivery area. Thus, the recommendation here is to take a corner or side of the room furthest away from the client/recipient area, perhaps one that is closest to the larger equipment in the adjoining room. This space should be enclosed with a thick leaded-glass window (to easily view the delivery space) and should also be 'shielded' on all sides with the use of copper mesh fabric, which is also externally-grounded.

Computer systems in this space should possess no wireless communication devices, or at least, components such as 'Bluetooth' and 'WiFi' should be completely disabled. Bear in mind that turning WiFi off on many systems does not disable the *device*. Usually, doing so will merely drop the active connection and, will allow the device to continue emitting its general operating frequencies.

All computers should he 'hard-wired' to any network using Ethernet or similar cabling systems. Of course, such cabling should be included in their own shielded conduits. Any router or hub connecting your system(s) should be located in the 'safe' room and also have wireless communication completely disabled.

These steps insure that only those signals that are intended to be distributed into the delivery/treatment area, actually reach the delivery area.

Likewise, each and every speaker and cable located in the delivery area should also be contained in its own Faraday 'container' in order to prevent secondary EM frequency propagation.

For instance, the motion of the cone element relative to the speaker magnet creates an EM induction field around the speaker. The larger the magnet, the larger and more powerful this induction field becomes at amplitude. As current science is divided on the negative effects of these EM fields to living tissue, it behooves the practitioner to exercise an abundance of caution in eliminating all but *intended* signals from the treatment space. In our case, intended signals are the primary sound waves and their propagated pressure waves.

Conclusion and Disclaimers

The writer has attempted to provide the audio production novice with sufficient, basic information to begin the design of an appropriate system that focuses on the ability to use alternate tuning systems with existing technology — all intended for the creation of 'music' geared toward sound and frequency therapy applications.

There certainly exist other methods and schools of thought in regards to creating these sounds and recording them. And, each DAW will have its own way of capturing the instruments' sound for recording. Experiment with what is available in your specific DAW software package.

While the writer always recommends using full waveform (.wav) recording, other so-named 'lossless' techniques will be available depending upon the DAW chosen. If your DAW does not provide a very high standard of lossless recording, please consider upgrading to better software before learning a product that may yield inferior results.

Because, each software package has its own way of doing things, it is important to make sure that the software you are learning is actually going to be useful for the intended purpose, which in our case, is the production of very high fidelity output that recreates the immersive atmosphere of an analog experience.

Having mastered the absolute basics above, one last point needs to be made. When recording your tracks, MIDI connections wherever practical, may need changing to include 'live' external connections.

What the heck does he mean by that?

Every available DAW has its own way of configuring and connecting external instruments. One purpose in doing so is to ensure that there are no unexpected sound 'layers' or filters creeping in to our recording process. That you are in-fact recording the full output *only*, of your analog synth (for instance).

The walk-through above should have all MIDI-capable instruments ready to be configured as external audio sources within your DAW. But, basically, any instrument that can not be electronically cabled to the system must somehow be 'configured' as a separate input channel.

We have gone to no small expense in purchasing an analog synthesizer as well as other useful instruments and hardware that are also analog output-MIDI-capable. Yet, we may have purchased other instruments which simply cannot be connected using MIDI and, must therefore be "mic'd." We now need to feed the live signal from these sound sources into our recording process — bypassing any digital manipulation. This means directly recording the instrument's track into your DAW as a live track, which (as previously mentioned) should be set to record in the best lossless format available.

The DAW's external input setup is the most straightforward way to do this. And, it works fine in most cases.

But, the better way is a bit more involved. And, it involves designing or renting a recording studio and using live microphones (of the highest quality) to capture those instruments and vocals which cannot be cabled to your MIDI system. This would include your hand-drums, bells, bowls, chimes, gongs, acoustic string instruments, etc. Obviously, these instruments must be recorded through high quality microphone/mixer setups. And, suddenly — here we are talking about a sound studio setup.

Either method you choose has its own particularly steep learning curve. But, the end result is being able to present high-definition, lossless audio in your sound and frequency healing sessions.

Simply put, live recording will most likely require adding a 'mixer' and one or more microphones to your setup. And, ideally constructing (or renting) a suitable studio for recording the sounds and backing tracks that you have spent days, weeks or even months preparing and practicing for your unique and amazing sound and frequency sessions.

A rental studio is a significant expense in any case. But, consider that; recording the perfect performance only to later realize the you have also recorded random noise (dogs barking, passing traffic, etc.) on your tracks, is an extremely frustrating experience. A professional studio is the only way this writer knows, to completely avoid environmental noise issues; outside of recording in a completely isolated area. Whether you see the long term need to build your own studio, or simply require a few hours studio rental, the funds will be well-spent to have clean, noiseless 'backing tracks' for your sound and frequency healing sessions.

At this point in your journey, you will be beyond the need for any kind of advice or tutelage from this writer. But, this verbose perspective is offered because it is simply too much information to jump right in to recording without understanding and practicing the barest essentials contained in this little walk-through.

Most practitioners were trained to deliver sound and frequency sessions with the use of acoustic instruments only. The development of computers and the associated technology both amazes and befuddles those of us who were 'raised' before any of this machinery existed in common usage. There are still many of the vanguard practitioners who resist its use. One must wonder if this entrenched attitude is due to technical or personal factors.

Again, for the record, this chapter is a very superficial outline of a very basic system and, is furthermore, based on the writer's personal struggles when getting started. Individual studio needs as well as practitioner methods vary widely. And, it should be noted that there really is more than one way to set up a personal studio.

In addition to peripheral amplifiers, loudspeaker arrays, and cabling concerns, every sound and frequency studio will be as unique as the practitioner's vision for these sessions.

**"All this machinery making modern music,
can still be open-hearted…" - Neil Peart**

The use of modern technology to deliver perfectly-tuned sound and frequency sessions (sound baths) that are restorative and healing on every level, is certainly an attainable objective. In this text, the writer has attempted to make the case that, with certain herein-outlined accommodations and modifications, modern music *technology* is a perfect partner in the further progress of music therapy as well as holistic sound and frequency applications, which are intended to promote healing and foster a more complete sense of wellness.

Well that's about it. That's all I've got for now.

Our website *https://www.sacredsonics.com* will be live in Spring of 2022. There, you will find information, updates, user experiences, and other pertinent data related to *Sacred Sonics* and our *Geometric tuning systems*.

Additional information regarding manufacturing partnerships will be made available as we work to make geometrically-tuned instruments available through strategic-partner retail channels.

Join us! And, help change the world of sound and frequency therapeutics - forever and for the better.

Look to **Available Light Press** for future offerings honoring and informing the world of holistic practice and healing practitioners. Together, we can make the world a 'brighter' place.

It has been this writer's *privilege* and pleasure to be the channel this work for the benefit of all sound and frequency healing practitioners. Thank you *so much* for reading!

Appendices

Appendix I

Sound & Wavelength Calculations for Session Spaces

Before beginning this discussion, it is important that the reader understand that performing waveform calculations for the purpose of tuning a session space is a task best left to professional acoustic engineers. That being said…

The following supplemental information is provided as base-line guidance to those who wish to construct their own sound and frequency therapy studio space. This basic information is provided for those who wish to present in larger spaces where acoustic effects such as echoing could become particularly troublesome. Smaller spaces or open spaces while having their own acoustic challenges may not find these suggestions quite as useful.

Of course, larger spaces, let's say greater than 2.5m high and/or more than 9m across will require some acoustic dampening materials in the plan, smaller spaces generally present the greatest challenges due to partial reflections and wave canceling effects.

When designing any presentation space, in many instances, you can do the preliminary calculations yourself (feasibility analysis) and then let the construction contractor figure out how to make your vision happen for you.

Of course, if you desire a truly tuned space for your sessions, the writer strongly urges the hiring of a professional acoustic contractor. They may give you some strange looks at first but, believe me! These contractors are used to getting some pretty odd and fairly difficult requests. It's part of the challenge for them.

Most of our acoustic space elements require the knowledge of wavelength for the range of frequency(ies) to which you wish to tune your space.

For instance, you need to understand why putting a decorative blanket ladder behind your primary gong is not such a great idea. It may look great. But, there are acoustic consequences. Going forward, in this discussion, the writer will assume 432Hz and/or 360Hz waveform tuning as the more desirable options. So, here is a little information to get you started.

Sonic Boom!

The speed of sound is the distance traveled per unit of time by a sound pressure wave as it propagates through a resistant, elastic medium. In our case, that 'medium' is the air in the session space. The speed of sound is dependent upon another factor however. And, that factor is the ambient temperature, which affects the 'viscosity' of the medium (i.e., The air.) The warmer the air, the less 'viscosity' the pressure wave must overcome as it propagates. Conversely, in a cooler environment, the pressure wave will move slightly slower due to the 'thickness' of the air.

At 21°C and assuming one Atmosphere air pressure, the speed of sound 'v' is accurately represented as 343.73 meters per second or 1127.72 feet per second.

This result could also be expressed as 768.9 mph or 1237.43 Kph. If performing the calculation in other units of length, you must be sure to use the correct units in all parts of the equation; otherwise, your results will not be accurate.

Generally, the use of 21°C is thought to be a safe assumption for mean temperature. If you prefer the session space warmer, please use the correct speed for the preferred air temperature. We mere mortals can't really hope to be more accurate than this... unless you simply love math and can locate the more precise calculations that account for barometric pressure variations and other factors.

Yes. The propagation speed of sound through air depends strongly on the air temperature and the atmospheric pressure through which the sound wave propagates.

We generally use 21°C (70°F) at one Atmosphere (Basically, room temperature at sea level) as our reference to arrive at the 343.73 m/s value used in all sound wavelength calculations used in this discussion. Additionally, if you present your sessions in a significantly colder or hotter environment, recalculations of all wavelengths for your particular application should be performed.

Although it is assumed that most practitioners will be performing in air-conditioned rooms at or near 21°C, the point is an especially valid consideration for those in open-air environments or generally warmer climates.

The equation used to determine wavelength* is expressed as:

$$\lambda = v/f$$

*Special thanks to Sir Isaac Newton for doing the hard work for us.

Where λ (lambda) is the wavelength (in meters), 'v' is the velocity (in meters per second), and 'f' is the frequency (in Hertz or cycles per second). Therefore the wavelength of a 432Hz sound wave at a velocity of 343.73 m/s is calculated as follows:

$$\lambda \text{ m} = 343.73 \text{ m/s} \div 432\text{Hz} = 0.79567 \text{ meters}$$
(or 79.567 centimeters)

Check your answer by reversing the math and multiplying the result **0.79567 x 432**. The check-result should be the original speed 'v' in the starting formula, i.e., 343.73.

Here, we have included a convenient table of the speed of sound at different Celsius temperatures (All assume one-atmosphere air pressure to keep calculations from becoming overly-complicated)

You may also perform these calculations in fps (feet per second) using the values displayed below. Convert your result to yards per second by dividing the given speed by 3fps to arrive at 'yards' per second.
To convert the speed to miles per hour, multiply the given rate in fps by 0.681818.

As you can see from the table, the maximum difference related to the usual 'comfortable' temperatures above is only about one centimeter.

Air Temp (°C)	Speed (m/s)	Speed (fps)	λ (432Hz wave)
17°C	341.39	1120.03	0.79025 m
18°C	341.97	1121.96	0.79296 m
19°C	342.56	1123.88	0.79296 m
20°C	343.15	1125.81	0.79432 m
21°C	343.73	1127.72	0.79567 m
22°C	344.31	1129.64	0.79701 m
23°C	344.90	1131.55	0.79838 m
24°C	345.48	1133.46	0.79972 m
25°C	346.06	1135.37	0.80106 m
26°C	346.64	1137.27	0.80241 m

So, one may wonder why I take such an issue with temperature. Well, it's basically due to the fact that exacting audio professionals have an issue with it. But, let's try to understand a little more about why the issue is important.

General Discussion

On a single wavelength scale, the difference of one centimeter may seem insignificant. However, let us consider the room or studio where the 'performance' or session is to be presented. The total length of the room can significantly compound acoustic design errors.

For the sake of simplicity, let's only consider one dimension of the room, its length. Let's call it ten meters.

At 21°C, a 432Hz sound front initiated at the back wall (again, for simplicity) will propagate once every 79.567 centimeters (peak-to-peak).

Theoretically, in a ten-meter room length, we have a reflective surface that is placed at 12.56 complete wave cycles. 12.5 would be a good fit. Exactly 12.0 would be a perfect fit. But, that extra 0.06 is a small problem resulting in a reflective discrepancy of several centimeters as the wave propagates back and forth from wall to wall, and this fact will likely give rise to undesirable imbalances in sound reflection. This defect invites unpleasant mid-wave collisions (interference) and reverberatory effects (echoing). Of course, this example is hyperbole but, is presented as an example of how small discrepancies in a tuned area cause things to go bad very quickly. Fortunately, utilizing geometric waveforms from within the same harmonic series, goes a very long way towards eliminating such interference in a properly-dimensioned space.

In this overly-simplified example, the wave must 'reflect' off the back wall at a point in its propagation that (nearly) perfectly reflects the sound wave, at either a propagation peak or a trough. Over ten meters, a miscalculation in temperature and, therefore, wavelength could cause an error up to 39.78 centimeters (Just under one-half wavelength) in the design of your studio walls' length. Again, hyperbole to illustrate a point.

You can do a little exercise to check this out for yourself. Perform the calculations for a 9.55-meter room length on your own. You will discover that there is only a 0.001 mathematical discrepancy - if

---

NOTE: The author is well aware of the many professional methods of mitigating echo and dissonance in a studio or performance hall. The information discussed here, is an example of a conceptual theory only. Here we are discussing the construction of a room/studio that intentionally and constructively reflects and perhaps even conducts sonic pressure waves through its structural components - contrary to standard practice in recording studio design. So, hold any critique for those trying to build a recording studio. We are trying to build a room that sings.

---

calculating for 432Hz room tuning. These dimensions are a MUCH better match for the tuning frequency with the reflection surface placed almost precisely at 12 full wavelengths. Of course, 9.55 meters may be a bit small for your studio 'guests' and all of your equipment. The example is presented to illustrate the critical relationship between the rooms dimensions and the performances tuning frequency.

Miscalculation can result in significant disappointment when discovering that your newly-designed and constructed session studio is nothing more than an expensive echo chamber. But, all is never lost! There are always professional fixes for these issues. But, performing the basic design calculations beforehand can possibly save a lot of time and money. Problems with echoes and 'dissonance' can often be remedied by adding acoustic panels or sound dampeners in the right places. However, these could stifle much of the very resonant quality initially desired if not done properly (usually with professional assistance.)

The beauty of using geometric and platonic solid frequencies is that they always lend themselves to the same numerical reductions (i.e., The digits of polygonal and platonic solid frequencies always summate to the number '9'). To save me a lot of trouble, I designed a studio that honors this strange and potentially mystical quality. I find that most frequencies calculated from our 432Hz-based work coexist very well within the 3-6-9 calculated spaces. Your mileage (and opinion) may vary.

The multiples of 3, 6, and 9 are key to designing a sound therapy studio. In fact, I recommend adherence to the 3-6-9 design-proportions concept for any 'healing' practice. For example; if your ceilings are three meters high, a proportional width and depth could be multiples of three. In this case, width would be nine meters (3m x 3) and the depth could be either 18 meters (3m x 6) or 27 meters (3m x 9). Play with the proportions and see what works best for you, your equipment, and your budget.

Alternatively, you could take that foundational 432Hz wavelength of 79.6cm and incorporate it into your math. If your ceiling can be 3 x 79.6cm high (2.39m), your width could be set to 7.17m (3 x 2.39m) and the depth could be either the same 7.17m or 14.34m (6 x 2.39m)

I suppose that Nikola Tesla was correct when he stated that 3, 6, and 9 were somehow a "key to the universe." It is certainly a convenient tool for achieving our purpose in designing a studio space for sound and frequency sessions.

If you happen to be renting your space, I suggest taking an instrument tuned to either 432Hz or 360Hz. Spend some time in the space playing these instruments and see how it works for you or perhaps what changes may need to be performed. You can record your mini-session and to later, evaluate for anything obvious you may have missed during your actual testing. It's a very personal thing; choosing the space for your sessions. Choosing wisely, with the best possible information, can serve to help your sessions be the very best they can be.

Appendix II

Piano Key Tones Using 'Even Tempered' Methodology

Comparison of 440Hz and 432Hz Standards Within the Modern Equal-Temperament Design Standard

Keyboard Position	Note Assignment	440Hz 12TET	432Hz 12TET
25	A2	110	108
24	G#2/A♭2	103.8263	105.7147
23	G2	97.9988	99.7814
22	F#2/G♭2	92.4987	94.1811
21	F2	87.3071	88.8950
20	E2	82.4070	83.9057
19	D#2/E♭2	77.7818	79.1964
18	D2	73.4162	74.7515
17	C#2/Db2	69.2957	70.5560
16	C2	65.4065	66.5959
15	B1	61.7355	62.8582
14	A#1/Bb1	58.2705	59.3302
13	A1	55	56
12	G#1/Ab1	51.9131	52.8572
11	G1	48.9994	49.8905
10	F#1/Gb1	46.2494	47.0903
9	F1	43.6536	44.4473
8	E1	41.2035	41.9527
7	D#1/Eb1	38.8910	39.5981
6	D1	36.7081	37.3756
5	C#1/Db1	34.6479	35.2778
4	C1	32.7033	33.2978
3	B0	30.8677	31.4290
2	A#0/Bb0	29.1353	29.6650
1	A0	27.5	28

Standard Piano Keys 1 through 25

Standard Piano Keys 26 through 63

Keyboard Position	Note Assignment	440Hz 12TET	432Hz 12TET
63	B5	987.7652	969.8117
62	A#5/B♭5	932.3286	915.3801
61	A5	880	864
60	G#5/A♭5	830.6100	815.5104
59	G5	783.9911	769.7390
58	F#5/G♭5	739.9895	726.5367
57	F5	698.4571	685.7591
56	E5	659.2552	647.2702
55	D#5/E♭5	622.2543	610.9415
54	D5	587.3300	576.6518
53	C#5/D♭5	554.3661	544.2866
52	C5	523.2513	513.7380
51	B4	493.8835	484.9039
50	A#4/B♭4	466.1638	457.6882
49	A4	440	432
48	G#4/A♭4	415.3050	407.7552
47	G4	391.9960	384.8695
46	F#4/G♭4	369.9943	363.2683
45	F4	349.2281	342.8795
44	E4	329.6276	323.6351
43	D#4/E♭4	311.1276	305.4707
42	D4	293.6650	288.3259
41	C#4/D♭4	277.1831	272.1433
40	C4	261.6261	256.8690
39	B3	246.9422	242.4520
38	A#3/B♭3	233.0824	228.8441
37	A3	220	216
36	G#3/A♭3	207.6525	211.4303
35	G3	195.9975	199.5636
34	F#3/G♭3	184.9976	188.3629
33	F3	174.6140	177.7908
32	E3	164.8138	167.8121
31	D#3/E♭3	155.5638	158.3935
30	D3	146.8320	149.5035
29	C#3/D♭3	138.5911	141.1125
28	C3	130.8126	133.1924
27	B2	123.4711	125.7168
26	A#2/B♭2	116.5412	118.6608

Standard Piano Keys 64 through 88, plus eleven more

Keyboard Position	Note Assignment	440Hz 12TET	432Hz 12TET
99	B8	7902.0713	7758.5862
98	A#8/B♭8	7458.5676	7323.1278
97	A8	7039.9555	6912.1099
96	G#8/A♭8	6644.8380	6524.1608
95	G8	6271.8964	6157.9858
94	F#8/G♭8	5919.8862	5812.3627
93	F8	5587.6326	5486.1380
92	E8	5274.0268	5178.2230
91	D#8/E♭8	4978.0220	4887.5901
90	D8	4698.6305	4613.2692
89	C#8/D♭8	4434.9199	4354.3448
*88	C8	4186.01	4109.9529
87	B7	3951.0702	3879.2777
86	A#7/B♭7	3729.3162	3661.5493
85	A7	3520	3456
84	G#7/A♭7	3322.4400	3262.0674
83	G7	3135.9681	3078.9806
82	F#7/G♭7	2959.9542	2906.1698
81	F7	2793.8322	2743.0581
80	E7	2637.0263	2589.1012
79	D#7/E♭7	2489.0173	2443.7853
78	D7	2349.3238	2306.6254
77	C#7/D♭7	2217.4644	2177.1638
76	C7	2093.0051	2054.9683
75	B6	1975.5304	1939.6311
74	A#6/B♭6	1864.6534	1830.7674
73	A6	1760	1728
72	G#6/A♭6	1661.2200	1631.0272
71	G6	1567.9840	1539.4842
70	F#6/G♭6	1479.977	1453.0791
69	F6	1396.9161	1371.5236
68	E6	1318.5084	1294.5455
67	D#6/E♭6	1244.5086	1221.8878
66	D6	1174.6619	1153.3081
65	C#6/D♭6	1108.7322	1088.5776
64	C6	1046.5025	1027.4801

Appendix III

Comparison of Even Tempered And Proposed Geometric Tuning System Frequencies

Based upon Geometric A-Major Tuning Grid [DRAFT]

Displayed Frequencies are expressed in Hertz (Hz)

21	F2	87.3071	88.8950	84.375
20	E2	82.4070	83.9057	81
19	D#2/E♭2	77.7818	79.1964	76.50
18	D2	73.4162	74.7515	72
17	C#2/Db2	69.2957	70.5560	67.5
16	C2	65.4065	66.5959	63
15	B1	61.7355	62.8582	60.75
14	A#1/Bb1	58.2705	59.3302	56.25
13	A1	55	56	54
12	G#1/Ab1	51.9131	52.8572	50.625
11	G1	48.9994	49.8905	47.25
10	F#1/Gb1	46.2494	47.0903	45
9	F1	43.6536	44.4473	42.1875
8	E1	41.2035	41.9527	40.5
7	D#1/Eb1	38.8910	39.5981	38.25
6	D1	36.7081	37.3756	36
5	C#1/Db1	34.6479	35.2778	33.75
4	C1	32.7033	33.2978	31.5
3	B0	30.8677	31.4290	30.375
2	A#0/Bb0	29.1353	29.6650	28.125
1	A0	27.5	28	27
0	G0#	25.95655	26.4286	25.3125
-1	G0	24.4997	24.94525	23.625
-2	F#0	23.1247	23.54515	22.5
-3	F0	21.8268	22.22365	21.09375
-4	E0	20.60175	20.97635	20.25
-5	D#0	19.4455	19.79905	19.125

62	A#5/B♭5	932.3286	915.3801	900
61	A5	880	864	864
60	G#5/A♭5	830.6100	815.5104	810
59	G5	783.9911	769.7390	756
58	F#5/G♭5	739.9895	726.5367	720
57	F5	698.4571	685.7591	675
56	E5	659.2552	647.2702	648
55	D#5/E♭5	622.2543	610.9415	612
54	D5	587.3300	576.6518	576
53	C#5/D♭5	554.3661	544.2866	540
52	C5	523.2513	513.7380	504
51	B4	493.8835	484.9039	486
50	A#4/B♭4	466.1638	457.6882	450
49	A4	440	432	432
48	G#4/A♭4	415.3050	407.7552	405
47	G4	391.9960	384.8695	378
46	F#4/G♭4	369.9943	363.2683	360
45	F4	349.2281	342.8795	337.5
44	E4	329.6276	323.6351	324
43	D#4/E♭4	311.1276	305.4707	306
42	D4	293.6650	288.3259	288
41	C#4/D♭4	277.1831	272.1433	270
40	C4	261.6261	256.8690	252
39	B3	246.9422	242.4520	243
38	A#3/B♭3	233.0824	228.8441	225
37	A3	220	216	216
36	G#3/A♭3	207.6525	211.4303	202.5
35	G3	195.9975	199.5636	189
34	F#3/G♭3	184.9976	188.3629	180
33	F3	174.6140	177.7908	168.75
32	E3	164.8138	167.8121	162
31	D#3/E♭3	155.5638	158.3935	153
30	D3	146.8320	149.5035	144
29	C#3/D♭3	138.5911	141.1125	135
28	C3	130.8126	133.1924	126
27	B2	123.4711	125.7168	121.5
26	A#2/B♭2	116.5412	118.6608	112.5
25	A2	110	108	108
24	G#2/A♭2	103.8263	105.7147	101.25
23	G2	97.9988	99.7814	94.5
22	F#2/G♭2	92.4987	94.1811	90

99	B8	7902.0713	7758.5862	7776
98	A#8/Bb8	7458.5676	7323.1278	7200
97	A8	7039.9555	6912.1099	6912
96	G#8/Ab8	6644.8380	6524.1608	6480
95	G8	6271.8964	6157.9858	6048
94	F#8/Gb8	5919.8862	5812.3627	5760
93	F8	5587.6326	5486.1380	5400
92	E8	5274.0268	5178.2230	5184
91	D#8/Eb8	4978.0220	4887.5901	4896
90	D8	4698.6305	4613.2692	4608
89	C#8/Db8	4434.9199	4354.3448	4320
*88	C8	4186.01	4109.9529	4032
87	B7	3951.0702	3879.2777	3888
86	A#7/Bb7	3729.3162	3661.5493	3600
85	A7	3520	3456	3456
84	G#7/Ab7	3322.4400	3262.0674	3240
83	G7	3135.9681	3078.9806	3024
82	F#7/Gb7	2959.9542	2906.1698	2880
81	F7	2793.8322	2743.0581	2700
80	E7	2637.0263	2589.1012	2592
79	D#7/Eb7	2489.0173	2443.7853	2448
78	D7	2349.3238	2306.6254	2304
77	C#7/Db7	2217.4644	2177.1638	2160
76	C7	2093.0051	2054.9683	2016
75	B6	1975.5304	1939.6311	1944
74	A#6/Bb6	1864.6534	1830.7674	1800
73	A6	1760	1728	1728
72	G#6/Ab6	1661.2200	1631.0272	1620
71	G6	1567.9840	1539.4842	1512
70	F#6/Gb6	1479.977	1453.0791	1440
69	F6	1396.9161	1371.5236	1350
68	E6	1318.5084	1294.5455	1296
67	D#6/Eb6	1244.5086	1221.8878	1224
66	D6	1174.6619	1153.3081	1152
65	C#6/Db6	1108.7322	1088.5776	1080
64	C6	1046.5025	1027.4801	1008
63	B5	987.7652	969.8117	972

Standard Keyboard 'Key numbers' are shown in the left column. 440Hz, 12-TET values in the third column, 432Hz, 12-TET in the fourth column and <u>A-Major Geometric Tuning Grid</u> tones in the fifth column

Appendix IV

Comparison of Even Tempered And Proposed Geometric Tuning System Frequencies

Based upon Geometric F#-Major Tuning Grid [DRAFT]

Displayed Frequencies are expressed in Hertz (Hz)

26	A#2/B♭2	116.5412	118.6608	112.5
25	A2	110	108	108
24	G#2/A♭2	103.8263	105.7147	101.25
23	G2	97.9988	99.7814	94.5
22	F#2/G♭2	92.4987	94.1811	90
21	F2	87.3071	88.8950	84.375
20	E2	82.4070	83.9057	81
19	D#2/E♭2	77.7818	79.1964	76.50
18	D2	73.4162	74.7515	72
17	C#2/Db2	69.2957	70.5560	67.5
16	C2	65.4065	66.5959	63
15	B1	61.7355	62.8582	60.75
14	A#1/Bb1	58.2705	59.3302	56.25
13	A1	55	56	54
12	G#1/Ab1	51.9131	52.8572	50.625
11	G1	48.9994	49.8905	47.25
10	F#1/Gb1	46.2494	47.0903	45
9	F1	43.6536	44.4473	42.1875
8	E1	41.2035	41.9527	40.5
7	D#1/Eb1	38.8910	39.5981	38.25
6	D1	36.7081	37.3756	36
5	C#1/Db1	34.6479	35.2778	33.75
4	C1	32.7033	33.2978	31.5
3	B0	30.8677	31.4290	30.375
2	A#0/Bb0	29.1353	29.6650	28.125
1	A0	27.5	28	27
0	G0#	25.95655	26.4286	25.3125
-1	G0	24.4997	24.94525	23.625
-2	F#0	23.1247	23.54515	22.5

Keyboard Position	Note Assignment	440Hz 12TET	432Hz 12TET	F# Major Geometric
62	A#5/B♭5	932.3286	915.3801	900
61	A5	880	864	864
60	G#5/A♭5	830.6100	815.5104	810
59	G5	783.9911	769.7390	756
58	F#5/G♭5	739.9895	726.5367	720
57	F5	698.4571	685.7591	675
56	E5	659.2552	647.2702	648
55	D#5/E♭5	622.2543	610.9415	612
54	D5	587.3300	576.6518	576
53	C#5/D♭5	554.3661	544.2866	540
52	C5	523.2513	513.7380	504
51	B4	493.8835	484.9039	486
50	A#4/B♭4	466.1638	457.6882	450
49	A4	440	432	432
48	G#4/A♭4	415.3050	407.7552	405
47	G4	391.9960	384.8695	378
46	F#4/G♭4	369.9943	363.2683	360
45	F4	349.2281	342.8795	337.5
44	E4	329.6276	323.6351	324
43	D#4/E♭4	311.1276	305.4707	306
42	D4	293.6650	288.3259	288
41	C#4/D♭4	277.1831	272.1433	270
40	C4	261.6261	256.8690	252
39	B3	246.9422	242.4520	243
38	A#3/B♭3	233.0824	228.8441	225
37	A3	220	216	216
36	G#3/A♭3	207.6525	211.4303	202.5
35	G3	195.9975	199.5636	189
34	F#3/G♭3	184.9976	188.3629	180
33	F3	174.6140	177.7908	168.75
32	E3	164.8138	167.8121	162
31	D#3/E♭3	155.5638	158.3935	153
30	D3	146.8320	149.5035	144
29	C#3/D♭3	138.5911	141.1125	135
28	C3	130.8126	133.1924	126
27	B2	123.4711	125.7168	121.5

Keyboard Position	Note Assignment	440Hz 12TET	432Hz 12TET	F# Major Geometric
99	B8	7902.0713	7758.5862	7776
98	A#8/B♭8	7458.5676	7323.1278	7200
97	A8	7039.9555	6912.1099	6912
96	G#8/A♭8	6644.8380	6524.1608	6480
95	G8	6271.8964	6157.9858	6048
94	F#8/G♭8	5919.8862	5812.3627	5760
93	F8	5587.6326	5486.1380	5400
92	E8	5274.0268	5178.2230	5184
91	D#8/E♭8	4978.0220	4887.5901	4896
90	D8	4698.6305	4613.2692	4608
89	C#8/D♭8	4434.9199	4354.3448	4320
*88	C8	4186.01	4109.9529	4032
87	B7	3951.0702	3879.2777	3888
86	A#7/B♭7	3729.3162	3661.5493	3600
85	A7	3520	3456	3456
84	G#7/A♭7	3322.4400	3262.0674	3240
83	G7	3135.9681	3078.9806	3024
82	F#7/G♭7	2959.9542	2906.1698	2880
81	F7	2793.8322	2743.0581	2700
80	E7	2637.0263	2589.1012	2592
79	D#7/E♭7	2489.0173	2443.7853	2448
78	D7	2349.3238	2306.6254	2304
77	C#7/D♭7	2217.4644	2177.1638	2160
76	C7	2093.0051	2054.9683	2016
75	B6	1975.5304	1939.6311	1944
74	A#6/B♭6	1864.6534	1830.7674	1800
73	A6	1760	1728	1728
72	G#6/A♭6	1661.2200	1631.0272	1620
71	G6	1567.9840	1539.4842	1512
70	F#6/G♭6	1479.977	1453.0791	1440
69	F6	1396.9161	1371.5236	1350
68	E6	1318.5084	1294.5455	1296
67	D#6/E♭6	1244.5086	1221.8878	1224
66	D6	1174.6619	1153.3081	1152
65	C#6/D♭6	1108.7322	1088.5776	1080
64	C6	1046.5025	1027.4801	1008
63	B5	987.7652	969.8117	972

Appendix V

Completed Draft Geometric Tuning Grids

V(a) Draft version of A-Major Geometric Tuning Grid:

Note	Interval	Ratio	Multiplier	Frequency (Hz)	Interval from Root (¢)	Step Interval (¢)
Tuning Grid Based on A-432Hz (7th Octave)						
A	Octave	2:1	2	**1728.00**	1200	111.731
G	Maj 7th	15:8	1.875	**1620.00**	1088.269	119.443
G	Sept min 7th	7:4	1.75	**1512.00**	968.826	84.467
F#	Major 6th	5:3	1.666666667	**1440.00**	884.359	111.731
F	Aug 5th	25:16	1.5625	**1350.00**	772.627	70.672
E	Perf 5th	3:2	1.5	**1296.00**	701.955	98.955
D#	dim 5/Aug4	17:12	1.416666667	**1224.00**	603.000	104.955
D	Perf 4th	4:3	1.333333333	**1152.00**	498.045	111.731
C#	M 3rd	5:4	1.25	**1080.00**	386.314	119.443
C	Sept min 3rd	7:6	1.166666667	**1008.00**	266.871	62.961
B	M 2nd	9:8	1.125	**972.00**	203.910	133.238
A#	5-Limit Semi	25:24	1.041666667	**900.00**	70.672	70.672
A	Root	1	1.00	**864.00**	—	—

V(a) Draft version of A#-Major Geometric Tuning Grid:

Note	Interval	Ratio	Multiplier	Frequency (Hz)	Interval from Root (¢)	Step Interval (¢)
Tuning Grid Based on A#-225Hz						
A#	Octave	2:1	2	**450.00**	1200	70.672
A	class. dim 8ve	48:25	1.92	**432.00**	1129.328	111.731
*A	sm. M 7th	28:15	1.8666667	**420.00**	1080.557	62.961
G#	m7th	9:5	1.8	**405.00**	1017.596	133.238
G	M 6th	5:3	1.66666667	**375.00**	884.359	70.672
F#	m 6th	8:5	1.6	**360.00**	813.686	111.731
F	Perf 5th	3:2	1.5	**337.50**	701.955	119.442
E	m 5th	7:5	1.4	**315.00**	582.512	84.467
D#	Perf 4th	4:3	1.33333333	**300.00**	498.045	111.731
D	M 3rd	5:4	1.25	**281.25**	386.314	70.672
C#	m 3rd	6:5	1.2	**270.00**	315.641	119.442
C	middle M 2nd	28:25	1.12	**252.00**	196.198	84.467
B	Semitone	16:15	1.06666667	**240.00**	111.731	111.731
A#	Root	1:1	1	**225.00**	—	—

V(a) Draft version of B-Major Geometric Tuning Grid:

			Tuning Grid Based on B-240Hz (4th Octave)			
Note	Interval	Ratio	Multiplier	Frequency (Hz)	Interval from Root (¢)	Step Interval (¢)
B	Octave	2:1	2	480.00	1200	111.731
A#	M 7th	15:8	1.875	450.00	1088.269	70.672
A	Sub min 7th	9:5	1.8	432.00	1017.596	48.770
G#	M 6th	7:4	1.75	420.00	968.826	155.140
G	m 6th	8:5	1.6	384.00	813.686	111.731
F#	Perfect 5th	3:2	1.5	360.00	701.955	119.443
F	dim 5th	7:5	1.4	336.00	582.512	62.961
E	Lg. M 4th	27:20	1.35	324.00	519.551	133.238
D#	M 3rd	5:4	1.25	300.00	386.314	70.672
D	5 limit m 3rd	6:5	1.2	288.00	315.641	111.731
C#	M 2nd	9:8	1.125	270.00	203.910	98.955
C	Sm Semitone	17:16	1.0625	255.00	104.955	104.955
B	Root	1	1.00	240.00	—	—

V(a) Draft version of C-Major Geometric Tuning Grid:

			Tuning Grid Based on C-252Hz (4th Octave)			
Note	Interval	Ratio	Multiplier	Frequency (Hz)	Interval from Root (¢)	Step Interval (¢)
C	Octave	2:1	2	504.00	1200	111.731
B	M 7th	15:8	1.875	472.50	1088.269	119.443
A#	Sub min 7th	7:4	1.75	441.00	968.826	35.697
A	Sept M 6th	12:7	1.714285714	432.00	933.129	111.731
*A	M 6th	5:3	1.66666667	420.00	884.359	62.647
G#	Large m 6th	45:28	1.607142857	405.00	821.398	119.443
G	Perfect 5th	3:2	1.5	378.00	701.955	84.467
F#	Sept Tritone	10:7	1.42857143	360.00	617.488	119.443
F	Perf 4th	4:3	1.33333333	336.00	498.045	111.731
E	M 3rd	5:4	1.25	315.00	386.314	119.443
D#	Sub m 3rd	7:6	1.16666667	294.00	266.871	62.961
D	M 2nd	9:8	1.125	283.50	203.910	84.467
C#	Just halftone	15:14	1.07142857	270.00	119.443	119.443
C	Root	1	1.00	252.00	—	—

V(a) Draft version of C#-Major Geometric Tuning Grid:

	Tuning Grid Based on C#-270Hz (4th Octave)					
Note	Interval	Ratio	Multiplier	Frequency (Hz)	Interval from Root (¢)	Step Interval (¢)
C#	Octave	2:1	2	540.00	1200	111.731
C	M 7th	15:8	1.875	506.25	1088.269	70.62
B	min 7th	9:5	1.8	486.00	1017.596	133.238
A#	M 6th	5:3	1.66666667	450.00	884.359	70.672
A	m 6th	8:5	1.6	432.00	813.686	111.731
G#	Perfect 5th	3:2	1.607142857	405.00	701.955	119.443
G	dim 5th	7:5	1.5	378.00	582.512	84.467
F#	Perf 4th	4:3	1.4	360.00	498.045	111.731
F	M 3rd	5:4	1.33333333	337.50	386.314	70.672
E	m 3rd	6:5	1.25	324.00	315.641	133.238
D#	JI Maj 2nd	9:8	1.2	303.75	203.910	92.179
D#	Small M 2nd	10:9	1.125	300.00	182.404	70.672
D	JI semitone	16:15	1.1111111	288.00	111.731	111.731
C#	Root	1	1.00	270.00	—	—

V(a) Draft version of D-Major Geometric Tuning Grid:

	Tuning Grid Based on D-288Hz (4th Octave)					
Note	Interval	Ratio	Multiplier	Frequency (Hz)	Interval from Root (¢)	Step Interval (¢)
D	Octave	2:1	2	576.00	1200	111.731
C#	M 7th	15:8	1.875	540.00	1088.269	119.443
C	min 7th	7:4	1.75	504.00	968.826	84.467
B	M 6th	5:3	1.66666667	480.00	884.359	111.731
A#	Aug 5th	25:16	1.5625	450.00	772.627	70.672
A	Perfect 5th	3:2	1.5	432.00	701.955	98.955
G#	Pseudo dim5th	17:12	1.416666667	408.00	603.000	104.955
G	Perf 4th	4:3	1.33333333	384.00	498.045	111.731
F#	M 3rd	5:4	1.5	360.00	386.314	119.443
F	Sub m 3rd	7:6	1.166666667	336.00	266.871	62.961
E	Maj 2nd	9:8	1.125	324.00	203.910	98.954
D#	sm. semitone	17:16	1.0625	306.00	104.955	104.955
D	Root	1	1.00	288.00	—	—

V(a) Draft version of D#-Major Geometric Tuning Grid:

Note	Interval	Ratio	Multiplier	Frequency (Hz)	Interval from Root (¢)	Step Interval (¢)
Tuning Grid Based on D#-300Hz (4th Octave)						
D#	Octave	2:1	2	600.00	1200	111.731
D	Maj 7th	15:8	1.875	562.50	1088.269	70.672
C#	Lg min 7th	9:5	1.8	540.00	1017.596	111.731
C	Pyth. M6th	27:16	1.6875	506.25	905.865	91.179
B	min 6th	8:5	1.6	480.00	813.686	111.731
A#	Perf 5th	3:2	1.5	450.00	701.955	119.443
A	Dim 5th	36:25	1.44	432.00	631.286	111.731
G#	harmonic 4th	27:20	1.35	405.00	519.551	133.238
G	M 3rd	5:4	1.25	375.00	386.314	70.672
F#	min 3rd	6:5	1.2	360.00	315.641	111.731
F	M 2nd	9:8	1.125	337.50	203.910	98.95859
E	sm. semitone	17:16	1.0625	318.75	104.955	104.9554
D#	Unison	1:1	1	300.00	—	—

V(a) Draft version of E-Major Geometric Tuning Grid:

Note	Interval	Ratio	Multiplier	Frequency (Hz)	Interval from Root (¢)	Step Interval (¢)
Tuning Grid Based on E-324Hz (4th Octave)						
E	Octave	2:1	2	648.00	1200	111.731
D#	Maj 7th	15:8	1.875	607.50	1088.269	119.443
D	min 7th	7:4	1.75	567.00	968.826	84.467
C#	Major 6th	5:3	1.666666667	540.00	884.359	111.731
C	Aug 5th	25:16	1.5625	506.25	772.627	70.672
B	Perf 5th	3:2	1.5	486.00	701.955	133.238
A#	Aug 4th	25:18	1.388888889	450.00	568.717	70.672
A	Perf 4th	4:3	1.333333333	432.00	498.045	111.731
G#	M 3rd	5:4	1.25	405.00	386.314	119.443
G	sub min 3rd	7:6	1.166666667	378.00	266.871	62.961
F#	M 2nd	10:9	1.1111111	360.00	182.404	77.448
F	sm. semitone	17:16	1.0625	344.25	104.955	104.955
E	Unison	1:1	1	324.00	—	—

V(a) Draft version of F-Major Geometric Tuning Grid:

	Tuning Grid Based on F-337.50Hz (4ᵗʰ Octave)					
Note	Interval	Ratio	Multiplier	Frequency (Hz)	Interval from Root (¢)	Step Interval (¢)
F	Octave	2:1	2	675.00	1200	119.443
E	Grave M 7ᵗʰ	28:15	1.866666667	630.00	1080.557	62.961
D#	min 7ᵗʰ	9:5	1.8	607.50	1017.596	133.238
D	Just Major 6ᵗʰ	5:3	1.666666667	562.50	884.359	70.672
C#	Just min 6ᵗʰ	8:5	1.6	540.00	813.686	111.731
C	Just Perf 5ᵗʰ	3:2	1.5	506.25	701.955	119.443
B	Aug 4ᵗʰ	7:5	1.4	472.50	582.512	84.467
A#	Just Perf 4ᵗʰ	4:3	1.333333333	450.00	498.045	70.672
A	dim 4ᵗʰ	32:25	1.28	432.00	427.373	111.731
G#	Just min 3ʳᵈ	6:5	1.2	405.00	315.641	119.443
G	mid M 2ⁿᵈ	28:25	1.12	378.00	196.198	84.467
F#	Semitone	16:15	1.066666667	360.00	111.731	111.731
F	Unison	1:1	1	337.50	—	—

V(a) Draft version of F#-Major Geometric Tuning Grid:

	Tuning Grid Based on F#-360Hz (5ᵗʰ Octave)					
Note	Interval	Ratio	Multiplier	Frequency (Hz)	Interval from Root (¢)	Step Interval (¢)
F#	Octave	2:1	2	720.00	1200¢	111.731¢
F	Major 7ᵗʰ	15:8	1.875	675.00	1088.269¢	119.4428¢
E	minor 7ᵗʰ	9:5	1.8	648.00	1017.596¢	133.238¢
E*	Sub minor 7ᵗʰ	7:4	1.75	630.00	968.826¢	84.4672¢
D#	Major 6ᵗʰ	5:3	1.6666667	600.00	884.359¢	70.6724¢
D	minor 6ᵗʰ	8:5	1.6	576.00	813.686¢	111.731¢
C#	Perfect 5ᵗʰ	3:2	1.5	540.00	701.955¢	119.4428¢
C	Aug 4ᵗʰ	7:5	1.4	504.00	582.512¢	84.4672¢
B	Perfect 4ᵗʰ	4:3	1.3333333	480.00	498.045¢	111.731¢
A#	Major 3ʳᵈ	5:4	1.25	450.00	386.314¢	70.6724¢
A	minor 3ʳᵈ	6:5	1.2	432.00	315.641¢	111.731¢
G#	Major 2ⁿᵈ	9:8	1.125	405.00	302.910¢	92.17872¢
G	Minor 2ⁿᵈ	16:15	1.0666667	384.00	111.731¢	111.731¢
F#	Root	1:1	1	360.00	—	—

V(a) Draft version of G-Major Geometric Tuning Grid:

	Tuning Grid Based on G-378.00Hz (Draft C - Orphaned)					
Note	Interval	Ratio	Multiplier	Frequency (Hz)	Interval from Root (¢)	Step Interval (¢)
G	Octave	2:1	2	768.00	1200	111.731
F#	Grave M7th	15:8	1.875	720.00	1088.269	119.443
F	Sub min 7th	14:8	1.75	672.00	968.826	62.961
E	Pyth M6th	27:16	1.6875	648.00	905.865	65.337
D#	Aug 5th	25:16	1.5625	600.00	772.627	70.672
D	Just Perf 5th	3:2	1.5	576.00	701.955	111.731
C#	Diat. Tritone	45:32	1.40625	540.00	590.224	88.800
C	harmonic	171:128	1.3359375	513.00	501.423	115.109
B	Just Maj 3rd	5:4	1.25	480.00	386.314	111.731
A#	dim m3rd	75:64	1.171875	450.00	274.582	70.672
A	M 2nd	9:8	1.125	432.00	203.910	98.955
G#	sm. Half step	17:16	1.0625	408.00	104.955	104.955
G	Unison	1:1	1	384.00	—	—

V(a) Draft version of G#-Major Geometric Tuning Grid:

	Tuning Grid Based on G#-405.00Hz (5th Octave)					
Note	Interval	Ratio	Multiplier	Frequency (Hz)	Interval from Root (¢)	Step Interval (¢)
G#	Octave	2:1	2	810.00	1200	111.731
G	M 7th	15:8	1.875	759.375	1088.269	92.179
F#	small m 7th	16:9	1.777777778	720.00	996.090	111.731
F	M 6th	5:3	1.666666667	675.00	884.359	70.672
E	m 6th	8:5	1.6	648.00	813.686	111.731
D#	Perf 5th	3:2	1.5	607.50	701.955	119.443
D	m 5th	7:5	1.4	567.00	582.512	84.467
C#	Perf 4th	4:3	1.333333333	540.00	498.045	111.731
C	M 3rd	5:4	1.25	506.25	386.314	70.672
B	m 3rd	6:5	1.2	486.00	315.641	111.731
A#	M 2nd	9:8	1.125	455.625	203.910	92.179
A	Semitone	16:15	1.066666667	432.00	111.731	111.731
G#	Unison	1:1	1	405.00	—	—

Appendix VI

Completed Solfeggio-Based Tuning Grids

SERIES-A Solfeggio fundamentals: (174, 285, and 396Hz)

	Tuning Grid Based on Solfeggio SERIES-A 174Hz					
Note	Interval	Ratio	Multiplier	Frequency (Hz)	Interval from Root (¢)	Step Interval (¢)
F	Octave	2:1	2	348.00	1200	111.731
E	Major 7th	15:8	1.875	326.25	1088.269	70.672
D#	minor 7th	9:5	1.8	313.20	1017.596	133.237
D	Major 6th	5:3	1.666666667	290.00	884.359	70.672
C#	minor 6	8:5	1.6	278.40	813.686	111.731
C	Perfect 5th	3:2	1.5	261.00	701.955	119.443
B	Aug 4th	7:5	1.4	243.60	582.512	84.467
A#	Perfect 4th	4:3	1.333333333	232.00	498.045	111.731
A	Major 3rd	5:4	1.25	217.50	386.314	70.672
G#	minor 3rd	6:5	1.2	208.80	315.641	111.731
G	Major 2nd	9:8	1.125	195.75	203.910	92.179
F#	minor 2nd	16:15	1.066666667	185.60	111.731	111.731
F	Root	1:1	1	174.00	—	—

	Tuning Grid Based on Solfeggio SERIES-A 285Hz					
Note	Interval	Ratio	Multiplier	Frequency (Hz)	Interval from Root (¢)	Step Interval (¢)
D	Octave	2:1	2	570.00	1200	111.731
C#	Major 7th	15:8	1.875	534.375	1088.269	70.672
C	minor 7th	9:5	1.8	513.00	1017.596	133.237
B	Major 6th	5:3	1.666666667	475.00	884.359	70.672
A#	minor 6	8:5	1.6	456.00	813.686	111.731
A	Perfect 5th	3:2	1.5	427.50	701.955	119.443
G#	Aug 4th	7:5	1.4	399.00	582.512	84.467
G	Perfect 4th	4:3	1.333333333	380.00	498.045	111.731
F#	Major 3rd	5:4	1.25	356.25	386.314	70.672
F	minor 3rd	6:5	1.2	342.00	315.641	111.731
E	Major 2nd	9:8	1.125	320.625	203.910	92.179
D#	minor 2nd	16:15	1.066666667	304.00	111.731	111.731
D	Root	1:1	1	285.00	—	—

Tuning Grid Based on Solfeggio SERIES-A 396Hz						
Note	Interval	Ratio	Multiplier	Frequency (Hz)	Interval from Root (¢)	Step Interval (¢)
G	Octave	2:1	2	792.00	1200	111.731
F#	Major 7th	15:8	1.875	742.50	1088.269	70.672
F	minor 7th	9:5	1.8	712.80	1017.596	133.237
E	Major 6th	5:3	1.666666667	660.00	884.359	70.672
D#	minor 6	8:5	1.6	633.60	813.686	111.731
D	Perfect 5th	3:2	1.5	594.00	701.955	119.443
C#	Aug 4th	7:5	1.4	554.40	582.512	84.467
C	Perfect 4th	4:3	1.333333333	528.00	498.045	111.731
B	Major 3rd	5:4	1.25	495.00	386.314	70.672
A#	minor 3rd	6:5	1.2	475.20	315.641	111.731
A	Major 2nd	9:8	1.125	445.50	203.910	92.179
G#	minor 2nd	16:15	1.066666667	422.40	111.731	111.731
G	Root	1:1	1	396.00	—	—

SERIES-B Solfeggio fundamentals: (417, 528, and 639Hz)

Tuning Grid Based on Solfeggio SERIES-B 417Hz						
Note	Interval	Ratio	Multiplier	Frequency (Hz)	Interval from Root (¢)	Step Interval (¢)
G#	Octave	2:1	2	834.00	1200	111.731
G	Major 7th	15:8	1.875	781.875	1088.269	70.672
F#	minor 7th	9:5	1.8	750.60	1017.596	133.237
F	Major 6th	5:3	1.666666667	695.00	884.359	70.672
E	minor 6	8:5	1.6	667.20	813.686	111.731
D#	Perfect 5th	3:2	1.5	625.50	701.955	119.443
D	Aug 4th	7:5	1.4	583.80	582.512	84.467
C#	Perfect 4th	4:3	1.333333333	556.00	498.045	111.731
C	Major 3rd	5:4	1.25	521.25	386.314	70.672
B	minor 3rd	6:5	1.2	500.40	315.641	111.731
A#	Major 2nd	9:8	1.125	469.125	203.910	92.179
A	minor 2nd	16:15	1.066666667	444.80	111.731	111.731
G#	Root	1:1	1	417.00	—	—

Tuning Grid Based on Solfeggio SERIES-C 852Hz

Note	Interval	Ratio	Multiplier	Frequency (Hz)	Interval from Root (¢)	Step Interval (¢)
A	Octave	2:1	2	1704.00	1200	111.731
G#	Major 7th	15:8	1.875	1597.50	1088.269	70.672
G	minor 7th	9:5	1.8	1533.60	1017.596	133.237
F#	Major 6th	5:3	1.666666667	1420.00	884.359	70.672
F	minor 6	8:5	1.6	1363.20	813.686	111.731
E	Perfect 5th	3:2	1.5	1278.00	701.955	119.443
D#	Aug 4th	7:5	1.4	1192.80	582.512	84.467
D	Perfect 4th	4:3	1.333333333	1136.00	498.045	111.731
C#	Major 3rd	5:4	1.25	1065.00	386.314	70.672
C	minor 3rd	6:5	1.2	1022.40	315.641	111.731
B	Major 2nd	9:8	1.125	958.50	203.910	92.179
A#	minor 2nd	16:15	1.066666667	908.80	111.731	111.731
A	Root	1:1	1	852.00	—	—

Tuning Grid Based on Solfeggio SERIES-B 639Hz

Note	Interval	Ratio	Multiplier	Frequency (Hz)	Interval from Root (¢)	Step Interval (¢)
E	Octave	2:1	2	1278.00	1200	111.731
D#	Major 7th	15:8	1.875	1198.125	1088.269	70.672
D	minor 7th	9:5	1.8	1150.20	1017.596	133.237
C#	Major 6th	5:3	1.666666667	1065.00	884.359	70.672
C	minor 6	8:5	1.6	1022.40	813.686	111.731
B	Perfect 5th	3:2	1.5	958.50	701.955	119.443
A#	Aug 4th	7:5	1.4	894.60	582.512	84.467
A	Perfect 4th	4:3	1.333333333	852.00	498.045	111.731
G#	Major 3rd	5:4	1.25	798.75	386.314	70.672
G	minor 3rd	6:5	1.2	766.80	315.641	111.731
F#	Major 2nd	9:8	1.125	718.875	203.910	92.179
F	minor 2nd	16:15	1.066666667	681.60	111.731	111.731
E	Root	1:1	1	639.00	—	—

SERIES-C Solfeggio fundamentals: (741, 852, and 963Hz)

Tuning Grid Based on Solfeggio SERIES-C 741Hz						
Note	Interval	Ratio	Multiplier	Frequency (Hz)	Interval from Root (¢)	Step Interval (¢)
F#	Octave	2:1	2	1482.00	1200	111.731
F	Major 7th	15:8	1.875	1389.375	1088.269	70.672
E	minor 7th	9:5	1.8	1333.80	1017.596	133.237
D#	Major 6th	5:3	1.666666667	1235.00	884.359	70.672
D	minor 6	8:5	1.6	1185.60	813.686	111.731
C#	Perfect 5th	3:2	1.5	1111.50	701.955	119.443
C	Aug 4th	7:5	1.4	1037.40	582.512	84.467
B	Perfect 4th	4:3	1.333333333	988.00	498.045	111.731
A#	Major 3rd	5:4	1.25	926.25	386.314	70.672
A	minor 3rd	6:5	1.2	889.20	315.641	111.731
G#	Major 2nd	9:8	1.125	833.625	203.910	92.179
G	minor 2nd	16:15	1.066666667	790.40	111.731	111.731
F#	Root	1:1	1	741.00	—	—

Tuning Grid Based on Solfeggio SERIES-C 852Hz						
Note	Interval	Ratio	Multiplier	Frequency (Hz)	Interval from Root (¢)	Step Interval (¢)
A	Octave	2:1	2	1704.00	1200	111.731
G#	Major 7th	15:8	1.875	1597.50	1088.269	70.672
G	minor 7th	9:5	1.8	1533.60	1017.596	133.237
F#	Major 6th	5:3	1.666666667	1420.00	884.359	70.672
F	minor 6	8:5	1.6	1363.20	813.686	111.731
E	Perfect 5th	3:2	1.5	1278.00	701.955	119.443
D#	Aug 4th	7:5	1.4	1192.80	582.512	84.467
D	Perfect 4th	4:3	1.333333333	1136.00	498.045	111.731
C#	Major 3rd	5:4	1.25	1065.00	386.314	70.672
C	minor 3rd	6:5	1.2	1022.40	315.641	111.731
B	Major 2nd	9:8	1.125	958.50	203.910	92.179
A#	minor 2nd	16:15	1.066666667	908.80	111.731	111.731
A	Root	1:1	1	852.00	—	—

Note	Interval	Ratio	Multiplier	Frequency (Hz)	Interval from Root (¢)	Step Interval (¢)
Tuning Grid Based on Solfeggio SERIES-C 963Hz						
B	Octave	2:1	2	1926.00	1200	111.731
A#	Major 7th	15:8	1.875	1805.625	1088.269	70.672
A	minor 7th	9:5	1.8	1733.40	1017.596	133.237
G#	Major 6th	5:3	1.666666667	1605.00	884.359	70.672
G	minor 6	8:5	1.6	1540.80	813.686	111.731
F#	Perfect 5th	3:2	1.5	1444.50	701.955	119.443
F	Aug 4th	7:5	1.4	1348.20	582.512	84.467
E	Perfect 4th	4:3	1.333333333	1284.00	498.045	111.731
D#	Major 3rd	5:4	1.25	1203.75	386.314	70.672
D	minor 3rd	6:5	1.2	1155.60	315.641	111.731
C#	Major 2nd	9:8	1.125	1083.375	203.910	92.179
C	minor 2nd	16:15	1.066666667	1027.20	111.731	111.731
B	Root	1:1	1	963.00	—	—

Appendix VII

Table of Polygonal Frequency Data

This table reveals the calculations on the first 250 regular polygons. For the purposes of this text, it is assumed that each polygon is 'equilateral', or that all sides possess equal length and, that all vertice angles are identical. The table is presented for reference and validation of the basic geometric data, used to formulate the criteria for the Geometric tuning grids, as well as those criterion's pertinence to the Solfeggio tuning grids.

Regular Polygonal Data		Internal Angles		Regular Polygonal Data		Internal Angles	
Number of Sides	Internal Angles	Sum of Internal Angles	Sum of Digits	Number of Sides	Internal Angles	Sum of Internal Angles	Sum of Digits
3	60	180	9	38	170.5263158	6480	18
4	90	360	9	39	170.7692308	6660	18
5	108	540	9	40	171	6840	18
6	120	720	9	41	171.2195122	7020	9
7	128.5714286	900	9	42	171.4285714	7200	9
8	135	1080	9	43	171.627907	7380	18
9	140	1260	9	44	171.8181818	7560	18
10	144	1440	9	45	172	7740	18
11	147.2727273	1620	9	46	172.173913	7920	18
12	150	1800	9	47	172.3404255	8100	9
13	152.3076923	1980	18	48	172.5	8280	18
14	154.2857143	2160	9	49	172.6530612	8460	18
15	156	2340	9	50	172.8	8640	18
16	157.5	2520	9	51	172.9411765	8820	18
17	158.8235294	2700	9	52	173.0769231	9000	9
18	160	2880	18	53	173.2075472	9180	18
19	161.0526316	3060	9	54	173.3333333	9360	18
20	162	3240	9	55	173.4545455	9540	18
21	162.8571429	3420	9	56	173.5714286	9720	18
22	163.6363636	3600	9	57	173.6842105	9900	18
23	164.3478261	3780	18	58	173.7931034	10080	9
24	165	3960	18	59	173.8983051	10260	9
25	165.6	4140	9	60	174	10440	9
26	166.1538462	4320	9	61	174.0983607	10620	9
27	166.6666667	4500	9	62	174.1935484	10800	9
28	167.1428571	4680	18	63	174.2857143	10980	18
29	167.5862069	4860	18	64	174.375	11160	9
30	168	5040	9	65	174.4615385	11340	9
31	168.3870968	5220	9	66	174.5454545	11520	9
32	168.75	5400	9	67	174.6268657	11700	9
33	169.0909091	5580	18	68	174.7058824	11880	18
34	169.4117647	5760	18	69	174.7826087	12060	9
35	169.7142857	5940	18	70	174.8571429	12240	9
36	170	6120	9	71	174.9295775	12420	9
37	170.2702703	6300	9	72	175	12600	9

Regular Polygonal Data		Internal Angles		Regular Polygonal Data		Internal Angles	
Number of Sides	Internal Angles	Sum of Internal Angles	Sum of Digits	Number of Sides	Internal Angles	Sum of Internal Angles	Sum of Digits
73	175.0684932	12780	18	108	176.6666667	19080	18
74	175.1351351	12960	18	109	176.6972477	19260	18
75	175.2	13140	9	110	176.7272727	19440	18
76	175.2631579	13320	9	111	176.7567568	19620	18
77	175.3246753	13500	9	112	176.7857143	19800	18
78	175.3846154	13680	18	113	176.8141593	19980	27
79	175.443038	13860	18	114	176.8421053	20160	9
80	175.5	14040	9	115	176.8695652	20340	9
81	175.5555556	14220	9	116	176.8965517	20520	9
82	175.6097561	14400	9	117	176.9230769	20700	9
83	175.6626506	14580	18	118	176.9491525	20880	18
84	175.7142857	14760	18	119	176.9747899	21060	9
85	175.7647059	14940	18	120	177	21240	9
86	175.8139535	15120	9	121	177.0247934	21420	9
87	175.862069	15300	9	122	177.0491803	21600	9
88	175.9090909	15480	18	123	177.0731707	21780	18
89	175.9550562	15660	18	124	177.0967742	21960	18
90	176	15840	18	125	177.12	22140	9
91	176.043956	16020	9	126	177.1428571	22320	9
92	176.0869565	16200	9	127	177.1653543	22500	9
93	176.1290323	16380	18	128	177.1875	22680	18
94	176.1702128	16560	18	129	177.2093023	22860	18
95	176.2105263	16740	18	130	177.2307692	23040	9
96	176.25	16920	18	131	177.2519084	23220	9
97	176.2886598	17100	9	132	177.2727273	23400	9
98	176.3265306	17280	18	133	177.2932331	23580	18
99	176.3636364	17460	18	134	177.3134328	23760	18
100	176.4	17640	18	135	177.3333333	23940	18
101	176.4356436	17820	18	136	177.3529412	24120	9
102	176.4705882	18000	9	137	177.3722628	24300	9
103	176.5048544	18180	18	138	177.3913043	24480	18
104	176.5384615	18360	18	139	177.4100719	24660	18
105	176.5714286	18540	18	140	177.4285714	24840	18
106	176.6037736	18720	18	141	177.4468085	25020	9
107	176.635514	18900	18	142	177.4647887	25200	9

Regular Polygonal Data		Internal Angles		Regular Polygonal Data		Internal Angles	
Number of Sides	Internal Angles	Sum of Internal Angles	Sum of Digits	Number of Sides	Internal Angles	Sum of Internal Angles	Sum of Digits
143	177.4825175	25380	18	178	177.9775281	31680	18
144	177.5	25560	18	179	177.9888268	31860	18
145	177.5172414	25740	18	180	178	32040	9
146	177.5342466	25920	18	181	178.0110497	32220	9
147	177.5510204	26100	9	182	178.021978	32400	9
148	177.5675676	26280	18	183	178.0327869	32580	18
149	177.5838926	26460	18	184	178.0434783	32760	18
150	177.6	26640	18	185	178.0540541	32940	18
151	177.615894	26820	18	186	178.0645161	33120	9
152	177.6315789	27000	9	187	178.0748663	33300	9
153	177.6470588	27180	18	188	178.0851064	33480	18
154	177.6623377	27360	18	189	178.0952381	33660	18
155	177.6774194	27540	18	190	178.1052632	33840	18
156	177.6923077	27720	18	191	178.1151832	34020	9
157	177.7070064	27900	18	192	178.125	34200	9
158	177.721519	28080	18	193	178.134715	34380	18
159	177.7358491	28260	18	194	178.1443299	34560	18
160	177.75	28440	18	195	178.1538462	34740	18
161	177.7639752	28620	18	196	178.1632653	34920	18
162	177.7777778	28800	18	197	178.1725888	35100	9
163	177.791411	28980	27	198	178.1818182	35280	18
164	177.804878	29160	18	199	178.1909548	35460	18
165	177.8181818	29340	18	200	178.2	35640	18
166	177.8313253	29520	18	201	178.2089552	35820	18
167	177.8443114	29700	18	202	178.2178218	36000	9
168	177.8571429	29880	27	203	178.226601	36180	18
169	177.8698225	30060	9	204	178.2352941	36360	18
170	177.8823529	30240	9	205	178.2439024	36540	18
171	177.8947368	30420	9	206	178.2524272	36720	18
172	177.9069767	30600	9	207	178.2608696	36900	18
173	177.9190751	30780	18	208	178.2692308	37080	18
174	177.9310345	30960	18	209	178.277512	37260	18
175	177.9428571	31140	9	210	178.2857143	37440	18
176	177.9545455	31320	9	211	178.2938389	37620	18
177	177.9661017	31500	9	212	178.3018868	37800	18

Regular Polygonal Data		Internal Angles		Regular Polygonal Data		Internal Angles	
Number of Sides	Internal Angles	Sum of Internal Angles	Sum of Digits	Number of Sides	Internal Angles	Sum of Internal Angles	Sum of Digits
213	178.3098592	37980	27	248	178.5483871	44280	18
214	178.317757	38160	18	249	178.5542169	44460	18
215	178.3255814	38340	18	250	178.56	44640	18
216	178.3333333	38520	18	251	178.5657371	44820	18
217	178.3410138	38700	18	252	178.5714286	45000	9
218	178.3486239	38880	27				
219	178.3561644	39060	18				
220	178.3636364	39240	18				
221	178.3710407	39420	18				
222	178.3783784	39600	18				
223	178.3856502	39780	27				
224	178.3928571	39960	27				
225	178.4	40140	9				
226	178.4070796	40320	9				
227	178.4140969	40500	9				
228	178.4210526	40680	18				
229	178.4279476	40860	18				
230	178.4347826	41040	9				
231	178.4415584	41220	9				
232	178.4482759	41400	9				
233	178.4549356	41580	18				
234	178.4615385	41760	18				
235	178.4680851	41940	18				
236	178.4745763	42120	9				
237	178.4810127	42300	9				
238	178.487395	42480	18				
239	178.4937238	42660	18				
240	178.5	42840	18				
241	178.5062241	43020	9				
242	178.5123967	43200	9				
243	178.5185185	43380	18				
244	178.5245902	43560	18				
245	178.5306122	43740	18				
246	178.5365854	43920	18				
247	178.5425101	44100	9				

Appendix VIII

Just Intonation Ratios and Interval Conventions

What follows, is a chart of the most common Just Intonation intervals used in this text. There are *many* more interval applications within the realm of Just Intonation than are presented here.

For more information on Just Intonation and Just Tuning, please refer to the *Just Intonation Primer* manual — available at popular on-line sources.

Common Just Intonation Intervals		
Interval Name	**Ratio**	**Total ¢**
Octave	2:1	1,200.000¢
Maj 7th	15:8	1,088.269¢
min 7th	9:5	1,017.597¢
Small min 7th	16:9	996.090¢
Harm minor 7th	7:4	968.826¢
Maj 6th	5:3	884.359¢
min 6th	8:5	813.687¢
Perfect 5th	3:2	701.955¢
Dim 5th	64:45	609.777¢
Aug 4th	7:5	582.512¢
min 5th*	7:5	582.512¢
Perfect 4th	4:3	498.045¢
Maj 3rd	5:4	386.314¢
min 3rd	6:5	315.641¢
Maj 2nd	9:8	203.910¢
minor 2nd tone	10:9	182.404¢
Semitone	16:15	111.731¢
Small semitone	17:16	104.955¢
Unison	1:1	0¢

Appendix IX

Harmonics and Interval Validation

When constructing any harmonic system, such as a tuning grid, it is important to observe, as much as possible, the inclusion of the harmonics and overtones. As mentioned in the main chapter titled 'Harmonics and Overtones', these frequencies can be calculated from any root tone. Once you have a list of the harmonics, it is relatively easy to see where the tones fit in to your system.

What follows is a brief diagram of a harmonic chart built from a F#-180Hz fundamental. You will notice that in the resulting calculations, that tones are 'predicted' in specific locations within the system. The resulting list is called a 'harmonic series.' In that case, the calculated harmonic series is based upon our venerable F# value and, reveals an entire, predictive series of tones that naturally show up in the F#-Major Tuning Grid — exactly where the harmonic series predicts they should appear.

First, a little theory; In the series of harmonics, there is an order of operations to observe. This flow pertains to the octave and intervals in which any tone should appear.

For example, regarding our 180Hz fundamental (also the first harmonic), the second harmonic is calculated as **180Hz x 2**. This, of course gives us 360Hz, the octave of 180. Thus, the second harmonic represents the octave tone of the fundamental.

To extend the example; if we want to know the third harmonic of 180Hz, we multiply **180Hz x 3**, which results in 540Hz. Obviously, 540Hz is not an octave value relative to the first harmonic tone. What it represents, is the natural 5th interval above the second harmonic. If one is to reference the F#-Major Tuning Grid in the Octave+Perfect 5th position, we will see that 540Hz is in fact, our C# above F#-360Hz. The F# to C# tonal interval, is indeed a Perfect 5th interval.

Even the most perfectly-balanced tuning system will appear to skip over some of the harmonic values. However, this is not a crisis situation by any means. While we do strive for perfect validation, few constructs will come close. And, chances are, that the desired value will pop up in the harmonic and overtone series produced by your well-balanced system.

Presented here, is a table of relationships to assist in building harmonic series to proof any work in building your own twelve-tone grids, or to use in examining those presented in this text. It is not always possible to adhere perfectly to this pattern. So, don't freak if your harmonics start to waver in the upper octaves.

For example, in the F#-Major Tuning Grid, the 11th harmonic is not present as a tone in the proposed tuning system. This is due to the choice of a Augmented 4th interval of 7:5, rather than the 11:8 that would yield a super-4th interval, which in the opinion of the writer, is simply too wide at that position.

The conflict became unresolvable with the present tools. Thus, the Aug 4th was adopted. Notwithstanding this complication, all of the other harmonics represented in this chart, are intact and, appear as mainline tones within the system as proposed.

Harmonic Relationships		
Harmonic	**Formula**	**Predicted Location**
1st (f_1)	$1(f_1)$	Equals the fundamental tone
2nd	$2(f_1)$	One Octave above fundamental
3rd	$3(f_1)$	Perfect 5th above 2f
4th	$4(f_1)$	Two Octaves above fundamental
5th	$5(f_1)$	3rd above 4f
6th	$6(f_1)$	5th above 4f
7th	$7(f_1)$	Minor 7th above 4f
8th	$8(f_1)$	Three Octaves above fundamental
9th	$9(f_1)$	Minor 2nd above 8f
10th	$10(f_1)$	3rd above 8f
11th	$11(f_1)$	4th above 8f*
12th ♪	$12(f_1)$	5th above 8f

The results of these calculations upon the fundamental tone of 180Hz, reveals a harmonic series of tones as follows:

Harmonic Series Based Upon 180Hz		
Harmonic	**Tone**	**Position**
1st (f$_1$)	180Hz	F$^{\#3}$
2nd	360Hz	F$^{\#4}$
3rd	540Hz	C$^{\#4}$
4th	720Hz	F$^{\#5}$
5th	900Hz	F$^{\#5}$
6th	1080Hz	A$^{\#5}$
7th	1260Hz	E^{5}
8th	1440Hz	F$^{\#6}$
9th	1620Hz	G$^{\#6}$
10th	1800Hz	A$^{\#6}$
11th	1980Hz	—
12th	2160Hz	C$^{\#7}$

As with so many things in this world of customized tuning, the structure and even the math of the harmonic series within any tuning system is somewhat subject to personal opinion and taste. However, within the systems intended for use in sound and frequency wellness, the writer and developer of the systems included in this text, would discourage significant deviation from the geometric purity these systems manage to accomplish.

That improvements are possible, the author does not deny. However, such modification and improvement should always tend toward perfection of geometric resonance and tonal balance — especially within the harmonic series produced by each of the proposed systems.

The author wishes to sincerely thank you for picking up 'Sacred Sonics' and supporting the sonic revolution for healing and wellness.

Sacred Sonics is produced by Available Light Intl. We are a small-but-determined group of healers, musicians, and supporting manufacturers that are dedicated to supporting and growing a worldwide network of sound and frequency healing professionals.

We are only at the beginning of our mission to make natural, healing frequencies the standard for sonic healing therapies.

To keep tabs on our growth, products and latest Sacred Sonics developments, please visit and bookmark our web site.

www.sacredsonics.com

This page is intentionally blank

Printed in Great Britain
by Amazon

41874518R00235